Improving Business Performance Through Innovation in the Digital Economy

Ionica Oncioiu
Titu Maiorescu University, Romania

IGI Global
DISSEMINATOR OF KNOWLEDGE

A volume in the Advances in Business Strategy and Competitive Advantage (ABSCA) Book Series

Published in the United States of America by
IGI Global
Business Science Reference (an imprint of IGI Global)
701 E. Chocolate Avenue
Hershey PA, USA 17033
Tel: 717-533-8845
Fax: 717-533-8661
E-mail: cust@igi-global.com
Web site: http://www.igi-global.com

Library of Congress Cataloging-in-Publication Data

Names: Oncioiu, Ionica, 1972- editor.
Title: Improving business performance through innovation in the digital economy / Ionica Oncioiu, editor.
Description: Hershey, PA : Business Science Reference, [2020] | Includes bibliographical references and index. | Summary: "This book examines the impact of digital computing. It investigates new economic and entrepreneurial approaches to enhancing community development"-- Provided by publisher.
Identifiers: LCCN 2019023677 (print) | LCCN 2019023678 (ebook) | ISBN 9781799810056 (hardcover) | ISBN 9781799810063 (paperback) | ISBN 9781799810070 (ebook)
Subjects: LCSH: Information technology--Management. | Electronic commerce--Management. | Community development.
Classification: LCC HD30.2 .I488 2020 (print) | LCC HD30.2 (ebook) | DDC 658.4/063--dc23
LC record available at https://lccn.loc.gov/2019023677
LC ebook record available at https://lccn.loc.gov/2019023678

This book is published in the IGI Global book series Advances in Business Strategy and Competitive Advantage (ABSCA) (ISSN: 2327-3429; eISSN: 2327-3437)

British Cataloguing in Publication Data
A Cataloguing in Publication record for this book is available from the British Library.

Advances in Business Strategy and Competitive Advantage (ABSCA) Book Series

Patricia Ordóñez de Pablos
Universidad de Oviedo, Spain

ISSN:2327-3429
EISSN:2327-3437

Mission

Business entities are constantly seeking new ways through which to gain advantage over their competitors and strengthen their position within the business environment. With competition at an all-time high due to technological advancements allowing for competition on a global scale, firms continue to seek new ways through which to improve and strengthen their business processes, procedures, and profitability.

The **Advances in Business Strategy and Competitive Advantage (ABSCA) Book Series** is a timely series responding to the high demand for state-of-the-art research on how business strategies are created, implemented and re-designed to meet the demands of globalized competitive markets. With a focus on local and global challenges, business opportunities and the needs of society, the **ABSCA** encourages scientific discourse on doing business and managing information technologies for the creation of sustainable competitive advantage.

Coverage

- International Business Strategy
- Core Competencies
- Resource-Based Competition
- Globalization
- Differentiation Strategy
- Small and Medium Enterprises
- Entrepreneurship & Innovation
- Adaptive Enterprise
- Strategic Management
- Strategic alliances

IGI Global is currently accepting manuscripts for publication within this series. To submit a proposal for a volume in this series, please contact our Acquisition Editors at Acquisitions@igi-global.com or visit: http://www.igi-global.com/publish/.

The Advances in Business Strategy and Competitive Advantage (ABSCA) Book Series (ISSN 2327-3429) is published by IGI Global, 701 E. Chocolate Avenue, Hershey, PA 17033-1240, USA, www.igi-global.com. This series is composed of titles available for purchase individually; each title is edited to be contextually exclusive from any other title within the series. For pricing and ordering information please visit http://www.igi-global.com/book-series/advances-business-strategy-competitive-advantage/73672. Postmaster: Send all address changes to above address.

Titles in this Series

For a list of additional titles in this series, please visit: www.igi-global.com/book-series

Handbook of Research on Entrepreneurship, Innovation, and Internationalization
Nuno Miguel Teixeira (Polytechnic Institute of Setúbal, Portugal) Teresa Gomes da Costa (Polytechnic Institute of Setúbal, Portugal) and Inês Margarida Lisboa (Instituto Politécnico de Leiria, Portugal)
Business Science Reference • ©2019 • 761pp • H/C (ISBN: 9781522584797) • US $395.00

Handbook of Research on Corporate Restructuring and Globalization
Antonio Carrizo Moreira (University of Aveiro, Portugal) and Pedro Silva (University of Aveiro, Portugal)
Business Science Reference • ©2019 • 408pp • H/C (ISBN: 9781522589068) • US $295.00

Responsible, Sustainable, and Globally Aware Management in the Fourth Industrial Revolution
Ziska Fields (University of KwaZulu-Natal, South Africa) and Stefan Huesig (Chemnitz University of Technology, Germany)
Business Science Reference • ©2019 • 396pp • H/C (ISBN: 9781522576389) • US $225.00

Handbook of Research on Entrepreneurial Leadership and Competitive Strategy in Family Business
José Manuel Saiz-Álvarez (Tecnológico de Monterrey, Mexico) and Jesús Manuel Palma-Ruiz (Universidad Autónoma de Chihuahua, Mexico)
Business Science Reference • ©2019 • 559pp • H/C (ISBN: 9781522580126) • US $345.00

The Belt and Road Strategy in International Business and Administration
Wei Liu (University of Sydney, Australia) Zhe Zhang (University of Sydney, Australia) Jin-Xiong Chen (Wuyi University, China) and Sang-Bing Tsai (University of Electronic Science and Technology of China Zhongshan Institute, China & Capital University of Economics and Business, China & Wuyi University, China)
Business Science Reference • ©2019 • 273pp • H/C (ISBN: 9781522584407) • US $225.00

Global Considerations in Entrepreneurship Education and Training
Luísa Cagica Carvalho (Instituto Politécnico de Setúbal, Portugal & CEFAGE - Universidade de Évora, Portugal) and Ana Dias Daniel (Universidade de Aveiro, Portugal)
Business Science Reference • ©2019 • 322pp • H/C (ISBN: 9781522576754) • US $215.00

Innovation and Social Capital in Organizational Ecosystems
Brychan Celfyn Thomas (University of South Wales, UK) and Lyndon John Murphy (Cardiff Metropolitan University, UK)
Business Science Reference • ©2019 • 341pp • H/C (ISBN: 9781522577218) • US $225.00

IGI Global
DISSEMINATOR OF KNOWLEDGE

701 East Chocolate Avenue, Hershey, PA 17033, USA
Tel: 717-533-8845 x100 • Fax: 717-533-8661
E-Mail: cust@igi-global.com • www.igi-global.com

Editorial Advisory Board

Table of Contents

Detailed Table of Contents

Disruptive technology has created radical change in the tourism industry, just like the emergence of the Internet. The cost of doing business has decreased, leading to more competition for customers and lowering of the barriers of entry. Customers have been the biggest winners, as competition has transferred more power into the hands of cunsumers, creating a consumer culture. The sharing economy has developed as a result of the Internet where consumers have become active players in the provision of services in the sharing economy against established businesses. The sharing economy created by technology platforms make it possible for a reduction in the costs of doing business, by lowering the barriers of entry and causing disruption in markets with low competition. The technology platform provided by sharing economy companies matches those that want to offer services and those that seek services, and Uber (taxi services) and Airbnb (accommodation) arc thc lcading pioneers.

The chapter considers a similarity between Maslow's and Corporate Social Responsibilities pyramids. Various groups of stakeholders may have opposite interests in relationship with related companies, generating moral dilemmas. An analysis of organizational and economic accounting patterns in commercial real estate is provided with examples of companies listed to Stock Exchange. These common patterns are in accordance with all professional standards, but still do not offer sufficient information for an informed investment decision of an average investor. The choice of accounting policy is one of the reasons why real estate industry is perceived as a high risk, as a high degree of subjectivity applies through the choices of accounting treatment. Conflicts between stakeholders should be avoided due to the direct impact on a company's development perspectives and value.

Today's technology has evolved greatly and influences us in different ways, more or less beneficial, depending on each user and the needs of each consumer. It has a beneficial influence on organizations, thanks to the continuous use of technologies being as innovative and topical as possible. So organizations need to keep pace and adapt to new technology requirements to thrive in their environment business and to be aware of market requirements. The role of marketing is to grasp the unfulfilled needs of people and to create new and attractive solutions.

The aim of the present study is to explore Digital Transformation frontiers using the lens of Open Innovation. By implementing bibliographic coupling method, the authors bring together segmental publications from different research fields and provide a comprehensive overview of the combined Open Innovation and Digital Transformation field's intellectual structure, revealing the different groups of thoughts, influential authors, and pressing topics. The research findings illustrate, the research area has polycentric composition with absence of overlaps between articles. Five main research groups are identified: Co-evolution of Digital Technologies and Open Innovation; Digital Peer-communities; Digital Ecosystems; Knowledge Management in the Open and Digital Era; and Open Innovation, Digital Technologies, and Businesses Performance. The current research contributes both Open Innovation and Digital Transformation fields by cross-exploring each phenomenon and revealing how Digital Transformation shapes the nature of innovation as a collaborative activity as part of an independent research area.

A complex evaluation of the activity of the enterprise is based on research of the results at the actual moment; this is why many managers use accountancy appreciation records such as: profit from invested capital or income at an asset. The indicators of income and profit are not objectives and depend on the method chosen by the record. Besides, the accountancy methods used today for analysis are short-time, being oriented towards the research, in a long period of the added value of the company. The objective of this chapter consists in developing the theoretical-methodological and substantiation mechanisms of perfecting the management enterprises. The results show that the methodological indications suggested may be used at the organization of the monitoring system in a stable-functioning enterprise, at the activities of re-establishment of the payment capacity of the debtor enterprises, and at the procedures of external management.

Sustainable economic intelligence, as a form of superior manifestation of an economy based on knowledge and innovation requires the management, quantification, monitoring, and reporting of non-financial information by economic entities (environmental issues, social and personnel aspects, respect the human rights and combating corruption) defined in relation to the average number of employees, total balance sheet, and net turnover. These elements, combined in the non-financial statements of economic entities, are decisive in achieving the transition to a sustainable global economy, combining profitability with social responsibility and environmental protection. The purpose of this scientific research is to achieve a systematization of the main non-financial performance indicators relevant to the activity of economic entities in Romania in order to favor sustainable economic growth and ensure transparency for stakeholders.

The economic environment of the Digital Age, characterized by the acceleration of technology innovation, fierce competition in gaining competitive advantage, increasing consumer expectations, and emerging market pressure, leads leadership to adapt Vision and Entity Strategy to new performance standards. Thereby, Leadership is the key active force that motivates and coordinates an organization to accomplish its objectives. A leader creates a vision for the others and then directs them towards achieving that vision. To be a leader, you must have followers who have confidence in you and who give you their support and commitment to a goal. The objective of this chapter is to demonstrate the role of contemporary leader in the digital economy.

This chapter presents the evolution and perspectives of management accounting in the digital economy. The main objectives of this chapter are to present the different conceptual approaches of the digital economy and Industry 4.0, the B20 pillars and their impact on the management accounting, the role of management accounting and of the management accountant in the new economy, forecasts and solutions regarding the adaptation of the management accounting to the digital economy, and cost management of the implementation of innovative information technology. All aspects presented are based on national and international professional studies and attempt to present the current state of the themes addressed. The chapter ends with the author's conclusions regarding management accounting in the digital economy. Through the authors' contribution, the chapter offers perspectives and solutions to increase knowledge to implement information technologies and adapt accounting management to these innovative waves.

Preface

The digital transformation produced by the fourth industrial wave or Industry 4.0 forces companies in all industries to re-orient their operation way and business policy. The holistic and well-coordinated approach to digital transformation initiatives has led in recent years to significant improvements in company performance, with increases in turnover, productivity and operational efficiency. Other positive effects produced by implementing innovative technologies have led companies to economic growth, reduced costs, or maintained customer numbers. With increasing competition, in the context of the interconnected digital economy, cooperation between pro-active and pro-competitive companies is required. Innovative technological advances in the digital markets lead to high investment rates among companies and this impact extends to all economy areas. Some of these effects and their impact on companies have been translated into this book; the purpose of continuing a previous edition is to present various and multidisciplinary approaches to improving companies' performance through innovation in the digital economy.

As suggested by its title, *Improving Business Performance through Innovation in Digital Economy* explores various areas where the digital economy is implemented and its consequences or impacts on the various activities of companies whose primary goal is maximizing profit. The target audience of this book is made up of researchers, professionals and teachers who have gained experience in information systems with real interest in innovation and business success in the digital economy. The results of the authors' studies of the chapters in this book provide some practical solutions to adapting to new innovative technologies and to successfully implementing the digital economy among large or small companies. Exploring the opportunities of the digital economy seeks to identify new successful ways to contribute to business success in companies, opening doors to unexplored and un-quantified issues.

Through the 15 chapters published in this book, we invite any specialist or simple reader to become the witness and decision maker of the digital economy by exploring ways to improve business performance while exploring the new opportunities of the topics debated by the authors. We hope that in this second edition, readers will find answers to many of their questions and that it will help broaden the topics discuss either at the academic or business level.

Some of the drivers and barriers brought by the Internet through technology innovation and the economy shared by the tourism industry in South Africa are presented by Unathi Sonwabile Henama in the first Chapter "The Sharing Economy in South Africa's Tourism Industry: The Case of Uber e-hailing taxi services". The Disruptive technology has created radical change in the tourism industry just like the emergence of the Internet. The cost of doing business has decreased, leading to more competition for customers and lowering of the entry barriers. Customers have been the biggest winners, as competition has transferred more power in the hands of consumers, creating a consumer culture. The sharing economy has developed along with the Internet where consumers have become active players in the provision of services in the sharing economy against established businesses. The sharing economy created by technology platforms make it possible for a reduction in the costs of doing business, by lowering the barriers of entry and causing disruption in markets with low competition. The technology platform provided by sharing economy companies matches those that want to offer services and those that seek services, and Uber (taxi services) and Airbnb (accommodation) are the leading pioneers.

An analysis based on the similarities between Maslow's and the corporate social responsibility pyramids revealed that different stakeholder groups may have opposite interests in relation to affiliated companies, generating moral dilemmas, as highlighted in Chapter 2, "Commercial Real Estate - Specific Approaches and Ethical Dilemmas in the Relationship between Stakeholders", by the authors Ionica Oncioiu, Dan Adrian Popovici, Hrisanta Cristina Ungureanu, and Florentina Raluca Bîlcan. An analysis of organizational and economic accounting patterns in commercial real estate is provided with examples of companies listed to Stock Exchange. Conflicts between stakeholders should be avoided due to the direct impact on the company's development perspectives and value. Companies have ethical dilemma in terms of social responsibilities due to differences between the stakeholder's interests. A conflict between stakeholders triggered by real facts or through allegations that are not verified will mean a loss of shareholders because even when the issue is solved, the market capitalization will be lower compared to its initial values, as suspicions will remain in place.

The impact of taxation on the online business environment in Romania and the results obtained from this study are presented in Chapter 3 "Tax Advice - An Essential Element in the Success of an E-Business" by the authors, Traian Ovidiu Calotă, Mihaela Ristache, Alin Eliodor Tănase. In the last 30 to 35 years, the world economy has been marked by a rapid development of the services sector, especially in economically developed countries, the degree of internationalization being a major feature of no doubt. The contribution of tax consultancy to the development of the economy has been remarkable in most areas of activity. The results asserted the research hypothesis: Romanian firms' strategies were influenced by the phenomenon of corruption reported, in particular, to tax evasion. Governments around the world are trying to respond to growing budgetary pressures by trying to introduce measures to combat tax evasion. Among them is Romania, which has lately changed its legislation on identifying undeclared revenues to tax. A continuous improvement of the strategy to identify and develop new processes leads to increased performance, efficiency of skills and harmonization of results.

The most important role in increasing the sustainability in digital business through the innovation of franchise via Netchising is highlighted in Chapter 4 "Sustainable Development through Franchise Innovation in Digital Economy" by the author Ye-Sho Chen. Franchising has been popular as a strategy for businesses to grow and innovate. It is even more so in today's business need of developing digital solutions for sustainability. In responding to the United Nations' Sustainable Development Goals, using franchise innovation to replicate proven sustainable solutions in other parts of the world is an effective approach to scaling up solutions to achieve Sustainable Development Goals. The essence of a successful franchise innovation lies in managing a good relationship between the franchisor and the franchisee. Specifically, it is debated that franchise innovation via Netchising, combining the digital power of the Internet for global demand-and-supply processes and the international franchising arrangement with local business solutions for sustainability is an entrepreneurial approach to the communities' development where economic and social aspects are mutually supportive.

Valuable, new information on the power of digital business transformation and its impact on accounting are brought to the fore in Chapter 5 "Cyberaccounting for the Leaders of the Future" by authors Alina Stanciu, Marius Petrescu, Anca Gabriela Petrescu, Florentina Raluca Bîlcan. To achieve this mission, it is necessary that leaders and accountants of the future should make the digital transformation visible in economic statistics and build a new modern economic infrastructure, through researching new performance indicators based on the use of AI technology and the capacity of interoperable teams to innovate in terms of cyber security threats. Digital transformation became the road map for any economic entity and together with financial capital; know-how capital assets and work are performance force driven. On the short term, cyber accounting will improve the international compatibility of current performance indicators and make statistical systems more flexible and responsive to the introduction of new and evolving, disruptive concepts such as Cloud, Edge Computing and 5G Technology. The true digital transformation will be achieved on the long term by the global economic community by redesigning a new, interdisciplinary platform protected from cyber-attacks and interconnected through partnerships between all the stakeholders involved with the powerful support of researchers.

Intelligent Assistance Systems for Marketing Decisions influences business development as a company's performance and its beneficial options are highlighted in Chapter 6 "Intelligent Assistance Systems for Marketing Decisions" by authors Mirela Dogaru, Dumitru Alexandru Stoica, Aurelian Vânceanu. Business intelligence software is the simplest way to analyze a company's data and information, just above other methods, and can be used for many purposes. The benefits of Business Intelligence software to Romanian companies are numerous. With the help of this software, many companies have identified their opportunities, valued their company, their capability, comparing strengths to competition, and have been able to identify market trends and rapidly change their requirements. A big asset of the companies was reporting, which is the basis of Business Intelligence, and a strong point in the evolution of the business; moreover, it helps in finding a solution for even better development, and with the help of financial reports they understood the company's situation regarding incomes and expenses. To choose business intelligence software is the best option because it allows you to import data from different locations, adjust your reports to variables, and make a forecast of them. It simplifies the working method and employees will no longer be stressed by managing the reports – everything will be at your fingertips, and with time you will be able to find solutions and plans for the future.

Digital transformation borders using Open Innovation lenses is presented through a polycentric research that provides an overview of the intellectual structure that combines Open Innovation and Digital Transformation in Chapter 7 "An Open Innovation Lens on Digital Transformation Frontiers" by authors Maryia Zaitsava, Elona Mark, Manuel Castriotta. By implementing bibliographic coupling method, the authors bring together segmental publications from different research fields and provide a comprehensive overview of the combined Open Innovation and Digital Transformation fields' intellectual structure, revealing the different groups of thoughts, influential authors and pressing topics. Five main research groups are identified: Co-evolution of Digital Technologies and Open Innovation; Digital Peer-communities; Digital Ecosystems; Knowledge Management in the Open and Digital Era; Open Innovation, Digital Technologies and Businesses Performance. The current research contributes both Open Innovation and Digital Transformation fields by cross-exploring each phenomenon and revealing how Digital Transformation shape the nature of innovation as a collaborative activity as part of an independent research area.

The development of the theoretical-methodological and substantive mechanisms for improving the management of enterprises is presented in Chapter 8 "Methodology of Monitoring the Financial Situation of Enterprise" by the authors Ionica Oncioiu, Nelu Mocanu, Ioana Ponagoreţ. Besides, the accountancy methods used today for analysis are made on short time being oriented towards research, in a long period of the added value of the company. The results show that the methodological indications suggested may be used at the organization of the monitoring system in an enterprise that has a stable functioning, at the activities of re-establishment of the payment capacity of the debtor enterprises, at the procedures of external management. It analyzes the strategic attitude in insolvency situations. Under the conditions of organizational stress, an increased ingeniousness and flexibility in the application of different strategies is required from the top-management of the industrial enterprise, that have as main purpose the drawing of the enterprise out of insolvency. This paper pointed out the types of strategy that must be applied in the actual situation of the enterprise: growth, stability, coming out.

A systematization of the main non-financial performance indicators relevant to the activity of economic entities in Romania in order to favor sustainable economic growth and ensure transparency for stakeholders is highlighted in Chapter 9 "Sustainable economic intelligence, a new dimension of information provided by non-financial indicators" by the authors Ionescu Constantin Aurelian, Mihaela Denisa Coman, Liliana Paschia, Nicoleta Luminita Gudanescu Nicolau, Sorina Geanina Stanescu. Sustainable economic intelligence, as a form of superior manifestation of an economy based on knowledge and innovation requires the management, quantification, monitoring and reporting of non-financial information by economic entities (environmental issues, social and personnel aspects, respect the human rights and combating corruption) defined in relation to the average number of employees, total balance sheet and net turnover. These elements, combined in the non-financial statements of economic entities, are decisive in achieving the transition to a sustainable global economy, combining profitability with social responsibility and environmental protection.

The role of the contemporary leader in the digital economy is presented by author Lavinia Essen in Chapter 10 "The Aspects of Leadership Development in Digital Economy". The economic environment of the Digital Age, characterized by the acceleration of technology innovation, fierce competition in gaining competitive advantage, increasing consumer expectations, emerging market pressure, leads the leadership to adapt Vision and Entity Strategy to new performance standards. Thereby, Leadership is the key active force that motivates and coordinates an organization to accomplish its objectives. A leader creates a vision for the others and then directs them towards achieving that vision. To be a leader you must have followers who have confidence in you and who give you their support and commitment to a goal.

The evolution and perspectives of management accounting and the role of the management accountant in the digital economy are presented in Chapter 11 "Management Accounting in the Digital Economy: Evolution and Perspectives" by the authors Sorinel Căpuşneanu, Dan Ioan Topor, Dana Maria (Oprea) Constantin, Andreea Marin-Pantelescu. The paper presents the different conceptual approaches of the digital economy and Industry 4.0, the B20 pillars and their impact on the management accounting, the role of management accounting and of the management accountant in the new economy, forecasts and solutions regarding the adaptation of the management accounting to the digital economy, and cost management of the implementation of innovative information technology. All aspects presented are based on national and international professional studies and attempt to present the current state of the themes addressed. The chapter ends with the authors' conclusions regarding management accounting in the digital economy. Through the authors' contribution, the chapter offers perspectives and solutions to increase knowledge and implement information technologies while adapting accounting management to these innovative waves.

A perspective of benchmarking in Romanian SMEs in terms of customer quality, cost, effectiveness and satisfaction is analyzed in Chapter 12 "Benchmarking - A Method to Improve Entity's Performance and Change Process" by the authors Ana Maria Ifrim, Alina Stanciu, Monika Brigitte Sürgün, Hrisanta Cristina Ungureanu. The results show that for many Romanian organizations, benchmarking is still a little overlooked, on the one hand because of the lack of necessary financial resources, and on the other hand, due to a poor awareness of the importance of these investments in the medium and long term. The implementation of performance management within an entity meets multiple requirements directly related to the level of achievement of the set goals. A first requirement refers to the need for leadership to evaluate and manage a low level of performance relative to objectives, which has other implications: focusing on the entity's strategic objectives, aligning resources with activities, feedback and future development directions. 2030 represents the new time horizon that has prompted entities to shape their vision, strategy and performance objectives as clearly and convincingly as possible. Although it seems remote as a time horizon, an in-depth knowledge of the resources of each entity with a potential to increase performance includes the management system as a whole, along with the methods and techniques implemented to define performance indicators.

The discovery of the socio-psychological consequences of the digital divide on Nigerian rural residents is presented in chapter 13 "Digital Divide and Its Socio-Psychological Implications on Rural Dwellers in Nigeria" by Afolayan Oluyinka Titilope. Unprecedented growth in the use of ICTs has contributed to digital divide in Nigeria. Despite global efforts in bridging the digital divide in developed and developing nations, digital equality is yet to be achieved in nations. The Government's effort in bridging the digital divide in Nigeria has become a daunting task due to several barriers hindering the use of ICTs by the rural dwellers such as low income, low deployment of telecommunication infrastructure, lack of skills, access, language and cultural challenges among others. The author further discusses the dimensions and perspectives to digital divide, the causes of digital divide, the global efforts in bridging it and the barriers militating against it, along with its social and psychological consequences on rural dwellers. Policy recommendations were made towards addressing the socio-psychological implications of digital divide on rural dwellers in Nigeria.

The unusual sources of funding and sustainability of the Nigerian SMEs and the ways they can be accessed are highlighted in Chapter 14 "Uncommon Sources of Finance and Sustainability, Growth and Development of Small Medium-sized Enterprises in Nigeria" by Abraham Oketooyin Gbadebo. In Nigeria, the lack of knowledge on non-traditional sources of funding has either contributed to the death or slow pace of development of SMEs. Some of the uncommon sources are crowd funding, merchant cash advance, elusive business grant and small business administration. The chapter exposes these sources as well as present guidelines on how they could be accessed. Finance is obviously not the factor militating against SME growth and development in Nigeria is certainly the most crucial. The chapter presents different definitions of SMEs in quantitative and qualitative terms. It also discusses the uncommon sources of financing SMEs in Nigeria. Finally, it presents arguments of scholars on the sources of financing SMEs in Nigeria, by showing that there is no consensus in the sources of finance identified by the researcher. Consequently, there is need for SMEs stakeholders to go beyond the traditional method of financing and explore the possibilities of the uncommon ones discussed in this chapter with a view to getting solutions to the paucity of funds that has been hindering the steady progress of SMEs in Nigeria.

Some interesting aspects related to the importance of information security and how to prevent cyber-attacks with the aim of damaging mobile phone users are presented in Chapter 15 "The Importance of Information Security and Strategies to Prevent Data Breaches in Mobile Devices" by Maulik Desai, Swati Jaiswa. Mobile devices have upgraded from normal java-based phones whose basic functionality was calling, messaging, storing contact information to a more adaptive operating system like Symbian, IOS, Android, who have smart features like e-mail, audio player, camera etc. Gradually, everyone started relying more and more on these mobile devices; this led to an increase in the number of cell phone hackers. Common ways that a hacker gets access to your phone is via phishing, shoulder surfing, piggybacking etc. There are countermeasures to this like bookmarking your most visited sites, using VPN, using encryption algorithms. Data theft and identity theft are a new concern for today's users; this chapter aims to educate the end user of different ways in which their privacy can be invaded via a mobile phone.

Acknowledgment

Looking back, we wish to thank all the persons who made the publishing of the present volume possible: Jan Travers, Melissa Wagner, Erin Wesser, Christina Henning, Nicole Elliott, Kristina Byrne, Lindsay Johnston, Joshua Witman, Nick Newcomer, Jaimie Watts, Josephine Dadeboe, Jordan Tepper, Sean Eckman, Marianne Caesar, Colby Conway and many other IGI – Global team members, reviewers, collaborators, and all the contributing authors: without your efforts and dedication this editorial project would have never been possible.

Chapter 1
The Sharing Economy in South Africa's Tourism Industry:
The Case of Uber E-Hailing Taxi Services

Unathi Sonwabile Henama
https://orcid.org/0000-0002-1111-0729
Tshwane University of Technology, South Africa

ABSTRACT

Disruptive technology has created radical change in the tourism industry, just like the emergence of the Internet. The cost of doing business has decreased, leading to more competition for customers and lowering of the barriers of entry. Customers have been the biggest winners, as competition has transferred more power into the hands of cunsumers, creating a consumer culture. The sharing economy has developed as a result of the Internet where consumers have become active players in the provision of services in the sharing economy against established businesses. The sharing economy created by technology platforms make it possible for a reduction in the costs of doing business, by lowering the barriers of entry and causing disruption in markets with low competition. The technology platform provided by sharing economy companies matches those that want to offer services and those that seek services, and Uber (taxi services) and Airbnb (accommodation) are the leading pioneers.

INTRODUCTION

The sharing economy has radically changed the world and even the world of work.Technological changes usually creates revolutionary changes in the world of business. "The emergence of new technology is frequently addressed and studies by looking into the interactions between technology supply and demand" Laurell & Sandstrom (2016, pp. 3). Technoloy has tended to create new markets, lowering barriers of entry and creating disintermediation in certain sectors. Laurell & Sandstrom (2016) noted that Uber's entry into the taxi market can therefore be analysed and understood as a new technological solution, competing with an established solution. "The travel industry is ideally suited to the Internet and was one of the first major industries to be disrupted by technology. Technology broke down the traditional

DOI: 10.4018/978-1-7998-1005-6.ch001

business channels, allowing businesses to be more efficient, creating exciting new opportunities and also empowered travellers by giving them much choice" De Waal (2015, pp. 1). "The phenomenon of the sharing thus emerges from a number of technological developments that have simplified sharing of both physical and non-physical goods and services through the availability of various information systems on the Internet" Hamari, Sjoklint & Ukkonen (2015, pp. 2). "The 'sharing economy' matches people who want to share assets online" Petropoulos (2016, pp. 1).The introduction of the sharing economy has decreased prices in the tourism industry, which has increased the critical tourism consumption through increased customers. "The market size of the tourism industry expands from the increase the number of visitors" Fang, Ye & Law (2016, pp. 1).

"Companies such as Airbnb and Uber are part of the sharing and collaborative economy which experiences an upward trajectory in growth. In the recent past, tourism companies were the exclusive providers of tourism products and services, and online platforms have allowed individuals to provide services. This involves an individual using a resource such as accommodation (Airbnb) and an automobile (Uber) to provide tourism services in the marketplace against established busiensses, thereby creating disruption" Manavhela & Henama (2018, pp. 610). "Since the take-off of disruptive travel consumer models such as Uber and Airbnb, conventional travel providers have been stressing about the impact of these industries will have on 'business as usual'" Steyn (2017, pp. 1). Disruption has emerged as the new normal as businesses face an ever increasing speed of change. "The disruptive Uber example demonstrates the effectiveness of the "on-demand economy" with allocation of physical possessions-how Uber does not need to own a car, relying, instead, on volunteers who subscribe to its mobile app and get connected to clients, who are competitively charged on a metered-cost basis"

The benefits of the sharing economy, are noted by Tatum (2017), as the following:

- Economically, one can save money and/or earn income.
- Environmentally, sharing than owning is more sustainable consumption.
- Practically, accessing rather than owning enables greatr choice; and
- Socially, one can meet new people and forge new relationships.

According to Queensland Tourism Industry Council (2014), the pros and the cons of the sharing economy are shown in Table 1.

Relationship Between Tourism and the Sharing Economy

The relationship between the sharing economy and tourism has led to the pooling of resources to provide services in the tourism industry. The tourism industry has certain parts that have low barriers of entry, whilst others such as aviation require deep pockets. The impact of the sharing economy has been one of lowering barriers of entry, which has increased tourism consumption as the cost of tourism consumption has decreased dramatically. The fact that the sharing economy is technology based, is an additional benefit for the tourism industry which has been responsive to technology. Technology had benefited the emergence of low cost carriers (LCC) that had reduced the cost of travel, as LCCs used technology to reduce their labour costs. LCCs such as companies located in the sharing economy have used technology to achieve lower costs. "The sharing economy has had a positive impact on tourism as well as a negative one. Its advocates think that it provides easy access to a wide range of services that are often of higher quality and more affordable than those provided by traditional business counterparts. Critics,

Table 1.

Factors	Regulated Tourism Businesses	Unregulated Sharing Companies
Price	The price of regulated products covers all overhead costs including licensing and permits.	The prices of unregulated products are typically lower than regulated products as compliance costs are not a factor.
Authenticity	Hotel rooms, taxis, and other tourism products provide a consistent approach, e.g. a hotel room in London and one in Sydoney may operate and even feel the same.	Consumers believe they are "living" in a similar way to a local resident and therefore believe they are experienced greater authenticity.
Environmental	Regulated businesses usually consume greater amounts as products are pucthased primarily for the consumer. This also include the physical buildings where businesses operate.	Sharing companies allow people to use their existing resources in a higher capacity.
Communication	There are established systems in place for response, complaints and queries. Consumers expect that the supplier will offer a quick-immediate response as risk of business loss would be higher.	Communicatiin with the consumer is depended on when the supplier has time and their willingness to respond. No real damage is incurred to the suppliers from lack of response.
Reliability	Booking systems are sophisticated and highly accurate. Where bookings are taken incorrectly, alternatives can in most cases be offered to the consumers.	The booking system relies on the supplier regularly updating their profile/status. The consumer may not be edequately compensated when the booking is taken incorrectly due to the detached relationshipbetween the supplier and the sharing company.
Transparency	Businesses are generally required to identify their address, cost, details their product and provide photographic or other evidence of the quality.	The potential for false listing is significantly higher. There are great ease in operating under a false guise, or provide a product that does not exist or is vastly different to how it is advertised.
Health and Safety	Businesss require all the necessary licenses, permits and safety equipment to operate, guaranteeing the health and safety of consumers.	There are no guarantees for the product. Consumers are subject to the risk and essentially responsible for their own personal safety and belogings.
Quality	A minimum standard of quality is guaranteed through compliance with regulations. Reviews, which often include exper reviews, also provide indication of the quality of a product.	The quality of the product is unknown and cannot be guaranteed. Peer reviews can be provided, however, these reviews are generally controlled by the sharing companies and therefore can be moderated.

on the other hand, claims that the sharing economy provides unfair competition, reduces job security, avoids taxes and poses a threat to seafety, health and disability compliance standards" Juul (2015, pp. 1). "In this milieu, the proliferation and diffusion of sharing economy are unbroken and several companies became global players like Uber or Airbnb" Boros et al. (2018, pp. 27). The sharing economy will continue to shape the tourism industry, and increase mass participation in the tourism industry, which would institutionalise th habit of holidays.

E-Hailing Taxi Services in South Africa

E-hailing taxi services have been able to compete with meter taxi drivers specifically and other transport providers generally by using technology platforms to match supply and demand better than existing competition. "Ridesourcing allows travellers to request a ride in real-tome through a smartphone application, which communicates the passenger's location to nearby drivers. After a driver accepts a ride request, the passenger can view the vehicle's real-time lcation and estimated arrival time. The app provides GPS-enabled navigation, which helps non-professional drivers find destinations and reduce the chances of taking a circuitous route. The payment-and sometimes tips-are automatically charged to the passengers credit card" Rayle et al. (2016, pp. 169). E-hailing services have succeeed in improving the response rate and reduced waiting times to get a taxi services.

Rayle et al. (2016) noted that ridesharing wait times were more consistent across day of week, time of day, and areas of the city. The advancement in matching supply and demand seamlessly, whilst ensuring predicatablity of waiting time has won e-hailing services a plethora of customers, making e-hailing service providers, the industry leader. "The rise of the Trabsport Network Company (TNC) modes proved that there are problemsn in the current conventional taxi service"). Paronda et al. (2017, pp. 7). The problems associated with TNC cannot be reduced to technology, as they are multicated. The high rate of urban congestion in major cities is a result of spatial planning that promoted urbanisation primarily for taxation purposes. TNC companies have not just been competition to metered taxis, they have led to mode switching.

People that have and own cars, may opt to use TNCs instead of driving their own cars. This is an aspect of TNC operation that has received scant attention, when compaed to mode switching that defined the emergence of low cost carriers (LCCs). TNCs might have a greater impact in developing counties when compared to developed, because of the inherent poor transport systems that exists in developing countries, In other words, TNCs can exist as the efficient part of the public transport system. Paronda et al. (2017) noted that convenience, safety, reliability, less hastle, ease to book, cashless paymets, and drivers that have undergone background checks are some o fthe reasons that people chose TNC operators. In addition, transparent pricing that is reflected upon trip request investigation, gives the custiomer additional rights which don't exist in conventional metered taxis.

History

"Uber, a high-tech ride-sharing platform company, was founded in March 2009 and was regarded as the highest-valued ventured-supported firm" Waanabe et al. (2016, pp. 2). "Uber connects drivers offering rides and passengers seeking them online. Potential passengers downloan an app that allows them to request the nearest available Uber car on their smartphone. The company does not own cars, but signs up private drivers willing to provide rides to paying passengers and passes the ride requests directly to them" Petropoulos (2016, pp. 2). E-hailing services just like Uber, have been able to lead the transport industry with innovation, whose speed of change has left many competing companies. "The term Uber has entered the global lexicon, complete with an advertbial expression-uberisation-symbolysing the impact disruptive technologies are meeting wherever we live anywhere on the planet" Mwaura (2016, pp. 1).

"Uber has taken over the taxi industry by storm with rival taxi associations in SA going so far as to protest against the ride-hailing service" Wheels24 (2016, pp. 1). Paronda et al. (2017) noted that Uber Technoloies Inc. was founded in March 2009, after a beta launch in the summer of 2010, it officially launched in San Francisco in 2011.According to Vetter (2016) Uber is not a taxi company-it's an online platform that connects popeple, a peer-to-peer business model. Uber become a market leader through institutioanlising excellent service as part of its taxi sevice. "Uber increased the amount of accountability by providing a two-way rating system for passengers and drivers. After each ride, both parties rated each other on a five-star scale. The rating system also allowed Uber to monitor and evaluate its drivers and determined if and when driver contracts needed to be determined, and provided information to passengers and drivers to decide if they wanted to choose a different driver/passengers before the ride began" O'Toole & Matherne (2017, pp. 563).

In 2016, cash paymenst were introduced in South Africa. It is not the first time, that Uber has introduced cash payments, as noted by Phakathi (2006) that Singapore's introduction of cash payments had a positive impact on demand. "In Europe and North America, Uber accounts are tied to a customer's credit card, eliminating the need for cash. But in sub-Saharan Africa, where only about a third of people own a bank account, low credit cards usage has presented another obstacle to Uber's growth" Jorgic (2016, pp. 2). Uber was able to adapt to the market conditions that exist in Southern Africa, where cash is king. Uber clearly understands that it must be at the forefront of innovation, and it has invested heavily in Research and Development. According to Huet (2017) Uber noted that it had hired NASA aircraft engineer Mark Moore to work on Uber Elevate, to create flying cars that are proposed to take-off in Dubai in 2020.

Uber signed a Space Act Agreement with NASA to create an air traffic control system to manage these low-flying possibly autonomous aircraft according to Hawkins (2017). Wired Transport (2017) noted that the 'modular vehicle' comprises of a car that, essentially, can disconnect from its wheels and can be picked-up by a flying set of rotors, and Airbus designed the concept with Italdesign. Uber designed the flying cars, understamding that urban congestion will increase, and Uber is providing a solution for urban congestion using flying cars. If the roads are congested, a passenger could take to sky. Uber will be pionnering "urban air mobility". This autonomous electric car will detach from the ground module when traffic ic bad, and be collected by self-piloting, 4.4 metre air-module, which picks up the capsule and delivers it and the occupants to the desired destination. According to Hawkins (2017) Uber's flying care project Elevate added Los Angeles as one of the cities where the aerial taxi service will be piloted in 2020.

Uber Employment

"In recent years, a number of firms have launched business modes that match demand for services to independent contractors providing these services. These businesses rely on independent contractors working intermittent or non standard hours. While these businesses do not offer many of the benefits of traditional employment relationships, they do provide an opportunity to service providers to earn compensation on a flexible schedule…The fastest growing part of this contract labour environment are digital platforms that instantaneously match buyers and sellers"Chen et al. (2017, pp. 2). "Uber drivers are considered independent contractors, so they are not entitled to minimum wage, paid vacations or health insurance" Petropoulos (2016, Pp. 6). Rawlins (2015) noted that Uber is an international transport that does not employ any driver or own any cares, but provides the technoloby platform that enables the conection between driver and passengers.

Without the technology platform, those that were traditionally outside of the taxi industry, would remain unable to provide taxi transport services. South Africa which is a constitutional democracy, where the rule of law is entrenched through an independent judiciary. The definition between independent contractor and employee has always been a grey agree for a sharing economy company such as Uber. South Africa has a strong labour unions, that participate in labour issue (labour bargaining) and in the political economy of South Africa, by determining the political dynamics of the country. Several unions approached the Commission for Conciliation, Mediation and Arbitration (CCMA) against Uber SA (a subsidirary of Uber BV based in the Netherlands). According to Sanlam (2017), the CCMA case of

Uber South Africa Technological Services (Pty) Ltd vs NUPSAW, SATAWU and other (2017) the commissioner concluded that the relationship between was one of employment, and that Uber South Africa was for all intents and purposes, the real employer of the drivers in South Africa.

This meant that Uber South Africa had to undertake labour relations processes to displine Uber partner drivers, instead of terminating their service, and therefore, the relationship. Chen et al. (2017) conceptualised that Uber drivers purchases the right to purchase the right to work during a shift for a fixed fee, during a "Uber shift" scenario, the driver has the right, but is not obligated to work each individual hours in a purchased shift. Uber has emerged as an attractive investment opportunity for many South Africans who have procured automobiles that would become Uber cars. Uber South Africa does provide a platform where Uber accredited drivers, can source opportunities for those who have their autombiles accredited to become Uber cars, providing an employment opportunity. According to Holmes (2016) DriverSelect allows Uber-approved vehicles to be rented out through UberSelect to drivers for between R2000 and R3000 a week. Uber had created a form of disruptive entrepreneurship which has changed the new world of work.

Minibus Taxis

South Africa has an absyam public transport system that is domninated by the minibus taxi industry. Minibus taxis are privately owned, actually in all honestly, South Africa does not have a public transport system. "South Africa's minibs taxi industry, scorned by other motorists for reckless driving and dogged by a reputation for violence, moves 15 million people everyday, most of them lower income blacks. More like buses thanthe taxis of New York or London, the rumbling 16-seaters are the wheels of Africa's largest economy" Dolan (2014). "The South African minibus taxi industry is a multi-million rand industry that has the majority of the ownership in the hands of black people" Henama (2013, pp. 63). The emergence of Uber has not direcrly challenged the minibus taxi industry, instead the direct competiton has been the metered taxi's who had charged customers excessives fees for their service.

Uber's emergence had substituted the services of the metered taxi's, whislt also activating a whole new market segment of people that have never used a metered taxi's before. This means that a critical mass of new customers were activated by Uberisation of taxi services in South Africa. Uber has had the impact of leading to leading to mode switching from other transport forms. "While Uber fares are typically higher than public transit fares, riders will subsititite Uber for public transit is Uber is fast enough and convenient enough to outweigh its additional cost. The case of Uber complementing public transit comes from the fat that most public transit systems use fixed routes with fixed schedules. It is Uber's ability to substitute for transit for those trips where transit works poorly that allows Uber to complement transit overall" Hall, Palsson & Prince (2017, pp. 15).

Surge Pricing

According to Uber (2018) the trip fare are calculated to take into account:

- Base fare: the price for pickup.
- Time: from start to end of a trip.
- Distance: miles or kilometres of route.

- Surge pricing (if applicable).
- Tolls and other fees (if applicable).

"Uber's model is designed to ensure that the supply of Uber drivers keep up with the demand for rides. When demand increases, the cost of a ride increase-know as 'surge pricing'-in order to encourage more drivers to become available. In this sense, Uber atleast reduces the challenges of finding a sober ride, although whether Uber is cheaper than a taxi service depends upon the prevailing demand at a given time" Brazil & Kirk (2016, pp. 3). Uber is able to match supply and demand is that it created a platform where the taxi services could be provided without the taxi license. "During periods of excessive demand or scarce supply, when there are far more riders than drivers, Uber increases its normal fares with multipliers whose value depends on scarcity of available drivers. This so-called surge pricing uses microeconomics to calculate a market price for riders and drivers alike.

The goal of surge pricing is to find the "equilibrium price" at which driver supply matches rider demand and riders' wait time is minimised. Studies show that surge pricing achieves what it was designed to do: it brings more drivers online, and it allocates available rides to those who value them more" Dholakia (2015, pp. 1-2). Surge pricing is the tax for ensuring demand is matches by supply, in times when traditionally wait time for getting a ride would be long because of low demand. According to Petropoulos (2016) Uber dynamic pricing policy, passengers can also be hurt when prices are high if there is a lack of alternative operators. In the case of South Africa, Uber has emerged as an extension of the public transport system for a country, that has an abysmal, under-funder public transport system. The abysmal public transport system has increased private automobile ownership, which has increased road congestions in major South African towns and cities.

According to Petropoulos (2016, pp. 4) " taxis are heavily regulated: rates are fixed and taxis must buy licenses to operate. Such licenses are issued rarely, and become more valuable as the urban population grows…However Uber has severely reduced the value of licenses, as Uber drivers do not need licenses to enter the market. Licenses no longer grant protection from competition". Uber has changed the rules, by breakingg the rules created by regulation, by creating more supply for taxi services that has been supported by customers. The taxi license system has been to benefit the taxi drivers at the expense of the customers, by creating a critical shortage of supply. Uber is able to flood the market with part-time drivers during peak periods, where the fares are higher. This ensures that heightened demand is matches by readily available supply. In the long term, Uber is discouraging customers from buying their own vehicles. In addition, it reduces the costs of owning a car, especially in cities and towns where there is limited parking.

Uber Crime in South Africa

"Most cities still employ a traditional roadside hailing taxi industry, meaning that the e-hailing mode competes with the traditional roadside hailing mode for both customers and taxi drivers" Wang et al. (2016, pp. 214). According to Petropoulos (2016) if taxis are unable to respond to the challenge of Uber, then they will be gradually be driven out of the market and Uber will become the dominant player. This is driven by customers undertaking mode switching towards Uber because of its convenience, transparent pricing and buit in safety features. When customers undertake mode switching, they hardly go back to the traditional suppliers of services, which may mean extinction of the metered taxi driver industry. E-hailing providers have remained relevant to customers, by spending money on research and development initiatives that have increased their ability to innovate. The e-hailing services have diversified from only providing taxi services, by focusing on other goods and services required by customers. Gabel (2016) noted that Uber is able to provide services at lower prices, in part, because its drivers are subject to less regulations. Crime against Uber partner drivers in South Africa is well documented, and has ranged from damage to property to several deaths with the metered taxi drivers being the main culprits. South Africa's International Airports are major crime hotspots between the Uber and the metered taxi drivers. The airports which are National Key Points, have tried to clamp down on violence at airports.

According to Lombard (2016) traffic law enforcement officials have clamped down on taxis and Uber drivers picking up travellers from drop-and-go areas in South Africa's airports. As a result of this, Lombard (2016) noted that Uber added a new R20 surcharge to compensate for parking. The Uber customer would then be directed by the Uber driver, where they have parked in order not to violate the rules of drop-and-go areas. In order to try and get Uber partner drivers and client, Uber South Africa launched an Incident Response Team (IRT) called ANN7 (2018) which is part of the Uber's Global Incident Response Team. The high rate of crime that has been directed towards Uber partner drivers and clients, had led to the IRT. The IRT is a call back line and safety related incidents line, providing riders and partner drivers with 24/7 access to Uber's global incident response team according to Broadband (2018). The IOL (2018) summarised the safety and support features of Uber offers:

- Uber has hired additional private security response teams in areas such as key Gautrain stations.
- They have partnered with multiple security response services that are able to dispatch security and medical services in emergency situations in a reduced time, in an effort to improve the safety of driver-partners who use the Uber appl.
- Their Incident Response Team (IRT) is available 24 hours a day, 7 days a week to respond immediately to any reported incidents or accidents globally.
- They also have a team of former law enforcement professionals who are working closely with the police to support any investigations.

Broadband (2018) noted that the IRT feature access is as follows:

- Clicking "Trip and Fare Review'.
- Select the trip in question.
- Select "I had a safety-related issues"
- Submit a ticket though the node.
- The rider will receive a call within minutes.

Uber reacted to the expectional nature of crime in South Africa by installing dashcam, which were digital cameras that would be installed in the front of the Uber cars. In addition, an SOS botton would be installed within the Uber cars. Van Zyl (2016b) noted that Uber began a dashcam pilot in Cape Town, as a means of additional security. The population of e-hailingcars which includes Uber and Taxify is three times larger than the metered taxi industry. Customer preferences have shifted towards e-hailing companies, as the acts of violence and the killing of Uber drivers has made customers to boycott the services of the metered taxi drivers. The acts of violence have actually done more to reduce customer demand for the metered taxi drivers.

CONCLUSION

By creating disruption, the technology platforms is able to dominate the markets that it operates by offering lower prices because of lower costs. The inputs are lower as the technology platform attracts a critical mass of people with resources that they use as collateral to offer services. People with autombiles, submit their vehicles for approval on the Uber system and offer taxi transport services. Those with rooms and whole houses offer them for on the Airbnb system, to become hosts. The net benefit is that created mass employment opportunities, in addition to entrepreneurship opportunities. The emergence of the sharing economy has led to collaborative consumption which in the case of Uber has allowed those with cars to provide trips, for those who require trips. This form of disruptive entrepreneurship had lowered the barriers of entry, and led to a collision course between Uber operators and the metered taxi drivers. Acts of intimidation, violence and loss of life has been the result of the turf war. South Africa which has an abysmal public transport system dominated by the minibus taxi industry. The emergence of Uber has filled an unmet transport need in South Africa. Uber has been used by locals and tourists as a cost-effective and safe transport system.

The cost-leadership pricing strategy of Uber, under cut the monopoly enjoyed by the metered taxi drivers. Surge pricing operated by Uber has allowed for demand to be always matched by supply, by creating the financial incentive for Uber partner drivers to become available at times of thin supply. Uber has forced metered taxi drivers to adapt to the emergence of a new competitor. Metered taxi drivers have developed their own online applications. Uber has remained relevant by diversifying to UberEats, offering a delivery service. UberAssist was initiated in South Africa to meet the needs of the elderly and the physically challenged. Uber self-driving cars will be a reality, and this will create disruption for the Uber partner drivers as they may no longer be needed as drivers. According to Petropoulos (2016) 'the presence of Uber might force the taxi industry to innovate and adopt new technologes to improve their service and survive. "In terms of work, Uber creates more jobs than it destroys. This leads to a clear increase in efficiency and provides overall income gains. Even if losers were fully compensated, the sume of the gains-shared by the firm, its mostly part-time workers, and its customers-woeld far outweigh the losses" World Economic Forum (2016, pp. 2). In the case of South Africa, the emergence of Uber has not stolen customers from metered taxi drivers, it has initiated and catalysed a whole new market. Rawlins (2015) noted that Uber drivers in South Africa noted that the most of their customers have never used a metered taxi before. In addition, private automobile owners would use Uber instead of driving their car, especially to get the Gautrain, the high speed train network.

Uber exists only in the major metropolitian cities of South Africa, and this excludes the rural hinterlands. Metered taxi drivers in South Africa can co-exist with e-hailing operators such as Uber, if only they can embrace technology. The emergence of Uber has lowered the barriers of entry into the taxi industry, and the metered taxi driver must adapt or die. The National Department of Transportation has already made amendments to legilstion to recognise e-hailing services. "The sharing economy is not a panacea (more on that below), nor a one-size-fitsall solution; however, it continues to outpace the "traditional" economy in terms of growth and investment" Tatum (2017, pp. 2). Scholar transportation is an avenue where metered taxi drivers can acquire a monthly anchor customers. Scholar transportation is funded by the Department of Basic Education, when a transport provider is accredited and has registed on the central database of government. Uber is at the forefront of innovation, and this means that it will pioneer new ways of transportation. Uber which has successfully tested self driving cars, will cause disruption to the Uber partner drivers. This means over time there will be a decline of employment opportunities for the Uber driver, as self-driving cars become the new standard. Possibly self-driving cars will co-exists for sometime with Uber partner driven cars, where the self-driving cars would come at a cheaper costs.

"Uber won't lock down its drivers with employee contracts, bit it could (eventually) control a fleet of self-driving cars. It's still possible autonomous vehicle provide the moat that helps Uber reach tech-giant status, but there are plenty of reasons to believe they will hand the advantage of Uber's competitors instead" Mims (2018, pp. 4). "The sharing economy, at certain developmental stages, plays an important role in solving the unemployment problem. Therefore, governments should formulate appropriate policies for its regulation" Fang, Ye & Law (2016, pp. 3). In the case of South Africa, it has created more jobs than destroying jobs. Any initiative that creates jobs in South Africa will get support from the government considering that South Africa has a high rate of unemployment. The emergence of Uber has created a new transport means for a country with an abysmal transport system. It has improved the economic performance of the Night Time Economy, through the reliability of the transport that it provides and has become an important source market for the Gautrain, which is a high speed train services in the economic hub of South Africa, Gauteng Province. Uber has not stopped to innovate, ranging from Uber self-driving carrs to flying cars that will be piloted in 2020 as part of Uber Elevate. As the world is grappling with the sharing economy, Uber will play a leading role in the fture of jobs and employment within the era of the Fourth Industrial Revolution.

REFERENCES

ANN7. (2018). *Uber SA launches Incident Response Team.* Retrieved from http://www.aan7.com/uber-sa-launches-incident-response-team/

Bhattacharya, A., & Balachandram, M. (2017). *Uber and Ola may soon have a new competitor: the government of India.* Retrieved from https://qz.com/103837/

Brazil, N., & Kirk, D. (2016). *Uber and Metropolitan Traffic Fatalities in the United States.* Retrieved from https://www.researchgate.net/publications/

Broadband. (2006). *Travel pioneer starts online roll-out in SA.* Retrieved from https://broadband.co.za/nephp/4021.html/

Broadband. (2018). *Uber South Africa adds call-back line for safety.* Retrieved from https://broadband.co.za/news/motoring/

Chen, M. K., Chevalier, J. A., Rossi, P. E., & Oehlsen, E. (2017). *The value of flexible work: Evidence from Uber drivers.* NBER Working Paper Series.

Competition Commission. (2015). *Uber: A game-changer in passenger transport in South Africa.* Retrieved from http:/.www.competition.org.za/

Cooper, A. (2016). Staying safe with strangers. Lifetech. *Sunday Independent,* Sept. 18.

Cramer, J., & Krueger, A. B. (2016). *Disruptive change in the taxi business: The case of Uber.* NBER Working Paper Series.

David, F. (2017). *Lawsuit spotlights regulation of sharing economy.* Tourism Update. Retrieved from http://www.tourismupdate.co.za/article/118539/

De Waal, P. (2015). *Technology is reshaping the travel industry.* Tourism Update. Retrieved from http://www.tourismupdate.co.za/artile/29777/Technology/

Dholakia, U. M. (2015). Everyone hates Uber's surge pricing-Here's how to fix it. *Harvard Business Review.* Retrieved from https://hbr.org/2015/12/

Dipa, K. (2016). Taxify to take on Uber in SA. Retrieved from http://www.iol.co.za/motoring/industry-news/

Dolan, D. (2014). Inside SA's R40bn taxi industry. Retrieved from http://www.moneyweb.co.za/archive/

Dube, S. H. (2015). Uber: A game changer in passenger transport in South Africa. Retrieved from https://www.competition.org.za/review/

Fahey, L., & Randall, R. M. (2001). *The Portable MBA in Strategy* (2nd ed.). New York, NY: Wiley & Sons.

Fang, B., Ye, Q., & Law, R. (2016). Effect of sharing economy on tourism industry employment. Research Notes and Report. *Annals of Tourism Research, 57*, 234–278. doi:10.1016/j.annals.2015.11.018

Gabel, D. (2016). Uber and the persistence of market power. *Journal of Economic Issues, 50*(2), 527–534. doi:10.1080/00213624.2016.1179060

Goodfellas. (2018). Reasons to Join. Retrieved from https://www.gfellas.co.za/index/php?option=com_content&view=article&id=3/

Govender, J. J. (2014). Public transport service quality in South Africa: A case study of bus and mini bus and mini-bus services in Johannesburg. *African Journal of Business Management, 8*(10), 317–326.

Guttentag, D., & Kirk, D. (2016). Uber and Metropolitan Traffic Fatalities in the United States. *American Journal of Epidemiology, 184*(3), 192–198. doi:10.1093/aje/kww062 PMID:27449416

Haas, A., & Bird, J. (2016). *Uber is arriving now: Driving urban mobility in Africa.* Retrieved from http://blogs.lse.ac.uk/africaatlse/

Hall, J. D., Palsson, C., & Prince, J. (2017). *Is Uber a substitute or complement for public transit?* Source Unknown.

Hamari, J., Sjoklint, M., & Ukkonen, A. (2015). The sharing economy: Why people participate in collaborative consumption. Retrieved from http://onlinelibrary.wiley.com/doi/10.1002/asi.23552/abstract/

Harding, S., Kandlikar, M., & Gulati, S. (2016). Taxi apps, regulation and the market for taxi journeys. *Transportation Research Part A, Policy and Practice, 88*, 15–25. doi:10.1016/j.tra.2016.03.009

Hawkins, A. J. (2017). *Uber's 'flying cars' could arrive in LA by 2020-and here's what it'll be like to ride one.* Retrieved from https://www.theverge.com/

Henama, U. S. (2013). A dream deferred? Santaco Airways, A low cost carrier that never launched in South Africa. *International Journal of Business, Economics and Law, 2*(2), 60–67.

Henderson, K. (2016). Innovators or Rule Breakers? Regulating Uber, Airbnb & the Sharing Economy. *(Unpublished Dissertation, University of Otago)*.

Holmes, T. (2016). Uber cited as example of sharing economy, but its vast resources suggest otherwise. *Mail & Guardian.* Retrieved from https://mg.co.za/article/

Huet, E. (2017). Uber plans to test flying cars in Dallas and Dubai by 2020. Retrieved from http://www.fin24.com/Tech/Companies/uber/

IOL. (2018). Uber introduces rider call back line for added safety. *Travel News.* Retrieved from https://www.iol.co.za/travel/travel-news/

Jorgic, D. (2016). Uber seeks to lure cabbies in Africa expansion plan. *Moneyweb.* Retrieved from http://www.moneyweb.co.za/news/tech

Juul, M. (2015). *The sharing economy and tourism: Tourist accommodation*. European Parliamentary Research Services.

Kalmbach, Z. (2015). The effect of ridesharing services on drunk driving. *(Undergraduate research thesis, Texas University).*

Kelly, R. W. (2016). *The Uber Effect. Undergraduate Awards.* Retrieved from http://ir.lib.uwo.ca/undergradawards_2016/8/

King, I., & Newcomer, E. (2018). *Uber spends $10.7bn in 9 years-here's how that stacks up.* Retrieved from https://www.iol.co.za/business-report/

Laurell, C., & Sandstrom, C. (2016). Analysing Uber in social media-disruptive technology or institutional disruption? *International Journal of Innovation Management*, *20*(5), 1–19. doi:10.1142/S1363919616400132

Lien, T. (2017). *As Uber spends big to compete with Lyft, profitability in the U.S. is not in sight.* Retrieved from http://www.latimes.com/business/technology/

Lombard, L. (2016). *Alert: Uber changes pick-up regulations at SA international airports.* Retrieved from http://traveller24.news24.com/TravelPlanning/

Madisha, K. (2018). Uber, Taxify drivers 'at risk'. *Afro Voice. Gauteng News.* May 16.

Manavhela, P., & Henama, U. S. (2018). Surge pricing as a new pricing model for transport services: The case of Uber in South Africa. *Conference proceedings of the 8th AHTMM Conference,* Bangkok, Thailand, (pp. 606-618).

Mims, C. (2018). *Uber's biggest problem: Its business model*. Source Unknown.

Moneyweb. (2017). *Namibia tells Airbnb hosts to register or face jail.* Retrieved from https://www.moneyweb.co.za/news-fast-news/

Mwaura, G. (2016). *Uber: The beauty and wrath of disruptive technologies in Africa.* Retrieved from http://www.newtimes.co.rw/section/article/

Naik, S. (2015). *We compare: Uber vs metered taxi.* Retrieved from https://www.iol.co.za/motoring/industry-news/

Ngcukana, L. (2017). Uber rival Taxify launches service in Eastern Cape. *City Press,* Nov. 12.

Nkanjeni, U. (2017). *Uber gift cards: A new offering across SA.* Retrieved from http://www.traveller24.com/TravelPlanning/uber-goft-card/

O'Toole, J., & Matherne, B. (2017). *Uber: Aggressive management for growth.* Retrieved from https://www.researchgate.net/publications/

Overly, S. (2017). Driver tips to change for Uber. *Business Report.* Retrieved from http://www.iol.co.za/business-report/international/

Parker, A. (2017). *Uber vs. meter taxis: The last of the professional drivers.* Retrieved from http://www.wheels24.co.za/News/Gear_and_Tech/

Parker, N. (2016). After exiting China, Uber shifts focus to Latin Maerica. *CNN Tech.* Retrieved from http://money.cnn.com/2016/12/06/technology/uber-latin-america/

Paronda, A. G., Regidor, J. R. F., & Gaabucayan-Napalang, S. (2017). *An exploratory study on Uber, GrabCar and Conventional Taxis in Metro Manila.* Conference Paper. Retrieved from http://www.researchgate.net/publication/31895959598/

Pearce, J. A., & Robinson, R. B. Jr. (2007). *Strategic Management: Formulation, Implementation and Control.* Boston, MA: McGraw-Hill.

Petropoulos, G. (2016). *Uber and the economic impact of sharing economy platforms.* Retrieved from http://bruegel.org/2016/02/02/

Phakathi, B. (2006). *Uber to experiment with cash payments.* Retrieved from http://www.bdlive.co.za/business/transport/

Porter, M. (1985). *Competitive Advantage: Creating and Sustaining Superior Performance.* New York, NY: The Free Press.

Queensland Tourism Industry Council. (2014). *The Sharing Economy: How it will impact the tourism landscape and what businesses can do.* Queensland Tourism Industry Council.

Rawlins, L. K. (2015). *Uber stifled by slow regulation.* Retrieved from http://www.itweb.co.za/

Rayle, L., Dai, D., Chan, N., Cervero, R., & Shaheen, S. (2016). Just a better taxi? A survey-based comparison of taxis, transit and ridesourcing services in San Francisco. *Transport Policy, 45,* 168–178. doi:10.1016/j.tranpol.2015.10.004

Reuters. (2017). *Malaysia legalises e-hailing services as Grab, Uber compete.* Retrieved from http://www.reuters.com/article/

Roy, B., Mamun, A., & Kuri, B. C. (2015). Sustainable tourism supply chain management for tourism industry in Bangladesh. *Global Journal of Management and Business Research for Real Estate, Event & Tourism Management, 15*(2), 1–7.

Salomon, R. (2016). Why Uber couldn't crack China. *Fortune.* Retrieved from http://fortune.com/uber-china-didi-chuxing/

Sanlam. (2017). *Independent contractor or employee-the Uber case.* Cape Town, South Africa: Sanlam.

Sigala, M. (2014). Customer involvement in sustainable supply chain management: A research framework and implications in tourism. *Cornell Hospitality Quarterly, 55*(1), 76–88. doi:10.1177/1938965513504030

Sithole, H. (2016). We don't feel safe: Uber drivers. Retrieved from http://www.sabc.co.za/news/a/

Steyn, L. L. (2017). Travelstart partners with Uber for half-price airport transfers. Retrieved from: http: //www.traveller24.com/TravelPlanning/travelstart

Szpilko, D. (2017). Tourism Supply Chain-Overview of Selected Literature. 7th International Conference on Engineering, Project and Production Management. *Procedia Engineering, 182*, 687–693. doi:10.1016/j.proeng.2017.03.180

Tau, P. (2017). Uber driver's death raises fears, tensions. *City Press,* July 23.

Tralac. (2017). *The sub-Saharan African services economy: Insights and trends.* Retrieved from https://www.tralac.org/news/article/

Uber. (2018). *How are fares calculated?* Retrieved from https://help.uber.com/

Van Zyl, G. (2015a). *Cape Town is Airbnb's top African market.* Retrieved from http://www.fin24.com/Tech/Companies/Cape-Town-is-Airbnb's-top-market/

Van Zyl, G. (2015b). *Uber, WesBank in R200 m car rental deal.* Retrieved from http://www.fin24.com/Tech/Companies/uber-wesbank/

Van Zyl, G. (2016a). *Travelstart receives $40m investment boost.* Retrieved from http://www.fin24.com/Tech/Companies/travelstart/

Van Zyl, G. (2016b). *Uber pilots dashcams, panic buttons in SA.* Retrieved from http://www.fin24.com/Tech/Companies/travelstart/

Vetter, S. (2016). *Uber, digital and disruption: what is happening and why does it work?* Retrieved from https://digital.pwc.co.nz/uber/

Waanabe, C., Naveed, K., Neittaanmaki, P., & Fox, B. (2016). Consolidated challenge to social demand for resilient platforms-lessons from Ube's global expansion. *Technology in Society.* doi:10.1010/J.TECHSOC.2016/10.006

Wang, X., He, F., Yang, H., & Gao, H. O. (2016). Pricing strategies for a taxi-hailing platform. *Transportation Research Part E, Logistics and Transportation Review, 93*, 212–231. doi:10.1016/j.tre.2016.05.011

Wheels24. (2016). *Would you tip your Uber driver? More than 6000 South Africans say NO*. Retrieved from http://www.wheels24.co.za/News/

Wired Transport. (2017). *Airbus has designed a part-car part-drone to help beat traffic*. Retrieved from http://www.wired.co.uk/article/airbus-flying-car/

World Economic Forum. (2016). *The regulatory challenges of disruptive companies*. Retrieved from https://www.weforum.org/agenda/

Chapter 2
Commercial Real Estate–Specific Approaches and Ethical Dilemmas in the Relationship Between Stakeholders

Ionica Oncioiu
European Academy of the Regions, Romania

Dan Adrian Popovici
Titu Maiorescu University, Romania

Hrisanta Cristina Ungureanu
Valahia University, Romania

Florentina Raluca Bîlcan
Valahia University, Romania

ABSTRACT

The chapter considers a similarity between Maslow's and Corporate Social Responsibilities pyramids. Various groups of stakeholders may have opposite interests in relationship with related companies, generating moral dilemmas. An analysis of organizational and economic accounting patterns in commercial real estate is provided with examples of companies listed to Stock Exchange. These common patterns are in accordance with all professional standards, but still do not offer sufficient information for an informed investment decision of an average investor. The choice of accounting policy is one of the reasons why real estate industry is perceived as a high risk, as a high degree of subjectivity applies through the choices of accounting treatment. Conflicts between stakeholders should be avoided due to the direct impact on a company's development perspectives and value.

DOI: 10.4018/978-1-7998-1005-6.ch002

INTRODUCTION

The manner in which business ethics is defined and the content is very different based on the industry specific, the level to which the term is applied (individual, organization, or environment), the time when the definition was created or the emphasis various authors put on aspects they want bring into community's attention (Marsh, 2013; Cowton & San-Jose, 2016). As in each language the meaning of words defines the problem, the returning to the basics seems the most reasonable. The word ethics is coming from Ancient Greek „êthos (ἦθος)" and has the meaning of character, moral nature. It results that we discuss about an entity (human being initially and extended to juridical) and his (it's) morality (Michel & Rosenbloom, 2011). In determining what it is moral, the definition provided by Stuebs and Wilkinson (2010) ethics represents "a set of concepts and principles that guide us in determining what behavior helps or harms sentient creatures", could be very useful because establishes a referential system.

In the case of a juridical entity, the „help or harm" guidance should refer to both, people and entities that represent the environment in which the company operates (Zang, 2012). This approach integrates both aspects of ethics: the character and the moral nature (Ajzen & Fishbein, 2005). Going further on, the environment can be defined as the stakeholders (employees, shareholders, government, customers, suppliers, financial institutions etc.).

Ethics can be defined as a code of conduct applicable to any situation when the correctness / inaccuracy of certain actions of an individual are involved, with the aim of achieving an expected outcome. In the financial and accounting field, ethics is an essential feature for optimal performance of micro and macro-economic activity (Armstrong, 1993; Greenfield, Norman & Wier, 2008; McDonald & Donleavy, 1995; Soltani, 2014).

Arsalidou (2017), in his work, wants to find solutions for global organizations to be able to change their actions so they become more ethical and, implicitly, more transparent. In this respect, it analyzes the main causes of a financial disaster, being closely related to bankers' attitude, mentality and behavior: excessive greed that pushes them into dangerous temptations (e.g. securitization and short maturity), behavioral limitations (e.g. trust and optimism excessive knowledge of financial products and risk awareness. From this point of view, the role of ethical education can be analyzed in a triple hypostasis. First, it can teach potential future leaders to act altruistically and act responsibly for social purposes. Secondly, it ensures commitment to a primary goal of sustainable development - pursuing all the interests of the parties involved in the smooth running of the activities of an entity, not just the interests of the shareholders. Thirdly, it is essential for future leaders to be aware of behavioral deficiencies that often characterize those who hold senior management positions; the risks of a biased judgment; the risks of lack of knowledge regarding the financial contrasts of the organization. Thus, ethical education helps to stabilize integrity at the entity level, increases transparency and improves corporate governance, all based on business ethics.

Englund and Gerdin (2018), in a study, both about the origin of business ethics and about the current state of research and development in this field, focuses its objectives on fundamental positions and key arguments in business education, business is based, mainly on a social function of entities, based strictly on the phenomena of values. Various research has been carried out in the literature on business ethics and its objectives (McDonald & Donleavy, 1995; Herndon, 1996, Schwartz, 2001; Hosbay, 2014; Gravelle, 2015).

This chapter wants to present similarities between the needs of human beings and companies because the set of morality rules are determined by these needs; discuss specificity of real estate industry and differences between moral and legal; argue about the fact that helping certain stakeholders could mean harming others and sometimes stakeholders group themselves to impose a certain „moral code" that offers them benefits detrimental to others; explain through a case studies how the above points apply for a real companies.

BACKGROUND

Real estate industry includes various aspects of property such as development, appraisal, marketing, selling, leasing, and management of commercial, industrial, residential, and agricultural properties (Oates & Dias, 2016; Webb, 1996; Alzola, 2017). The analysis below refers only to commercial segment and more specific to groups listed to stock exchange that are the owners of property and the reporting is done in accordance with International Financial Reporting Standard (IFRS).

Specific to the organizational structure of the group: only the holding company is listed to the stock exchange for the obvious reason to raise capital; the financing from banks is usually negotiated at holding level and is afterwards distributed to the individual companies as share capital or loans; the obligation to issue financial statements for investors in accordance with IFRS refers only to Group, not to individual entities; each property is included within a single company – a Special Purpose Vehicle (SPV) – usually a limited liability one; it is common that the ownership of SPVs is not directly linked to the company listed to Stock Exchange, but through holdings located in countries that offer tax advantages; for Groups that include a large number of companies the SPVs do not have employees (Book, 2012; Giacomino, 1992; Hoffman et al., 2006). All the services are provided through specific entities (subsidiary or not), creating synergies and decreasing costs; the SPVs usually do not have their own employees (McCuen, 1994; Vladu, Amat & Cuzdriorean, 2016; Ponemon, 1995).

Specific to economic accounting: International Accounting Standard (IAS) 40 allows an entity to treat the property at fair value or at cost; the fair value model, unlike the valuation model where the valuation surplus goes into a reserve account, require that any difference should go in profit and loss; the cost model requires the recognition of property, after the initial measurement at cost, at „depreciated cost (less any impairment accumulated losses)" in accordance with IAS 16; fair value of property is done by a specialized company that could use any method considered appropriate (discounted cash flow alone or combined with residual value, market value etc.); profits are generated mainly through rental revenues (property is provided in operational leasing to tenants) and fair value differences; the SPV's may act in economic environments with different currencies compared to the currency in which the holding presents the consolidated financial statements; while it is a common practice to link the cost of services provided (rent, communication) to a stable internationally accepted currency such as US$ or EUR, the transactions performed by the SPVs could be considered a mix of stable currency and local one; in such cases IAS 21 allows the use of judgement and the usual manner the group proceeds is to establish the stable currency as functional one (Johnson, Fleishman, Valentine & Walker, 2012; Gino, 2015; Albrecht, 1991).

The real estate industry is recognized for the level of risk (Ashkanasy & Windsor, 1997; Dechow, P., Hutton, A., Kim, J. H., & Sloan, 2012; Keen, 2006). High attention is provided by the auditors before accepting an assignment for a company acting in this area and special approval procedures are required (Roxas & Stoneback, 2004; Guthrie & Parker, 2016). The risk results also from the fact that the financial crisis in 2008 was triggered by subprime mortgage – the valuation of properties created the bubble - and afterwards expanded through the investment banks.

The financing is realized in a centralized manner, justified through the scale economies (Applbaum, 2000; Dechow, Ge & Schrand, 2010). It is obtained from the shareholders or financial institutions. In the first case the shareholders will feel more comfortable as the business risk can be dissipated due to portfolio (SPVs) spread and location, in the second case it could be obtained better interest rates and offered required warranties to financial institutions (Hassan, 2005). The dilemma appears when the holding uses the money obtained not only to purchase SPV, but also to provide financing to SPV for construction of property or working capital. The financing can be provided as share capital or as interest bearing loan. The use of share capital method should not raise questions except when the investment is done in a non-stable country and the holding needs to be able to quit it quickly to protect its shareholders. In the case of loans the problem is linked to transfer price value of the interest rate perceived. If furthermore the loan provided is obtained from raising capital, the holding acts as a bank, without being one. The purpose for which the group was created initially and for which the share capital was raised changed without consulting the providers of capital and, in conjunction with other factors, as we will see, could harm an uninformed investor (Johns, 1998; Mele, 2005; Pilaj, 2015).

It is common for the groups acting in real estate market to purchase an SPV, to improve it in terms of rental revenues and occupancy, automatically influencing its fair value, with the difference reflected directly in the profit and loss account of the group and afterwards to sell the shares held by the holding company located in a country providing fiscal advantages and being taxed there. In economic terms this business model maximizes the profit of shareholders by decreasing the taxation and eliminating the expenses and taxes to be paid in the case of selling only the property. But let's consider the stakeholders of SPV and in particular the state where the property is located. One of the roles of the state is the redistribution of wealth through reallocation and in order to be able to do it, as stakeholder, the state should maximize its revenues. It results a potential conflict between 2 stakeholders of SPV, with opposite interests and a moral dilemma for the group – how should it be distributed the increase of value between the shareholders and the environment that generated the profit.

The obligation of issuing only the Group Financial Statements, without providing the individual financial statements of SPVs can be justified through the relevance and the volume of information to be processed and efficiency (resources used versus result). However, it opens a large area of judgement and opportunities for creative accounting and business models such as:

- The use of different accounting policies, allowed by IFRS, for the financial statements of the Group versus the financial statements of SPV.
- Restrictions in the distribution of profits through dividends, resulting from the impossibility of SPV's with losses to distribute dividends to holding, the latest one not being disclosed to the investors.
- Reclassification per type and value of expenses by choosing, based on judgement, a stable currency as functional currency of entities instead the use of local currency and the translation of this currency as presentation one in accordance with IAS 21.

The above matters comply with the legal and professional requirements, but raise questions about ethical aspects and put in potential conflict the interest of various stakeholders: shareholders that have the right to be fully informed, company's employees and in particular the management that is interested in not presenting the possible complications if not required, the state through the taxes that should be received.

Let's focus for the beginning to the choice of accounting treatment for property. It is well-known that the global economy has cycles consisting in expansion (growth) and contraction (recession). Each industry is influenced by the global economy cycle in different ways. The real estate cycle is usually 6-8 years long and varies from country to country (Saunders, 1995; Campbell & Cowton, 2015).

Almost all real estate industry that we defined in the scope of this article uses to treat in Group Financial Statements their properties based on fair value model. If we establish a link between the accounting treatment and the economic cycle, the profits will be extremely important during the growth phase, while in recession, the loss will be amplified. This choice compared to the more conservative way of using IAS 16 will motivate the potential investor in the stock exchange to invest based on the return computed, without considering the economic cycle. Supplementary we can remark that the increase in the value of property is a non cash item and would eventually contribute only to the transactional share value.

When an investor (the potential shareholder) takes an investment decision, the consideration is provided to the increase of share value and the dividend provided after the entity succeeds to obtain the financial resources needed for development and working capital (Johns, 1998). As the profit that has a cash correspondence results from rent revenues less operating, financial expenses and taxes, it results that the only internal source for dividend payment, growth and day to day activities is limited. The increase of share value due to total profit, out of which a very material or determinant part relies on the fair value model, is only on paper (as part of it is on cash) and is realizable as long as it is accepted by the market in general, potential shareholders in particular.

If the group decided to use the business model of holding acting as a bank – previously described - and to use in the case of SPV statutory books IAS 16 for the treatment of property in order to minimize the tax, the SPV could have statutory losses. In this case it is extremely possible that the Group reports profits, while the SPVs report losses. One of the implications is that the Group cannot distribute the profit reported as dividends. Due to different accounting treatment in statutory books, the SPV has not profits and consequently cannot pay dividends. Even more, the SPV based on statutory books requirement, could reach negative equity and request the increase of share capital from the holding company. As the professional standards do not require disclosure of previous matters, we can discuss again about a potential conflict between stakeholders (shareholders, employees and state) and about a moral dilemma (Loeb, 1988).

Based on the differences of taxation system in the jurisdictions where the holding and the SPV operates it is possible that the group structure does not insure the minimum total corporate tax. To understand the previous statement let's consider a simple case – 2 entities that represent a Group and operate in the same country. If these entities are not related parties and do not have common interests, entity A will have a gross profit of 100 and entity B will have 10. The taxable base will be 110. If the Group will use the bank approach and entity A, instead of providing share capital to entity B will provide a bearing interest loan, using the market interest rate, it is possible that the entity A will have a profit of 120 while B will have a loss of 10. The taxable base becomes 120 and if this policy continues at Group level the deferred tax from losses carried forward cannot be recognized (entity B will continue to have a loss), a higher cash flow and a lower net profit occurs. The shareholders and the group will have a disadvantage in terms of net profit and liquidity, while the state will benefit from the arrangement. In practice the things could change due to the different taxation system in the countries where A and B operate, but still the capitalization requirements of B could become a problem. Again an ethic issue and different interests of stakeholders (state, company, shareholders).

RESEARCH METHODOLOGY

The shareholders are interested in increasing the value of their investment (Gray, Bebbington & McPhail, 1994). The key indicators they follow-up relate to dividend's yield, value of share, growth of business. Certain aspects such as the associated risk is not assessed because they do not have the financial knowledge of the industry and even if they have it, the information required to be disclosed is incomplete to allow them to take an informed decision.

The most sensitive area of this industry is the fair value of properties. Group's management usually hires a reputable, multinational company, with subsidiaries in all the countries where SPVs exist, to perform the appraisal. There are a set of criteria (demographics, GDP, location, country risk, demand and offer, class of property etc.) that should be taken in consideration when determining the fair value, but the manner in which the yield and the residual value is computed remains subjective and often not transparent, even for a knowledgeable investor. The impact of the valuation is more than significant. Let's consider a valuation performed based on discounted cash flow. A usual yield, provided by the valuation company is 9%. Let's assume that the yield next year reached 8% (a 1% movement) because the country GDP increased, the interest rates provided by the banks on deposits decreased etc. The impact on the profit and loss account will be 12.5% from the fair value of properties existing in last year balance sheet. As usually the value of property represents over 75% of company's assets, while the rental revenues are around 10% of property value, it is obvious the impact of this professional opinion on the final result reported to shareholders.

Let's assume now that all the stakeholders (real estate group, evaluators, state) act in good faith. Still the subjectivity and the impossibility to compute accurate values remain. The supporting example would be the highest rating provided by international agencies to the investment banks that created the 2008 global crisis.

In practice, apart from the professional judgement, it could be pressures from the company's management over the evaluators, errors of statistic data used to determine the yield, tentation to put on the market studies showing a growing trend of real estate sector, as this will stimulate the investments and the consumption (if an increase of residential prices is expected, people will feel urged to purchase houses). All the above – including the professional judgement - could create a cascade effect and a growth on paper until the moment when the increase is not any more sustainable and the „bubble" explodes. The impact of the explosion could be small – a simple economic cycle of industry- or can trigger a global crisis – depending on how conservative the whole mechanism was. Again it is possible to discuss different approaches from stakeholders, this time the employees of real estate company, the evaluators, the state having similar interest that do not match the safety interest of shareholders – as they will be the ultimate stakeholders loosing from the above cycle if they maintained the investment for a long period based on market analysts opinion. A question that could arise is how ethic is the above system and whether the reporting and legal aspects serves the interest of economic environment in which they act and are sufficient for insuring a fair distribution of information.

Employees and company's management should have similar interest with shareholders in order to have a workplace and benefit of bonuses. They could be tempted to artificially increase the profitability and company's value by using legal means such as accounting policies that maximize the profit, not disclosing important information that is not specifically required by professional standards and create a potential „bubble", favoring economic cycles that could be used to earn money by a specialist with access to inside information. The shareholder's protection through the Stock Exchange regulations usually is not enough. The extreme non ethical attitude could result in manipulating the value of shares traded over the valuators of property to increase the fair value.

Financial institutions that provide loans to a real estate company maintain a discrete presence, as their interest is to be able to recover the money lend. The valuation of buildings is not an issue for them as long as Debt / Equity ratio is under 1 because usually the loan recovery is insured through a collateral – the property – and even if the fair value of property is overvalued, based on the ratio mentioned, they will be able to not record losses. We can say that the banks are one of the most neutral stakeholders.

The state is interested to indirectly create jobs and have a maximum of resources for redistribution. These are somehow balanced and it can be decided to favorite specific sectors that need to be developed by providing facilities (reduced taxation of labor, subsidies etc.). Especially within the real estate industry, in the phase of property / building construction, the access to utilities could raise moral problems. While the connection cost to gas, electricity, water, sewerage paid by the municipality is perfectly legal, what benefit will be provided to a specific real estate company remains debatable. The state could in particular cases to not pursue the best interest of citizens. Same dilemma can extend to the change of height allowed to the buildings in different areas and to the issuance of construction permits.

The clients (tenants) are interested usually in how the real estate owner is seen by the economic environment and it became common to have a clause in the contract through which they may renounce without penalty to it if the owner changes or his reputation on the market is bad. Their interest is to decrease the rent value (opposite to real estate company shareholders) and sometime ask free periods based on claims – real or not – for the services provided by the facility management, quality of building, maintenance work etc. Another questionable practice refers to the request for which the landlord pays the improvements of the space to a supplier company that is client's related party.

The suppliers of utilities remain neutral. However, the valuation companies' subjectivity and transparence in determining the fair value could create a risk for the real estate sector. In the modern world the search of clients is more and more done through agencies that receive a commission to bring a tenant that signs the contract. The strategy of these agencies is to maximize their profit and control the market. By controlling this information, a morally questionable practice but perfectly legal, is to contact the real estate company two years before the contract expires and to ask the extension of the period on behalf of the tenant by receiving twice a commission for the two-year period. As they are in control of market information, the threat is that at the end of the two-year period the real estate company loses its client.

The dividends distribution and the need of increasing share capital are based on statutory books and no sufficient information is available to aggregate and compare versus the cash flows needed to occur between the holding company and SPVs in 2 aspects: need for capitalization and possibility to distribute retained earnings through dividends. Meantime no restriction about the possible distribution of retained earnings appear in the Group Financial statements, as this is not required by professional standards.

Economic accounting contains also patterns in order to minimize taxes (applied to the manner in which the property is treated in statutory books and Group financial statements), but also in the manner of presentation by choosing the functional currency.

Professional judgment of specialized valuators is subjective, and we can remark differences between methods of valuation and discount rates for same geographic areas from one Valuation Company to another. By choosing IAS 40 treatment for the property, the professional, but subjective opinion of valuators can completely change the economic perspective and the investor decision. In any case, even if the approach of property evaluators is conservative, the impact is material compared to group rental revenues and net profit.

The information required to be disclosed by professional standards, while sufficient for the average investor is not sufficient for a professional one to make informed decisions. The level of information disclosed is highly dependent upon Company's management (for example the impact of foreign exchange rates is disclosed in detail by Immofinanz, but not so detailed by the other 2 companies).

Lack of full information may be speculated by stakeholders to pursue their own interest. A conflict between stakeholders, even if solved in company's favor will decrease the market capitalization. Parties loosing from these conflicts are the existing shareholders at the moment of conflict and the company - the first ones through their investment value, the second one through the perspectives of development (raise funds, reputation, and trust of all stakeholders).

SOLUTIONS AND RECOMMENDATIONS

In the context of the current economic situation, if we compare Maslow's and Archie's pyramids it results:

- the basic level for each one insures the existence of the entity; without satisfying physiological need and without being profitable, the entities cease to exist;
- both entities need safety; while in the case of human beings we discuss about security, shelter, medical services, in the case of companies the corresponding need is compliance with legal responsibilities that insures their protection by the state (for example through insolvency, distribution of dividends only after the financial exercise is closed) and also the protection of the environment in which the entity operates versus the actions of the company.
- third level – belongingness – does not exist in the case of companies because it is a psychological need of human beings;
- ethical and philanthropic responsibilities should be grouped together and compared with the last 2 levels in Maslow's pyramid; they are related to moral behavior, the help provided to and by the environment as a consequence of subject's attitude.

In conclusion a parallel can be performed between the needs of human beings and those of companies, and we can expect similarities in their motivations and actions. The difference is that in the case of human beings we discuss about one entity, while in the case of companies we should consider the combination of stakeholder's needs and the people that represent them.

FUTURE RESEARCH DIRECTIONS

Future research directions can be numerous, from detailed analysis of what professional accountants understand through ethical / unethical conduct and the determination of the real factor for which they adopt one of the two conducts. Moreover, further studies can be made on the difference between the adoption of IFAC standards and AICPA standards in terms of reporting and ethical conduct from the perspective of multinationals that respond financially to jurisdictions that apply these standards distinctly. Also, detailed studies have not been made on emerging market companies but with foreign ownership and administrative headquarters in tax havens. Future research opportunities are in the field of taxation when it is possible to measure the impact of the adoption of new tax regulations in combating unfair and unethical fiscal conduct of large corporations.

CONCLUSION

Professional standards leave a large area uncovered in terms of manner the business is presented. Integrity and importance of management's ethical behavior is critical. Also, there are major concerns regarding the development of the educational system regarding professional ethics from the very early age (Baylis & Downie, 1991). Also, more and more corporations are training their staff to adopt ethical professional conduct.

Specific practices and accounting treatment allowed and chosen by real estate companies management, while justified by the need to attract investors and report profit, as condition of juridical entity existence, are the main reason for the risk and volatility of this industry. The conservative treatment would not attract sufficient funds and arguable do not reflect economic reality as perceived by investors market.

Companies have ethical dilemma in terms of social responsibilities due to differences between stakeholder's interests. A conflict between stakeholders, triggered by real facts or through not verified allegations will mean a loss of shareholder because even when the issue is solved the market capitalization will be lower compared versus initial values, as suspicions will remain in place.

REFERENCES

Ajzen, A., & Fishbein, M. (2005). *The Influence of Attitude on Behavior. The handbook of attitudes.* Mahwah, NJ: Erlbaum.

Albrecht, W. S. (1991). Fraud in government entities: The perpetrators and the types of fraud. *Government Finance Review, 7*(6), 27–30.

Alzola, M. A. (2017). Beware of the watchdog: Rethinking the normative justification of gatekeeper liability. *Journal of Business Ethics, 140*(4), 705–721. doi:10.100710551-017-3460-3

Applbaum, A. I. (2000). *Ethics for Adversaries. The Morality of Roles in Public and Professional Life.* Princeton, NJ: Princeton University Press. doi:10.1515/9781400822935

Armstrong, M. B. (1993). Ethics and Professionalism in Accounting Education: A Sample Course. *Journal of Accounting Education, 11*(1), 77–92. doi:10.1016/0748-5751(93)90019-F

Arsalidou, D. (2017). Educating Bankers on Law, Ethics and Social Values: A Perspective from the US, the UK and Europe. *European Company and Financial Law Review, 14*(4), 569–608. doi:10.1515/ecfr-2017-0026

Ashkanasy, N. M., & Windsor, C. A. (1997). Personal and Organisational Factors Affecting Auditor Independence: Empirical Evidence and Directions for Future Research. *Research on Accounting Ethics*, *3*, 35–48.

Baylis, F., & Downie, J. (1991). Ethics Education for Canadian Medical Students. *Academic Medicine*, *66*(7), 413–414. doi:10.1097/00001888-199107000-00009 PMID:2059268

Book, L. (2012). Symposium Introduction: Offshore Accounts, Corporate Income Shifting, and Executive Compensation. *Villanova Law Review*, *57*(3), 421–432.

Campbell, D., & Cowton, C. J. (2015). Method issues in business ethics research: Finding credible answers to questions that matter. *Business Ethics (Oxford, England)*, *24*(S1), S3–S10. doi:10.1111/beer.12093

Cowton, C. J., & San-Jose, L. (2016). On the ethics of trade credit: Understanding good payment practice in the supply chain. *Journal of Business Ethics*, *140*(4), 673–685. doi:10.100710551-016-3050-9

Dechow, P., Hutton, A., Kim, J. H., & Sloan, R. G. (2012). Detecting earnings management: A new approach. *Journal of Accounting Research*, *50*(2), 275–334. doi:10.1111/j.1475-679X.2012.00449.x

Dechow, P. M., Ge, W., & Schrand, K. M. (2010). Understanding earnings quality: A review of the proxies, their determinants and their consequences. *Journal of Accounting and Economics*, *50*(2-3), 344–401. doi:10.1016/j.jacceco.2010.09.001

Giacomino, D. E. (1992). Ethical Perceptions of Accounting Majors and Other Business Majors: A 402 Steven Dellaporta Empirical Study. *Accounting Educators' Journal*, *4*(2), 126–132.

Gino, F. (2015). Understanding ordinary unethical behavior: Why people who value morality act immorally. *Current Opinion in Behavioral Sciences*, *3*, 107–111. doi:10.1016/j.cobeha.2015.03.001

Gray, R. H., Bebbington, J., & McPhail, K. J. (1994). Teaching Ethics and the Ethics of Teaching: Educating for Immorality and a Possible Case for Social and Environmental Accounting. *Accounting Education*, *3*, 51–75. doi:10.1080/09639289400000005

Greenfield, A. C. Jr, Norman, C. S., & Wier, B. (2008). The effect of ethical orientation and professional commitment on earnings management behavior. *Journal of Business Ethics*, *83*(3), 419–434. doi:10.100710551-007-9629-4

Hassan, M. K. (2005). Management accounting and organizational change: An institutional perspective. *Accounting & Organizational Change*, *1*(2), 125–140. doi:10.1108/18325910510635326

Herndon, N. C. Jr. (1996). A New Context for Ethics. Education Objectives in a College of Business: Ethical Decision-Making Models. *Journal of Business Ethics*, *15*(5), 501–510. doi:10.1007/BF00381926

Hoffman, W. M., Brown Kamm, J., Frederick, R. E., & Petry, E. S. (Eds.). (2006). *The Ethics in Accounting & Finance: Trust, Responsibility and Control*. Westport, PA: Quorum Books.

Hoşbay, D. (2014). Organizational Misbehavior: A Research about Perceptions of Managers and Employees in Banking Sector. *The WEI International Academic Conference Proceedings*, (pp. 7-20).

Jane, G., & Gravelle, I. (2009). Tax Havens: International Tax Avoidance and Evasion. *National Tax Journal*, *62*(4), 727–753. doi:10.17310/ntj.2009.4.07

Johns, G. (1998). *Organizational behavior*. Bucharest, Romania: Economic Publishing House.

Johnson, E., Fleishman, G., Valentine, S., & Walker, K. (2012). Managers' ethical evaluations of earnings management and its consequences. *Contemporary Accounting Research*, *29*(3), 910–927. doi:10.1111/j.1911-3846.2011.01135.x

Keen, L., & Ligthart, J. E. (2006). Information Sharing and International Taxation: A Primer. *International Tax and Public Finance*, *13*(1), 81–110. doi:10.100710797-006-3090-7

Loeb, S. E. (1988). Teaching Students Accounting Ethics: Some Crucial Issues. *Accounting Education*, *3*, 316–329.

Marsh, C. (2013). Business executives' perceptions of ethical leadership and its development. *Journal of Business Ethics*, *114*(3), 565–582. doi:10.100710551-012-1366-7

McCuen, R. H. (1994). Constructivist Learning Model for Ethics Education. *Journal of Professional Issues in Engineering Education and Practice*, *120*(3), 273–278. doi:10.1061/(ASCE)1052-3928(1994)120:3(273)

McDonald, G. M., & Donleavy, G. D. (1995). Objections to the Teaching of Business Ethics. *Journal of Business Ethics*, *14*(10), 839–853. doi:10.1007/BF00872350

Mele, D. (2005). Ethical Education in Accounting: Integrating Rules, Values and Virtues. *Journal of Business Ethics*, *57*, 97–109. doi:10.100710551-004-3829-y

Michel, S. D., & Rosenbloom, H. D. (2011). Teaching Clinical Ethics as a Professional Skill: Bridging the Gap Between Knowledge About Ethics and its Use in Clinical Practice. *Journal of Medical Ethics*, *21*, 97–103. PMID:7608948

Oates, G., & Dias, R. (2016). Including ethics in banking and finance programs: Teaching "we shouldn't win at any cost". *Education + Training*, *58*(1), 94–111. doi:10.1108/ET-12-2014-0148

Pilaj, H. (2015). The choice architecture of sustainable and responsible investment: Nudging investors toward ethical decision making. *Journal of Business Ethics*, *140*(4), 609–613.

Ponemon, L. A. (1995). The Objectivity of Accountants' Litigation Support Judgments. *The Accounting Review*, *70*(3), 467–488.

Roxas, M. L., & Stoneback, J. Y. (2004). The importance of gender across cultures in ethical decision-making. *Journal of Business Ethics*, *50*(2), 149–165. doi:10.1023/B:BUSI.0000022127.51047.ef

Saunders, M. (1995). The Forgotten Curriculum: An Argument for Medical Ethics Education. *Journal of the American Medical Association*, *274*(9), 768–769. doi:10.1001/jama.274.9.768 PMID:7650832

Schwartz, M. (2001). The Nature of the Relationship between Corporate Codes of Ethics and Behaviour. *Journal of Business Ethics*, *32*(3), 247–262. doi:10.1023/A:1010787607771

Soltani, B. (2014). The anatomy of corporate fraud: A comparative analysis of high profile American and European corporate scandals. *Journal of Business Ethics*, *120*(2), 251–274. doi:10.100710551-013-1660-z

Stuebs, M., & Wilkinson, B. (2010). Ethics and the Tax Profession: Restoring the Public Interest Focus. *Accounting and the Public Interest*, *10*(1), 13–35. doi:10.2308/api.2010.10.1.13

Vladu, A. B., Amat, O., & Cuzdriorean, D. D. (2016). Truthfulness in accounting: How to discriminate accounting manipulators from non-manipulators. *Journal of Business Ethics*, *140*(4), 633–648. doi:10.100710551-016-3048-3

Webb, J. (1996). Inventing the Good: A Prospectus for Clinical Education and the Teaching of Legal Ethics in England. *The Law Teacher*, *30*(3), 270–294. doi:10.1080/03069400.1996.9992956

Zang, A. Y. (2012). Evidence on the trade-off between real activities manipulation and accrual-based earnings management. *The Accounting Review*, *87*(2), 675–703. doi:10.2308/accr-10196

ADDITIONAL READING

Englund, H., & Gerdin, J. (2018). Management accounting and the paradox of embedded agency: A framework for analyzing sources of structural change. *Management Accounting Research*, *38*(1), 1–11. doi:10.1016/j.mar.2017.12.001

Guthrie, J., & Parker, L. D. (2016). Whither the accounting profession, accountants and accounting researchers? Commentary and projections. *Accounting, Auditing & Accountability Journal*, *29*(1), 2–10. doi:10.1108/AAAJ-10-2015-2263

KEY TERMS AND DEFINITIONS

Education Ethics: It includes a relatively broad range of ethical concerns about education.

Ethical Conduct: A conduct allowed by a code of conduct.

Ethical Misconduct: A conduct which is not allowed by a code of conduct.

Financial Information Users: External - potential investors, state, business partners, internal - employees, managers.

Morality: Set of personal principles which allow a person to distinguish between right and wrong.

Tax Avoidance: The way an entity reduces its taxable income and tax liability.

Tax Evasion: Illegal way an entity uses in order to reduce to completely erase tax liability.

Chapter 3
Tax Advice:
An Essential Element in the Success of an E-Business

Traian Ovidiu Calotă
Titu Maiorescu University, Romania

Mihaela Ristache
Titu Maiorescu University, Romania

Alin Eliodor Tănase
Titu Maiorescu University, Romania

ABSTRACT

This chapter investigates the impact of taxation on the online business environment in Romania. In the last 30 to 35 years, the world economy has been marked by a rapid development of the services sector, especially in economically-developed countries, with the degree of internationalization being a major feature of no doubt. The contribution of tax consultancy to the development of the economy has been remarkable in most areas of activity. The results asserted the research hypothesis: Romanian firms' strategies were influenced by the phenomenon of corruption reported, in particular, to tax evasion. Governments around the world are trying to respond to growing budgetary pressures by trying to introduce measures to combat tax evasion. Among them is Romania, which has lately changed its legislation on identifying undeclared revenues to tax. Continuous improvement of the strategy to identify and develop new processes leads to increased performance, efficiency of skills, and harmonization of results.

INTRODUCTION

In the context of a transition process that Romania has proposed, from the Communist economy to a modern economy, commonly referred to as a "market economy", the economic analysis of the application of economic policy efficiency can provide a guide for political decision-makers and leaders public administration. In this regard, two main objectives, namely the design of economic policies based on efficiency criteria and the creation of management systems for these economic policies that meet the

DOI: 10.4018/978-1-7998-1005-6.ch003

minimum criteria such as: optimal size, low consumption of resources, small time response, and disturbance protection (Ahmed, Neel & Wang, 2013; Dennis, 2014; Florou & Pope, 2012).

The management of modern economies is based on a combination of economic policy instruments to achieve the desired results (Caylor, 2010; Ozkan, Singer & You, 2012). They can be cited as the main instruments of economic policy: taxes (internal taxation), budget allocations (subsidies), customs duties, public investment, and interest rate (Damayant, 2013). By using them, according to the public choice (choice of society), the structure and objectives of the national economic system inevitably change (Jackson & Liu, 2010).

Many of the reported deficiencies were corrected during the reform (Barth, Landsman & Lang, 2008; Cahan & Sun, 2015; Lukka, 2010). Moreover, the principle "nothing is perfect, everything is perfect" also works in accounting. In our opinion, any accounting system, however modern, converging with International Financial Reporting Standards, will never be perfect, because the world economy and, implicitly, the national economy is constantly changing (Richardson, 2011). New trends, new informational needs are emerging, and they pose a challenge to the accounting system and an invitation to reflection for accountants (Chen, Qu & Sun, 2017).

On the other hand, given that companies can choose their accounting policies within certain limits, the results obtained reflect their objectives and not the reality (Baker & Bettner, 1997; Soltani, 2014). In this situation, is the outcome credible and relevant? The objectives of accounting policies differ according to the size of the enterprise and the economic environment in which it operates (Ahrens, 2008; Bettner & Kate, 2013). As an example, it is possible to mention the reduction of the published losses, the decrease of the taxable profit, the increase or decrease of the current result, the increase or the decrease of the profit to be distributed, the temporary arrangement of the accounting results in order to reduce the risk perceived by the financial environment.

Thus, this chapter investigates the impact of taxation on business environment in Romania, by reference to the development of the tax consultancy sector. We will propose innovative methods as well as personalized and customized systems tailored to the needs of its clients in order to attract the interest of the potential clients but especially to serve the current clients as best as possible, developing communication relations that ultimately determine the success of the business developed by the firm.

BACKGROUND

Given the recent history of scandals involving accounting conduct, the credibility of the public accounting profession has dropped significantly, losing one of the core responsibilities of the professional accountant (Doukakis, 2014). According to specialty studies, the share of services in world trade has increased significantly over the last period, with "invisible" exchanges currently accounting for 30% of total world goods and services flows (Byard, Li & Yu, 2011; He, Pan & Tian, 2017). An important place for this is tax consultancy.

At the same time, the population evolves both quantitatively and qualitatively, which leads to a continuous increase and diversification of requirements (Ramanna, 2008). The level of training, increasing for every person as well as for social groups and nations, leads to a significant diversification of the requirements for the basic characteristics of products and services, as well as the inclusion of new requirements for social, safety, prestige needs. Therefore, Brown (2010) supports the importance of increasing demands on reliability, maintainability, technical level, etc. In this context, the success of a tax consultancy firm depends on the quality of all activities directly or indirectly linked to the performance of the services (Holthausen & Watts, 2001). Today's customers have multiple sources of information, are much better informed, can formulate their requirements more precisely and find easy buying alternatives (Li, Qi, Tian & Zhang, 2017). There is also a change in the structure of clients in terms of age, level of training, habitat categories, and occupations (Ball, 2013). These changes lead to a change in the structure of the requirements and, in general, to the orientation towards higher quality goods and services (Alzola, 2017).

Tax advisory activity is defined by the Romanian legislation in Ordinance no. 71 of August 30, 2001, regarding the organization and the exercise of the fiscal consultancy activity, published in the Official Gazette, Part I no. 538 of 1 September 2001. Accordingly, it is in accordance with the provisions in force that it provides professional assistance services in the preparation of tax and tax declarations, tax assistance and budgetary claims, such as fines, penalties, as well as representation before the tax authorities, and in front of the judiciary, as an expert (Chen, Tang, Jiang & Lin, 2010).

Under the terms of the present law, we can characterize the tax consultancy sector through competition, corporate strategy aimed at maintaining and consolidating in an increasingly fierce market, the resources used, and through related areas of accounting, auditing, management consultancy, legal advice (Schleicher, Tahoun & Walker, 2010). In this context, taxation as a whole can be perceived as a tax and tax collection and collection system, but also as a legal ensemble to regulate taxpayers' taxation and to substantiate the mechanism for establishing taxes and duties which is why tax consultancy services must be strictly based on tax, accounting and related regulations in force.

The flexibility of the provisions of the Fourth ECE Directive, concretized through the four models of presentation, as well as the possibility of choosing them by companies, is the expression of the conciliation of cultural differences between the countries of the European Union (Barth et al., 2014). French companies prefer the presentation of the profit and loss account in the form of an account, with the classification of expenses and incomes by nature, while Anglo-Saxon companies interested in meeting the information needs of investors prefer the drafting of the profit and loss account with the classification expenditure by function.

Increasing profitability is essential for the healthy and sustainable development of a business (Andon, Baxter & Chua, 2007). To this end, organizations have a range of ways, each with its advantages and disadvantages. But the greatest challenge in this case is to find that method or that mix of factors that will lead to an optimal increase in term profitability long, with an important role to play in securing tax security, which can only be achieved by calling for tax advisory services (Ball, Li & Shivakumar, 2015). But the market for consulting services is constantly changing, with many firms in Romania offering services in the field of tax consultancy. An accurate record of these firms is difficult to obtain, but there are some sources of information that can provide an overview of this area. Relevant is the analysis carried out by Alin Negrescu, Tax Director at KPMG Romania. Therefore, the intensification of ANAF controls to combat tax evasion has increased the market for tax advisory services by 15-20% in 2015. According to the consultant, this increase was largely due to the anticorruption activity of DNA and other prosecutor's offices (Parker, 2012).

Starting with 2014, these actions, coupled with those of ANAF, brought the consulting firm a portfolio of clients requesting tax and tax assistance. This is especially necessary to investigate the tax implications of strategic decisions to reorganize the activity that are reflected in implementation plans whose stages need to be detailed, including from the perspective of tax costs.

However, sometimes consultants are regarded by business people as characters who say things already known (Fan, Li & Zheng, 2016). This is often true, because there are quite a few situations where consultants are more "creative" than Romanian businessmen. The reality is that no one knows a business better than its owner. Therefore, it is absolutely necessary to create a close collaboration between the two parties involved (entrepreneur and consultant) so that the final result can be properly evaluated and advantageous for each. It should be noted that the activity of tax consultants does not overlap with that of business consultants (management) but is complementary to it. Therefore, the tax consultant has an auxiliary role in the reorganization activity (similar to the role of the management consultant), with the central role of the entrepreneur / manager as a decision-maker.

There are situations in which the cases that entrepreneurs ask for are vaguely formulated or contain unrealistic objectives, such as the expression that they do not want to pay taxes and / or taxes, and / or use sufficient knowledge of tax legislation and the legal consequences of non-compliance. In these situations, it is clear that the role of the consultant is not understood and what he can do (Hou, Jin, Yang, Yuan & Zhang, 2015). Therefore, in the opinion of the above-mentioned authors, the role of tax consultants is to identify the options allowed by the legislation in force, to make them known to entrepreneurs and to support their implementation, according to the entrepreneur's decision.

Probably many entrepreneurs are wondering what he is doing all day in the office as a tax consultant and, especially, why someone would need a tax consultant as long as they have an accountant, called by the authors, "cheap and good-natured" (Barth, 2013). One answer might be that the tax consultant deals with "tricks" to lower the amount of taxes owed to the state. This answer is only partially true because, however much we would like to find "legal loopholes" to diminish the value of taxes, this is very rare and is easy to cancel by the state.

In practice, working with external consultants is, in some cases, a positive experience: consultants come up with a new perspective on a key issue or, by working effectively with client staff, get visible and meaningful results, which results in profits bigger. Other times, their involvement is less successful, or even so much so that the client wonders what else he would ever want to call upon (Allen & Ramanna, 2013).

To assume a failure is an act of courage (Li, 2010). The relationship between the consultant and the client may fail for a number of reasons. Sometimes the consultant does not know about the item or spends the time and energy it needs. But this is rare, most consultants being competent and conscientious people who take their work seriously and really want to offer their customers a quality job. Most often, problems arise at the beginning of the relationship and result from a lack of mutual understanding between the consultant and the client, about the needs of one and the offer of the other. Most consultancy projects do not end so badly, but the most important thing is that the poor performance of consultancy work is often due to a lack of communication.

RESEARCH METHODOLOGY

The Fiscal Consultant profession is an extremely interactive one, consisting of operational work, communication and direct customer relationship. In order to be a Fiscal Consultant, individuals must promote an examination organized by the Fiscal Consultants Chamber on the basis of a regulation approved by the Board of Governors and published in the Official Gazette Part I.

A tax consultant is required to be a graduate of a faculty with an economic profile, to have at least 5 years' professional experience, of which at least 3 years in one or more activities aimed at applying tax and accounting legislation. Another strong point is the lack of a criminal record for committing offenses punishable by fiscal, financial, accounting, customs, and financial discipline. Practically, the work of a tax consultant must be based on certain principles such as objectivity, based on an independent analysis of the risks, opportunities and peculiarities of each client, personal engagement, the development of optimal relationships with clients, and implicitly the building of personalized solutions, as well professional rigor, details, knowledge and experience to find the most appropriate solutions.

The consultant may work as a specialist or expert. In this role, he has to be more informed than his client, the quality of the expert assuming a very narrow field of specialization. The consultant then discusses the client and understands the entire activity of the client, proposing a unique solution tailored to the needs of the client.

In general, a consultant's workflow may vary, depending on the strategy each person adopts. For example, in the case of a request for tax consultancy services from a customer, the consultant has the obligation to prepare the service offer. Tenders must be given a registration number, and must be kept in the required data base. If the customer accepts the proposed service offer, the next step, or the conclusion of a contract, is taken. The contract will be drawn up and completed with the necessary elements for signing by the designated person, to be issued in two copies. Contracts receive a registration number from the entry-exit register and are signed by the partner. The signed contract is sent by email (scanned) or by fax and by post / courier (as the case may be), after which it is kept in the customer file. Depending on the type of contract made available to the client, monthly activity reports are prepared.

Usually, if the customer contract is terminated or terminates by the expiration of the period, for any reason, there is an obligation to end a Contract termination note with the customer. In this regard, any request for termination of the consultancy contract must be immediately communicated to the partner / supervisor.

The profession of consultant is a relatively new profession in Romania, at least in the sense of market economy, based on principles such as economic efficiency, independence, objectivity, assuming professional conduct and ethical code. Practically, the consultant is an independent and qualified person who initiates and implements technological, organizational and behavioral changes within the client organization. He conducts organizational studies and assessments, designs systems and procedures, performs work efficiency studies, measures organization performance, and prepares manuals and procedures to assist the organization's management to lead the work effectively and effectively.

In a functional organizational system, product quality and enterprise efficiency are considered indispensable to each other. Under these conditions, a strong correlation is formed between the organization's performance indices, such as the company's market share, the return on investment, and the quality of the products marketed. Also, the starting point for developing a quality management system is to identify customers and their requirements. This is all the more important as the role of customers is almost decisive in doing business.

For all that, in the field of tax consultancy, the application of the "customer focus" principle implies: understanding all customer needs and expectations about products and services, their features, price, etc.; ensuring a balance between how to address the needs of customers and other stakeholders (owners, organization staff, suppliers, local community, society in general); communicating these needs and expectations throughout the organization; assessing customer satisfaction for continuous improvement of results; customer relationship management.

Taking into consideration the above-mentioned aspects, the following can be highlighted as components of the quality of consulting services:

1. Quality of the consultancy service availability. The availability of the consultancy service is conditional on the observance of the deadlines set for delivery, but especially the timeliness of the customer service and the provision of the service at the right time (e.g. training of the client's personnel, drafting the specific project documentation, etc.);
2. The quality of the provision of the advisory service. The quality of the consultancy service is determined by the quality of the staff (consultants, trainers, etc.), the equipment and other resources used, the available space, the environment in which the service is provided;
3. The quality of access to the consulting service. The quality of access to the consulting service depends on the possibility of contacting the service provider, for example, by phone, to meet him without difficulty, to find out all the necessary information about the services offered;
4. The quality of the relationship with the consultant service provider. The quality of the relationship with the consultant's service provider is determined by the way the customer is received, the attention paid to him, the way his / her wishes, the solicitude of the staff, the personalization of the relationship with the client are received;
5. The quality of the information provided to the client. The information provided must be clear, precise, so as not to give rise to ambiguities, different interpretations by customers (for example, a clear distinction can be made between free and over-the-counter services);
6. The quality of the suggestions made to the client. The quality of the suggestions made can be assessed by the relevance of customer responses, advice on calling to certain services, their adaptation to the specific situation of a particular customer, etc.);
7. The quality of customer satisfaction.

The issues presented may put the private environment in a hurry to face an avalanche of rapid change. Consultants need to quickly understand changes to respond to customer requests. The risk of mistakes is greater, especially in those who are in their early career and have little experience, which can compromise not only promotion, but even the busy job.

Over the last period, it has been observed that this normative act has made numerous changes since its publication. As a positive aspect, it can be mentioned that these changes lead to an increase in the volume of activity because the persons working in the economic field must be up to date and apply the latest changes in the field. But there is also the reverse in the sense that investors, especially foreign ones, cannot realize a timely business plan or give up investment, so there is a reduction in the volume of activity and even the number of clients.

At the end of my study, we identified the most important indicators that can influence taxation in Romania. Therefore, depending on the weighting we have awarded a score of 1 to 5, we have come to the conclusion that taxation, both private and public, presents some risks that may affect, in various forms, the economic sector in Romania.

SOLUTIONS AND RECOMMENDATIONS

In the context of the current economic situation, in the field of activity of any profession, and therefore of the fiscal consultancy, it is necessary to lay it on fundamental principles, meant to ensure high standards of professionalism and quality. In pursuing this profession, the tax consultant must conduct his / her work on the basis of certain principles and values, namely moral, competence and quality.

When we relate to the future, we often try to aspire to changes that inevitably influence the work done. Therefore, it is very important to anticipate these changes in order to meet the challenges in the business environment. Therefore, another aspect that strongly affects the area under consideration and represents a local risk is the continued change in tax legislation. For example, since 2003, when Law no. 571/2003 regarding the Fiscal Code and GD no. 44/2003 on the methodological norms for the application of the Fiscal Code, numerous amendments were made to these normative acts (approximately 68 amendments to the Law No. 571/2003 and 32 to the implementing rules). Also, these changes are not always clear, often creating confusion over the interpretation of the legislation. However, frequent changes to legislation can be considered a beneficial risk because blurring may prompt customers.

FUTURE RESEARCH DIRECTIONS

The decisive factors must be reconciled from the beginning for the consultancy project to evolve towards a happy ending and the following elements should be considered:

- what the customer wants: who thinks it's the problem and how it thinks it should be resolved.
- what the consultant offers is independence, professionalism, uninterrupted care for finding solutions to customer problems.
- what the client needs can sometimes be (albeit not impartial) totally different from what he wants. That is why the consultant needs to understand as accurately as possible the present and future wishes of the client, seeking to solve, according to his experience and competence, the real problems the client is facing and not necessarily what the client wants.

The activity of a tax advisor is often risky for making strategic decisions. It is important to note that a problem with an unclear statement will receive a responsive response. Practically, before addressing a problem to solve a consultant, it is the client who needs to understand the content of the problem, i.e. the tax issues that are to be solved.

CONCLUSION

Every company must expect many obstacles, especially of a technical and managerial nature, to deal with in order to survive and thrive. That is why it is very important to ensure an updated database and a detailed knowledge of the trends in the field. From this perspective, we can refer to some recommendations to get the highest level of quality in managing customer interaction. Thus, the continuous growth of the quality of consulting services can be achieved by increasing customer satisfaction with zero objective complaints from them, the continuous increase of the "good" and "very good" ratings in the surveys for the customer satisfaction assessment, as well as the development of the associated services taking into account market requirements. It can also be noticed that the most important aspects in the client-consultant relationship are: understanding the client's business and its specific needs; quality of communication flow and compliance with established agreements.

It is therefore necessary for a consultant to permanently pursue these goals. Last but not least, customers want a consultant to have a broader approach and develop communication solutions that go beyond the brief, so the company has the opportunity to use increasingly unconventional projects for which customers would be willing to pay more.

REFERENCES

Ahrens, T. (2008). Overcoming the subjective–objective divide in interpretive management accounting research. *Accounting, Organizations and Society, 33*(2), 292-297.

Allen, A., & Ramanna, K. (2013). Towards an understanding of the role of standard setters in standard setting. *Journal of Accounting and Economics*, *55*(1), 1–66. doi:10.1016/j.jacceco.2012.05.003

Alzola, M. A. (2017). Beware of the watchdog: Rethinking the normative justification of gatekeeper liability. *Journal of Business Ethics*, *140*(4), 705–721. doi:10.100710551-017-3460-3

Andon, P., Baxter, J., & Chua, W. F. (2007). Accounting change as relational drifting: A field study of experiments with performance measurement. *Management Accounting Research*, *18*(2), 273–308. doi:10.1016/j.mar.2006.06.007

Baker, C., & Bettner, M. (1997). Interpretive and Critical Research in Accounting: A Commentary on its Absence from Mainstream Research||. *Critical Perspectives on Accounting*, *8*(4), 293–310. doi:10.1006/cpac.1996.0116

Ball, R. (2013). Accounting informs investors and earnings management is rife: Two questionable beliefs. *Accounting Horizons*, *27*(4), 847–853. doi:10.2308/acch-10366

Barth, M., Landsman, W., & Lang, M. (2008). International accounting standards and accounting quality. *Journal of Accounting Research*, *46*(3), 467–498. doi:10.1111/j.1475-679X.2008.00287.x

Barth, M. E. (2013). Global comparability in financial reporting: What, why, how, and when? *China Journal of Accounting Studies*, *1*(1), 2–12. doi:10.1080/21697221.2013.781765

Barth, M. E., Landsman, W. R., Young, D., & Zhuang, Z. (2014). Relevance of Differences between Net Income based on IFRS and Domestic Standards for European Firms. *Journal of Business Finance & Accounting*, *41*(3-4), 297–506. doi:10.1111/jbfa.12067

Bettner, M., & Kate, K. (2013). Changes in annual reporting rituals of financial services firms in periods of market crisis. *International Journal of Critical Accounting*, *5*(6), 577–593. doi:10.1504/IJCA.2013.059027

Brown, J. (2010). Accounting and visual cultural studies: Potentialities, challenges and prospects. *Accounting, Auditing & Accountability Journal*, *23*(4), 482–505. doi:10.1108/09513571011041598

Byard, D., Li, Y., & Yu, Y. (2011). The effect of mandatory IFRS adoption on financial analysts' information environment. *Journal of Accounting Research*, *49*(1), 69–96. doi:10.1111/j.1475-679X.2010.00390.x

Cahan, S. F., & Sun, J. (2015). The effect of audit experience on audit fees and audit quality. *Journal of Accounting, Auditing & Finance*, *30*(1), 78–100. doi:10.1177/0148558X14544503

Caylor, M. L. (2010). Strategic revenue recognition to achieve earnings benchmarks. *Journal of Accounting and Public Policy*, *29*(1), 82–95. doi:10.1016/j.jaccpubpol.2009.10.008

Chen, H., Tang, Q., Jiang, Y., & Lin, Z. (2010). The role of international financial reporting standards in accounting quality: Evidence from the European Union. *Journal of International Financial Management & Accounting, 21*(3), 220–278. doi:10.1111/j.1467-646X.2010.01041.x

Chen, M., Qu, X., & Sun, X. (2017). Whose cost of equity capital reduces after IFRS convergence and why? Heterogeneity evidence from Chinese stock market. *China Journal of Accounting Studies, 5*(1), 1–27. doi:10.1080/21697213.2017.1304539

Damayant, T. (2013). Who is afraid of Qualitative Research? A Compromise Accounting Research Failure in Improving Accounting Practices. *International Journal of Advances in Management and Economics, 2*(2), 89-94.

Dennis, I. (2014). *The Nature of Accounting Regulation*. New York, NY: Routledge.

Doukakis, L. C. (2014). The effect of mandatory IFRS adoption on real and accrual-based earnings management activities. *Journal of Accounting and Public Policy, 33*(6), 551–572. doi:10.1016/j.jaccpubpol.2014.08.006

Florou, A., & Pope, P. (2012). Mandatory IFRS adoption and institutional investment decisions. *The Accounting Review, 87*(6), 1993–2025. doi:10.2308/accr-50225

He, K., Pan, X., & Tian, G. (2017). Legal liability, government intervention, and auditor behavior: Evidence from structural reform of audit firms in China. *European Accounting Review, 26*(1), 61–95. doi:10.1080/09638180.2015.1100547

Holthausen, R. W., & Watts, R. L. (2001). The relevance of the value-relevance literature for financial accounting standard setting. *Journal of Accounting and Economics, 31*(1-3), 3–75. doi:10.1016/S0165-4101(01)00029-5

Hou, Q., Jin, Q., Yang, R., Yuan, H., & Zhang, G. (2015). Performance commitments of controlling shareholders and earnings management. *Contemporary Accounting Research, 32*(3), 1099–1127. doi:10.1111/1911-3846.12111

Jackson, S. B., & Liu, X. K. (2010). The allowance for uncollectible accounts, conservatism, and earnings management. *Journal of Accounting Research, 48*(3), 565–601. doi:10.1111/j.1475-679X.2009.00364.x

Li, L., Qi, B., Tian, G., & Zhang, G. (2017). The contagion effect of low-quality audits at the level of individual auditors. *The Accounting Review, 92*(1), 137–163. doi:10.2308/accr-51407

Li, S. (2010). Does mandatory adoption of international accounting standards in the European Union reduce the cost of equity capital? *The Accounting Review, 85*(2), 607–636. doi:10.2308/accr.2010.85.2.607

Lukka, K. (2010). The roles and effects of paradigms in accounting research. *Management Accounting Research, 21*(2), 110–115. doi:10.1016/j.mar.2010.02.002

Parker, L. (2012). Qualitative management accounting research: Assessing deliverables and relevance. *Critical Perspectives on Accounting, 23*(1), 54–70. doi:10.1016/j.cpa.2011.06.002

Ramanna, K. (2008). The implications of unverifiable fair-value accounting: Evidence from the political economy of goodwill accounting. *Journal of Accounting and Economics*, *45*(2-3), 253–281. doi:10.1016/j.jacceco.2007.11.006

Richardson, A. (2011). Myth, Paradigms and Academic Accounting Research: A Comment on Reading and Understanding Academic Research in Accounting. *Global Perspectives on Accounting Education*, *8*, 67–77.

Schleicher, T., Tahoun, A., & Walker, M. (2010). IFRS adoption in Europe and investment-cash flow sensitivity: Outsider versus insider economies. *The International Journal of Accounting*, *45*(2), 143–168. doi:10.1016/j.intacc.2010.04.007

Soltani, B. (2014). The anatomy of corporate fraud: A comparative analysis of high profile American and European corporate scandals. *Journal of Business Ethics*, *120*(2), 251–274. doi:10.100710551-013-1660-z

ADDITIONAL READING

Ahmed, A., Neel, M., & Wang, D. (2013). Does mandatory adoption of IFRS improve accounting quality? Preliminary evidence. *Contemporary Accounting Research*, *30*(4), 388–423. doi:10.1111/j.1911-3846.2012.01193.x

Ball, R., Li, X., & Shivakumar, L. (2015). Contractibility and transparency of financial statement information prepared under IFRS: Evidence from debt contracts around IFRS adoption. *Journal of Accounting Research*, *53*(5), 915–963. doi:10.1111/1475-679X.12095

Fan, J. P. H., Li, J., & Zheng, G. (2016). Revisiting the bright and dark sides of capital flows in business groups. *Journal of Business Ethics*, *134*(4), 509–528. doi:10.100710551-014-2382-6

Ozkan, N., Singer, Z., & You, H. (2012). Mandatory IFRS adoption and the contractual usefulness of accounting information in executive compensation. *Journal of Accounting Research*, *50*(4), 1077–1107. doi:10.1111/j.1475-679X.2012.00453.x

KEY TERMS AND DEFINITIONS

Cost: The money form of all material and labor expenses made by the company to produce and market material goods, execution works and service works.

Economic management: The achievement of the budget objectives with minimum costs so that when the activity is completed the revenue exceeds the costs, namely there is a profit that ensures a level of profitability as high as possible both at general level and by product, department or service performed.

Financial Accounting Standards Board (FASB): Set up and develop generally accepted accounting principles.

Financial management: A tool in the decision-making relating to the collection and analysis of information in order to increase the performance level of the economic entity.

Integrity: The prohibition amendment - by deleting or adding - or the unauthorized destruction of information; integrity refers to confidence in the data and resources of a system by which to manage information.

Chapter 4
Sustainable Development Through Franchise Innovation in the Digital Economy

Ye-Sho Chen
Louisiana State University, USA

ABSTRACT

Franchising has been popular as a strategy for businesses to grow and innovate. It is even more so in today's business need of developing digital solutions for sustainability. In responding to United Nations' Sustainable Development Goals, using franchise innovation to replicate proven sustainable solutions in other parts of the world is an effective approach to scaling up solutions to achieve Sustainable Development Goals. The essence of a successful franchise innovation lies in managing the good relationship between the franchisor and the franchisee. In this paper, we show that digital business solutions for sustainability play an important role in growing and nurturing such a good relationship. Specifically, we discuss that franchise innovation via Netchising, combining the digital power of the Internet for global demand-and-supply processes and the international franchising arrangement with local business solutions for sustainability, is an entrepreneurial approach to communities' development where economic and social aspects are mutually supportive.

INTRODUCTION

International franchising as a global growth strategy is gaining its popularity (Justis, & Judd, 2002; Thomas & Seid, 2000; Chen, & Justis, 2006). For example, the U.S. Commercial Service estimated that India has an estimated market size of $50.4 billion in the franchise industry and international franchising is a growing industry for U.S. franchises to expand in India (U.S. Commercial Service, 2018). In addition, Brazil has 1,643 franchising chains and 79,988 franchising units, ranking the Brazilian franchising market as the 6th largest in the world (in number of units) and the 4th largest (in number of franchise chains) (U.S. Commercial Service, 2018). The popularity of franchising continues to increase, as we witness an emergence of a new digital business model, Netchising, which is the combination the digital

DOI: 10.4018/978-1-7998-1005-6.ch004

power of the Internet for global demand-and-supply processes and the international franchising arrangement with local responsiveness (Chen, Justis, & Yang, 2004; Chen, Chen & Wu, 2006). For example, Entrepreneur magazine – well known for its Franchise 500 listing – in 2001 included Tech Businesses into its Franchise Zone that contains Internet Businesses, Tech Training, and Miscellaneous Tech Businesses. At the time of this writing, 33 companies are on its list (TBF, 2019).

In the 21st century, there is a need to develop digital business solutions for sustainability achieving the 17 sustainable development goals (SDGs) set by the United Nations in 2015 (UNSDG, 2015). For example, the Better Business, Better World (BBBW, 2019) shows that it makes good business sense for companies to pursue the SDGs to address the interconnections of global risks as indicated in the Global Risks Interconnections Map 2019 (World Economic Forum, 2019). New evaluation tools, such as The Chemical Sector SDG Roadmap (WBCSD, 2018) and Trucost – part of S&P Dow Jones Indices, a division of S&P Global (SB, 2018), help companies develop SDGs-aligned business strategies. Furthermore, Impact 2030 (IMPACT2030, 2019), a private sector led coalition, help companies align employee volunteer programs to meet the SDGs. Social franchising, i.e., using franchise innovation to replicate proven sustainable solutions where economic and social aspects become mutually supportive to enhance their impact on communities' development, is an effective entrepreneurial approach to scaling up solutions to achieve SDGs (Eggers, & Macmillan, 2013; Asemota, & Chahine, 2017; Samsudin, & Wahab, 2018).

In his best seller, *Business @ the Speed of Thought*, Bill Gates (1999) wrote: "Information Technology and business are becoming inextricably interwoven. I don't think anybody can talk meaningfully about one without talking about the other." (p. 6) Gates' point is quite true when one talks about digital business solutions using franchise innovation. Thus, to see how digital business solutions can be "meaningfully" used in franchise innovation for sustainable development, one needs to know how franchising really works and how to effectively engage in digital business management for franchise innovation (Eggers, & Macmillan, 2013). As a prelude to examining the chapter, we discuss how to build the franchisor-franchisee relationship in franchising for franchise innovation; how to develop digital business for franchise relationship management, how to harness information technologies to implement the digital business around the franchisee life cycle, how to align the digital business and media management implementation with application service providers, how to focus the attention to grow the franchisees at different stages of the franchisee life cycle; and how to go global through a "Flying High, Landing Soft" platform to leverage established social networks to reduce risks, using an illustrative example of making cities resilient to show how to advance SDGs through university-industry partnerships, and finally we conclude the chapter with some future trends.

FRANCHISE INNOVATION: MANAGING THE FRANCHISOR-FRANCHISEE RELATIONSHIPS

Franchising is "a business opportunity by which the owner (producer or distributor) of a service or a trademarked product grants exclusive rights to an individual for the local distribution and/or sale of the service or product, and in return receives a payment or royalty and conformance to quality standards. The individual or business granting the business rights is called the franchisor, and the individual or business granted the right to operate in accordance with the chosen method to produce or sell the product or service is called the franchisee." (Justis, & Judd, 2002, pp. 1-3) Developing a good relationship between the franchisor and the franchisee is the key for a successful franchise (Justis, & Judd, 2002).

Figure 1 describes how to build a good franchisor-franchisee relationship through franchise innovation. The franchisor needs to learn and innovate continuously for the growth of the franchise. The learning and innovation process is developed through five stages (Justis, & Judd, 2002): (1) Beginner – learning how to do it; (2) Novice – practicing doing it; (3) Advanced – doing it; (4) Master – teaching others to do it; and (5) Professional – becoming the best that you can be. Once reaching the "Advanced" stage, most preceding struggles have been overcome. However, further challenges will arise as the franchise continues growing. This is especially true once the system reaches the "Professional" stage, where various unpredicted and intricate problems could arise. Bud Hadfield (1995), the founder of Kwik Kopy franchise and the International Center of Entrepreneurial Development, aptly stated: "The more the company grows, the more it will be tested." (p. 156). To capture the learning and innovation process, a counter-clockwise round arrow surrounding the franchisor is used to depict the increasing intensity of learning and innovation as the franchisor continues to grow.

The franchisee also goes through five stages of franchisee life cycle (Schreuder, Krige, & Parker, 2000): (1) Courting: both the franchisee and the franchisor are eager with the relationship; (2) "We": the relationship starts to deteriorate, but the franchisee still values the relationship; (3) "Me": the franchisee starts to question the franchisor that the success so far is purely of his/her own work; (4) Rebel: the franchisee starts to challenge the franchisor; and (5) Renewal: the franchisee realizes the "win-win" solution is to continue working with the franchisor to grow the system through franchise innovation. Similar to the franchisor, a counter-clockwise round arrow surrounding the franchisee is used in Figure 1 to depict the increasing intensity as the franchisee continues growing. As the franchisee progresses through the life cycle, the good relationship gradually develops an influencing process (Justis, & Vincent, 2001), depicted in Figure 1 with a bi-directional arrow. By going through the processes of learning and influencing, both the franchisor and the franchisee gain the progressive working knowledge of relationship management with the consumers and suppliers. The franchisor, the franchisee, the consumers, and the suppliers in Figure 1 are surrounded with dashed lines, indicating that there is no limit to the learning and innovation process. For examples, Figure 1 show several environmental factors which may have significant impacts on the franchisor-franchisee relationship including extreme weather and its impact on the franchise's operations, eco-innovation, circular business models, constraint management

Figure 1. Franchise Innovation: Managing the Franchisor-Franchisee Relationships

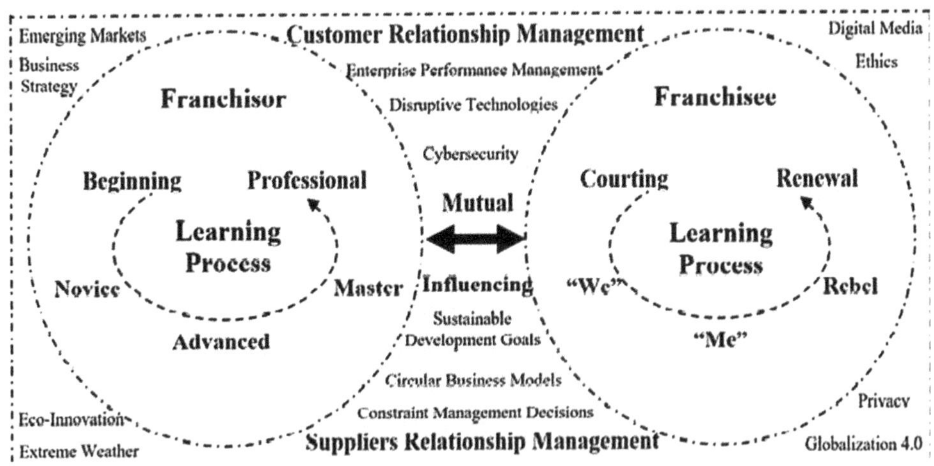

decisions, privacy, ethics, Globalization 4.0 (World Economic Forum, 2018), enterprise performance management, disruptive technologies, cybersecurity, risks and opportunities in emerging markets, business strategy, digital media engagement, and achieving SDGs. As such, there is a constant need for the members of the franchise community to learn and innovate so that the franchisor-relationship relationship can remain strong.

FRANCHISE INNOVATION IN THE DIGITAL ECONOMY

With the advancement of Internet technology, franchise companies are adapting digital business strategies for perfecting the franchisor-franchisee relationship to innovate and grow their franchises globally. Figure 2 is a visual depiction of deploying digital business strategy in franchise innovation: (1) Intra-enterprise collaboration through Intranet for franchisee relationship management, enabling the franchisor to build up relationships with the board of directors, multi-unit franchisees, new franchisees, prospective franchisees, franchisor management and employees; (2) Collaboration with consumers through Internet for consumer relationship management, enabling the franchisor and the franchisees to build up relationships with customers, prospective customers, investors, competitors, media, blogs, advocacy groups, and government; and (3) Collaboration with suppliers through Extranet for supplier relationship management, enabling the franchisor and the franchisees to build up relationships with members and affiliates of international franchise association, law firms, co-branding partners, goods distributors, real estate agents, information systems consultants, accounting firms, and marketing agents.

The digital platform shall also have the capacities to monitor, sense and respond to the changes of the environment. Figure 2 shows some examples. For Intranet, the capabilities include the best working knowledge practices in the industry, how to transform the workers to be the star performers (Seidman, & Grbavac, 2013; Force 2014), how to effectively telling the stories of the star performers, and how

Figure 2. Digital Platform for Franchise Innovation

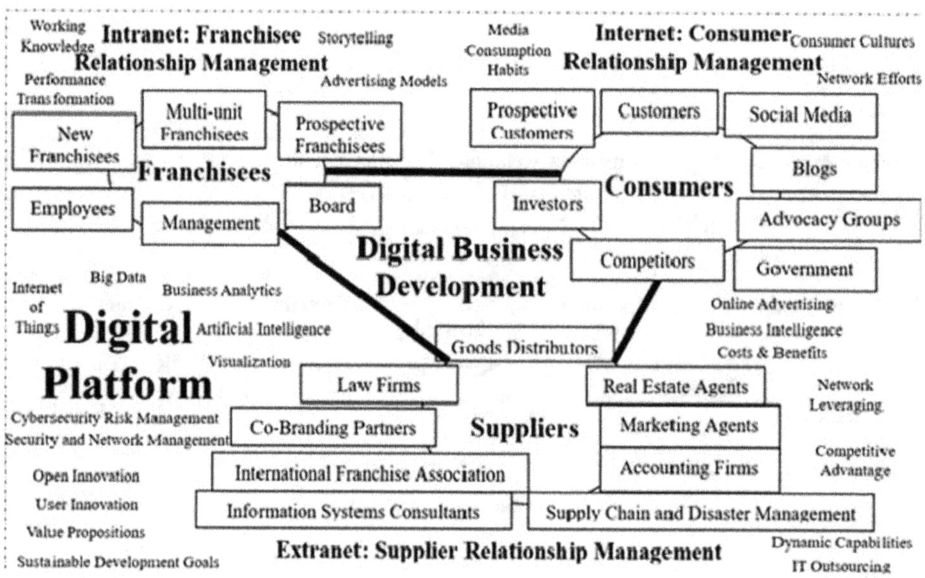

to recruit the prospective franchisees using the most effective advertising models with the storytelling of the star performers. For Internet, the capabilities include understanding consumer cultures, media consumption habits, online advertising, business intelligence, media structure ownership and competition and network efforts for effective consumer relationship management. For Extranet, the capabilities include understanding the suppliers' dynamic capabilities, competitive advantage, network leveraging, costs and benefits for effective supplier relationship management, and IT outsourcing. Finally, the digital business development team shall also plan for the evolution of the digital platform with the evaluation and adoption of new technologies such as Internet of Things, big data, business analytics, artificial intelligence, cybersecurity risk management, security and network management, open innovation and user innovation. The value propositions for the new version of the digital platform shall include how to advance the franchise's SDGs.

Table 1 shows a customer-service-life-cycle (CSLC) (Ives, & Mason, 1990) digital business strategy in franchising (Chen, Chong, & Justis, 2002) for relationship management and franchise innovation depicted in Figure 2. Here we define the franchisee as the customer of the franchisor and the franchisee's customer as the customer's customer of the franchisor. The stages of CSLC are based on two well-known franchising books by Justis and Judd (2002) and Thomas and Seid (2000). There are four major components in the digital business strategy: (1) Benchmarking the Requirements and Acquisition stages. The CSLC model shown in Table 1 is a comprehensive guide for a franchise to develop its web site, especially at the stages of Requirements and Acquisition. The model may be used to compare a franchise's digital business strategy with its competitors. As the industry progresses, best practices based on the CSLC model will evolve and become a standard for benchmarking and websites enhancements. (2) Helping the franchisees serve their customers in the Ownership stage without the Internet encroachment. There is a rich collection of studies in digital business in franchising (Chen, Chong, & Justis, 2002) showing how the Internet can help the franchisees serve their customers in the Ownership stage, including "Marketing & Promoting the Franchise Products/Services" and "Managing the Franchise System". (3) Cultivating the Ownership and Renewal/Retirement stages with effective knowledge management. As mentioned earlier, the greatest challenge in the Ownership stage is to build up the relationship between the franchisor and franchisee. To cultivate the Ownership stage so that "Professional" franchisee can advance to the Renewal stage instead of retiring, Chen, Chong, and Justis (2000a; 2000b) suggest building an Intranet-based Franchising Knowledge Repository. The Repository provides a framework based on which a franchise system may transform into a learning organization. Partnering with the "disruptive technology" providers to enhance the CSLC stages. Innovative entrepreneurs will reengineer their franchise businesses around the CSLC model shown in Table 1. Their ability to track, analyze, and leverage the buying behaviors of their customers in the CSLC sub-stages is their real competitive advantage. For example, Statability.com is a "visionary Web-based Reporting" portal for the hospitality industry. In terms of the CSLC model, Statability.com is a focused business that reengineers around the sub-stages of Ownership. Its "disruptive technology" of reporting is adopted by many franchises in the hospitality industry. As discussed earlier, partnering with those "disruptive technology" providers will make the franchise system more competitive.

Although Internet technology can help deploy the franchise's digital business strategy, the immediate question is: at what cost? Because of the need for digital business processes to monitor the linkage of internal information technologies with external processing and services, the digital business investment could be very expensive and complicated. Many franchise companies, especially small ones, find it financially difficult to invest in the digital business technologies; however, a new type of service in

Table 1. The Customer-Service-Life-Cycle (CSLC) Digital Business for Franchise Innovation

<table>
<tr><th>CSLC</th><th>Sub-stages</th><th>Internet Strategy</th><th>Intranet Strategy</th><th>Extranet Strategy</th></tr>
<tr><td rowspan="4">Requirements</td><td>Understanding How Franchising Works</td><td rowspan="7">Developing an interesting and informative website with rich content and effective storytelling professionally written
Gaining online visibility with key phases in the industry and the search engine capabilities
Using the web site as the friendly customer relationship management tool to address potential franchisees' concerns at various stages (Chen, Chong & Justis, 2002)
Providing useful information on financing and showing how the franchise system may help finance the franchise investment
Conducting comprehensive social media and social network analysis to identify prospective franchisees and develop effective strategies to recruit them
Engaging effectively in the community relationship building by helping address the needs in the environment
Sponsoring local events, such as cultural and sport, to identify prospective franchisees, develop relationships, and recruit them at the appropriate time</td><td rowspan="7">Transforming the organizational structure and corporate culture to support the digital business operation enabled by the Intranet systems (Zeng, Chen & Huang, 2008)
Designing an environment for more team work opportunities and establishing digital learning environment to transform employees to become high performers
Recruiting media creative workers and developing talent management for retention
Developing media platforms with focused media audience and attention management
Building big data and business analytics with visualization capabilities to identify regions with high growth potential
Using digital media to alert entrepreneurial opportunities and provide social sources of information to cultivate the creation of the local franchise unit (Chen, Lu & Zeng, 2014)</td><td rowspan="11">Developing effective strategies of supplier sourcing linking the digital platforms of the supply chain seamlessly and securely
Managing the control and ownership of the supply chain, including the transportations and logistics, effectively according the size of the franchise
Partnering with suppliers to enhance the various stages of CSLC continuously (Chen, Justis & Wu, 2006), e.g., a franchise system may need to partner with banks to deliver good services at the stage of "Financing the Franchise Business".
Aligning the Internet and Intranet Strategy with reputable Application Service Providers (ASP) having focused businesses reengineering around the stages of CSLC (Chen, Ford, Justis & Chong, 2001).
Making the supply chain links stable and resilient especially during the extreme weather seasons
Being able to adapt to the environmental and political changes in the supply chain of the franchise system
Learning from the best practices in franchise networks to leverage the network effects. For example, Statability.com is a "visionary Web-based Reporting" portal for the hospitality industry. It has the focused business reengineering around the stage of "Managing the Franchise System". Its focused service is being respected by franchise companies in the hospitality industry, as is evidenced from the ever-increasing list of its client base, including Hilton and Marriott.
Supply chain models of development and the digital platform revolution</td></tr>
<tr><td>Investigating Franchise Opportunities</td></tr>
<tr><td>Obtaining Franchisee Prospectus</td></tr>
<tr><td>Making the Choice</td></tr>
<tr><td rowspan="3">Acquisition</td><td>Preparing Business Plan</td></tr>
<tr><td>Financing the Franchise Business</td></tr>
<tr><td>Signing the Contract</td></tr>
<tr><td rowspan="3">Ownership</td><td>Marketing & Promoting the Franchise Products or Services</td><td>Benchmarking and enhancing the web site continuously (Chen, Chong & Justis, 2002; Chen, Justis & Chong, 2008)
Identifying frequently the best practices of web design in the industry and improving the web site accordingly</td><td rowspan="4">Helping the franchisees make sales and serve their customers with proper policies dealing with the Internet encroachment issues
Cultivating the franchisor-franchisee relationship with effective knowledge management tools (Chen, Chong, Justis 2000a and 2000b)
Providing basic communications support, distance learning, and centralized franchise applications such as employee recruitment and online ordering (Chen, Hammerstein, & Justis, 2002; Chen, Seidman, & Justis, 2005)
Connection between sustainability and successful franchisees for local community innovation</td></tr>
<tr><td>Managing the Franchise System</td><td rowspan="3">Understanding consumer cultures & media consumption habits and developing effective media branding strategies accordingly
Cultivating an open innovation culture with user innovation and co-creation to develop value propositions for consumers through effective media platforms
Localized customizations based on the geopolitical evolution and demographic characteristics</td></tr>
<tr><td>Building the Relationship between the Franchisor and the Franchisee</td></tr>
<tr><td>Renewal or Retirement</td><td>Becoming a Professional Multi-unit Franchisee or Retiring from the Franchise System</td></tr>
</table>

digital business called Application Service Providers (ASP) promises to make digital business more economical and affordable to the franchise systems. The concept of subscribing information technologies through ASPs has special appeal in the franchising industry because an ASP can duplicate success for other similar franchises quickly and inexpensively (Chen, Ford, Justis, & Chong, 2001). When aligning the CSLC-based digital business strategy with ASPs, a franchise company should focus on (Chen, Ford, Justis, & Chong, 2001): (1) Develop an overall vision of the applications, including software and hardware, needed for the company. (2) Determine what applications and the specific services, e.g., to be available 24 hours a day and 7 days a week with 99.999% of reliability, you want an ASP to host, which have to be clearly defined in the Service Level Agreement. (3) Evaluate ASP providers, i.e., vendors who provide the applications services, using flexibility and trust relationship as the two primary factors.

SUSTAINABLE DEVELOPMENT THROUGH FRANCHISE INNOVATION IN THE DIGITAL ECONOMY: UNIVERSITY-INDUSTRY PARTNERSHIPS IN ACHIEVING SDGS

The Sustainable Development Goals (UNSDG, 2015), also known as the Global Goals, consist of 17 global goals set by the United Nations in 2015. As an example, consider Making Cities Resilient, a part of SDG 11: Sustainable Cities and Communities, is a campaign started in 2010 by the United Nations International Strategy for Disaster Reduction. The campaign provides a list of ten essentials for cities to implement their resilience (UNISDR, 2019): (1) organize for disaster resilience; (2) identify, understand and use current and future risk scenarios; (3) strengthen financial capacity for resilience; (4) pursue resilient urban development and design; (5) safe guard natural buffers to enhance the protective functions offered by natural ecosystems; (6) strengthen institutional capacity for resilience; (7) understand and strengthen societal capacity for resilience; (8) increase infrastructure resilience; (9) ensure effective disaster response; and (10) expedite recovery and build back better. The campaign also encourages cities to exchange their experiences with each other to help enhance their resilience. One example is the New Orleans / Gothenburg Exchange in 2015 during the ten-year anniversary of the devastating Hurricane Katrina in Louisiana and five years after the disastrous oil spill in 2010. This exchange produced a report of 323 pages documenting how the two cities learning from each other to make their cities more resilient to disasters with respect to Essentials 1, 4, 5, 7, 8, 9, and 10 (NOGE, 2015). As reported in the New Orleans / Gothenburg Exchange, one of the effective developments of making coastal cities resilient is conducting extensive wetland growth and regrowth to maintain healthy ecology and protect land losses.

Louisiana people and industries, working with organizations such as universities, have risen up to develop wetland entrepreneurship businesses to provide solutions to help address the issues of wetland losses and maintain healthy wetland ecosystems. Table 2 shows some success stories. As the stories show, the university-industry partnerships for making cities resilient can better connect entrepreneurs with opportunities and resources to start up and scale up their businesses for restoring Louisiana's coast. For example, consider Marsh Dog. Working with the LSU Food Incubator (Randall, 2015), the founder was able to turn the invasive species Nutria into dog treats to help Louisiana ecosystem. For pet service franchises, there could be many opportunities by working with universities to turn other invasive species into pet foods and help make cities resilient. Digital tools are needed to help develop the solutions. Exemplar technology tools for wetland recovery and restoration are (1) Coastal Emergency Risks Assessment (CERA, 2019): A useful storm surge guidance with interactive maps, enabled by a science-based

Table 2. Examples of Wetland Entrepreneurship through University-Industry Partnerships

Solutions	Examples
Turning invasive species into business solutions	• Nutria (NUTRIA, 2019) is an invasive species that significantly damages Louisiana wetlands. Louisiana entrepreneurs turn this invasive species into value-added products such as Marsh Dog (MD, 2019) dog treats made of nutria meat and Righteous Fur (RF, 2019) for the contemporary fashion market made of nutria fur and teeth. • The New York Times report "The Drowning Coast" (Sack & Schwartz, 2018) also pointed out new invasive species, such as small sap-sucking insects and feral hogs, are on the rise and altogether they are destroying the vegetation essential for restoring wetlands. More entrepreneurial solutions are very much needed. • Asian carp is another invasive species damaging Louisiana wetlands. Can't Beat 'EM, Eat 'EM (CBEEE, 2019) turns Asian carp into value-added natural protein food products for human consumption.
Constructing wetland ecosystems using oysters	• Seventy percent of the oysters caught in the USA are from the Coast of Gulf of Mexico and Louisiana's oyster industry contributes US$317 million annually to the state economy. • In addition, oyster reefs along with other bioengineered reefs are being built by entrepreneurial businesses such as ORA Estuaries (ORAE, 2019) and Oyster Bed (OB, 2019) to help protect Louisiana's shoreline and coastal wetlands.
Helping save Louisiana's coastal wetlands through alligators	• Alligators are common in wetlands and Louisiana accounts for 80 percent of American alligators' production (Millar, 2012) with a total annual economic impact of $104 million (LS, 2019). To make the alligator economy environmentally sustainable, Louisiana State developed rules and regulations in the alligator industry (AP, 2019). • This balanced approach empowers the landowners to maintain their healthy wetlands and helps save Louisiana's coastal wetlands (Lewis, & Lallo, 2013).
Investing in wetland forests for carbon financing	• Tierra Resources (TR, 2019) focuses on innovative carbon financing that allows companies to invest in wetland restoration projects in Louisiana to offset their greenhouse gas emissions.
Cleaning up oil spills with floating islands	• Martin Ecosystems (ME, 2019) is another Louisiana startup that developed floating islands to clean polluted lakes, recycle water bottles (Propeller, 2016), support a wildlife habitat, protect wetland erosion, and facilitate wetland restoration. • The SHORE|LINKS® system (SL, 2019) provides a unique, cost- effective technology that prevents and repairs erosion damage through the creation of living shorelines.
Scaling up the proven solutions through the investments of multinationals	• Multinationals are also investing in making Louisiana cities more resilient. For example, energy companies such as Conoco Phillips and Entergy (Abrams, 2019) supported Tierra Resources to plant mangroves using crop duster planes to spread the seed through the air. • Similarly, through the support of Shell and Entergy (RT, 2019), Martin Ecosystems work with Coastal Conservation Association's Building Conservation Trust and 100 Lafourche Parish school students to help build the Floating Islands Restoration Project in Grand Isle, a frontier city in Louisiana fighting the eroding wetlands. • On the other hand, Dow (2016) helped students along the shores of Louisiana's Lake Pontchartrain explore wetland conservation and encouraged students in the Netherlands to build their own wetland chain reactions.

computer model, for first responders, emergency managers and decision makers; (2) Coastal Resilience Decision-Support (CRDS, 2019): A science-based computer tool enabling the five U.S. Gulf states to visualize the coastal hazards risks and examine ways to increase coastal resilience through conservation and restoration activities; (3) EPA's Climate Resilience Evaluation and Awareness (ECREA, 2019): A risk assessment tool helping utilities to adapt to extreme weather events by discovering, assessing, and sharing current and long-term weather conditions; (4) Microsoft AI for Earth (MAE, 2019): Cloud and AI tools educating and training people to develop innovative, scalable solutions to address environmental challenges across the globe; (5) NOAA Sea Level Rise Viewer (NSLRV, 2019): A tool allowing people to view sea level rise and potential coastal flooding impact areas and relative depth; (6) Social Vulnerability Index Mapping Dashboard (SVIMD, 2019): A tool providing specific information to help public health officials and local planners better prepare communities to respond to emergency events; and (7) The Nature Conservancy Climate Wizard (TNCCW, 2019): A tool enabling people to access climate change information in the history and visualize the impacts anywhere on the earth.

In the 21st century, combining information and communication technology with globalization, produces an environment where everyone is facing the problem of information overload. Simon (1971) spoke for us all when he said that ‘a wealth of information creates a poverty of attention.” (p.41) Getting the franchisee’s attention on training in an information rich world is a major challenge. Ocasio (1997) proposed an attention-based theory of the firm, which allows the firm to shield off irrelevant information and gain access to information relevant to what the firm focuses on. According to Ocasio (1997), attention is defined to “encompass the noticing, encoding, interpreting, and focusing of time and effort by organizational decision-makers on both (a) issues: the available repertoire of categories for making sense of the environment: problems, opportunities, and threats; and (b) answers: the available repertoire of action alternatives: proposals, routines, projects, programs, and procedures.” (p.188) Ocasio (1997) further classifies attention into three principles: (1) focus of attention, what decision makers do primarily depends on the selective issues and answers they focus attention on; (2) situated attention, what decision makers focus on and do depends primarily on the particular contextual environment they are located in; and (3) structural distribution of attention, how decision makers attend to the particular contextual environment they are in depends on how the firm’s attention structure (including rules, resources, and relationships) channels and distributes various issues, answers, and decision makers into specific communications and procedures.

In the context of sustainable development through franchise innovation in the digital economy, what do focus of attention, situated attention, and attention structures look like? How does a franchise design an attention-based training and innovation program for the growth of the franchisees? We propose an attention-based framework in Table 3 for the franchisee training. Such a framework has two dimensions. The first dimension is the franchisee life cycle, consisting of Beginner in the Courting Phase, Novice in the “We”-Phase, Advanced in the “Me”-Phase, Master in the Rebel Phase (since the rebel ones tend to be those who know the system well and are capable of influencing others to follow them), and Professional in the Renewal Phase. It is vital for relationship building to understand which stage the franchisee is situated and allocate appropriate resources at different touch-points to help them perform their focuses of attention. The second dimension is the demand-and-supply value networks (Chen, Justis, & Wu, 2006), the attention structures of the franchise, consisting of customers, franchisee outlet, franchisor headquarters, suppliers and partners, and franchise community. The main body of the framework is the focus of attention of the franchise of different levels.

Global markets, such as BRICS (Brazil, Russia, India, China, and South Africa) commonly known as the emerging markets, have growing opportunities for international franchising. Consider the following statistics estimated by the U.S. Commercial Service: (1) Brazil has 2,845 franchising chains and 146,134 franchising units, ranking the Brazilian franchising market as the 6th largest in the world (in number of units) and the 4th largest (in number of franchise chains) (U.S. Commercial Service, 2018). (2) Russia formally adopted franchise legislation in 1994 and the number of franchise concepts has grown steadily over 2,500 in 2017 (U.S. Commercial Service, 2018). (3) India has an estimated market size of $50.4 billion in the franchise industry. Franchising is considered to be a growing industry for U.S. franchises (U.S. Commercial Service, 2018). (4) China has over 2,600 brands with 200,000 franchised retail stores in over 80 sectors and is now the largest franchise market in the world (U.S. Commercial Service, 2007, 2008). (5) South Africa has 531 franchise systems with 28,620 units contributing 12.5% to the country’s

Table 3. An Attention-based Framework for the Sustainable Development through Franchise Innovation in the Digital Economy

<table>
<tr><th colspan="2" rowspan="2">Situated Attention: Relationship Touch-points</th><th colspan="5">Attention Structures: Demand & Supply Value Networks</th></tr>
<tr><th>Customers</th><th>Franchisee Outlet</th><th>Franchisor Headquarters</th><th>Suppliers & Partners</th><th>Franchise Community</th></tr>
<tr><td rowspan="5">Franchisee Life Cycle</td><td>Beginner in the Courting Phase: Beginner Guide</td><td colspan="5">Focus of Attention: Learning how to become a franchisee with subjects such as:
• Understanding how franchising works
• Investigating franchise opportunities
• Obtaining franchisee prospectus
• Making the choice
• Preparing business plan
• Financing the franchised business
• Signing the contract</td></tr>
<tr><td>Novice in the "We"-Phase: Practicing</td><td colspan="5">Focus of Attention: Practicing how to do activities such as:
• How to get training and services from the headquarters
• How to find a good site
• How to find suppliers
• How to serve the customers
• How to manage the franchised unit
• How to work with the franchisor
• How to work with fellow franchisees</td></tr>
<tr><td>Advanced in the "Me"-Phase: Doing</td><td colspan="5">Focus of Attention: Doing activities such as:
• How to do effective marketing and media management
• How to acquire and keep customers
• How to hire, train, and fire employees
• How to manage inventory
• How to manage the back office operations
• How to manage the supply chain more efficiently</td></tr>
<tr><td>Master in the Rebel Phase: Teaching Others</td><td colspan="5">Focus of Attention: Teaching others how to do activities such as:
• How to teach others
• How to work as team
• How to do the bulleted processes above for Beginner, Novice, and Advanced franchisees</td></tr>
<tr><td>Professional in the Renewal Stage: Creative Learning and Innovation</td><td colspan="5">Focus of Attention: Becoming the best he/she can be by:
• Learning to creatively improve activities such as:
o How to cut the cost of the operations
o How to increase the profit of the operations
o How to acquire other franchises and brands
o How to do localized customizations based on the geopolitical evolution and demographic characteristics?
o How to develop supply chain models of development and the digital platform revolution?
• Looking for opportunities for innovation such as:
o Are there any new growth opportunities we can create based on our intangible assets of demand & supply value chains?
o How do we avoid the loss of this new venture?
o Are there any partnership opportunities with our customers and suppliers so that their customers could become ours and vice versa.
o What are the major concerns in the communities and how can we help to deal with them and build a good media relationship?
o How to connect between sustainability and successful franchisees for local community innovation?</td></tr>
</table>

GDP in 2008 (U.S. Commercial Service, 2010). A "Flying High, Landing Soft" platform (Chen et al., 2010, 2011, 2013), grounded in the theory of Strategic Entrepreneurship and docility-based distributed cognition, is proposed to implement the digital business in the new global market.

Strategic entrepreneurship (Hitt et al., 2011), rooted in the resource-based view of the firm (Barney, 1991), creates value for individuals, organizations, and society in three dimensions: (1) resource inputs, consisting of environmental factors, organizational resources, and individual resources; (2) resource orchestration processes (Sirmon et al., 2011), consisting of structuring the firm's resource inputs into portfolios, bundling resource portfolios into capabilities, and leveraging the capabilities to create value for shareholders; and (3) outputs, consisting of creating individual benefits, organizational benefits, and societal benefits. Docility is "the tendency to depend on suggestions, recommendations, persuasion, and information obtained through social channels as a major basis of choice" (Simon, 1993, p.156). Furthermore, "because of docility, social evolution often induces altruistic behavior in individuals that has net advantage for average fitness in the society. Altruism includes influencing others to behave altruistically" (Simon, 1993, p.157). The docility-based distributed cognition (Secchi, 2010) has three dimensions: (1) developing learning communities with communication standards and docile people who are willing to share resources and networks to help others in advancing the common interests of the communities; (2) developing coaching procedures for advice giving and taking through accessible social channels; and (3) telling success stories with bandwagon effects as the feedbacks to the communities.

Specifically, the "Flying High, Landing Soft" platform consists of four major components as is shown in Table 3: Resource Inputs, Processes of Resource Orchestration, Outputs, and Expanded Resource Inputs. The Resource Inputs, based on the success model of KFC in China (Liu, 2008), consisting of docility-based learning communities in franchising with shareable networked resources. In Table 4, the Processes of Resource Orchestration consists of developing coaching procedures through accessible

Table 4. A "Flying High" Platform for the New Global Market

<table>
<tr><th>Outputs</th><th>Processes of Resource Orchestration</th></tr>
<tr><td>Cultivating storytellers with effective media engagement & management for positive network effects</td><td>Developing interactive, value-added coaching procedures through accessible social channels with five steps of preparing the franchise company to venture into the new global market:
• Step 5: Signing the international franchising agreements
• Step 4: Developing relationships with partners
• Step 3: Identifying partners for the new global market venture
• Step 2: Knowing how to do business in the new global market
• Step 1: Market opportunities in the new global market</td></tr>
<tr><th colspan="2">Resource Inputs</th></tr>
<tr><td colspan="2">Docility-based learning communities with communication standards enabled by communication systems & technologies and docile people who are willing to share networked resources to help the franchise company venture into the new global market. The resources may include:
• Individual resources, such as human capital, social capital, and financial capital.
• Organizational resources, such as local partnerships, culture, etiquette, leadership, and headquarter support in the new global market. Supply chain models of development and the digital platform revolution.
• Environmental factors, such as government regulations and relations; local knowledge of product, marketing, supply chain, real estate development; and disaster management. Localized customizations based on the geopolitical evolution and demographic characteristics</td></tr>
</table>

social channels with five "flying high" steps of preparing the franchise company to venture into the new global market. In Table 5, the Processes of Resource Orchestration consists of developing coaching procedures through accessible social channels with five steps of soft landing based on the attention-based framework for the franchisee training shown in Table 2. Soft landings, originally developed by the National Business Incubation Association (NBIA, 2014), is a process of helping a company from one country land softly – without crashing – into the new market of another country through a designated incubator. The purpose is to help the soft landings companies reduce risks/costs and find business opportunities to succeed in the new market. The Outputs in Table 3 focuses on cultivating storytellers and empowering them to tell their stories. Those storytellers and the networked resources behind the success stories become the Expanded Resource Inputs, fostering a virtuous cycle of continuous improvement in the entrepreneurial platform.

Future trends of digital business in international franchising are to enrich the theories and practical applications of the four major components of the "Flying High, Landing Soft" platform shown in Table 3: (1) Resource Inputs, increasing docility-based learning communities to help franchise companies venture into new global markets. Three trends are emerging: networking with leading universities globally for global talent recruiting and retention; partnering with leading research universities globally to develop innovative products/solutions for local markets; and leveraging new technologies such as the Internet of Things for managing the global supply chains efficiently and effectively; (2) Processes of Resource Orchestration, improving coaching procedures for venturing into the new global market. Two trends are

Table 5. A "Landing Soft" Platform for the New Global Market

Outputs	Processes of Resource Orchestration
Cultivating and empowering storytellers via networking, team building, and coaching	Developing coaching procedures through accessible social channels with five steps of soft landing based on the attention-based framework for the growth of the franchisee as shown in Table 2: • Step 1: Beginner in the Courting Phase: Beginner Guide • Step 2: Novice in the "We"-Phase: Practicing • Step 3: Advanced in the "Me"-Phase: Doing • Step 4: Master in the Rebel Phase: Teaching Others • Step 5: Professional in the Renewal Stage: Creative Learning and Innovation
Resource Inputs	
Docility-based learning communities with communication standards enabled by communication systems & technologies and docile people who are willing to share networked resources to help the franchise company venture into the new global market. The resources may include: • Individual resources, including human capital, social capital, and financial capital. • Organizational resources, including local partnerships, culture, etiquette, leadership, and headquarter support in the new market. Supply chain models of development and the digital platform revolution. • Environmental factors, including government regulations and relations; local knowledge of product, marketing, supply chain, real estate development; and crisis management. Connection between sustainability and successful franchisees for local community innovation.	

emerging: developing social style profiles to help achieve high performances; proactively engaging in local communities with projects of high corporate social responsibilities; (3) Outputs, developing effective storytelling via social media. An emerging trend is to develop listening analytics and engage storytelling in the right context of conversations (Chen et al., 2014); and (4) Expanded Resource Inputs, fostering a virtuous cycle of continuous improvement in the "Flying High, Landing Soft" platform. An emerging trend is to cultivate innovation brokers (Macchi et al., 2014) to develop open innovation paradigms to foster positive virtuous cycles.

CONCLUSION

Franchising has been popular as a strategy for businesses to grow and innovate. It is even more so in today's business need of developing digital solutions for sustainability (Chen, Chen, and Wu, 2005). In responding to United Nations' Sustainable Development Goals (SDG), using franchise innovation to replicate proven sustainable solutions in other parts of the world is an effective approach to scaling up solutions to achieve Sustainable Development Goals. The essence of a successful franchise innovation lies in managing the good relationship between the franchisor and the franchisee. In this chapter, we show that digital business solutions for sustainability play an important role in growing and nurturing such a good relationship. We discussed that franchise innovation via Netchising, combining the digital power of the Internet for global demand-and-supply processes and the international franchising arrangement with local business solutions for sustainability, is an entrepreneurial approach to communities' development where economic and social aspects are mutually supportive.

Specifically, we discussed: (1) managing the franchisor-franchisee relationship through the Customer-Service-Life-Cycle (CSLC) approach, where organizational learning is believed to be the key to building the good relationship; (2) harnessing the digital business strategy around the CSLC approach, where four major components are discussed: benchmarking the requirements and acquisition stages, helping the franchisees serve their customers in the ownership stage and avoiding Internet encroachment, cultivating the ownership and renewal/retirement stages with effective knowledge management, and partnering with the "disruptive technology" providers to enhance the CSLC stages continuously; (3) aligning the CSLC-based digital business strategy with application service providers, where trust relationship is the major issue; (4) developing an attention-based framework for the growth of the franchisee; (5) proposing a "flying high, landing soft" platform to help franchise companies go global with less risks and costs; and (6) using an illustrative example of making cites resilient, we showed how the university-industry partnerships can help sustainable franchises achieve SDGs.

REFERENCES

Abrams, R. (2019). USA Today recognizes Tierra Resources in leading the charge to prevent the next Katrina, *Tierra Resources*. Retrieved from https://tierraresourcesllc.com/usa-today-recognizes-tierra-resources-leading-charge-prevent-next-katrina

AP. (2019). Alligator Program, *Louisiana Wildlife & Fisheries*. Retrieved from http://www.wlf.louisiana.gov/wildlife/alligator-program

Asemota, J., & Chahine, T. (2017). Social franchising as an option for scale. *Voluntas*, *28*(6), 2734–2762. doi:10.100711266-016-9763-7

Barney, J. B. (1991). Firm resources and sustained competitive advantage. *Journal of Management*, *17*(1), 99–120. doi:10.1177/014920639101700108

BBBW. (2019). *Better Business, Better World*. Retrieved from http://report.businesscommission.org

CBEEE. (2019). Can't Beat 'Em, Eat 'Em. Retrieved from http://www.cantbeatemeatem.us

CERA. (2019). *Coastal Emergency Risks Assessment*. Retrieved from https://cera.coastalrisk.live

Chen, Y., Chen, G., & Wu, S. (2006). A Simonian approach to digital business research: A study in netchising. Advanced Topics in Digital business Research: Digital business Innovation and Process Management, Vol. 1.

Chen, Y., Chong, P., & Justis, R. T. (2000a, November). Information technology solutions to increase franchise efficiency and productivity. *Proceedings of the 2000 Franchise China Conference and Exhibition*, Beijing, Guangzhou, and Shanghai, China.

Chen, Y., Chong, P., & Justis, R. T. (2000b). Franchising knowledge repository: A structure for learning organizations. *Proceedings of the 14th Annual International Society of Franchising Conference*, San Diego, CA.

Chen, Y., Chong, P., & Justis, R. T. (2002). Digital business Strategy in Franchising: A Customer-Service-Life-Cycle Approach. *Proceedings of the 16th Annual International Society of Franchising Conference*, Orlando, FL.

Chen, Y., Ford, C., Justis, R. T., & Chong, P. (2001). Application service providers in franchising: Opportunities and issues. *Proceedings of the 15th Annual International Society of Franchising Conference*, Las Vegas, NV.

Chen, Y., Hammerstein, S., & Justis, R. T. (2002). Knowledge, learning, and capabilities in franchise organizations. *Proceedings of the 3rd European Conference on Organizational Knowledge, Learning, and Capabilities*, Athens, Greece.

Chen, Y., Justis, R., & Wu, S. (2006). Value networks in franchise organizations: A study in the senior care industry. *Proceedings of the 20th Annual International Society of Franchising Conference*, Palm Springs, CA.

Chen, Y., & Justis, R. T. (2006). Chinese franchise brands going globalization. *1st Annual China Franchise International Summit*, International Franchise Academy, Zhuhai, China.

Chen, Y., Justis, R. T., & Chong, P. P. (2008). Data mining in franchise organizations. In J. Wang (Ed.), *Data Warehousing and Mining: Concepts, Methodologies, Tools, and Applications* (pp. 2722–2733). doi:10.4018/978-1-59904-951-9.ch169

Chen, Y., Justis, R. T., & Yang, H. L. (2004). Global digital business, international franchising, and theory of netchising: A research alliance of East and West. *Proceedings of the 18th Annual International Society of Franchising Conference*, Las Vegas, NV.

Chen, Y., Lu, B. Z, & Zeng, C.F. (2014). Business analytics in franchising. *Encyclopedia of Information Science and Technology*, Third Edition, July.

Chen, Y., Seidman, W., & Justis, R. T. (2005). Strategy and docility in franchise organizations. In the *Proceedings of: 19th Annual International Society of Franchising Conference*, London, UK.

Chen, Y., Watson, E., & Azevedo, R. F. L. (2011). Soft landings curriculum of U.S.-China entrepreneurship. China Currents, 10(2).

Chen, Y., Watson, E., Cornacchione, E., & Azevedo, R. F. L. (2013). "Flying High, Landing Soft": An innovative entrepreneurial curriculum for Chinese SMEs going abroad. *Journal of Chinese Entrepreneurship*, *5*(2), 122–143. doi:10.1108/JCE-10-2012-0025

Chen, Y., Watson, E., Liu, C., Cornachione, E., & Wu, S. (2010). Soft landing curriculum of entrepreneurship in emerging markets, *Academy of International Business 2010 Annual Meeting*, Rio de Janeiro, Brazil.

CRDS. (2019). *Coastal Resilience Decision-Support*. Retrieved from http://maps.coastalresilience.org/gulfmex/#

Dow. (2016). Going Back to School: Ambassadors for Science – How Dow is working to increase STEM literacy and prepare tomorrow's workforce to develop the innovative solutions we all need. Retrieved from https://corporate.dow.com/en-us/science-and-sustainability/earth-day/stem-outreach

ECREA. (2019). *EPA's Climate Resilience Evaluation and Awareness*. Retrieved from https://www.epa.gov/crwu/creat-risk-assessment-application-water-utilities

Eggers, W. D., & Macmillan, P. (2013). The Solution Revolution: How Business, Government, and Social Enterprises Are Teaming Up to Solve Society's Toughest Problems. Brighton, MA: Harvard Business Review Press.

Force, C. (2014). The Star Factor-Discover What Your Top Performers Do Differently-and Inspire a New Level of Greatness in All. *The Journal of Applied Management and Entrepreneurship*, *19*(1), 127–129. doi:10.9774/GLEAF.3709.2014.ja.00012

Gates, B. (1999). Business @ the Speed of Thought: Succeeding in the Digital Economy. New York, NY: Warner Books. doi:10.1111/1467-8616.00097

Hadfield, B. (1995). Wealth Within Reach. Tallahassee, FL: Cypress Publishing.

Hitt, M. A., Ireland, R. D., Sirmon, D. G., & Trahms, C. A. (2011). Strategic entrepreneurship: Creating value for individuals, organizations, and Society. *The Academy of Management Perspectives*, *25*(2), 57–75.

IMPACT2030. (2019). *Impact (Sydney), 2030*. Retrieved from https://www.impact2030.com

Ives, B., & Mason, R. O. (1990). Can information technology revitalize your customer service? *The Academy of Management Executive*, *4*(4), 52–69.

Justis, R. T., & Judd, R. J. (2002). *Franchising*. DAME Publishing.

Justis, R. T., & Vincent, W. S. (2001). *Achieving Wealth Through Franchising*. Avon, MA: Adams Media Corporation.

Lewis, S., & Lallo, E. (2013). *Alligators are helping save Louisiana's coastal wetlands*. Retrieved from http://gulfseafoodnews.com/2013/09/18/the-business-of-alligator-part-four-the-thick-skinned-environmentalists

Liu, W. K. (2008). *KFC in China: Secret Recipe for Success. John Wiley & Sons (Asia)*. PTE LTD.

LS. (2019). *The economy of seafood in Louisiana*. Retrieved from http://www.louisianaseafood.com/industry

Macchi, M., Rizzo, U., & Ramaciotti, L. (2014). From services dealers to innovation brokers: How open innovation paradigm affects incubator activities. Evidence from Italy. *Journal of Intellectual Capital*, *15*(4), 554–575. doi:10.1108/JIC-06-2014-0078

MAE. (2019). *Microsoft AI for Earth*. Retrieved from https://www.microsoft.com/en-us/aiforearth

MD. (2019). *Marshdog.com*. Retrieved from http://www.marshdog.com

ME. (2019). Martin ecosystems. Retrieved from http://www.martinecosystems.com

Millar, D. (2012). Louisiana alligator industry stages a comeback, thanks to growing demand for skins. *The Times-Picayune*, June 17. Retrieved from https://www.nola.com/business/2012/06/louisianas_alligator_industry.html

NBIA. (2014). National Business Incubation Association. Retrieved from http://www.nbia.org/member_services/soft_landings

NOGE. (2015). *Making cities resilient: New Orleans / Gothenburg Exchange*. Retrieved from http://sdmi-resilient-cities.com

NSLRV. (2019). *NOAA Sea Level Rise Viewer*. Retrieved from https://coast.noaa.gov/slr

NUTRIA. (2019). *Nutria.com*. Retrieved from https://nutria.com/site.php

OB. (2019). *Oyster Bed*. Retrieved from https://theoysterbed.com

OB. (2019). *The Oyster Bed*. Retrieved from https://theoysterbed.com

Ocasio, W. (1997). Towards an attention-based view of the firm. *Strategic Management Journal*, *18*(S1), 187–206. doi:10.1002/(SICI)1097-0266(199707)18:1+<187::AID-SMJ936>3.3.CO;2-B

ORAE. (2019). *ORA Estuaries*. Retrieved from https://www.oraestuaries.com

Propeller. (2016). *Water challenge winner recycles water bottles to protect coasts & reduce pollutants*. March 15, Propeller.com. Retrieved from http://gopropeller.org/news/1583

Randall, K. (2015). Local company helps Louisiana ecosystem with dog treats, The Daily Reveille, Nov 18. Retrieved March 31, 2019 from http://www.lsunow.com/daily/local-company-helps-louisiana-ecosystem-with-dog-treats/article_383e337a-8e48-11e5-b788-3391e5941165.html

RF. (2019). Righteousfur.com. Retrieved from http://www.righteousfur.com

RT. (2019). Louisiana kids help build Floating Islands Restoration Project, *Riding Tide*. Retrieved from https://risingtide.joincca.org/news3

Sack, K., & Schwartz, J. (2018). The Drowning Coast. *New York Times*. Retrieved from https://www.nytimes.com/interactive/2018/02/24/us/jean-lafitte-floodwaters.html

Samsudin, F., & Wahab, S. A. (2018). Sustainable Development in Franchising: Measuring the Impacts of Strategic Direction in Franchise Organization. Retrieved from https://www.researchgate.net/publication/325816508_SUSTAINABLE_DEVELOPMENT_IN_FRANCHISING_MEASURING_THE_IMPACTS_OF_STRATEGIC_DIRECTION_IN_FRANCHISE_ORGANIZATION

SB. (2018). *Trucost's new evaluation tool will help companies align strategy with the SDGs*, Sustainable Brands. Retrieved from https://sustainablebrands.com/read/new-metrics/trucost-s-new-evaluation-tool-will-help-companies-align-strategy-with-the-sdgs

Schreuder, A. N., Krige, L., & Parker, E. (2000). The franchisee lifecycle concept – A new paradigm in managing the franchisee-franchisor relationship. *Proceedings of the 14th annual International Society of Franchising Conference*, San Diego, CA.

Secchi, D. (2010). Extendable Rationality: Understanding Decision Making in Organizations. New York, NY: Springer.

Seidman, W., & Grbavac, R. (2013). *The Star Factor: Discover What Your Top Performers Do Differently--and Inspire a New Level of Greatness in All*. AMACOM.

Simon, H. A. (1971). Designing organizations for an information rich world. In M. Greeberger (Ed.), Computers, Communications, and the Public Interest, pp. 38-52. Baltimore, MD: The Johns Hopkins Press.

Simon, H. A. (1993). Altruism and economics. *The American Economic Review*, *83*(2), 156–161.

Sirmon, D. G., Hitt, M. A., Ireland, R. D., & Gilbert, B. A. (2011). Resource orchestration to create competitive advantage: Breadth, depth, and life cycle effects. *Journal of Management*, *37*(5), 1390–1412. doi:10.1177/0149206310385695

SL. (2019). SHORE|LINKS. Retrieved from http://www.shore-links.com

SVIMD. (2019). *Social Vulnerability Index Mapping Dashboard*. Retrieved from https://svi.cdc.gov/map.aspx?txtzipcode=70806&btnzipcode=Submit

TBF. (2019). *Tech Business Franchises*. Retrieved from https://www.entrepreneur.com/franchises/category/tech

Thomas, D., & Seid, M. (2000). Franchising for Dummies. Foster City, CA: IDG Books.

TNCCW. (2019). *The Nature Conservancy Climate Wizard*. Retrieved from http://www.climatewizard.org/index.html

TR. (2019). *Tierra Resources*. Retrieved from https://tierraresourcesllc.com

UNISDR. (2019). *Making cities resilient: My city is getting ready*. United Nations International Strategy for Disaster Reduction. Retrieved from https://www.unisdr.org/campaign/resilientcities

UNSDG. (2015). *Sustainable development goals: 17 goals to transform our world.* Retrieved from https://www.un.org/sustainabledevelopment/sustainable-development-goals

U.S. Commercial Service. (2007). *China Franchising Industry: Access Dynamics and Emerging Markets*, The JLJ Group, September. Retrieved from http://export.gov/china/build/groups/public/@eg_cn/documents/webcontent/eg_cn_027119.pdf

U.S. Commercial Service. (2008). *China Franchising Industry*, The JLJ Group, April.

U.S. Commercial Service. (2010). *Doing Business in South Africa - 2010 Country Commercial Guide for U.S. Companies*. Retrieved from http://www.franchise.org/uploadedFiles/Franchise_Industry/International_Development/Country_Profiles/South%20Africa_2010.pdf

U.S. Commercial Service. (2018). *India - Franchising*. Retrieved from https://www.export.gov/article?id=India-Franchising

U.S. Commercial Service. (2018). *Brazil - Services - Franchising*. Retrieved from https://www.export.gov/article?id=Brazil-Services-Franchising

U.S. Commercial Service. (2018). *Russia - Franchising Industry*. Retrieved from https://www.export.gov/apex/article2?id=Russia-Franchising-Industry-Sector

WBCSD. (2018). *The Chemical Sector SDG Roadmap*, World Business Council for Sustainable Development. Retrieved from https://sdgroadmaps.wbcsd.org/overview

World Economic Forum. (2018). *Globalization 4.0 – What Does It Mean?* Retrieved from https://www.weforum.org/agenda/2018/11/globalization-4-what-does-it-mean-how-it-will-benefit-everyone

World Economic Forum. (2019). *The Global Risks Report 2019*. Retrieved from https://www.weforum.org/reports/the-global-risks-report-2019

Zeng, Q., Chen, W., & Huang, L. (2008). Digital business transformation: An analysis framework based on critical organizational dimensions. *Journal of Tsinghua Science and Technology*, *13*(3), 408–413. doi:10.1016/S1007-0214(08)70065-8

KEY TERMS AND DEFINITIONS

Customer Service Life Cycle: Serving customers based on a process of four stages: Requirements, Acquisition, Ownership, and Retirement. Many companies are using the approach to harness the Internet to serve the customers.

E-Business: Coined by IBM's marketing and Internet teams in 1996 it is defined as the application of information and communication technologies in support of all the business activities and processes in the entire value and supply chain.

E-Business Innovation: Innovation originating from innovative e-business applications that impact established business models and collaborations with stakeholders. (Lin and Hsia, 2011).

Franchising: A business opportunity based on granting the business rights and collecting royalties in return.

Franchisee: The individual or business who receives the business rights and pay the royalties for using the rights.

Franchisee Life Cycle: The stages a franchisee goes through in the franchise system: Courting, "We", "Me", Rebel, Renewal.

Franchisor: The individual or business who grants the business rights.

Franchisor-Franchisee Learning Process: The stages of learning, including Beginner, Novice, Advanced, Master, and Professional.

Franchisor-Franchisee Relationship Management: The vital factor for the success of a franchise, including: Knowledge, Attitude, Motivation, Individual Behavior, and Group Behavior.

Soft Landings: A process to help a company from one country land softly – without crashing – into the market of another country through a designated incubator.

Chapter 5
Cyberaccounting for the Leaders of the Future

Alina Stanciu
1 Decembrie 1918 University, Romania

Marius Petrescu
Valahia University, Romania

Anca Gabriela Petrescu
Valahia University, Romania

Florentina Raluca Bîlcan
Valahia University, Romania

ABSTRACT

The new volatile, uncertain, complex and ambiguous economic context generates the evolution of a global, integrated, and permanently connected world, in which territoriality and temporality have almost disappeared. Fluctuations and changes in economic power poles, past financial crises, but also signs of new recession periods, rising capital, multiplying variables, and cause-effect factors outline the current economic environment. Simultaneity and interconnection of Industrial Revolution 4.0, Globalization 4.0, Artificial Intelligence, Internet of Things, Data Revolution, and Digital Enterprise have determined the emergence of new concepts such as: Digital Ecosystems, Cyber counting, Cybersecurity, Platform Architecture for Financial, Digital Interface, concepts directly related to business performance in the new economic environment: Digital Economy.

INTRODUCTION

The global economic entities are facing growing transformation pressures - moving from product-driven business models to new models focused on creating and capturing different sources of new value (Agrawal, & Tapaswi, 2017; Tiago, Manoj, & Espadanal, 2014; Lee, & Kim, 2017). As a result, innovation is becoming more and more complex. The Fourth Industrial Revolution 4.0 rewrite the new global architecture: Globalization 4.0 developing technology, skills and new innovation. And this unprecedented,

DOI: 10.4018/978-1-7998-1005-6.ch005

exponential shift of rhythm is increasingly based on collaborative platforms to achieve more radical innovations driven by shifts in technology (Gandino, Celozzi, & Rebaudengo, 2017).

The performance of the digital enterprise has exceeded its profitability boundaries, and any development strategy involves the KPI's performance indicators predictability and sustainability indicators, but also "digital platform business models, ecosystems and partnerships, as the important angles of responsibility, trust and governance, from multiple levels - corporate, national and international" (Katzenbach, & Smith, 2015). Under the action of these forces the new performance concept is divided into three pillars of action: Sustainable Performance, Finding & Retaining Talents, as a source of added value in a global competitive market, and Research & Innovation. "High Performance Organizations" which "record exceptional financial results, have satisfactory customers and employees, high productivity, encourage innovation and leadership" are the result of their evolution, trough digital transformation in a Digital Economy (Wang, & Hu, 2014).

To better understand why is necessary to develop a structured process of information security risk within the organization, it must be borne in mind that, regardless of the type of organization, the field of activity or form of organization, there is uncertainty both in organization and in the environment in which it operates (Andress, 2003; Stepchenko, & Voronova, 2015). The uncertainty may take the form of either threats or opportunities. In this contest, each manager must handle threats, because otherwise the organization's objectives cannot be met, and, on the other hand, capitalize the opportunities to the benefit of the organization, proving efficiency (Collins, & McCombie, 2012; Karim, 2007). Given that uncertainty is a fact of life, then the uncertainty response should become a permanent managerial concern (Landoll, 2010; Karanja, 2017).

The present chapter analyzes from the future leader's perspective the impact of business digital transformation, the strengths and opportunities created by Artificial Intelligence, but also the threats and vulnerabilities on managing accounting information system, which from our point of view represent the Core of the Business.

BACKGROUND

The complete digitization of economic environment changes the way that leaders of the future relate with their business (McQuade, 2006; Yang, Wu, & Wang, 2014). Leading technologies, Artificial Intelligence (AI), Internet of Things (IoT) involve all the levels of the business, all the functions and all the stakeholders, transforming "the structures of economic interaction: the twin trends of digitization and virtualization are creating an economy of near-unlimited mobility in which cyberspace is home to all data" (Chen, Ge, & Xie, 2015), including indicators, accounting and global financial data. Reports, Charts, Technical Indicators, Trend Analysis, Research, Cloud Computing and Mobile Application, today all are interconnected, vertical integrated "creating smart systems that are not just analytical but also predictive and prescriptive" (Hiller, & Russel, 2013) in cross-country surveys with all stakeholders linked.

Recent research and studies are strengthening the opinion that "businesses are experiencing massive disruption as they respond and attempt to capitalize on the on-going changes (Schwab, 2019; Zangeneh, & Shajari, 2018; Lin, Lin, & Pei, 2017). Digital transformation is more far-reaching than just technology (Hadžiosmanović, Bolzoni, & Hartel, 2012). If we look at how the digital market is evolving, it is very clear that people are a constant and at the heart of digital evolution (Lee, Lee, & Kim, 2016). Harnessing the collective intelligence of employees, partners and customers is a critical success factor for digital transformation" (Choi, Lee, Kim, Jung, Nam, & Won, 2014; Khan, Gani, Wahab, Shiraz, & Ahmad, 2016).

In the opinion of Klaus Schawb, Founder and Executive Chairman of the World Economic Forum, these technologies have the power to connect the businesses in a "global digital and virtual system and the related flow of ideas and services" (Singh, & Fhom, 2017). The impact of digital transformation on business is remove all borders and to replace old economies of scale (Yar, 2006; Kurosawa, Ohta, & Kakuta, 2017).

In 2016, a study made by McKinsey & Company calculated that "digital flows—which were practically nonexistent just 15 years ago—now exert a larger impact on GDP growth than the centuries-old trade in goods" (Friedberg et al., 2016). The study reveals a "45-fold increase in the amount of cross-border bandwidth from 2005 to 2016 and predicted another 5-fold increase by 2022" (Kurosawa, Ohta, & Kakuta, 2017).

In 2019, another study "Measuring the Digital Transformation - A Roadmap for the future" made by the Organization for Economic Cooperation and Development – OECD, reveal a roadmap with nine action steps that if they are prioritized and implemented would help the countries to monitor the process of digital transformation and its impacts on economic environment (Schwab, 2019). First four action steps are directed to build with a new generation of stakeholders, a new generation of data and indicators capable of dealing with challenges of digital transformation: make the digital economy visible in global economic statistics, understand the cross-countries economic impacts of business digital transformation, measuring well-being in the digital age, and design new and interdisciplinary approaches to data collection. The next five action steps are directed towards specific areas of interests: fast accelerating transformative digital technologies, global data infrastructure, data flows, and skills in the digital era, trust in online environments, and governments' digital strengths and policies.

Digital Transformation is about cloud computing, mobility, Internet of Things (IoT), Artificial Intelligence related science and technologies, Big Data Analytics, replacing the power of one with the power of many and develop a new practical paradigm of economic value (Fischbacher-Smith, 2016).

A survey from 2019 reveals that between 2013 and 2016, five economies of the World – USA, China, Chinese Taipei, Japan, and Korea, develop between 70% - 100% of cutting-edge digital technologies. Digital business transformation under the digital are the based-tech entities. In less than 25 years, Amazon grew from a startup e-commerce store to the world's second-largest traded company, revolutionizing retail, cloud computing, and other Web services. Apple became the world's first trillion-dollar company in 2018, barely a decade after it released the first iPhone. In Asia, Alibaba Group registered a market value of $ 499.4B (Schwab, 2019).

Digital Transformation subject has challenged practitioners and theoreticians to analyze this business expansion and to outline new horizons' (He, Chen, Chan, & Bu, 2012; Broadbent, & Schaffner, 2016; Liaudanskienel, Ustinovicius, & Bogdanovicius, 2009). Business expansion is based on two directions (Malatras, Geneiatakis, & Vakalis, 2016; Arukonda, & Sinha, 2015). First are the economic entities that have included on their business model the new industries: cloud computing, healthcare, loans and payments. The second direction is represented by economic entities that have disrupted social patterns trough global tech platforms, without any physical assets as a support for their services, but having a strong ally: Artificial Intelligence, Big Data and a capacity to build the necessity of their services (Peltier, 2010; Hjortdal, 2011; Agrawal, & Tapaswi, 2017). Tech entities, including computers and mobile phones succeeded this in past 12 to 14 years and they continue expanding at global level, worldwide, becoming digital conglomerates, gaining market power and counting billion of users (Tropina, & Callanan, 2015; Gaidelys, & Valodkiene, 2011).

RESEARCH METHODOLOGY

Business expansion and digital transformation have produced significant changes at all business levels, on vertical and horizontal plan (Hong, Kim, & Cho, 2010). Therefore, on vertical plan the digital transformation changes the perspective of stakeholders represented by" broad group interested in the success or failure of a business: shareholders, creditors and customers, employees, the local community, and the government" (Kesan, & Hayes, 2012). At the top of pyramid the founders, investors and other shareholders and at the bottom the employees replaced step-by-step with different forms of Artificial Intelligence (Krombholz, Hobel, Huber, & Weippl, 2015). On horizontal plan, digital transformation rewrites the organizational structure of economic entity, the organizational culture, the human resource participation and also the operations.

Studies and reports from the industry reveal the positive impact of Artificial Intelligence implication on accounting area, reshaping the vision of data on stakeholders based on the association between the Artificial Intelligence and natural language interfaces with high change potential (Mittelman, 2011; Smith, 2005; Lee, & Kim, 2017). From the perspective of an economic entity, Cyber accounting is the new force of accounting in Digital Economy. The purpose is to make a significant, reliable and positive impact on the finance department, by redefining key performance indicators and especially real profits, creating new business models, develop revolutionary business solutions for all type of economic entities, covering Accounting Services, Bookkeeping, TAX filing and VAT reporting services as "technology building blocks" (Okamoto, & Takashima, 2015) with the expansion in maximizing the value of financial data even if the threat of cybersecurity risk still exists.

In the vision of practitioners, Cyber Accounting will be the new language in which Accounting and Finance will speak to the world. The impact of Artificial Intelligence with innovations in technology include "bookkeeping apps, tax software, auditing automation, and platforms that generate financial projections and visualized data" (Willems, 2011). By adding block chain technology between them and financial institutions, auditing and anti-fraud race to automation, we sustain our opinion that Cyber Accounting will help the leaders of the future to build a strong economic entity by developing a better business model.

The classical accounting procedures in which accountants "processed invoices, purchase orders, or deliver orders on paper documents which manually were introduced in computer systems, coded, and finally transmitted to the managers for approval and payment" is replaced by "automated workflow process and software that analyzes, recognizes, directs, and exports data into a company's ERP/financial system"(Karanja, 2017).

Based on cloud solutions which are available in real time for millions of economic entities and users, the force of Cyber accounting is reflected in: the improvement of cloud-based software solutions (SaaS/software-as-a-service) for managing financial documents with variable structure, in automatically recognition with no prior configuration, in the usage of optical recognition of codes using OCR/optical recognition technology, processes and routes invoices, in accuracy to rebuild an automatized relation with suppliers and in the clear vision offered to leaders on payment deadlines, approval workflows, management decisions based on financial reports, in improvements in invoice processing time from 30 days to 2 days, processing costs per invoice reduced from $13.00 to about $2.00, and the opportunities to capture early payment discounts rise from only 20% of the time to 80% of the time (Chen, Ge, & Xie, 2015).

The self-learning—machine learning—capabilities of cloud-based software solutions for data processing, verifications, referrals, and fraud detection are constantly improving and up-date. These solutions essentially learn from their mistakes and do not make them again once accountants correct them. Based on that, their productive time directed towards value-added for economic entities trough analysis, strategy, creative thinking, meaningful reporting and decision-making will increasing exponentially with the business force of Cyber accounting.

As practitioner and a cloud AP automation user, Bryan Schmidt, controller for Unite Here Health support the idea of a better business model through cyber accounting: "The improvements are due to capturing, automatically coding and storing invoices instead of handling paper or sending around PDF files. The system observes and learns from clerks' keystrokes, continuously improves GL coding, and reduces errors" (Tropina, & Callanan, 2015). Therefore, another impact of cyber accounting is on human resource. Studies reveal that the jobs with repeatable actions will be replaced by automated: "bookkeepers have a 97.6 percent chance of seeing their jobs automated, accountants and auditors 93.5 percent chance and financial analysts 23.3 percent chance"(Zangeneh, & Shajari, 2018), while those that require human resource skills, analysis and reporting capacity will become key positions looking for key persons.

In our opinion, the leaders of the future are the key persons who will implement and encourage the emerging technologies of automating accounts payable processes in the economic entities, streamlining the entire financial process. Cyber accounting must be seen more as a driving force than a threat. The advantages that Artificial Intelligence create on the businesses are multiples: building a clear representation of financial incoming and outgoing with real time control on payment, offering the possibility of creating new business models in which a central role is played by algorithms. The solutions offered by Artificial Intelligence are flexible, adaptable at multiple variables, with the capacity of automatically "data recognition in an exhaustive and reliable way, with no prior configuration" (Stepchenko, & Voronova, 2015). Is for the first time in the economic environment when "the value of financial data in an accounting information system is extremely high" and for the first time when Accounting Information Systems (AIS) is able to support all accounting functions and activities: financial reporting, auditing, taxation, and management accounting (Lin, Lin, & Pei, 2017).

Forbes predicts that "by 2020, accounting tasks including tax, payroll, audits and banking will be fully automated using Artificial Intelligence - based technologies, which will disrupt the accounting industry in a way it never was for the last 500 years, bringing both huge opportunities and serious challenges" (Schwab, 2019).

We believe that Artificial Intelligence, with all the advantages is not capable to build a connection with the leader vision and is not able to listen, even if cyber accounting reveal 90 percent of client profile. The rest 10 percent is related only with human resources capabilities, accountants experience and their capability to connect a leader's financial, numbers-based profile with its vision, goals, strengthens, weaknesses, opportunities and threats. And those goals, weaknesses and threats are the real seeds of accountants advisory.

As we have presented the theoreticians and practitioners are preoccupied to support the stakeholders with the real impact of the cyber threats which can disrupt business. On that basis, IT and Accounting become the most powerful "defensive weapons" for the leaders of the future, and accountants have the mission to protect the economic entities in front of cyber-attacks, mitigate and help them recover. As a consequence, for all the economic entities that acts in actual and future Digital Economy, a guide adapted at the economic entity characteristics was developed: The NIST Cybersecurity Framework. A six core components correspond at five Cybersecurity Framework's Functions: Predict, Identify, Prevent, Detect, Respond and Recover. Around this Cybersecurity Framework the business is organized with a cybersecurity management at first level of importance and with leaders' decisions based on risk management analyzes. The Cybersecurity Function represent three parts: "Framework Core, Framework Implementation Tiers, and Framework Profiles" rewriting the connection between stakeholders and the IT and Accountants representatives, who translate in reality the strategic directions of action (Schwab, 2019).

SOLUTIONS AND RECOMMENDATIONS

Practitioners in the field present a similarity between Accounting and Cybersecurity reflected in their mutual capacity of being "detailed oriented and fluent with numbers" (Kurosawa, Ohta, & Kakuta, 2017). The analytical cyber reveal that working in a digitized environment, where numbers and mathematical algorithms rule supreme, offer possibility for accountants to touch a field of cybersecurity. The difference between them is that accountants are able to analyze, summarize, interpret and present the complex economic entity and financial area, while cybersecurity experts provide to the stakeholders the cybersecurity framework based on risk management system.

In practice, changes produced by business digital transformation are the result of digital technology waves: increase demand of cloud computing services, rise of AI and Big Data analytics, the necessity of building a global data infrastructure, mapping AI economic entities from all sectors, impact of digitization on operations, work process and young generations and the evolution of "digital divides" (Landoll, 2010). Digital Era Trends are the reflection of a new Digital Integrated Global Framework Policy where all the stakeholders are involved: The increasing of AI and the human replacement with algorithms who manage the financial documents, learning machine and deep learning lead to the emergence and development of new related concepts at the new digital economy: Accounting Intelligence or Cyber Accounting, a new force who will reshape the business financial information through use of "computers that recognize and analyze documents automatically" (Agrawal, & Tapaswi, 2017) and improvement of accounts payable processes. Cyber Accounting is about capture the financial anticipation, about using Cloud, Edge and 5G Technology to build a new Modern Economic Infrastructure and about believe in the magic of tech innovations (Chen, Ge, & Xie, 2015).

Still a question remains for the leaders of the future: "Is Accounting Information Systems capable to offer the answers according with their Vision?" In our opinion, based on latest theoretical interpretation of digital transformation and the emerging cyber accounting, we sustain that AI impact on accounting will increase and expand the volume of processed data with the help of algorithms in order to improve the process of making decisions in an empirical way.

Nevertheless, the predictions of the business future require leader vision expansion until the core of the business, in a complex and intuitive medium, where all the business growth capabilities are waiting to be augmented. Real business growth is based on strategy, on the ability to develop a real, powerful, and trust-based relation between leader of the future and accountants, in order to reshape the business on digital transformation requirements.

Prevention means that the attack will be prevented (Fischbacher-Smith, 2016). Typically, prevention involves implementation of mechanisms that users not be able to counteract and are implemented correctly, unaltered, so the attacker cannot alter those (Singer, & Friedman, 2014). Prevention mechanisms are cumbersome and often interfere with the use of the system to the point that, sometimes hamper normal use thereof (Winkler, 2010). But some simple preventive mechanisms with as passwords (which are designed to prevent unauthorized users from using the system) have become widely accepted plan (Gandino, Celozzi, & Rebaudengo, 2017). Once implemented, the resources protected by mechanisms not are monitored to identify any security issues, at least in theory (Ruževičius, & Gedminaitė, 2007).

FUTURE RESEARCH DIRECTIONS

IBM vision on cyber security is that "Security doesn't need more tools. It needs new rules", while Patrick Buono in Cybersecurity for Accountants reveal that "global cost of cybercrime will reach $2 trillion by 2019" (Schwab, 2019). In the vision of Warren Buffett cyber-attacks represent "a bigger threat to humanity than nuclear weapons," and for Ginni Rometty, IBM President & CEO, cybercrime as "the greatest threat to every profession, every industry, every company in the world" (Schwab, 2019). Statistics conducted by The National Computer Security Survey, U.S. Department of Justice's Bureau of Justice Statistics, found 68% of cyber theft victims will incur losses of $10,000 or more, and victims of cyber-attacks will experience downtime of 24 hours or more (Lee, & Kim, 2017).

Based on that, our conclusion is that "proactively taking measures to prevent cybercrimes is a business necessity" (Gandino, Celozzi, & Rebaudengo, 2017). The complexity of economic entity cybersecurity strategy is reflected on vertical axe by the complexity of use and popularity of approach and on horizontal axe by specificity and generality of application in sectors and is applied by the leaders of the future trough the building of Cybersecurity Action Pilon:

- The acceptance of the Fourth Industrial Revolution challenges without any border, interconnected, and interdependent than the global economy of integrated supply chains.
- Global cooperation with focus on the governance issues at the Core of the Business digital transformation: cybersecurity, the use of AI, intellectual property and data protection agreements.
- Develop interoperable teams: management accountants, cloud service experts, legal advisors, able to promote awareness and use of the cybersecurity framework in reshaping the architecture of cloud system.
- Improving the communication at all levels and between all the stakeholders, internally and externally, in order to evaluate the effectiveness of the economic entity controls in achieving its cybersecurity objectives.
- Creating a Cybersecurity Action Plan based on privacy-preserving sensitive data approaches in cloud computing: privacy threat model and privacy enhancing protocols and solutions.
- Real engagement of interoperable teams for the leaders in order to present a description of cybersecurity risk management program with the possibility to identify its cybersecurity processes and to assess the leaders in applying cybersecurity risk management program.

Future research is important because certain events with a negative impact on the objectives to be transformed into opportunities if they are identified early. One of the limitations of this study is that the collected data was cross-sectional, and all hypotheses were examined for a particular period. In addition, the data in this study was collected within particular urban areas. Hence, special care should be taken when generalizing our findings to other country's businesses. Furthermore, the effects of demography are not included in this study, but some demographic factors may have more explanatory power than others which can be investigated in future research. Best practices will consist of technical and procedural security measures whose effectiveness in combating specific threats and vulnerabilities has been proven.

CONCLUSION

Cyber accounting for the Leaders of the Future represent our interdependence manifesto of two knowledge areas related to the future of the business: Accounting and Artificial Intelligence. The present chapter provide to readers valuable information, new insights regarding the force of business digital transformation and its impact on accounting, reinforcing the beliefs that business digital transformation at the end is about: "Going Digital, Shaping Policies, Improving Lives."

To achieve this mission, is necessary that leaders and accountants of the future make the digital transformation visible in economic statistics and build a new modern economic infrastructure, through researching of new performance indicators based on the use of AI technology and the capacity of interoperable teams to innovate in terms of cybersecurity threats. Digital transformation became the road map for any economic entity and together with financial capital, know-how capital assets and work are performance force driven.

On short term, cyber accounting will improve the international compatibility of current performance indicators and make statistical systems more flexible and responsive to the introduction of new and evolving, disruptive concepts such as Cloud, Edge Computing and 5G Technology. The true digital transformation will be on long term achieved by the global economic community with redesign of a new, interdisciplinary, and protected from cyber-attacks platform and interconnected through partnerships between all the stakeholders involved with the powerful support of researchers.

REFERENCES

Agrawal, N., & Tapaswi, S. (2017). Defense schemes for variants of distributed denial-of-service (DDoS) attacks in cloud computing: A survey. *Information Security Journal: A Global Perspective, 26*(1), 1-13.

Andress, A. (2003). *Surviving Security: How to Integrate People, Process, and Technology*. Boca Raton, FL: Auerbach Publications. doi:10.1201/9780203501405

Arukonda, S., & Sinha, S. (2015). The innocent perpetrators: Reflectors and reflection attacks. *Advanced Computer Science*, *4*, 94–98.

Broadbent, A., & Schaffner, C. (2016). Quantum cryptography beyond quantum key distribution. *Designs, Codes and Cryptography*, *78*(1), 351–382. doi:10.100710623-015-0157-4

Chen, H., Ge, L., & Xie, L. A. (2015). User Authentication Scheme Based on Elliptic Curves Cryptography for Wireless Ad Hoc Networks. *Sensors (Basel, Switzerland)*, *15*(7), 17057–17075. doi:10.3390150717057 PMID:26184224

Choi, Y., Lee, D., Kim, J., Jung, J., Nam, J., & Won, D. (2014). Security Enhanced User Authentication Protocol for Wireless Sensor Networks Using Elliptic Curves Cryptography. *Sensors (Basel, Switzerland)*, *14*(6), 10081–10106. doi:10.3390140610081 PMID:24919012

Collins, S., & McCombie, S. (2012). Stuxnet: The emergence of a new cyber weapon and its implications. *Journal of Policing. Intelligence and Counter Terrorism*, *7*(1), 80–91. doi:10.1080/18335330.2012.653198

Fischbacher-Smith, D. (2016). Breaking bad? In search of a (softer) systems view of security ergonomics. *Security Journal*, *29*(1), 5–22. doi:10.1057j.2015.41

Friedberg, I., McLaughlin, K., Smith, P., Laverty, D., & Sezer, S. (2016). STPA-SafeSec: Safety and security analysis for cyber-physical systems. *Journal of Information Security and Applications*, *29*, 1–12.

Gaidelys, V., & Valodkiene, G. (2011). The Methods of Selecting and Assessing Potential Consumers Used of by Competitive Intelligence. *Inzinerine Ekonomika-Engineering Economics*, *22*(2), 196–202.

Gandino, F., Celozzi, C., & Rebaudengo, M. (2017). A Key Management Scheme for Mobile Wireless Sensor Networks. *Applied Sciences*, *7*(5), 490. doi:10.3390/app7050490

Hadžiosmanović, D., Bolzoni, D., & Hartel, P. H. (2012). A log mining approach for process monitoring in SCADA. *International Journal of Information Security*, *11*(4), 231–251. doi:10.100710207-012-0163-8

He, D., Chen, C., Chan, S., & Bu, J. (2012). Secure and efficient handover authentication based on bilinear pairing functions. *IEEE Transactions on Wireless Communications*, *11*(1), 48–53. doi:10.1109/TWC.2011.110811.111240

Hiller, J., & Russel, R. (2013). The challenge and imperative of private sector cybersecurity: An international comparison. *Computer Law & Security Review*, *29*(3), 236–245. doi:10.1016/j.clsr.2013.03.003

Hjortdal, M. (2011). China's use of cyber warfare: Espionage meets strategic deterrence. *The Journal of Strategic Studies*, *4*(2), 1–24.

Hong, J., Kim, J., & Cho, J. (2010). The trend of the security research for the insider cyber threat. *International Journal of Future Generation Communication and Networking*, *3*(2), 31–40.

Karim, H. V. (2007). Strategic security management: a risk assessment guide for decision makers. Amsterdam, The Netherlands: Elsevier.

Katzenbach, J. R., & Smith, D. K. (2015). *The Wisdom of Teams: Creating the High-Performance Organization*. Boston, MA: Harvard Business Review Press.

Kesan, P. J., & Hayes, M. C. (2012). Mitigative counterstriking: Self-defense and deterrence in cyberspace. *Harvard Journal of Law & Technology*, *25*(2), 474–529.

Khan, S., Gani, A., Wahab, A. W. A., Shiraz, M., & Ahmad, I. (2016). Network forensics: Review, taxonomy, and open challenges. *Journal of Network and Computer Applications*, *66*, 214–235. doi:10.1016/j.jnca.2016.03.005

Krombholz, K., Hobel, H., Huber, M., & Weippl, E. (2015). Advanced social engineering attacks. *Journal of Information Security and Applications*, *22*, 113–122. doi:10.1016/j.jisa.2014.09.005

Kurosawa, K., Ohta, H., & Kakuta, K. (2017). How to make a linear network code (strongly) secure. *Designs, Codes and Cryptography*, *82*(3), 559–582. doi:10.100710623-016-0180-0

Landoll, D. J. (2010). The security risk assessment handbook: a complete guide for performing security risk assessment. Second Edition. Boca Raton, FL: CRC Press, Taylor & Francis Group.

Liaudanskienel, R., Ustinovicius, L., & Bogdanovicius, A. (2009). Evaluation of Construction Process Safety Solutions Using the TOPSIS Method. *Inzinerine Ekonomika-Engineering Economics*, *64*(4), 32–40.

Lin, Z., Lin, D., & Pei, D. (2017). Practical construction of ring LFSRs and ring FCSRs with low diffusion delay for hardware cryptographic applications. *Cryptography and Communications*, *9*(4), 431–440. doi:10.100712095-016-0183-8

Malatras, A., Geneiatakis, D., & Vakalis, I. (2016). On the efficiency of user identification: A system-based approach. *International Journal of Information Security*, *15*(1), 1–19.

McQuade, S. (2006). *Understanding and Managing Cybercrime*. Boston, MA: Allyn & Bacon.

Mittelman, J. H. (2011). Global (in) security: The confluence of intelligence and will. *Global Change, Peace & Security*, *23*(2), 135–139. doi:10.1080/14781158.2011.580954

Okamoto, T., & Takashima, K. (2015). Achieving short ciphertexts or short secret-keys for adaptively secure general inner-product encryption. *Designs, Codes and Cryptography*, *77*(2), 725–771. doi:10.100710623-015-0131-1

Peltier, T. R. (2010). Information security risk analysis. Third Edition. Boca Raton, FL: CRC Press, Taylor & Francis Group, Auerbach Publications. doi:10.1201/EBK1439839560

Ruževičius, J., & Gedminaitė, A. (2007). Business Information Quality and its Assessment. *Inzinerine Ekonomika-Engineering Economics*, *52*(2), 18–25.

Schwab, K. (2019). *Globalization 4.0. A New Architecture for the Fourth Industrial Revolution. A call for engagement.* Geneva, Switzerland: World Economic Forum.

Singer, W. P., & Friedman, A. (2014). *Cyber Security and Cyber War: What Everyone Needs to Know*. New York, NY: Oxford University Press.

Singh, A., & Fhom, H. C. S. (2017). Restricted usage of anonymous credentials in vehicular ad hoc networks for misbehavior detection. *International Journal of Information Security*, *16*(2), 195–201. doi:10.100710207-016-0328-y

Smith, D. (2005). Dancing with the mysterious forces of chaos: Issues around complexity, knowledge and the management of uncertainty. *Clinician in Management, (3/4)*, 115–123.

Stepchenko, D., & Voronova, I. (2015). Assessment of Risk Function Using Analytical Network Process. *Inzinerine Ekonomika-Engineering Economics*, *26*(3), 264–271.

Tiago, O., Manoj, T., & Espadanal, M. (2014). Assessing the determinants of cloud computing adoption: An analysis of the manufacturing and services sectors. *Information & Management*, *51*(5), 497–510. doi:10.1016/j.im.2014.03.006

Tropina, T., & Callanan, C. (2015). *Self- and Co-regulation in Cybercrime, Cybersecurity and National Security*. New York, NY: Springer International Publishing. doi:10.1007/978-3-319-16447-2

Wang, W., & Hu, L. (2014). A secure and efficient handover authentication protocol for wireless networks. *Journal of Sensors, 14*(7), 11379–11394. doi:10.3390140711379 PMID:24971471

Willems, E. (2011). Cyber-terrorism in the process industry. *Computer Fraud & Security, 3*(3), 16–19. doi:10.1016/S1361-3723(11)70032-X

Winkler, I. (2010). Justifying IT Security – Managing Risk & Keeping your network Secure. Foster City, CA: Qualys Inc.

Yang, C. N., Wu, C. C., & Wang, D. S. (2014). A discussion on the relationship between probabilistic visual cryptography and random grid. *Information Sciences, 278*, 141–173. doi:10.1016/j.ins.2014.03.033

Yar, M. (2006). *Cybercrime and Society*. London, UK: Sage.

ADDITIONAL READING

Agrawal, N., & Tapaswi, S. (2017). Defense schemes for variants of distributed denial-of-service (DDoS) attacks in cloud computing: A survey. *Information Security Journal: A Global Perspective, 26(1)*, 1-13.

Karanja, E. (2017). The role of the chief information security officer in the management of IT security. *Information & Computer Security, 25*(3), 300–329. doi:10.1108/ICS-02-2016-0013

Kurosawa, K., Ohta, H., & Kakuta, K. (2017). How to make a linear network code (strongly) secure. *Designs, Codes and Cryptography, 82*(3), 559–582. doi:10.100710623-016-0180-0

Lee, C., Lee, C. C., & Kim, S. (2016). Understanding information security stress: Focusing on the type of information security compliance activity. *Computers & Security, 59*, 60–70. doi:10.1016/j.cose.2016.02.004

Lee, W., & Kim, N. (2017). Security Policy Scheme for an Efficient Security Architecture in Software-Defined Networking. *Information, 8*(2), 65. doi:10.3390/info8020065

Zangeneh, V., & Shajari, M. (2018). A cost-sensitive move selection strategy for moving target defense. *Computers & Security, 75*, 72–91. doi:10.1016/j.cose.2017.12.013

KEY TERMS AND DEFINITIONS

Availability: Ensuring the conditions necessary for easy retrieval and use of information and system resources, whenever necessary, with strict conditions of confidentiality and integrity.

Cyber Physical Systems: They are being set up by the internet of things that are machines, employees, products and products facilities being digitally interconnected by the internet.

Integrity: The prohibition amendment - by deleting or adding - or the unauthorized destruction of information; integrity refers to confidence in the data and resources of a system by which to manage information.

Prevention: Implementation of mechanisms that users not be able to counteract and are implemented correctly, unaltered, so the attacker cannot alter them.

Risk Management: The implementation and updating of methods and tools to minimize risks associated with the information system of an organization, such as the Information Security policies, procedures and practices associated formalized and adopted other means in order to bring these risks to acceptable levels.

Threats: The possibility of accidental or deliberate compromise of information security, the loss of confidentiality, integrity or availability or impaired functions that provide authenticity and non-repudiation of information.

Chapter 6
Intelligent Assistance Systems for Marketing Decisions

Mirela Dogaru
Dimitrie Cantemir Christian University, Romania

Dumitru Alexandru Stoica
Valahia University, Romania

Aurelian Vânceanu
Valahia University, Romania

ABSTRACT

Today's technology has evolved greatly and influences us in different ways, more or less beneficial, depending on each user and the needs of each consumer. It has a beneficial influence on organizations, thanks to the continuous use of technologies being as innovative and topical as possible. So organizations need to keep pace and adapt to new technology requirements to thrive in their environment business and to be aware of market requirements. The role of marketing is to grasp the unfulfilled needs of people and to create new and attractive solutions.

INTRODUCTION

The definition of marketing according to Kotler and Keller (2015) is: "Marketing is the science and art of exploring, creating and delivering value to meet the needs of a target market at a profit. Marketing also identifies unfulfilled needs and desires. It defines, measures and quantifies the size of the identified market and the potential profit, points out the segments that the company is capable of serving best, and projects and promotes the right products and services".

A department within the organization often does marketing. This is both good and bad. It's a good thing because it unites a group of trained people, focuses on the task of marketing, and the bad thing is that marketing activities should not be done in a single department, but they should be in all the organization's activities. Marketing is a totally misunderstood topic, in business circles and in the minds

DOI: 10.4018/978-1-7998-1005-6.ch006

of the public, companies believe that marketing exists on the market as a manufacturing support and to escape the company's products (Agha, Alrubaiee, & Jamhour, 2012).

Truth is at the opposite end, manufacturing supports marketing, and the company can always outsource manufacturing through its marketing offers and ideas. Functions that support the company's business are: manufacturing, purchasing, research and development, finance, and more.

Often marketing is confused with the sale, but this is just the "tip of the iceberg" marketing, which is not seen is the extensive market investigation, research and development of the right products, the challenge to set a fair price, the start of the distribution, product market, making marketing more comprehensive than selling (Arsenault, & Faerman, 2014).

Marketing and sale are at opposite ends, long ago Kotler and Keller (2015) said: "Marketing is not the art of finding smart ways to dispose of what you are doing. Marketing is an art of creating real value for the client, is the art of helping customers become better. The keywords in marketing are: quality, services and value. "

The sale begins when you have a product, and marketing starts before you have the product. Marketing is the theme of the company, it has to discover the needs of consumers and what product they should do. Marketing determines how to launch, price, distribute and promote product / service offerings on the market, monitors results and supply improvements over time, and decides when the offer ends (de Waal, & Kourtit, 2013).

Marketing has appeared in the United States in the early part of the 20th century in courses dealing with distribution, especially in wholesale or retail. Economists, out of pure passion for theory, have neglected institutions that have helped to operate the economy, the supply and demand curve appeared when the price could be established, and the price chain would not be explained, the way from the producer through wholesalers and retailers (Kotler, & Keller, 2015).

So marketing has filled the intellectual gaps left by economists, and yet economics is the mother science of marketing (Tong, & Arvey, 2015). At the same time, people have brilliant ideas, not being trained in marketing, so creativity is a big part of marketing success, which means not everything is limited to it (Akgün, Keskin, & Byrne, 2009).Also, science is very important in marketing, marketers make interesting discoveries through marketing research, market modelling, and predictive analytics.

Marketers use marketing models to make decisions and focus on investment. They develop marketing values to indicate their impact on sales and profit (Alhyari, Alazab, Venkatraman, Alazab, & Alazab, 2013).

The notion of marketing has at least three missions, one of them is that: the marketing mission is to sell any and all products to the company to anyone and everyone, a second, slightly more sophisticated mission is that: the marketing mission is to create products that meet the unsatisfied needs of the target markets, a third, more philosophical mission is that: the marketing mission is to raise the living standard of life throughout the world as well as the quality of life (Cameron, & Quinn, 2011).

The role of marketing is to grasp the unfulfilled needs of people and to create new and attractive solutions. According to Davila (2012), the marketing definition is: "Marketing is a modern concept, an attitude in the orientation of enterprises, embodied in a coherent set of practical activities, programmed and organized through the use of scientific methods and techniques, respectively specific instruments". The marketing term is of Anglo-Saxon origin and comes from the "to market" verb, which means market transactions (Kotler, & Keller, 2015). According to the etymology of the word marketing, it is defined as a process of exchange in market space (Ashkanasy, 2011).

Today the Internet plays an important role in businesses because it is a means of communicating with both customers and their suppliers. With the help of the Internet, most people are looking for a job, consumers find information and services, with the help of the Internet, and news and advertising messages are transmitted. It's a communication tool that reaches millions of users, so those who chose to do online marketing have had lower spending on offline marketing.Before making the decision to make online marketing, it must be taken into account that online marketing does not replace the classic one, but it complements it (Ben-Asher, & Gonzalez, 2015).

BACKGROUND

Nowadays, the term "cyber" is the nonphysical "virtual" place where computers and communications meet and communicate (Li, Xu, & Zhao, 2018). Orzan (2001) defines cyber marketing as "Using the power of computing and on-line communication networks and the interactive digital environment to achieve marketing goals." Another definition given by Orzan (2001) is: "Cyber marketing means the process of creating and maintaining a customer relationship through on-line activities to exchange ideas, products and services to meet the needs of both parties."

The marketing mix refers to combining some of the organization's marketing policy instruments, helping to conduct business in optimum conditions. The elements of the marketing field may vary depending on the theoretician or practitioner (Yadav, & Sagar, 2013).

In all these years, various elements have been proposed such as product creation, pricing, branding, services, shelf product exposure, product promotion, promotion, and place of sale (Ahearne, Lam, Mathieu, & Bolander, 2010; Tajeddini, 2015).

The digital environment is a fast environment, there are always changes, because most companies are changing sites and new services are emerging. Software packages and hardware components are on the rise, coming from even non-traditional sources. In the digital environment, you can develop a business with great ease because it creates a revenue stream, management and distribution of information. In cyber marketing, the 4Ps have a totally different approach to the offline environment (Li, Xu, & Zhao, 2018).

Products in the on-line environment include both products and services. In this case, product policy is based on the product category on which the business is based, for example: material goods, services and software or products that can be converted into digital form. Goods are variable, such as machines, machines, and books where product policy is done in a classic way. In the case of these products, online marketing is based on their presentation in catalos, electronic magazines, and on-line documentation. Products that can be changed in digital form are the products that can be given up on body and body parts (Orzan, 2001).

The price is similar to offline, only some organizations change it due to the large number of competitors when it comes to the on-line environment. In the case of online prices, the same rule applies as in the offline environment; the same strategies and factors are taken into account. In the on-line environment, pricing is much easier than the offline environment because competitors' prices can be easily and quickly checked just by accessing sites or by simply searching on one of the existing search engines.

Distribution is less costly in terms of: packaging, transporting, delivering and storing products, all done in real time. Also, distribution strategies for cyber marketing involve direct or short distribution channels, channel width is selective by intermediary or exclusive by product category, using varied distribution control patterns.

Table 1. Promotion techniques in offline and online environments

Techniques to Promote in Traditional Marketing	Techniques to Promote in Cyber Marketing
Advertising by television, radio, press	Advertising by banners
Outdoor advertising	Promote through site content
Printed advertising: catalogs, flyers, brochures, brochures	Online Catalog Online Brochures
Public Relations: press releases, conferences, etc.	Pressroom site
Direct marketing: telemarketing, email	Email marketing: opt-in lists, newsletter, discussion groups
Fairs and exhibitions	Information marketing
Sponsorship	Online sponsorship
Promotions	Online events
Word of mouth	Virtual Marketing

Website promotion, product and service information, and even products and services per se are highly effective regardless of the marketing environment used. The important elements used to promote products online are: content, text, graphics, video, sound, multimedia, Java Scripts, and programs. The forms of on-line promotion are: information marketing, press releases, sponsorships and Internet advertising.

In Romania, online advertising appeared in 1999, and the number of users was 900,000 because it was not seen with consumer confidence (Orzan, 2001). On-line advertising is done using static or dynamic type messages, which are displayed on users' screens. There are many marketing techniques in Romania, based on the needs of each company and the development of the Internet. Unfortunately, in Romania we are very little used, but for those who have opted for this promotion is a very high advantage, such a campaign must be very well planned and adapted according to the objectives to be achieved (Table 1).

In order to develop an internet marketing strategy, it takes steps, these steps consist of identifying the problem, which depends on the company's involvement in the online environment, if the company is at the beginning of the online launch, it should see the opportunity to launch online, and for those who are already in the online environment, they need to investigate if there were any marketing issues that year, and they need updating the site based on new image changes or business activity (Alstete, & Beutell, 2018).

Another strategy that the company can adopt is to set goals, these goals being the result of the marketing effort, they can be: the visibility of the site, the number of visitors or the good communication with the customers (Hartnell, Ou, & Kinicki, 2011).

The company must determine what type of strategy it uses based on market characteristics, and in this case the same strategy applies as in the case of classic marketing. Another step to be taken is to allocate resources, each organization has a budget made available for a proposed project, and so it is appropriate for the launch in the online environment to allocate a rich budget so that it reaches the end of the program in order to be successful but not failure. Running the plan is another step that needs to be followed carefully because the plan to launch you into the marketing environment should be implemented, not just theoretically (Taticchi, Tonelli, & Cagnazzo, 2010).

IMPLICATIONS OF CUSTOMER RELATIONSHIP MARKETING IN ORGANIZATION RESULTS

Customer Relationship Marketing (CRM) is a business process in which customer relationships, customer loyalty and brand value are built through marketing strategies and activities that enable companies to develop long-term relationships with both established and new customers, while contributing to the rationalization of corporate performance. Customer relationship marketing includes customer-specific business and employee strategies through employee training, marketing planning, relationship building, and advertising (Ahearne, Lam, Mathieu, & Bolander, 2010).

CRM also offers a way to directly evaluate customer value, for example: a business is truly interested in its customers; it is rewarded with customer loyalty to the brand. Because CRM is mutually beneficial, market share advances viable at an alert pace (Arsenault, & Faerman, 2014).

It offers cross-selling opportunities, where, depending on customer approval, a business can prove a marketing or branding strategy more than one customer. Customer relationship marketing should not be confused with "customer relationship management," is a related but unique concept that uses the same acronym for CRM (Davila, 2012).

Marketers started the new millennium in one of two groups: those who practice CRM, and those who do not. Those who do so recognize their marketing programs to create and strengthen loyalty to the brand, have put as much emphasis on customer retention as they are part of attracting customers. The same marketers also give up the idea that advertising work ends with the sale, that its purpose is to carry a "take your hands" to the house register (Li, Xu, & Zhao, 2018).

They admit that selling is the beginning of an opportunity to create a lasting brand relationship, profitability with the client, and those who do not practice CRM, they can not yet, but they will and will do it if they want to survive this millennium, if they support a profitable growth in the face of diminishing, they are returning to the marketing waves that preceded the CRM. There are three such waves, which collectively have led the market since the Second World War.

Customer relationship marketing has many implications for market planning, employee training, advertising, promotion, public relations, direct marketing, packaging design, etc. CRM asks us to redirect our attention to the economic value of brands, CRM applications that we consider the brand's cost of exploitation versus the brand-building benefits.

The goal of customer marketing is to win and maintain customer loyalty to the brand (Orzan, 2001). Advertising and promotion should work in a concentrated way, not in conflict; the key to this combination is to achieve the right balance. Researchs show that there is a "point of danger", a point that says too much of the marketing mix is spent on promoting prices instead of building loyalty to the brand (Tajeddini, 2015; Yadav, & Sagar, 2013).

Customer relationship marketing is a side of customer relationship management that focuses on customer loyalty and long-term engagement of clients rather than short-term goals such as customer acquisitions and individual sales. The purpose of relationship marketing (or relationship with the marketing client) is to create strong customer relationships, even emotional, a brand can lead a business, can promote free of charge through Word-of-mouth, and the information gathered by customers leads further to promotion.

Customer Relationship Marketing is in contrast to the traditional approach to marketing transactions that focuses on increasing individual sales. In the transactional model, the return on the customer's purchase cost may be insufficient.

A customer can be convinced to select that brand once, but without a strong marketing strategy, the customer cannot come back to that brand in the future. While organizations combine the elements of both transactional marketing relationships, customer relationship marketing is starting to play a more important role for many companies.

Marketing relationships are based on customer experience management principles, focusing on improving customer integration to better promote brand loyalty. While these interactions can still occur personally by phone, much of the marketing relationship and customer experience has emerged through the web.

With plenty of information on the web and the thriving use of the media, most consumers expect to have easy access tailored to details about a brand and expect the possibility of influencing services and products through media outlets and comments online. Today, the marketing relationship involves the easy creation of two-way communication between customers and businesses, customer tracking activities and the provision of customized information based on these activities.

For example, a merchant site could track a client's activity by allowing them to create a user profile so their information is conveniently saved for future visits so that the site can push more information to accommodate them for the next time on the next visit. Visitors to the site can also connect with Facebook or another social media channel, allowing users a simpler experience and linking them to the social media presence of the automated brand.

This is also the case with CRM and automated marketing software that can support a customer relationship marketing strategy by tracking and tracking customer information more easily. A Social CRM goes further by helping to expand marketing relationships in the social media, allowing companies to monitor in a simpler way and to respond to customer problems on social channels, which in turn helps to maintain an image better brand.

There are five reasons why Customer Relationship Marketing is important in a business (Alstete, & Beutell, 2018), these being:

- **Builds knowledge, just like the trust factor**. To take into account the following knowledge, such as the confidence factor, start by thinking about your own shopping habits as a consumer. Nowadays, will you buy online from an alien? Will you buy something from a random randomly visited site? Will you hire a consultant, coach or assistant you did not see and did not hear of him, with whom you did not work and did not see him? The answer to these questions is a great NO. In the era of today's technology, we have the luxury of knowing and deciding and trusting the people or the company behind each acquisition. To do this, it's important to be constantly active on social media, site, and offline networks on the network. For example, in social media you want to attract new followers, respond to comments and create relevant content that is both educational and entertainment.
- **Word of mouth recommendations**. When it comes to owning your own business, Word of mouth recommendations are gold, and when you focus on building a business based on the person-to-person connection, a "WOW" factor is created that makes the client talks. There are clients who want to feel special and important, because they often do not feel the same in other areas throughout their lives, and this is essential to remember, as customers rarely purchase services or products solely on the basis of the expected results.By building the ability of marketing relationships, meet these additional needs, offer you more than a product or service, it gives you experience. To gain experience, highlight your customer's successes, answer questions promptly, and respond to

concerns instead of reacting to them. Responding to a concern means that you will find a way to answer the question your company and the person who deals with.

- **Creating opportunity in the business**. When you build your marketing relationship skills, it will also open the door to more business opportunities because a personal connection experience leaves a long-lasting impression. The memory created with the client will come to their minds more quickly and frequently, so when a client's friend talks to you asking for a business risk report, the customer will remember you.
- **Keep up to date with your customers' needs**. With the person-to-person marketing relationship model you can learn firsthand, and at no cost, in terms of your customers' wishes. For example, Starbucks offered Wi-Fi customers, and thanks to this choice, stores are always filled with customers who know they can do business and enjoy a good coffee. The other frontiers have not listened to consumers' demands, companies have not made the necessary changes, improving to keep customers coming back, and as a result the company has disappeared.
- **Adds your business style**. In our new economy, in the case of insecure jobs, more and more people are opening their own business, to survive in the new, booming, small business market, they need to stand out, have their own luminous signal, and to be unique. Having an instant marketing relationship, you can grow quickly and easily by adopting a unique style. It gives you space to learn more about consumer needs, and to develop confidence with your own techniques, you do not have to match the model of someone else's business, you just have to be yourself and respond with confidence to your customers. Faces have changed since the media appeared, businesses have to change how they acted until that time, and have to focus on building relationships with people to enable them to improve their brand and create relationships lasting, which will lead to long-term profits.

Business Intelligence (BI) can be defined as a set of techniques and tools for the acquisition and transformation of raw data into meaningful and useful information in business analysis (Li, Xu & Zhao, 2018). Business Intelligence technologies are capable of manipulating a large amount of unstructured data that helps identify and develop and create new strategic business opportunities. The Business Intelligence mission is to facilitate the interpretation of a large amount of data. Identifying opportunities and implementing an effective forward-looking strategy can give businesses market advantage and long-term stability. Business Intelligence technologies can provide data from the past, present and future of business operations. The Business Intelligence features are: reporting; online analytical processing; data exploitation; business performance management; Benchmarking; predictive analysis; prescription analysis (Li, Xu, & Zhao, 2018).

Business Intelligence is used to support a wide range of business decisions, from operational to strategic, and basic decisions are those that include the position or price of the product. The high efficiency of Business Intelligence is noticeable when combining data from a company operating on an external market with the data of a company operating in an internal market such as data and financial operations. When the internal data is combined with external data, a complete image is provided; creating "intelligence" that cannot be derived from a single set of data (Li, Xu, & Zhao, 2018). Among the innumerable uses, Business Intelligence tools help empower organizations by gaining a new market outlook by assessing demand, appropriate products and services for different market segments, and assessing the impact of marketing efforts.

The Software Advice Team has made a sample of these interactions taken over the past two years; this report reveals key discovery trends such as: more than 70% of potential Business Intelligence buyers are not IT professionals, but according to job titles listed correspond to business professionals; approximately half of potential buyers are looking for Business Intelligence software in order to better view their data. Similarly, the most requested Business Intelligence tools among buyers are dashboards and scorecards; a small fraction of all potential Business Intelligence buyers want integrated suites, but they remain safe on an implementation model (Li, Xu, & Zhao, 2018).

Separate job titles, 70% of users were not IT professionals, but they had roles such as: Financial Officer, Operations Manager or Marketing Director, and 37% were IT Professionals serving either Chief Information Officer or IT leadership. Certainly, demand is higher among business professionals, they want to capitalize not only on prospects gathered through Business Intelligence software but also to do this without the help of the IT department (Orzan, 2001).

Buyers want a better view of data from the information systems used, whether the organization evaluated the Business Intelligence software for the first time or an existing system, 40% rated the software because they wanted a better view of the data on who collects them. Another 25% were either looking for an existing software update or never implemented a business intelligence system; others have been looking for ways to automate and unify a previously scattered data collection system.

Dashboards and scorecards are the buyers' preferences, being the most sought-after tools. On the top of the list of companies that have rated these solutions; only two of the companies have rated the integrated suites. Depending on the preferences of each user, data warehousing, extraction, transformation and upload (ETL) and on-line analytical processing tools (OLAP) are also sought. 6% integrated buyers acquired data exploitation and predictive analysis of the least needed category.

Most BI software buyers are those in the healthcare and manufacturing industries, banking / finance, and retail sales; however, most buyers were from disparate industries with the category "other ", which includes areas such as: non-profit, education and distribution.

The general steps and objectives of a Business Intelligence system (Orzan, 2001) are as follows:

- *Measurement*: This part of the business intelligence process gives managers value for benchmarking and benchmarking of the company, as well as ways to compare a business in terms of goals set with real-life performance statistics.
- *Analysis*: Here is the bulk of Business Intelligence processing, including data extraction, modelling and statistical analysis. Data is processed by developers and informed decision-making. The analysis refers to the data standardization process and its organization for lower consumption.
- *Reporting*: Refers to data viewing, takes place in the analysis stage, where it generates reporting infrastructure for business management, and the organized data is presented to the users in the reporting phase.
- *Collaboration*: Here is the exchange of data and their transfer, the activity segments work together to exchange knowledge and process the output of Business Intelligence. Collaboration is important because each business segment has its own set of important information, and only by comparing their BI-specific results, they can get a real global look with an „overall picture".
- *Knowledge Management*: The real world, the real world of business intelligence, at this stage is the management of the knowledge, the data actually applied in the decision-making and planning process.

The major players in the Business Intelligence industry are: IBM Congo's, SAP, Oracle and many others (Li, Xu, & Zhao, 2018). These companies provide the hardware and software needed to process large amounts of data in Business Intelligence systems; these data are received from end users from a data repository, passing through three layers:

- **Staging:** Developers gather raw data, standardize it for easy comparison, and prepare it for classification and analysis;
- **Integration:** raw data is classified, organized and catalogued for easy access to the end user.
- **Access:** Data is easy to use and delivered to end-user applications.

Undoubtedly, business intelligence is the most used word in the modern business landscape. New Business Intelligence models are easier to use, have simpler interfaces and can be operated and understood even by the most technologically advanced member of the side team in a company. Given the accessibility of today's Business Intelligence software, the questions now are: "Do the manager really need a Business Intelligence system in my company?" or "How can this information help make better business decisions?"

SOLUTIONS AND RECOMMENDATIONS

SQL Server Reporting Services is a server-based reporting platform that allows us to create and manage a large variety of different reports and deliver them in a wide range of formats. On this platform you can create tables and charts, you can view complex data using charts, maps and spark lines. Finished reports can be submitted directly from the Reporting Services site, called Reports Manager, or can be viewed by users directly from their Web or Windows application. We can also install SQL Server Reporting Services (SSRS), so we can run reports directly from SharePoint. The basics of SSRS report development (Li, Xu & Zhao, 2018) are as follows:

- **Building SSRS Reports**: Refers to the basics of SSRS, demonstrates how to quickly build simple reports, and helps familiarize yourself with the Report Designer core environment.
- **Customizing SSRS Reports**: refers to the use of custom and aggregate functions, sub-reporting, matrix control, drill-downs, and sorting.
- **Visual Inspection of SSRS**: Refers to in-depth look at visual controls of SSRS, especially control charts.
- **Running SSRS Reports**: Leads the user through reports, deploying reports-building tools.

An SSRS implementation must be associated with a SQL Server instance; this instance will be two databases by default. The first database named Report Server, which contains report definitions, configuration, history, security of reports, and more, the second database is called Report Server Temped just like temped, is used as a workspace for construction reports, and not permanently maintain no objects.

There are several ways to implement Reporting Services for a department or company, with SharePoint integrated mode gaining popularity. Earlier versions of SQL Server used the Business Intelligence Development Studio (BIDS) as an SSRS development tool. However, since SQL Server 2017, SQL Server

Data Tools (SSDT-BI) has been used, which may or may not be in the SQL Server media, depending on the version. Each tool runs as an add-in for Visual Studio (Li, Xu & Zhao, 2018).

On the other hand, SQL Server Management Studio is a management and administration environment based on Visual Studio 2005, mainly used for administration of Analysis Services instances, SQL Server, Integration Services and Reporting Services. With SQL Server Management Studio, you can manage the Analysis Services objects, and you can also create new objects directly on existing analysis services, for example, by using XMLA scripts. SQL Server Management Studio provides an analysis script project where you can develop and save scripts written in Multidimensional Expressions (MDX), Data Mining Extensions (DME), and XML. Script project analysis is used to perform tasks for managing or re-creating objects such as databases and cubes.

Both Business Intelligence Development Studio and SQL Server Management Studio provide projects that are organized in solutions. A solution may contain several projects, and a project contains several elements. A new solution is automatically generated when you create a project, and you can add additional projects needed for an existing solution. Objects that a project contains depend on the project type. The elements a project contains are saved as files in project documents in the file system.

FUTURE RESEARCH DIRECTIONS

Power Business Intelligence is a Cloud-based Microsoft Business Intelligence solution and includes the following tools: *Data Analysis* (power Business Intelligence can unify all of your organization's data, whether in Cloud or local, and provides quick and easy access to data owned by the organization. With Power Business Intelligence, customers get a 360-degree view of their business, where data can be explored and quickly discovered); *Interactive Reporting* (customers can view all data through a glass pane, Power Business Intelligence Mobile applications are automatically updated with data changes, allowing them to access date, data, and reports whenever needed); *Financial Performance* (power Business Intelligence provides a complete picture on different data sources in just a few seconds; you can view financial data in a single image from the summary statements to the detailed account level); *Easily Used Interface* (with one click, users can access the data behind the dashboard using initiative tools, discovering the easy answers); *Data View* (can be creative and productive with what you built, combining disparate database data, web files and services with visual tools that help you better understand and solve data quality issues and format them in an automated way) (Li, Xu, & Zhao, 2018).

CONCLUSION

Business today has evolved a lot, and companies are forced to adapt if they want to survive on the market. Using and interpreting information has become an essential one, and small organizations have begun to focus their attention on the business intelligence system in order to have an edge over competition. A business intelligence system is quite expensive, but due to the evolution of technology, prices have begun to decline, so those who have small businesses can afford to acquire this system and benefit from the benefits of business intelligence software.

Business intelligence software is the simplest way to analyze a company's data and information, just above other methods, and can be used for many purposes. The benefits of Business Intelligence software to Romanian companies are numerous. One very important benefit for organizations in Romania is the increase in sales due to the analysis of information. By simply sending an email to a customer by a company that contains a link to the web page, when the customer has accessed this link, it can monitor its behavior through an analytical tool, it can also be used to predict sales, and in depending on that, you will be able to make a decision to reach a proposed target.

With the help of this software, many companies have identified their opportunities, valued the company's value, their capability, comparing strengths and strengths to competition, have been able to identify market trends and rapidly change their requirements. As is known, the center of attention of any small company is the customer, and the support service has to be considered, so there is a tool that gathers customer feedback, and through this support companies can find problems to solve them in a timely manner.

A big asset of the companies was the reporting, which is the basis of Business Intelligence, and the strong point in the evolution of the business, more than that helps to find a solution for even better development, and with the help of the financial reports they understood the company's situation regarding the incomes and expenses. Business Intelligence software greatly influences business development as company performance depends on a large number of factors and this solution to choose a business intelligence software is the best option because it allows you to import data from different locations, adjust your reports to variables, and make a forecast of them. It simplifies the working method and employees will no longer be stressed by managing the reports and everything will be at your fingertips, and with time you will be able to find solutions and plans for the future.

REFERENCES

Agha, S., Alrubaiee, L., & Jamhour, M. (2012). Effect of core competence on competitive advantage and organizational performance. *International Journal of Business and Management*, *7*(1), 192–204.

Ahearne, M., Lam, S. K., Mathieu, J. E., & Bolander, W. (2010). Why are some sales people better at adapting to organizational change? *Journal of Marketing*, *74*(3), 65–79. doi:10.1509/jmkg.74.3.065

Akgün, A. E., Keskin, H., & Byrne, J. (2009). Organizational emotional capability, product and process innovation, and firm performance: An empirical analysis. *Journal of Engineering and Technology Management*, *26*(3), 103–130. doi:10.1016/j.jengtecman.2009.06.008

Alhyari, S., Alazab, M., Venkatraman, S., Alazab, M., & Alazab, A. (2013). Performance evaluation of e-government services using balanced scorecard. *Benchmarking: An International Journal*, *20*(4), 512–536. doi:10.1108/BIJ-08-2011-0063

Alstete, J. W., & Beutell, N. J. (2018). Designing learning spaces for management education: A mixed methods research approach. *Journal of Management Development*, *37*(2), 201–211. doi:10.1108/JMD-08-2017-0247

Arsenault, P., & Faerman, S. R. (2014). Embracing paradox in management: The value of the competing values framework. *Organizational Management Journal*, *11*(3), 147–158. doi:10.1080/15416518.2014.949614

Ashkanasy, N. (2011). International happiness; a multilevel perspective. *The Academy of Management Perspectives*, (February): 23–29.

Ben-Asher, N., & Gonzalez, C. (2015). Effects of cyber security knowledge on attack detection. *Computers in Human Behavior*, *48*, 51–61. doi:10.1016/j.chb.2015.01.039

Cameron, K. S., & Quinn, R. E. (2011). *Diagnosing and Changing Organizational Culture: Based on the Competing Values Framework*. San Francisco, CA: Jossey-Bass.

Davila, A. (2012). New trends in performance measurement and management control. In Performance Measurement and Management Control. *Global Issues (Washington, D.C.)*, *25*, 65–87.

de Waal, A. A., & Kourtit, K. (2013). Performance measurement and management in practice. *International Journal of Productivity and Performance Management*, *62*(5), 446–473. doi:10.1108/IJPPM-10-2012-0118

Hartnell, C. A., Ou, A. Y., & Kinicki, A. (2011). Organizational culture and organizational effectiveness: A meta-analytic investigation of the competing values framework's theoretical suppositions. *The Journal of Applied Psychology*, *96*(4), 677–694. doi:10.1037/a0021987 PMID:21244127

Kotler, Ph. T., & Keller, K. L. (2015). *Marketing Management* (15th ed.). USA: Pearson.

Li, Sh., Xu, L. D., & Zhao, S. (2018). 5G Internet of Things: A survey. *Journal of Industrial Information Integration*, *10*, 1–9. doi:10.1016/j.jii.2018.01.005

Orzan, G. (2001). *Cybermarketing*. Bucharest, Romania: Uranus Publishing House.

Tajeddini, K. (2015). Exploring the antecedents of effectiveness and efficiency. *International Journal of Hospitality Management*, *49*(7), 125–135. doi:10.1016/j.ijhm.2015.06.007

Taticchi, P., Tonelli, F., & Cagnazzo, L. (2010). Performance measurement and management: A literature review and a research agenda. *Measuring Business Excellence*, *14*(1), 4–18. doi:10.1108/13683041011027418

Tong, Y. K., & Arvey, R. D. (2015). Managing complexity via the Competing Values Framework. *Journal of Management Development*, *34*(6), 653–673. doi:10.1108/JMD-04-2014-0029

Yadav, N., & Sagar, M. (2013). Performance measurement and management frameworks. *Business Process Management Journal*, *19*(6), 947–971. doi:10.1108/BPMJ-01-2013-0003

ADDITIONAL READING

Barnes, C. M., Dang, C., Leavitt, K., Guarana, C., & Uhlmann, E. L. (2018). Archival data in micro organizational research: A toolkit for moving to a broader set of topics. *Journal of Management*, *44*(4), 1453–1478. doi:10.1177/0149206315604188

Cumming, D., & Groh, A. P. (2018). Entrepreneurial finance: Unifying themes and future directions. *Journal of Corporate Finance*, *50*, 538–555. doi:10.1016/j.jcorpfin.2018.01.011

Fan, J. P. H., Li, J., & Zheng, G. (2016). Revisiting the bright and dark sides of capital flows in business groups. *Journal of Business Ethics*, *134*(4), 509–528. doi:10.100710551-014-2382-6

KEY TERMS AND DEFINITIONS

Data Security: Data security is provide storage and transmit security by using encryption algorithm.

Economic Management: The achievement of the budget objectives with minimum costs so that when the activity is completed the revenue exceeds the costs, namely there is a profit that ensures a level of profitability as high as possible both at general level and by product, department or service performed.

Efficiency: A measurable concept, quantitatively determined by the ratio of useful output to total input.

Financial Management: A tool in the decision-making relating to the collection and analysis of information in order to increase the performance level of the economic entity.

Chapter 7
An Open Innovation Lens on the Digital Transformation Frontiers

Maryia Zaitsava
University of Cagliari, Italy

Elona Marku
University of Cagliari, Italy

Manuel Castriotta
University of Cagliari, Italy

ABSTRACT

The aim of the present study is to explore Digital Transformation frontiers using the lens of Open Innovation. By implementing bibliographic coupling method, the authors bring together segmental publications from different research fields and provide a comprehensive overview of the combined Open Innovation and Digital Transformation field's intellectual structure, revealing the different groups of thoughts, influential authors, and pressing topics. The research findings illustrate, the research area has polycentric composition with absence of overlaps between articles. Five main research groups are identified: Co-evolution of Digital Technologies and Open Innovation; Digital Peer-communities; Digital Ecosystems; Knowledge Management in the Open and Digital Era; and Open Innovation, Digital Technologies, and Businesses Performance. The current research contributes both Open Innovation and Digital Transformation fields by cross-exploring each phenomenon and revealing how Digital Transformation shapes the nature of innovation as a collaborative activity as part of an independent research area.

INTRODUCTION

In today's extremely dynamic environment characterized by the rapid technological progress, globalization, unlimited knowledge sharing, and collaborative innovation with the new active role of users, businesses have no alternative but to take into account this new realm in order to be sustainable and competitive in the long run. The fundamental transformation of business models and work practices toward open and collaborative mode brought by digital technologies is witnessed in all levels of economic activity

DOI: 10.4018/978-1-7998-1005-6.ch007

(Eaton, 2015). Open Innovation (OI) of today goes far beyond licensing, spin-offs and traditional collaborative methods of OI coined by Chesbrough back in 2006 as innovation process that intentionally manages knowledge flows across organizational boundaries. It is recognized that modern mode of OI has become a new space for each level of the society to collaborate and co-innovate (Nieto et al., 2007; Cassiman et al., 2009; Cassiman et al., 2010; Lichtenthaler, 2011; Rayna et al., 2015; Cassiman et.al, 2016). This transition has been thrust forward by a variety of factors, where among the most important are fast-developing ICT, digital technologies that made possible the valuable knowledge to be widely diffused and easily accessible (von Hippel, 2005; Barrett et.al., 2012; Yoo, 2012; Fitzgerald et al., 2014; & Parviainen et al., 2017). Indeed, the coexistence of OI and digital transformation (DT) has fueled the emergence of the new perception of innovation in the digital era, which favors extensive networking and co-creative collaboration between a variety of stakeholders - from users (Baldwin et al., 2011; Afonso et al., 2012) to public sector, SMEs, industry incumbents (Curley et al., 2013; Skarzauskiene et al., 2016).

Most of prior OI reviews have offered *qualitative* attempts to assess and structure the current state of development of the field. More specifically, Gassmann (2006; 2010) revealed research streams and developed a situational approach and a comprehensive structure of OI management, taking into account various aspects form industry to firm level. Elmquist and colleagues (2009) deepened the research domain and identified new OI themes while rethinking the concept of OI, its strengths, and weaknesses, and proposing conceptual models. Lichtenthaler (2011) put his efforts on compiling existing view and future perspectives of OI, while West and Bogers (2014) changed the research focus moving towards business models, commercialization of OI. In contrast, a few reviews adopted a *quantitative* approach. In particular, Kovacs et al. (2015) represented both overviews of decade literature of OI domain and its research fronts; however, while focusing predominantly on the OI phenomenon, it neglected specific insights on DT dynamics making this "digital advent" gap more than evident. Van Oorschot et al. (2018) although provided a comprehensive picture of an innovation adoption field in their recent bibliometric review work, they investigated especially the adoption of open systems.

Although the latest research highlights that DT is an undeniable side of the future research topics on OI (Bogers et al. 2017; 2018), and co-evolution and co-influence effects are observed (Christensen et al., 2005; Ernkvist, 2015; Bogers et al., 2016), knowledge is still unstructured and unable to describe and understand the phenomenon and its outcomes for organizations. In the light of increasing interest, the extant scientific literature definitely requires an objective overview of the intellectual structure and well-articulated pressing research topics.

In this vein, this chapter has the goal to provide a comprehensive overview of the field's intellectual structure while highlighting the different groups of thoughts among the combined OI and digital technologies studies, defining research fronts, and revealing influential authors and pressing topics. The authors adopt the bibliographic coupling method which is widely used in management research to recognize the shift from traditional research focus to current trends (Boyack et al., 2010; Vogel et al., 2013; Zupic et al., 2015), and used the Viewer software algorithm for the visualization of results (van Eck et al., 2009). The final sample consists of 45 articles published in top-journals between 2005 – 2018 period.

The present research contributes both to the OI and to DT research fields by identifying emerging research trends and elaborating on OI and DT co-evolution. The research puts the brick into the understanding of OI evolution through the lens of digital technologies development and their ubiquitous nature. The paper also contributes to the understanding of the DT process happening in conditions of knowledge sharing and OI boundaries. The results presented in this paper can be used for mapping future research agenda or for contributing to the identified research topics. Finally, the research can have managerial implications for leaders and OI policymakers by synthesizing knowledge on the emerging topic, shedding light on opportunities and challenges of the OI and digital technologies synergy, and analyzing in depth the most influential papers and findings.

METHODOLOGY

Bibliographic Coupling

In this article, one of the bibliometric methods—namely bibliographic coupling—is adopted to identify the intellectual structure of the emerging topics in OI and DT. Bibliometrics are widely recognized to be effective in summarizing and mapping the most representative bibliographic documents (Pritchard, 1969; Broadus, 1987; Di Guardo, & Harrigan, 2012; Loi et al., 2016; Castriotta, & Di Guardo, 2016). These quantitative methods are based on the fundamental assumption that two articles are more like their bibliographies. In other words, a focal publication cites papers, which are at some degree related to the topic of the focal paper (Kovacs, 2015).

Thus, the bibliometric coupling (BC) method, introduced in 1963 by Kessler (Kessler, 1963) aims at representing the research fronts by identifying the intellectual structure's clusters, based on linking documents that reference the same set of cited documents (Boyack, & Klavans, 2010). Moreover, BC method is able to cluster very recent papers in longitudinal studies (Kovacs et al., 2015). Therefore, the bibliographic coupling is widely used in research to recognize the shift from traditional research focus to current trends, including management studies (Boyack, & Klavans, 2010; Vogel, & Güttel, 2013; Zupic, & Čater, 2015).

This method captures ongoing trends (Boyack, & Klavans, 2010; Kovacs et al., 2015) and future priorities within a field (Vogel, & Güttel, 2013). As long as the topic of DT and OI is emerging, the bibliographic coupling is considered a beneficial method to orientate in the research trends, and identifying the intellectual structure and new streams.

Visualization of Similarities Approach: VOSviewer Software

This research relies on the visualization of similarities (VOS) technique (Van Eck, & Waltman, 2007). This relatively new technique, introduced by Van Eck and Waltman (2007) in 2007, aims at providing a low-dimensional visualization of the distance between pairs of objects, where the distance captures the similarities in the most accurate way (Van Eck, & Waltman, 2007). For example, the strong relation between two items is represented by the short distance between them, and the weak relation is represented by the longer distance from items. The technique is recognized to be the sort of alternative to the one of the most popular techniques in constructing bibliometric maps multidimensional scaling (MDS) (Van Eck et al., 2010). It is worth to mention, both techniques persuade the same goal to represent the distance between items, which reflects the relatedness level of items, but do it differently. Thus, VOS uses the optimization algorithm of minimizing a weighted sum of the squared distances between items and weighting the squared distance by the similarity between papers (Van Eck et al., 2010). It helps to reduce the influence of some artifacts MDS technique suffers from. Using the VOS clustering algorithm, which adopted modularity function to measure the quality of the clustering into groups (Newman, & Girvan, 2004), publications are then clustered into networks.

The authors use VOSviewer software package, which combines both VOS optimization and clustering algorithms to visualize the results. VOSviewer has been used to design bibliographic maps based on a co-word analysis or bibliographic coupling method in various research domains to identify the research trends and fronts (Van Eck, & Waltman, 2017; Marku et al., 2017; Laengle et al., 2017; Ferreira, 2018; Martínez-López et al., 2018; Castriotta et al., 2019).

Sample Selection

Our empirical study follows the general process for bibliographic coupling method: 1) identifying a set of recent papers; 2) calculating the similarity measures; 3) assigning papers to clusters using the similarity values (Boyack, & Klavans, 2010). In order to get units of analysis, the authors use the Web of Science Core Collection database. Using two keywords "Open Innovation" and "Digital*" the researchers extract articles from the WoS Core Collection. As the topic of DT on the crossroad with OI has an emerging nature, a relatively small amount of papers in this sphere can be observed. Therefore, the authors decided not to restrict keywords specifically to "Digital Transformation" and apply the broader term "Digital*" to grasp the vaster amount of papers and get the "big picture" of the research field. All extracted publications were published in top-journals between 2005-2018 period, while conference proceedings and editorials were excluded.

The choice of the timespan period has two reasons. First, following Nosella (2012) a seminal work triggering the literature was published by Christensen et al. in 2005. The authors introduced new research directions on OI and technology dynamics co-existence (Vogel, & Güttel, 2013). Second, it provides a comprehensive picture of the literature. In fact, although there is no exact indication of time limits while using bibliographic coupling methods, it is mentioned about a decade as the most frequently used time span (Zupic, & Čater, 2015). Further, the authors found out that previous literature justifies the slightly extended time-period in cases where an article considered as a foundational is taken as a starting point (Nosella, 2012).

Thus, in total 13 500 articles have been identified in OI topic and 384 926 in digital. Using the Boolean operator "AND", the final amount of 885 papers dealing with both OI and digital was selected. By applying "Management" and "Business" filters, authors then narrowed the results until 150 papers presented in the final selection. To perform bibliographic coupling and cluster analysis the authors use VOSviewer software algorithms (van Eck et al., 2009). The matrix of raw intermediate results was processed using the full counting approach (Leydesdorff, & Park, 2017). 51 articles out of 151 met the selected treshold of four citations (Small, 1973; Zupic, & Cater, 2015). Furthermore, the analysis of the similarities shows that three papers were not connected with each other. Therefore, the unit of analysis was reduced to 48 articles. Finally, through the reading of all the abstracts and full texts three articles have been considered false positive and excluded while considered not eligible or on topic. The final sample consists of 45 articles.

RESULTS

The Foundations of Open Innovation and Digital Transformation Research

Total number of 45 papers on OI and DT publications is shown in Table 1. Overall, each cluster consists of almost the same number of papers, which makes all clusters relatively equal in terms of research interest of scholars. Meaningful insights are revealed after analysis of the number of citations of each cluster: the number of citations of each cluster does not show strong connection with an average year of items publications (Table 1). Clusters which are relatively younger and logically should have had fewer citations, overall, have the same amount of citations as "older" clusters. The most logic explanation of it is the presence of paper-influencer affecting the number of citations inside younger clusters. However, scholars prove that the presented data sample does not suffer from this bias either. Thus, the cluster *Co-evolution of DT and OI* has the most influencing paper (Christensen et al., 2005) not only of the cluster

Table 1. Grouping obtained through cluster analysis

Clusters	Co-evolution of Digital Technologies and OI	Digital Peer-communities	Digital Ecosystems	Knowledge Management in the Open and Digital Era	OI, Digital Tech. Advances, and Businesses Performance
Publications	1. Christensen et al. (2005) 2. Malhotra et al. (2007) 3. Nylén & Holmström (2015) 4. Bogers et al. (2016) 5. Lee et al. (2008) 6. Obal, M. & Lancioni, R. A. (2013) 7. Bogers et al. (2018) 8. Greenstein et al. (2013) 9. Benghozi & Salvador (2016)	1. Kohler, T. et al. (2009) 2. Arakji & Lang (2007) 3. Benner & Tushman (2015) 4. Austin et al. (2012) 5. Parmentier & Mangematin (2014) 6. Harryson (2008) 7. Martínez-Torres et al. (2010) 8. Bauer & Gegenhuber (2015) 9. Wilfredo Bohorquez Lopez & Esteves (2013) 10. Pera & Viglia (2015). 11. Abdelkafi et al. (2009)	1. Yoo et al. (2012) 2. Boudreau (2012) 3. Eaton et al. (2015). 4. Nambisan et al. (2017) 5. Boudreau & Jeppesen (2015) 6. Parker et al. (2016) 7. Lopez-Berzosa & Gawer (2014) 8. Ghazawneh & Henfridsson (2015) 9. Täuscher (2017)	1. Selander et al. (2013) 2. Carayannis & Turner (2006) 3. Barrett et al. (2016) 4. Trantopoulos et al. (2017) 5. Faraj et al. (2016). 6. Schildt (2017) 7. Ho et al. (2011) 8. Kyriakou et al. (2017)	1. Scuotto et al. (2016) 2. Scuotto et al. (2017) 3. Scuotto et al. (2017) 4. Ernkvist (2015) 5. Solima et al. (2016) 6. Angelidou et al. (2018) 7. Nucciarelli et al. (2017) 8. Pal (2016)
Total number of citations	469	362	468	104	111
Number of citations without paper-influencer	212	244	279	104	68
Average year of an item publication	2012.333	2011.55	2014.78	2014.13	2016.5

but also of the whole data set which has got 257 citations and literally doubles the number of citations of the cluster. The cluster *Digital Ecosystems* has its own influencer cited 198 times since 2012 (Yoo, et al., 2012). For the sake of non-biased results, the authors analyze outcomes after removing papers-influencers from each cluster (except *Knowledge Management in the Open and Digital Era,* as there was no discovered influencing paper). It has been identified that even with a significantly lowered number of citations of some of the clusters, relatively the same picture remained and with the relatively small amount of publications in data set, when one single paper can influence the degree of significance of a cluster, there is small bias in the revealed intellectual structure.

From the analysis of the dynamics of publications over years (2005 – 2018) emerges that number of publications on the topic has two phases: the first phase of relatively low interest to the topic (10 articles), and more than triple growth of the number of publications in the period 2012 – 2018 (35 articles), indicating an increasing research interest towards the topic in the research community. Moreover, looking at the same aspect but from a single cluster perspective, it has become evident that this sharp increase has happened due to new topics joining the discussion. Thus, initially scholars have been mostly interested in understanding the nature of co-evolution of DT and OI, digital peer-communities (2005– 2011). Nevertheless, with time, the interest towards management of digital ecosystems and deeper understanding of how exactly OI and digital advances influence businesses have linked up to existing topics (2012 – 2018).

Finally, the journal-wise analysis of papers reveals additional insights. The most active conversation, in particular one third, occurs only in top-4 journals: *MIS Quarterly, Technological Forecasting and Social Change, Organization Science, Technovation.* These four strong players mostly focus their research interest on *Knowledge Management in the Open and Digital* Era and *Digital Ecosystems* clusters. Overall, quite fragmented nature of journals only supports the fact that the phenomenon of DT and OI is broad and be focused on only a few aspects would be rather difficult.

Bibliographic Coupling and Overview of the Intellectual Structure of the Research Topic

The intellectual structure of the sample based on the bibliographic coupling of 45 papers grouped in 5 clusters is presented in Fig. 1. Firstly, the authors have analyzed keywords, abstracts, and introductions in order to get the meaningful explanation of the algorithm-based mapping of the papers in 5 clusters listed below:

- ***Cluster 1***: Co-evolution of Digital Technologies (DT) and Open Innovation (OI)
- ***Cluster 2***: Digital Peer-communities
- ***Cluster 3***: Digital Ecosystems
- ***Cluster 4***: Knowledge Management in the Open and Digital Era
- ***Cluster 5***: OI, Digital Technologies and Businesses Performance

The bibliographic network presented on the Fig. 1 is coherent; clusters are positioned logic-wise on the map. Thus, clusters that are closer to the center of the knowledge map play the focal role on the research area, on the analogy, clusters on the periphery have no so central role and most probably have more niche nature. The most central cluster is represented by the *Co-evolution of DT and OI group* which is surrounded by four other clusters. It has a logic explanation: while other four clusters are focused on

Figure 1. The literature mapping and network

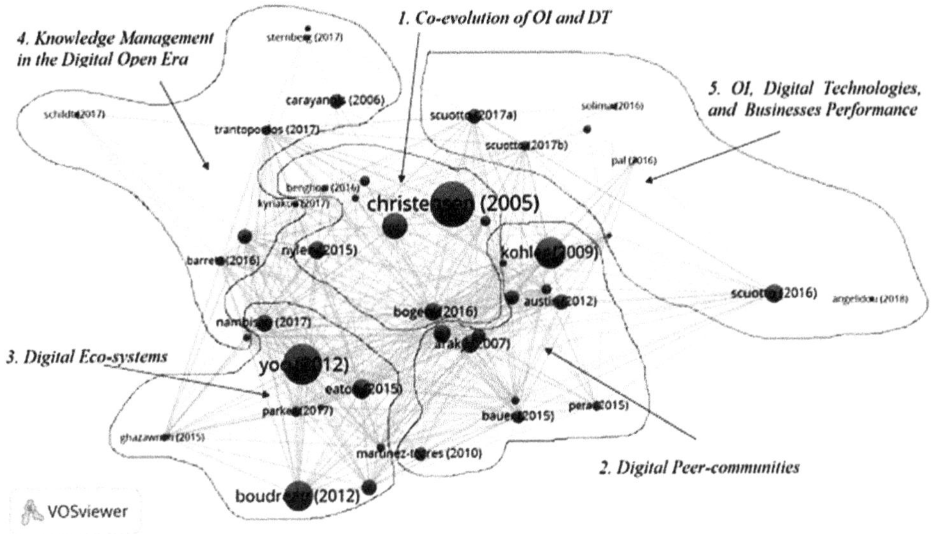

exploring specific aspects of DT and OI, *Co-evolution of DT and OI* cluster is interested in understanding the phenomenon of the co-existence of DT and OI per se. Therefore, this cluster is at a certain degree connected with all knowledge groups. The highest total number of citations (see Table 1) also supports the choice of Co-evolution of DT and OI as the focal cluster.

The analysis of the more general picture of the knowledge map reveals that three clusters *Digital Peer-communities, Co-evolution of DT and OI,* and *Digital Ecosystems* are more synthesized and grouped closer to the center of the map, have the highest number of total citations (see Table 1), and form the core of the knowledge map. On the other hand, two other clusters *Knowledge Management in the Open and Digital Era* and *OI, Digital Technologies and Businesses Performance* are positioned on the periphery of the knowledge map and are spread through the knowledge space. Moreover, some of the papers within these two clusters are "outsiders" with the significant gaps even within clusters. This can signalize about the existing research gap and new research dynamics in knowledge groups. The trend is enhanced with the fact that these two research groups are younger than three other clusters.

In order to identify the focal papers of each cluster, the principle of size variation according to citation number is implemented. Based on this visualization feature, it is evident that although all clusters are quite well divided and relatively independent from each other, some single papers with a high number of citations are placed on the borders with other clusters, if not particularly on the area of neighboring cluster. These "line-crossers" are among the most significant papers in terms of citations within the whole data set. Their positioning emphasizes their role in building the research domain at whole, not only within single cluster.

Co-Evolution of Digital Technologies and Open Innovation Group

This cluster is ground-breaking in its nature, as it groups the scientific papers exploring the complementarities of OI and digital technologies, discussing cross-effects and influences. As the perspectives on this topic are various and path breaking, so is the visualization of the cluster: papers are mostly spread through borders with another clusters. Although, it is possible to distinguish two main research flows: understanding the new nature of digital and open era and challenges brought by OI and digital advances to businesses.

The focal and most cited paper of the map in general and this cluster in particular (Christensen et al., 2005) celebrates the opening of the era of discussion on OI and DT and triggers the rise of interest to the topic, from the industrial dynamics' perspectives. Authors argue that with the maturing of a technology and overall digitalization of goods, services, processes within single industry, strategic choices and modes of OI will be influenced. Thus, at the early ferment phase of a technology development, small companies more probably will need complementary contributions from multiple players of an industry, in order to be commercially viable. As a technology becomes more mature, smaller businesses tend to collaborate with one or two incumbents in order to protect their position on the market. The key assumption of the time is that "by sharing technology, new technology is created" (Lee, 2008). Therefore, technological standardization and standard-based cross-industry alliances have become the crucial feature of technological convergence. This process of convergence sculptures industries and technological boundaries in the mode of collaboration rather than just competition. Overall, boundary spanning ability of new electronic information exchange channels and OI ease a technological standardization and encourage strategic alliances (Malhotra et al., 2007).

After a period of silence on cross-influences of DT and OI, the topic started being the focus of the interest again from the middle of 2010th. Scholars witnessed that with the technological advent, science and innovation become more open and collaborative. In order to facilitate idea creation, innovation sector combines physical and digital from now on. This combinatorial type of innovation puts users at the core, where innovation is no longer a linear process from a producer to a user, but happens on multiple levels due to technological maturing (Obal, & Lancioni, 2013; Bogers et al., 2016). Moreover, technological development directly influences the emergence of completely new markets with new business models characterized by the high level of openness and user engagement (Bogers et al., 2016). As witnessed, innovation process in creative industries firstly responded to the new challenges brought by digital economy by increasing interest towards innovative and strategic models. Following creative industries, businesses that are more traditional, have started transforming value chains toward open ecosystems empowered by digital technologies (Benghozi, & Salvador, 2016).

However, together with the bright opportunity of getting "outsider perspectives", involving users in co-creation process, more efficient R&D, companies should consider also some challenges. Thus, there is a threat to lose internal knowledge (Obal, & Lancioni, 2013), therefore, companies need to rethink intellectual property and privacy setting control (Greenstein et al, 2013). Another challenge is innovation process itself, which can become now uncontrollable and unpredictable with entire industries shifting from physical goods to digital platforms instead, with users engaged into final product creation. Therefore, the need in effective tools to manage this new digital and OI process is salient (Nylén, & Holmström, 2015). Finally, the recent work of Bogers in co-authorship with Chesbrough and Moedas, more than 10 years after Christensen (2005) work on industrial perspectives on innovation, gives fresh view on OI in the digital era emphasizing the importance of combination of three key flows: OI research, practices, and policies (Bogers et al., 2018).

Digital Peer-communities Group

The thematic orientation of this cluster is best described with the label "Digital Peer-communities" as all papers discuss different aspects of the phenomenon of peer-communities in digital space, such as emergence of user-driven innovation, changes and challenges it brought to the existing order of innovation and discussing some peculiarities of digital communities comparing them with real ones. Scholars are interested in exploring these four directions: user-led innovation phenomenon, premises of digital communities' emergence, changes in a firms' organizational structure and management, and human aspects of digital communities.

Traditional approach of innovation being the prerogative of producers only, with the passive or consuming role of users, has been disrupted by DT and OI. From now on, digital peer-communities are favored to design goods and services to meet real needs of the market. Thus, the focal paper of this cluster highlights the importance of user–centric innovation or avatar-based innovation (Kohler et al., 2009) in digital spaces for real-world innovation and successful products design with "real-world potential". This successful "migration" from digital to the real world or from open source software projects to hardware co-design smoothed by user-centric innovation in peer-communities is an opportunity companies should leverage. Companies open their innovation process not only for collaboration, but also for modifications and improvements by peers (Abdelkafi et al., 2009).

Scholars reasonably argue that the phenomenon of online peer-communities has been triggered by rapid technological development. As (Benner, & Tushman, 2015) in their landmark study claim, dramatic decrease of the communication and computational costs triggered by DT pushed the trajectory of innovation beyond boundaries of a firm and caused the emergence of open or peer communities. In particular, not only did technological advances enable new open digital nature of interactions (Kohler et al., 2009), but also an emergence of new types of producer–consumer collaboration in the product development process and profit maximization enabled by opening content to users and outsourcing design to digital networks (Arakji, & Lang, 2007).

DT and openness of boundaries for peer- and user innovation have led to the profound changes in a firms' organizational structure. Thus, due to this transformation of firm and product boundaries towards open ones, a new typology of peers "working consumers" and "consuming producers" is emerging (Bauer, & Gegenhuber, 2015), firm's identity and reducing property rights are reshaping (Parmentier, & Mangematin 2014). Overall, an innovation model in peer-communities has changed from top-down to bottom-up modes of idea creation and communication (Martínez-Torres et al., 2010). In order to advance knowledge acquisition, the reorganization and integration of both external and internal knowledge streams to promote innovation within companies are required (Bohorquez Lopez, & Esteves, 2013). Moreover, Parmentier & Mangematin (2014) argue that companies will have to balance between collaborative creation, production and post-production both internally (inside a firm) and externally (within digital communities). All these lead to the transformation of management approaches.

Orchestrating peer-communities rather than just managing them may cover mentioned above complexities. For example, the structure and dynamics of local digital networks is important aspect of an effective orchestration of peer-communities in digital space (Martínez-Torres et al., 2010). However, many networks perform collaborative innovation across the globe, therefore, understanding phases and types of relationships within communities is a crucial point for moving from creativity and collaboration to commercialization at a global scale (Harryson, 2008). Thus, three types of networks, creativity networks, transformation networks and process networks, are responsible for different tasks and goals, and require different approaches of leadership and master mechanism.

However, notwithstanding strict orchestrating of digital peer-communities, there should be a room for creative discoveries as in co-creative innovation happening in reality. The phenomenon of accidental innovation as the means to get valuable ideas is something that companies need to consider while managing digital peer-communities (Austin et al., 2012). Another "human aspect" of being part of a virtual community is a subjective well-being (SWB) – an important psychological insight of effective co-production and digital fabrication in peer-communities (Pera, & Viglia, 2015).

Digital Ecosystems Group

This cluster organizes knowledge on digital ecosystems, which with the advance of technologies have become very rich in their variety: from knowledge sharing, work execution platforms, crowdsourcing and crowdfunding, virtual worlds, to digital makerspaces or app stores, and social media. As in previous clusters, papers explore various aspects of the topic, however, it is possible to schematically knowledge into four knowledge sub-flows: understanding the nature of digital ecosystems, discussing the new role of developers, network effects, and exploration of crowdsourcing aspect.

The focal publication of this cluster in terms of number of citations highlights the importance of digital platforms in shifting innovation process nature (Yoo et al., 2012) and signalizes about the changing mindset. Thus, firms tend to innovate by developing platforms instead of single products. Moreover, as digital technologies become more ubiquitous, digital ecosystems play even more crucial role in companies, allowing to design, create new goods or services, collaborate among collectives, control various products, sub-systems, manage various heterogeneous actors using one single digital ecosystem and do not use different digital tools (Nambisan et al., 2017; Yoo et al., 2012).

OI and digital technologies have influenced the way end users and developers exchange goods, applications and triggered the emergence of marketplaces or app-stores. Going further, with the time, app-stores have crystallized into specific types of market places (closed, censored, focused, and open). Open models play important role in this typology breakdown influencing focused ecosystems (with generalized scope of a platform) and open (with non-generalized scope) marketplaces to have a distributed control over exchanging apps and digital products among variety of users and developers (Ghazawneh, & Henfridsson 2015). With the clear trend of distributed control, the role of developers becomes more central, companies tolerate external value creation rather than internal one. Moreover, high-risk innovation with more developers is more profitable than low-risk innovation with fewer amount of developers, this fact leads to even more openness of boundaries of digital ecosystems (Parker et al., 2016).

Unlike common understanding of competition and innovation, when too much competition can suppress innovation incentives, innovation in digital ecosystems and app stores, in particular, is based on the attracting large numbers of independent software producers and growing competition to generate a vast number of app software (Boudreau K. J., 2012). This phenomenon has two sides of the network effect. On the one hand, it increases innovation incentives, and leads to a more attractive range of applications, raised consumer demand. On the other hand, larger number of producers leads to lower interest of app developers within the same software field. Moreover, digital ecosystems suffer from the dual nature of co-creation: open and collaborative nature of innovation should be combined with the control of ecosystem boundaries. This tension can be reduced by the effective managing of boundary resources (Eaton et al., 2015). While many product-developing companies start adopting ecosystem-centric modes expecting network effects being a great advantage, in fact, the network effect value works not in every case. Thus, despite the fact that the variety of personal incentives to contribute to a platform on the non-sales base is witnessed, it is also true that zero network effect exists in crowd-platforms with unpaid contributors. The phenomenon can be explained by a positive growth rate of a platform usage and at the same time a negative response to growing numbers of complementors, which neglect each other, eventually (Boudreau, & Jeppesen, 2015).

Digital ecosystems open up new opportunities of leveraging crowd-intelligence and outsource some of the business activities to independent contributors and lead to the emergence of new crowd-based business models (CBBMs) (Täuscher, 2017). However, with all positivism around crowd-based business models, as any traditional business models, CBBM should be questioned on their ability to create and capture value. Overall, collective intelligence has raised a number of issues, such as facilitating collective innovation while preserving the private interests of companies and keep on the level of healthy competition. IP rights, policy regulations and high royalty rate can have a positive effect on preserving the right balance in firms (Lopez-Berzosa, & Gawer, 2014).

Knowledge Management in the Open and Digital Era

This group organizes various points of view on specifics of knowledge management while performing digital shift with OI. The fragmented nature has been reflected on the knowledge map: some papers are placed on the very periphery of the map and have the weakest links with other clusters and papers within their cluster. Although this knowledge group presents mostly findings based on a specific industry case study, it reveals some aspects potentially important for anyone willing to digitally transform a company and move towards open modes of innovation. Thus, discussion on the variety of knowledge flows, the technological aspect of knowledge management, and the emerging topic on challenges of knowledge sharing has been started.

With online communities evolving through time, different actors and participants produce different types of value (financial, epistemic, ethical, service, reputational, platform) (Barrett et al., 2016). Moreover, likewise in real communities, the collective flow within digital networks is divided into various sub-flows among community contributors (Faraj et al., 2016). Overall, ecosystem-centric models in digital spaces can be characterized by the presence of focal (market leaders) and periphery actors. There is an evidence that the behavior of focal and periphery market actors in searching for capabilities and new knowledge sources differ (Selander et al., 2013). Thus, non-focal players can benefit more from operating across different digital ecosystems and relating to external knowledge in order to advance their existing capabilities. The source of knowledge flows in the digital era vary, the new sources of knowledge flows emerge. Data-driven decision-making based on open and big data, AI and ML algorithms is a constant source of innovation and organizational design changes. Not only creates it new type of "algorithmic management", but also ever-increasing knowledge flows for organizations, empowers organizational learning and disrupts the hierarchical structure within organizations (Schildt, 2017). Therefore, a better understanding of the typology and differences of knowledge flows in online communities and ecosystems and encouraging knowledge collaboration will help to sustain the dynamics of digital communities, value co-creation and capturing in platform-based ecosystems.

Another aspect of knowledge management in the open digital era is a technology itself and opportunities it opens for better knowledge use. Thus, in the world of the rapid adoption of online communication, interactions and knowledge sharing, the question of cyber security technology adoption is indisputably important. Modern security-related technologies for, name a few, securing transmissions, verifying identities, enabling the safety of data, asymmetric encryption and digital certificates are more and more demanding by companies with open business models involving peer-to-peer communication and various stakeholders' interactions (Carayannis,, & Turner 2006). Moving further, with emerging technologies expansion, such as 3D printing, open source, open design companies and communities went to another level of knowledge reuse. Could they not only innovate or replicate ideas, but also reuse knowledge for improving customization and be even more consumer-oriented in their innovation (Kyriakou et al., 2017). However, operating openly and online and sharing knowledge does not mean being without geographical limits. Yet, international openness is important aspect in the context of international e-commerce ecosystems. Not only influences it a country e-commerce growth in the business-to-customer sphere, but also it works as an exogenous power that captures knowledge overflows from countries that have a positive impact on the technological advance of another trading countries (Ho et al., 2011).

Finally, with all positivism on DT coupled with an easy or open access to external knowledge sources, companies should bring into proper correlation strategies for sourcing external knowledge and investment in digital technologies to enhance their innovation performance (Trantopoulos et al., 2017).

Open Innovation, Digital Technologies and Businesses Performance Group

The last cluster talks it all about benefits of DT and OI applied together. As long as DT has a different degree of maturity in different industries, scholars are mostly focused on case studies analysis. While, it seems not possible to distinguish any knowledge sub-flows in this cluster, the potential of the collaboration of these two phenomena for improved business and innovation performance is salient. Thus, new technologies and open models enable accessibility, interconnectivity and technological intelligence for the physical world. Openness and digitalization promise to become a single digital experience instead of two different phenomena (Solima et al., 2016). The direct positive relationship can be witnessed between an ability to successfully pass the so-called phase of ferment for new entrants and open and collaborative way of establishing new regulations. Collaborative commitments and a high level of involvement of industry actors such as regulators, interest organizations, firms and other stakeholders can lead to more rapid adaptation of innovation on the industry level (Ernkvist, 2015). Moreover, improved ROI (Return on Investments) evidences that shift from traditional approaches of innovation to collaborative ones drives the innovation and facilitates the innovation search in some industries (Scuotto et al., 2017).

An orientation of intra (R&D) and inter organizational (open) innovation to ICT can have a positive effect on the performance of a company. In particular, SMEs will benefit from the digitalization of data and the knowledge management process significantly (Scuotto et al., 2017). Manufacturing companies, in their turn, could leverage the support of collaborative partnership and platform-enabled networking in their servitization initiatives aimed at building integrated product-service offer, which enables value in use (Pal, 2016). Crowd-based open business models, in particular, reward-based crowdfunding, go far beyond just fundraising campaigns - together with capital values it brings technical and market knowledge (Nucciarelli, 2017). Finally, smart cities are the classic case of a successful collaboration of OI strategies and rapid DT. It has been proved, wise usage of technologies, big data, IoT empowered by collaborative innovation, user-driven ecosystems help to build smart and sustainable urban environment (Scuotto et al., 2016; Angelidou et al., 2018).

DISCUSSION AND CONCLUSION

Current research provides an objective intellectual structure on the crossroad of two research fields, OI and DT. The main premise of this research is to explore digital transformation shaping the nature of innovation as a collaborative activity as part of an independent research area, identify focal knowledge areas and papers, spot the research dynamics and gaps. For this, the authors brought together segmental publications from different research fields, such as technology innovation, service innovation, OI, marketing, information technology management and other research fields, and gathered them in unified knowledge group by implementing bibliographic coupling method. Therefore, on the one hand, the current research complements both OI and DT research fields by cross-exploring each phenomenon through the lens of DTs development or OI boundaries. On the other hand, the paper attempts to break the inertia of discussing OI and technological advances exclusively as part of OI or technology innovation literature by identifying emerging research trends in common and elaborating on the co-evolution phenomenon.

The nature of the research area is predominantly based on case study analysis both of firm and industry level. However, the main focus is on the analysis of creative and technological industries, which reasonably respond to the technological changes first. Thus, e-printing, mobile, smart cities, virtual games, e-commerce fields are at the forefront of the research focus. While qualitative approach predominates, few contributions are mix-methods oriented; several works have quantitative nature, using big data analysis, such as co-patent analysis, or assessing techniques, exemplary, technology adoption rate.

Overall, the articles analyzed can be distinguished into three parts: (1) case study analysis to derive some valuable implications and test hypothesis; (2) conceptual papers aimed at theoretical models and frameworks building or testing (based on case studies, rarely, on existing literature); and (3) essays and reviews aimed at witnessing and describing the aspect of digital and open transformation co-existence from different points of view. Mostly highly cited papers form this third group. Some of these influential papers celebrate the opening of the era of discussion on co-influence of OI and DT (Christensen et al., 2005), highlight the emergence of the new aspects of the open digital era, such as user-centric innovation (Kohler, 2009), or reflex on previous paradigm and innovation trajectory change (Benner, & Tushman, 2015). Other works emphasize the importance of being prepared to innovation in digitalized world by building modern coherent OI practices and policies, moving towards platforms and ecosystems, rethinking crowd-models in the digital era (Bogers et al., 2018; Boudreau, 2012; Yoo, 2012). All these bring to the conclusion, although some efforts have already been done on conceptualizing new phenomena, such as exploring the evolution path and co-existence of OI and DT in depth based on industry-focused case studies, the research area is only emerging.

Moreover, the positioning of articles on the knowledge map suggests the two dimensions: vertical and horizontal. Vertical dimension refers to different sides of the topic analysis: from the technology side to humans' crowdsourcing one. In its turn, horizontal dimension the level of research: from conceptualizing extant knowledge into conceptual frameworks to narrow industry-specific case studies. Our results reveal a polycentric structure of the field with absence of overlaps between articles and highlighted five groups: (1) *Co-evolution of Digital Technologies and Open Innovation Group* represents the core of the intersection between OI and DT fields as it signalized on the opening discussion in scientific; (2) *Digital Peer-communities Group* gathers around contributions on peer-communities in digital space focusing on the user-led innovation phenomenon, premises of digital communities' emergence, changes in a firms' organizational structure and management, and "human" aspects of digital communities; (3) *Digital Ecosystems Group* is the most controversial in terms of research findings as authors question network effects presence in virtual ecosystems, point out at the aspect of positivism while adopting crowdsourcing models, emphasize the new role of developers in market places; (4) *Knowledge Management in the Open and Digital Era Group* discusses various points of view on types of knowledge flows, technological side of knowledge management, and challenges of knowledge sharing; (5) *Open Innovation, Digital Technologies Advances, and Businesses Performance Group* is the youngest one and it gathers around papers discussing the potential of the collaboration of OI and DT for improved business and innovation performance.

Some suggestions for future research can be articulated. The influence and dominance of the OI research domain in this data set are evident. However, some attempts to start developing independent research domains can be observed, and could be supported by the research community in the future. Thus, with all opportunities OI and DT brought to businesses, little has been said yet on challenges of this phenomenon. Papers describing failure case studies or putting attention at challenges will be of interest for policy makers and scientists. While the whole domain is technology-driven mostly, pointing out at the opportunities of technological advances, the field lacks strategy-driven papers. For example, questioning opportunistic behavior of adopting open models and digitally transform a company without a risks and opportunities estimation, or new economics and financial evaluation perspectives on OI and DT could contribute to the emerging topic of improved ROI, innovation performance. New scientific methods could be a potential direction to push forward the development of the research thought and reply to the hegemony of qualitative case studies. Overall, quantitative works are needed in order to provide less subjective and biased results and generalize findings. Finally, not only the research map has gaps within each cluster, but also polarity of research groups, therefore, research papers positioned on the crossroad with other domains are needed to fully describe the potential of the phenomenon.

While bibliographic coupling is an effective method to provide a structured picture of the emerging research domain, it also has some limitations. Firstly, the data set presented here consists of works containing the terms "Open Innovation" and "Digital* in a title, abstract, keywords area, and main text body of the WOS Core Collection database, which makes it possible to miss publications where these terms are not used while still covering the topic. Secondly, some important publications can be influenced by biased citing behavior, such as self-justification or micro-politics. Thirdly, the selection of the final threshold of a minimum four citations for a cited reference, can lead to missing publications, especially those which are younger, and therefore have fewer opportunities to be cited. Finally, publications with longer reference list could been overweight, thus, the more references a publication has the more possibilities of crossovers with other reference lists, and the higher possibility to have network centrality.

REFERENCES

Abdelkafi, N. B., Blecker, T., & Raasch, C. (2009). From open source in the digital to the physical world: A smooth transfer? *Management Decision*, *47*(10), 1610–1632. doi:10.1108/00251740911004718

Afonso, O., Monteiro, S., & Thompson, M. (2012). A growth model for the quadruple helix. *Journal of Business Economics and Management*, *13*(5), 849–865. doi:10.3846/16111699.2011.626438

Angelidou, M. P., Psaltoglou, A., Komninos, N., Kakderi, C., Tsarchopoulos, P., & Panori, A. (2018). Enhancing sustainable urban development through smart city applications. *Journal of Science and Technology Policy Management*, *9*(2), 146–169. doi:10.1108/JSTPM-05-2017-0016

Arakji, R. Y., & Lang, K. R. (2007). Digital consumer networks and producer-consumer collaboration: Innovation and product development in the video game industry. *Journal of Management Information Systems, 24*(2), 195–219. doi:10.2753/MIS0742-1222240208

Austin, R. D., Devin, L., & Sullivan, E. E. (2012). Accidental innovation: Supporting valuable unpredictability in the creative process. *Organization Science, 23*(5), 1505–1522. doi:10.1287/orsc.1110.0681

Baldwin, C. V., & von Hippel, E. (2011). Modeling a paradigm shift: From producer innovation to user and open collaborative innovation. *Organization Science, 22*(6), 1399–1417. doi:10.1287/orsc.1100.0618

Barrett, M., Oborn, E., & Orlikowski, W. (2016). Creating value in online communities: The sociomaterial configuring of strategy, platform, and stakeholder engagement. *Information Systems Research, 27*(4), 704–723. doi:10.1287/isre.2016.0648

Barrett, M., Oborn, E., Orlikowski, W., & Yates, J. (2012). Reconfiguring boundary relations: Robotic innovations in pharmacy work. *Organization Science, 23*(5), 1448–1466. doi:10.1287/orsc.1100.0639

Bauer, R. M., & Gegenhuber, T. (2015). Crowdsourcing: Global search and the twisted roles of consumers and producers. *Organization, 22*(5), 661–681. doi:10.1177/1350508415585030 PMID:27524930

Benghozi, P. J., & Salvador, E. (2016). How and where the R&D takes place in creative industries? Digital investment strategies of the book publishing sector. *Technology Analysis and Strategic Management, 28*(5), 568–582. doi:10.1080/09537325.2015.1122184

Benner, M. J., & Tushman, M. L. (2015). Reflections on the 2013 Decade Award—"Exploitation, exploration, and process management: The productivity dilemma revisited" ten years later. *Academy of Management Review, 40*(4), 497–514. doi:10.5465/amr.2015.0042

Bogers, M., Chesbrough, H., & Moedas, C. (2018). Open innovation: Research, practices, and policies. *California Management Review, 60*(22), 5–16. doi:10.1177/0008125617745086

Bogers, M., Hadar, R., & Bilberg, A. (2016). Additive manufacturing for consumer-centric business models: Implications for supply chains in consumer goods manufacturing. *Technological Forecasting and Social Change, 102*, 225–239. doi:10.1016/j.techfore.2015.07.024

Bogers, M., Zobel, K., Afuah, A., Almirall, E., Brunswicker, S., Dahlander, L., ... Ter Wal, A. L. J. (2017). The open innovation research landscape: Established perspectives and emerging themes across different levels of analysis. *Industry and Innovation, 24*(1), 8–40. doi:10.1080/13662716.2016.1240068

Bogers, M. C., Chesbrough, H., & Moedas, C. (2018). Open innovation: Research, practices, and policies. *California Management Review, 60*(2), 5–16. doi:10.1177/0008125617745086

Bohnsack, R. H. (2018). Same, same, but different!? A systematic review of the literature on digital transformation. Academy of Management Proceedings, 2018(1), 16262.

Boudreau, K. J. (2012). Let a thousand flowers bloom? An early look at large number of software app developers and patterns of innovation. *Organization Science, 23*(5), 1409–1427. doi:10.1287/orsc.1110.0678

Boudreau, K. J., & Jeppesen, L. B. (2015). Unpaid crowd complementors: The platform network effect mirage. *Strategic Management Journal, 36*(12), 1761–1777. doi:10.1002mj.2324

Boyack, K. W., & Klavans, R. (2010). Co-citation analysis, bibliographic coupling, and direct citation: Which citation approach represents the research front most accurately? *Journal of the American Society for Information Science and Technology*, *61*(12), 2389–2404. doi:10.1002/asi.21419

Broadus, R. (1987). Toward a definition of "bibliometrics". *Scientometrics*, *12*(5-6), 373–379. doi:10.1007/BF02016680

Carayannis, E. G., & Turner, E. (2006). Innovation diffusion and technology acceptance: The case of PKI technology. *Technovation*, *26*(7), 847–855. doi:10.1016/j.technovation.2005.06.013

Cassiman, B., Di Guardo, M. C., & Valentini, G. (2009). Organising R&D projects to profit from innovation: Insights from co-opetition. *Long Range Planning*, *42*(2), 216–233. doi:10.1016/j.lrp.2009.01.001

Cassiman, B., Di Guardo, M. C., & Valentini, G. (2010). Organizing links with science: Cooperate or contract?: A project-level analysis. *Research Policy*, *39*(7), 882–892. doi:10.1016/j.respol.2010.04.009

Cassiman, B., & Valentini, G. (2016). Open innovation: Are inbound and outbound knowledge flows really complementary? *Strategic Management Journal*, *37*(6), 1034–1046. doi:10.1002mj.2375

Castriotta, M., & Di Guardo, M. C. (2011). Open innovation and crowdsourcing: the case of mulino bianco. Information Technology and Innovation Trends in Organizations (pp. 407–414). Heidelberg, Germany: Physica-Verlag HD. doi:10.1007/978-3-7908-2632-6_46

Castriotta, M., & Di Guardo, M. C. (2016). Disentangling the automotive technology structure: A patent co-citation analysis. *Scientometrics*, *107*(2), 819–837. doi:10.100711192-016-1862-0

Castriotta, M., Loi, M., Marku, E., & Naitana, L. (2019). What's in a name? Exploring the conceptual structure of emerging organizations. *Scientometrics*, *118*(2), 407–437. doi:10.100711192-018-2977-2

Chesbrough, H., & Bogers, M. (2014). *Explicating Open Innovation: Clarifying an Emerging Paradigm for Understanding Innovation* (Vol. 3). Oxford, UK: Oxford University Press. doi:10.1093/acprof:oso/9780199682461.003.0001

Chesbrough, H. W. (2006). Open innovation: The new imperative for creating and profiting from technology. Brighton, MA: Harvard Business Press.

Christensen, J. F., Olesen, M. H., & Kjær, J. S. (2005). The industrial dynamics of Open Innovation: Evidence from the transformation of consumer electronics. *Research Policy*, *34*(10), 1533–1549. doi:10.1016/j.respol.2005.07.002

Curley, M. S. B. (2013). Open Innovation 2.0: A New Milieu. OISPG Open Innovation 2.0 Year Book 2014, European Commission, 1-14.

Dahlander, L. G., & Gann, D. M. (2010). How open is innovation? *Research Policy*, *39*(6), 699–709. doi:10.1016/j.respol.2010.01.013

Di Guardo, M. C., & Harrigan, K. R. (2012). Mapping research on strategic alliances and innovation: A co-citation analysis. *The Journal of Technology Transfer*, *37*(6), 789–811. doi:10.100710961-011-9239-2

Eaton, B., Elaluf-Calderwood, S., Sorensen, C., & Yoo, Y. (2015). Distributed tuning of boundary resources: The case of Apple's iOS service system. *MIS Quarterly: Management Information Systems, 39*(1), 217–243. doi:10.25300/MISQ/2015/39.1.10

Elmquist, M., Fredberg, T., & Ollila, S. (2009). Exploring the field of open innovation. *European Journal of Innovation Management, 12*(3), 326–345. doi:10.1108/14601060910974219

Ernkvist, M. (2015). The double knot of technology and business-model innovation in the era of ferment of digital exchanges: The case of OM, a pioneer in electronic options exchanges. *Technological Forecasting and Social Change, 99*, 285–299. doi:10.1016/j.techfore.2015.02.001

Faraj, S., von Krogh, G., Monteiro, E., & Lakhani, K. R. (2016). Special section introduction—Online community as space for knowledge flows. *Information Systems Research, 27*(4), 668–684. doi:10.1287/isre.2016.0682

Ferreira, F. A. (2018). Mapping the field of arts-based management: Bibliographic coupling and co-citation analyses. *Journal of Business Research, 85*, 348–357. doi:10.1016/j.jbusres.2017.03.026

Fitzgerald, M., Kruschwitz, N., Bonnet, D., & Welch, M. (2014). Embracing digital technology: A new strategic imperative. *MIT Sloan Management Review*, 1–12.

Gassmann, O. (2006). Opening up the innovation process: Towards an agenda. *R & D Management, 36*(3), 223–228. doi:10.1111/j.1467-9310.2006.00437.x

Gassmann, O. E. (2010). The future of open innovation. *Research Management, 40*(3), 213–221.

Gawer, A., & Cusumano, M. A. (2014). Industry Platforms and Ecosystem Innovation. *Journal of Product Innovation Management, 31*(3), 417–433. doi:10.1111/jpim.12105

Ghazawneh, A. H., & Henfridsson, O. (2015). A paradigmatic analysis of digital application marketplaces. *Journal of Information Technology, 30*(3), 198–208. doi:10.1057/jit.2015.16

Gobble, M. M. (2018). Digitalization, Digitization, and Innovation. Research-Technology Management. *Research Technology Management, 61*(4), 56–59. doi:10.1080/08956308.2018.1471280

Greenstein, S. L., Lerner, J., & Stern, S. (2013). Digitization, innovation, and copyright: What is the agenda? *Strategic Organization, 11*(1), 110–121. doi:10.1177/1476127012460940

Harryson, S. J. (2008). Entrepreneurship through relationships–navigating from creativity to commercialisation. *R & D Management, 38*(3), 290–310. doi:10.1111/j.1467-9310.2008.00516.x

Ho, S. C., Kauffman, R. J., & Liang, T.-P. (2011). Internet-based selling technology and e-commerce growth: A hybrid growth theory approach with cross-model inference. *Information Technology Management, 12*(4), 409–429. doi:10.100710799-010-0078-x

Kessler, M. M. (1963). Bibliographic coupling between scientific papers. *American Documentation, 14*(1), 10–25. doi:10.1002/asi.5090140103

Kohler, T. M., Matzler, K., & Füller, J. (2009). Avatar-based innovation: Using virtual worlds for real-world innovation. *Technovation, 29*(6-7), 395–407. doi:10.1016/j.technovation.2008.11.004

Kovacs, A., Van Looy, B., & Cassiman, B. (2015). Exploring the scope of open innovation: A bibliometric review of a decade of research. *Scientometrics, 104*(3), 951–983. doi:10.100711192-015-1628-0

Kyriakou, H. N., Nickerson, J. V., & Sabnis, G. (2017). Knowledge reuse for customization: Metamodels in an open design community for 3D printing. 2017. *MIS Quarterly, 41*(1), 315–332. doi:10.25300/MISQ/2017/41.1.17

Laengle, S. M., Merigó, J. M., Miranda, J., Słowiński, R., Bomze, I., Borgonovo, E., ... Teunter, R. (2017). Forty years of the European Journal of Operational Research: A bibliometric overview. *European Journal of Operational Research, 262*(3), 803–816. doi:10.1016/j.ejor.2017.04.027

Lee, Y. G., Lee, J.-H., Song, Y.-I., & Kim, H.-J. (2008). Technological convergence and open innovation in the mobile telecommunication industry. *Asian Journal of Technology Innovation, 16*(1), 45–62. doi:10.1080/19761597.2008.9668646

Leydesdorff, L., & Park, H. W. (2017). Full and fractional counting in bibliometric networks. *Journal of Informetrics, 11*(1), 117–120. doi:10.1016/j.joi.2016.11.007

Lichtenthaler, U. (2011). Open innovation: Past research, current debates, and future directions. *The Academy of Management Perspectives, 25*(1), 75–93.

Lichtenthaler, U. (2017). Shared value innovation: Linking competitiveness and societal goals in the context of digital transformation. *International Journal of Innovation and Technology Management, 14*(4), 1–14. doi:10.1142/S0219877017500183

Liu, X. Y. (2010). Weighted hybrid clustering by combining text mining and bibliometrics on a large-scale journal database. *Journal of the American Society for Information Science and Technology, 61*(6), 1105–1119.

Loi, M., Castriotta, M., & Di Guardo, M. C. (2016). The theoretical foundations of entrepreneurship education: How co-citations are shaping the field. *International Small Business Journal, 34*(7), 948–971. doi:10.1177/0266242615602322

Lopez-Berzosa, D. G., & Gawer, A. (2014). Innovation policy within private collectives: Evidence on 3GPP' s regulation mechanisms to facilitate collective innovation. *Technovation, 34*(12), 734–745. doi:10.1016/j.technovation.2014.07.005

Malhotra, A. G., Gosain, S., & El Sawy, O. A. (2007). Leveraging standard electronic business interfaces to enable adaptive supply chain partnerships. *Information Systems Research, 18*(3), 260–279. doi:10.1287/isre.1070.0132

Marku, E., Castriotta, M., & Di Guardo, M. C. (2017). Disentangling the intellectual structure of innovation and M&A literature. *Technological Innovation Networks: Collaboration and Partnership, 47.*

Martínez-López, F. J.-F., Merigó, J. M., Valenzuela-Fernández, L., & Nicolás, C. (2018). Fifty years of the European Journal of Marketing: A bibliometric analysis. *European Journal of Marketing, 52*(1/2), 439–468. doi:10.1108/EJM-11-2017-0853

Martínez-Torres, M. R. (n.d.). The role of Internet in the development of future software projects. *Internet Research, 20*(1), 72-86.

Nambisan, S., Lyytinen, K., Majchrzak, A., & Song, M. (2017). Digital Innovation Management: Reinventing innovation management research in a digital world. *Management Information Systems Quarterly*, *41*(1), 223–238. doi:10.25300/MISQ/2017/41:1.03

Nambisan, S. S., Siegel, D., & Kenney, M. (2018). On open innovation, platforms, and entrepreneurship. *Strategic Entrepreneurship Journal*, *12*(3), 354–368. doi:10.1002ej.1300

Newman, M. E., & Girvan, M. (2004). Finding and evaluating community structure in networks. *Physical Review E, 69*(2), 026113 - 026113/15.

Nieto, M. J., & Santamaría, L. (2007). The importance of diverse collaborative networks for the novelty of product innovation. *Technovation*, *27*(6-7), 367–377. doi:10.1016/j.technovation.2006.10.001

Nosella, A. C., Cantarello, S., & Filippini, R. (2012). The intellectual structure of organizational ambidexterity: A bibliographic investigation into the state of the art. *Strategic Organization*, *10*(4), 450–465. doi:10.1177/1476127012457979

Nucciarelli, A. L., Li, F., Fernandes, K. J., Goumagias, N., Cabras, I., Devlin, S., ... Cowling, P. (2017). From value chains to technological platforms: The effects of crowdfunding in the digital game industry. *Journal of Business Research*, *78*, 341–352. doi:10.1016/j.jbusres.2016.12.030

Nylén, D. H., & Holmström, J. (2015). Digital innovation strategy: A framework for diagnosing and improving digital product and service innovation. *Business Horizons*, *58*(1), 57–67. doi:10.1016/j.bushor.2014.09.001

Obal, M. L., & Lancioni, R. A. (2013). Maximizing buyer–supplier relationships in the Digital Era: Concept and research agenda. *Industrial Marketing Management*, *42*(6), 851–854. doi:10.1016/j.indmarman.2013.06.002

Pal, R. (2016). Extended responsibility through servitization in PSS: An exploratory study of used-clothing sector. *Journal of Fashion Marketing and Management: An International Journal*, *20*(4), 453–470. doi:10.1108/JFMM-12-2015-0100

Pallot, M. (2015). Open Innovation 2.0: Living Labs . Open Innovation Ecosystems: A Study on Matchmaking between Living Labs and other Organisations within Horizon 2020 Calls. *Open Innovation YearBook 2015 European Commission.*

Parker, G. V., Van Alstyne, M., & Jiang, X. (2016). Platform ecosystems: How developers invert the firm. 2017. *Management Information Systems Quarterly*, *41*(1), 255–266. doi:10.25300/MISQ/2017/41.1.13

Parmentier, G. M., & Mangematin, V. (2014). Orchestrating innovation with user communities in the creative industries. *Technological Forecasting and Social Change*, *83*, 40–53. doi:10.1016/j.techfore.2013.03.007

Parviainen, P., Tihinen, M., Kääriäinen, J., & Teppola, S. (2017). Tackling the digitalization challenge: How to benefit from digitalization in practice. *International Journal of Information Systems and Project Management*, *5*(1), 63–77.

Pera, R. V., & Viglia, G. (2015). Turning ideas into products: Subjective well-being in co-creation. *Service Industries Journal*, *35*(7-8), 388–402. doi:10.1080/02642069.2015.1015521

Pritchard, A. (1969). Statistical bibliography or bibliometrics. *The Journal of Documentation*, *25*(4), 348–349.

Rayna, T., & Striukova, L. (2015). Open innovation 2.0: Is co-creation the ultimate challenge? *International Journal of Technology Management*, *69*(1), 38–53. doi:10.1504/IJTM.2015.071030

Rogers, E. M. (1962). *Diffusion of Innovation*. New York, NY: Free Press of Glencoe.

Schildt, H. (2017). Big data and organizational design–the brave new world of algorithmic management and computer augmented transparency. *Innovation-Management Policy & Practice*, *19*(1), 23–30. doi:10.1080/14479338.2016.1252043

Scuotto, V., Del Giudice, M., della Peruta, M. R., & Tarba, S. (2017). The performance implications of leveraging internal innovation through social media networks: An empirical verification of the smart fashion industry. *Technological Forecasting and Social Change*, *120*, 184–194. doi:10.1016/j.techfore.2017.03.021

Scuotto, V., Ferraris, A., & Bresciani, S. (2016). Internet of Things: Applications and challenges in smart cities: a case study of IBM smart city projects. *Business Process Management Journal*, *22*(2), 357–367. doi:10.1108/BPMJ-05-2015-0074

Scuotto, V., Santoro, G., Bresciani, S., & Del Giudice, M. (2017). Shifting intra-and inter-organizational innovation processes towards digital business: An empirical analysis of SMEs. *Creativity and Innovation Management*, *26*(3), 247–255. doi:10.1111/caim.12221

Selander, L. H., Henfridsson, O., & Svahn, F. (2013). Capability search and redeem across digital ecosystems. *Journal of Information Technology*, *28*(3), 183–197. doi:10.1057/jit.2013.14

Simeoni, F., & Cassia, F. (2019). From vehicle suppliers to value co-creators: The evolving role of Italian motorhome manufacturers. *Current Issues in Tourism*, *22*(2), 218–236. doi:10.1080/13683500.2017.1293619

Skarzauskiene, A., & Zaitsava, M. (2016). Exploring the Potential of Open Innovation 2.0 and Web 3.0 for SMEs. *3rd European Conference on Social M di R h Media Research EM Normandie*, (p. 369). Caen, France.

Solima, L. D., Della Peruta, M. R., & Maggioni, V. (2016). Managing adaptive orientation systems for museum visitors from an IoT perspective. *Business Process Management Journal*, *22*(2), 285–304. doi:10.1108/BPMJ-08-2015-0115

Suseno, Y., Laurell, C., & Sick, N. (2018). Assessing value creation in digital innovation ecosystems: A Social Media Analytics approach. *The Journal of Strategic Information Systems*, *27*(4), 335–349. doi:10.1016/j.jsis.2018.09.004

Täuscher, K. (2017). Leveraging collective intelligence: How to design and manage crowd-based business models. *Business Horizons*, *60*(2), 237–245. doi:10.1016/j.bushor.2016.11.008

Tilson, D., Lyytinen, K., & Sørensen, C. (2010). Research commentary—Digital infrastructures: The missing IS research agenda. *Information Systems Research*, *21*(4), 748–759. doi:10.1287/isre.1100.0318

Trantopoulos, K., von Krogh, G., Wallin, M. W., & Woerter, M. (2017). External knowledge and information technology: Implications for process innovation performance. *Management Information Systems Quarterly*, *41*(1), 287–300. doi:10.25300/MISQ/2017/41.1.15

Van Eck, N., & Waltman, L. (2009). Software survey: VOSviewer, a computer program for bibliometric mapping. *Scientometrics*, *84*(2), 523–538. doi:10.100711192-009-0146-3 PMID:20585380

Van Eck, N. J., & Waltman, L. (2007). *Advances in data analysis. VOS: A new method for visualizing similarities between objects* (pp. 299–306). Berlin, Germany: Springer. doi:10.1007/978-3-540-70981-7_34

Van Eck, N. J., & Waltman, L. (2017). Citation-based clustering of publications using CitNetExplorer and VOSviewer. *Scientometrics*, *111*(2), 1053–1070. doi:10.100711192-017-2300-7 PMID:28490825

Van Eck, N. J., Waltman, L., Dekker, R., & van den Berg, J. (2010). A comparison of two techniques for bibliometric mapping: Multidimensional scaling and VOS. *Journal of the American Society for Information Science and Technology*, *61*(12), 2405–2416. doi:10.1002/asi.21421

van Oorschot, J. A., Hofman, E., & Halman, J. I. (2018). A bibliometric review of the innovation adoption literature. *Technological Forecasting and Social Change*, *134*, 1–21. doi:10.1016/j.techfore.2018.04.032

Vogel, R., & Güttel, W. H. (2013). The dynamic capability view in strategic management: A bibliometric review. *International Journal of Management Reviews*, *15*(4), 426–446.

von Hippel, E. (2005). *Democratizing Innovation*. Cambridge, MA: MIT Press. doi:10.7551/mitpress/2333.001.0001

West, J. B., & Bogers, M. (2014). Leveraging external sources of innovation: A review of research on open innovation. *Journal of Product Innovation Management*, *31*(4), 814–831. doi:10.1111/jpim.12125

Wilfredo Bohorquez Lopez, V., & Esteves, J. (2013). Acquiring external knowledge to avoid wheel reinvention. *Journal of Knowledge Management, 17*(1), 87-105.

Yoo, Y. B., Boland, R. J. Jr, Lyytinen, K., & Majchrzak, A. (2012). Organizing for innovation in the digitized world. *Organization Science*, *23*(5), 1398–1408. doi:10.1287/orsc.1120.0771

Zupic, I., & Čater, T. (2015). Bibliometric methods in management and organization. *Organizational Research Methods*, *18*(3), 429–472. doi:10.1177/1094428114562629

ADDITIONAL READING

Benner, M. J., & Tushman, M. L. (2015). Reflections on the 2013 Decade Award—"Exploitation, exploration, and process management: The productivity dilemma revisited" ten years later. *Academy of Management Review*, *40*(4), 497–514. doi:10.5465/amr.2015.0042

Bogers, M., Chesbrough, H., & Moedas, C. (2018). Open innovation: Research, practices, and policies. *California Management Review*, *60*(22), 5–16. doi:10.1177/0008125617745086

Christensen, J. F., Olesen, M. H., & Kjær, J. S. (2005). The industrial dynamics of Open Innovation: Evidence from the transformation of consumer electronics. *Research Policy*, *34*(10), 1533–1549. doi:10.1016/j.respol.2005.07.002

Curley, M. S. B. (2013). Open Innovation 2.0: A New Milieu. OISPG Open Innovation 2.0 Year Book 2014, European Commission, 1-14.

Eaton, B. E.-C., Elaluf-Calderwood, S., Sørensen, C., & Yoo, Y. (2015). Distributed tuning of boundary resources: The case of Apple's iOS service system. *MIS Quarterly: Management Information Systems*, *39*(1), 217–243. doi:10.25300/MISQ/2015/39.1.10

Ernkvist, M. (2015). The double knot of technology and business-model innovation in the era of ferment of digital exchanges: The case of OM, a pioneer in electronic options exchanges. *Technological Forecasting and Social Change*, *99*, 285–299. doi:10.1016/j.techfore.2015.02.001

Ernkvist, M. (2015). The double knot of technology and business-model innovation in the era of ferment of digital exchanges: The case of OM, a pioneer in electronic options exchanges. *Technological Forecasting and Social Change*, *99*, 285–299. doi:10.1016/j.techfore.2015.02.001

KEY TERMS AND DEFINITIONS

Bibliographic Coupling: Bibliographic method that uses citation analysis to establish meaningful relationships between documents.

Digital Ecosystems: Distributed and open socio-technical networks with various stakeholders and entities. Usually are built for tasks connected with competition and collaboration.

Digital Peer-communities: Self-organizing communities made of individuals, exist in digital space, and create a shared outcome, such as goods, services, knowledge.

Digital Transformation: A transformation of a business or an industry by the use of digital technologies to enable major business improvements, such as developing new business models, providing advanced customer experience, optimizing processes, creating and getting value in new ways, creating new digital revenue streams.

Open Innovation: Type of innovation when valuable ideas can come from inside or outside the company and can go to market from inside or outside the company as well.

Chapter 8
Methodology of Monitoring the Financial Situation of Enterprise

Ionica Oncioiu
European Academy of the Regions, Belgium

Nelu Mocanu
Tomis University, Romania

Ioana Ponagoreț
Valahia University, Romania

ABSTRACT

A complex evaluation of the activity of the enterprise is based on research of the results at the actual moment; this is why many managers use accountancy appreciation records such as: profit from invested capital or income at an asset. The indicators of income and profit are not objectives and depend on the method chosen by the record. Besides, the accountancy methods used today for analysis are short-time, being oriented towards the research, in a long period of the added value of the company. The objective of this chapter consists in developing the theoretical-methodological and substantiation mechanisms of perfecting the management enterprises. The results show that the methodological indications suggested may be used at the organization of the monitoring system in a stable-functioning enterprise, at the activities of re-establishment of the payment capacity of the debtor enterprises, and at the procedures of external management.

INTRODUCTION

The dynamic economic systems of different enterprises intensively compete among them (Parveen, & Noor Ismawati, 2015). Today all the events are so focused and the processes are so interdependent that the slightest delay in this competition would mean defeat, moreover in the loss will not only the economy in the abstract meaning of the word, but also the standard of living of each human being (Bloodgood, & Morrow, 2000). That is why all the countries, regardless the level of developing must look at each other

DOI: 10.4018/978-1-7998-1005-6.ch008

permanently and to take over the best accomplishments of competitors, as well as the way of developing of questions regarding the insolvability (Brown, & Harvey, 2006).

The implementation of market economy in Romania could not help generating a series of new problems, one of the most important being the problem of insolvability (Bolman, & Deal, 1999). Many enterprises could not adapt to the new economic conditions, which were in favor for the general political instability, the inconsistency of the implementation of the market reform, unfavorable investment climate, inefficient fiscal policy and other macro-economic factors (Pfeffer, 2012).

The analysis of the activity of enterprise where the arbitrary management is implemented shows that only a single type of insolvability may be present, which is due to many causes (Pettigrew, Woodman & Cameron, 2001). Some real measures of drawing the enterprises out of insolvability are different based on the initial causes and the conditions of insolvability (Kets de Vries, & Miller, 1984; Munro, 2014). It is important to be taken into account the previous situation. Insolvability develops step by step (Frahm, & Brown, 2007). If today the enterprise could not pay its liabilities it is possible to be happening due to external macro-economic reasons but other causes may exist as the wrong choice of the type of activity, errors in the evaluation of the volume of the market, irrational organization of management, investment policy.

The strict delimitation of the internal and external causes is almost impossible, the emphasis and analysis of previous errors contributing to the financial stability in the presence of unfavorable external factors (Levy, & Merry, 1986).

Insolvability appears under the form of misunderstanding of cash flows, when in the presence of entries cash flows of financial resources, the enterprise is insolvable and passes from the stage of falling in the curve of cycle of life to the disappearance (Pfeffer, 2012). The fact that shows that the enterprise passes to the stage of disappearance is the stagnation of production in the enterprise and the cause of stagnation is the non-payment (Peters, 1998). Thus, it appears the necessity of starting the procedure of bankruptcy.

Bankruptcy is an economic problem that is solved at certain legal levels (Day, 1999; Wong, 2013). The most important in the contemporary regulation of the process of bankruptcy is the emphasis of the balance between the creditors' interests and the tendency to keep the business (Witherspoon, & Wohlert, 1996).

In this chapter it is presented the he theoretical-methodological and the substantiation mechanisms for perfecting the management enterprises. The novelty, originality and the main scientific results are determined by the purpose and the task of the research, by the problems that are formulated and the solving methods, by the results obtained further to the complex analysis of organization and applying the technologies of management within the autonomous stage directions, by the conclusions and results of the research made.

BACKGROUND

One of the major tasks of insolvability management in the industrial enterprises is the maintenance of balance for satisfying the investors' interests (shareholders) and workers (personnel). The decisive condition of the improving of insolvability situation is the finding of reasons and resources for the consolidation of the common actions of opponent subjects of the enterprise.

For determining the signals of appearance of the phenomenon of insolvency situation in the enterprise it is necessary the monitoring of its finances, which means a permanent surveillance of business and financial indicators and not just the work with accountancy reports. The analysis of these indicators allows the quantitative appreciation of the probability of payment incapacity, as basic factor of the insolvability of the enterprise.

The purpose of the suggested methodology- offering an algorithm of monitoring with the use of calculation methods and normative values of the indexes. The methodology given is projected for the enterprises in any domain of activity, with different forms of property and different territories of location. These methodological indications suggested may be used at the organization of the monitoring system in an enterprise that has a stable functioning, at the activities of re-establishment of the payment capacity of the debtor enterprises, at the procedures of external management. All the analyzed indicators are divided in four groups depending on the importance in the management, which allows the succession of making the calculations.

As for the choice of main strategy of insolvability management in the industrial enterprise, the most advantageous is „the differentiate strategy" (Buchanan, & Boddy, 1992). The enterprise in insolvability has a lot of funds in excess, as well as free collaborators, which does not allow that in short term to reach the minim level at the basic production and to become leader in low costs. In the same time the existence of the potential surplus can allow the fast taking of measures regarding the modification of operating quality (consumption) of products, in correspondence with the preferences of different groups of consumers, increasing the sales and the profit, implicitly. The combining of the strategies mentioned above (leader in low and differentiate costs), in the insolvability management not only will double the effect but also lead to the reduction of the increase. That is why it is preferable to be chosen a single strategy, in our case – „ the differentiate strategy" (Antoni, 2004).

In essence the strategy represents a multidimensional category that describes the functioning technology of the organization for obtaining and achieving some purposes (Latham, & Pinder, 2005).

Usually there are focused the following four groups of rules that shape the strategy of the organization: group 1: rules of evaluation of the results of activity (they determine the direction of orientation and form the plan); group 2: rules referring to the relations with the external environment (they shape the market strategy: what, whom and how much must be delivered); group 3: rules referring to the relations and procedures within the organization (organizational conception); group 4: rules of daily activity (operative procedures).

The indicators of the business activity are calculated based on the sizes that make the flows. The indicators, determined from the sizes – flow, may deviate in some limits, and their establishing may be calculated by the average sizes or the appreciation of the variations from average or wanted values. If by analysis it is observed a process of deviation with amplitude in growth, this proves instability of the business activities. At their turn, the indicators are calculated based on sizes – flow, being the indicators of liquidity and profitability.

Based on the analysis of the index of profitability conclusions may be drawn about capacity or incapacity of the enterprise to function in the given direction. The indicators of liquidity are very important as they signal in a bigger extent the possibility of a bankruptcy of the enterprise in future.

The indicators stated must be analyzed in interdependence and on stages:

- **Stage 1:** The index of liquidity is analyzed.
- **Stage 2:** It is analyzed the working capital and the index of maneuverability.
- **Stage 3:** It is analyzed the „quality" of assets.
- **Stage 4:** The liquidity at the mobilization of resources is analyzed.

Along each stage may be focused disturbances of stability. For instance, the working capital and the index of liquidity may be analyzed. If the index of working capital tends to be zero or becomes negative this means that the current assets are not enough for covering the short-term debts and the index of liquidity related to the working capital, if its value tends also towards zero, it reflects the damages in production.

The analysis of the "quality" of assets is reduced at the analysis of two indicators:

- The share of assets which are difficult to make in the total of current assets.
- The relation between the assets that are difficult to be made and assets that are easily made.

The increase of the share of the assets that are difficult to be made is a signal of some deficiencies in production. The decrease of the liquidities of the enterprise may cause mistrust from the creditors of the enterprise and, as a consequence the creditors may reduce the terms of the credits, which influences unfavorably the payment capacity of the enterprise. The excessive production reserves increase the cost of production and decrease the profit.

The analysis of indicators of financial situation of the enterprise is more difficult than the analysis of liquidity. The indicators of the financial situation are less limited by some steps. Taking into account that they are calculated based on the sizes of the flow, a certain average size may be determined and the percentage of variation around it. If the values of the indicators of financial situation vary in the limits of some deviance, then a stability of the financial situation of the enterprise is noticed. If the values of the indicators deviate in time around the curve with positive bending, then it is noticed an increase and consequently the good perspectives of the enterprise. If the values of the indicators deviate in time around the curve with negative bending, then it is noticed a period of decline. Such an analysis must be made with the index of financial stability, financial independence. A particularity of the insolvability strategy is the closed characteristic of the application period and its content. The strategy is considered to be accomplished once with the passing of the organization to the balanced functioning and stable work condition. The purposes of the organization represent an assembly of desired results of its functioning, which are reflected in figures, graphics and other ways of picturing its dynamic and statics condition.

THE METHODOLOGY OF MONITORING THE FINANCIAL SITUATION OF ENTERPRISE

Each organization has an assembly of purposes which reflect the goals of society (macro-environment), of the business environment, of shareholders (including of investors), as well as of the hired personnel (Frahm, & Brown, 2007).

As for the top management, although it takes part from the hired personnel, its goals are specific (Pfeffer, 2012). They represent a balance; on the one hand the founder's interest and on the other hand the hired personnel, as both groups can determine the fate of the general director, top manager that in some situations of insolvability the enterprise is very unstable.

In this condition the attention of the strategic management should be focused to the second group of purposes – operating, as their achieving may draw the organization out of the vulnerable situation.

The insolvency strategies of autonomous stage directions are essentially different from the common ones (Rojon, McDowall, & Saunders, 2015). This is due to their high dynamic, the intense drawing of resources and obtaining both positive and negative results.

One of the permanent insolvency strategies is the evaluation and forecast of the possibility of the enterprise to reach in insolvency condition (Wong, 2013). If the enterprise function in a sedate way this task has a forecast-analytical character, and in insolvency stage the character of the strategy is on short term.

Usually the insolvency is produced both from internal and external causes (Sementelli, 2016). Though, in order to track down in due time the insolvency, firstly it must be evaluated the external environment and must be made the analysis of its probable condition on short and long term.

The metamorphoses of the external environment considerably influence the reproduction dynamic of industrial enterprises, as they are dependent on the request of their products and the financial policy at macro-level.

The particularity of the competitive environment at macro-level consists in the fact that it may initiate insolvency processes in all the stages of the cycle of life of industrial enterprises; this can happen both with the whole company and with some of its products.

The periodic insolvency conditions with a short duration represent a permanent phenomenon in the functioning of the enterprise, especially in the conditions of instability of the external environment (Latham, & Pinder, 2005). This fact allows the forecast in time of the insolvency in its incipient stages as well as the drawing of a set of measures regarding the reduction of damages and drawing enterprise out of insolvency.

The particularity of the competitive environment at macro-level consist in the fact that it can initiate insolvency processes in all the stages of the cycle of life of enterprises happening both with the entire company and with some of its products. If the indicators of the entrepreneurial activity of the external environment deviate slowly, a profound insolvency in the industrial enterprise appears gradually. This does not allow the forecast in due time of the insolvency in the incipient stages or the drawing of a set of measures regarding the reducing of damages and drawing the enterprise out of insolvency.

In the insolvency management, the strategic component plays a special role (Piderit, 2000). Its essence consists in the systematic drawing of the rules, scheduled decisions, „formulas of actions", for the internal management in different situations of the changeable environment (Weiss, 2001). It is determined by the fact that in industrial enterprises with a complicated internal structure the superior managers do not succeed to control the modifications of the situations in all the subdivisions of the enterprise and to draw operatively proper solutions. This is more actual in the insolvency period of organization, when the reaction to the changes of the situations must be immediate. Such working conditions require the existence of an assembly of "managerial formulas" that have to be applied after receiving the decisions in the changeable conditions (Kets de Vries, 2003).

Generally, the optimum solving of the problems that appear in the insolvency management requires the systematic use of prognosis-analytical methods with frequent application of the economic-mathematic instruments, calculation technique, activities of experts, analysts and those who draw different systems.

One of the most frequent forms of supplying insolvency management is the modeling of insolvency strategies (Lichtenstein, 2000).

Taken into account that each organization has a unique content, for drawing adequate insolvency strategies it is necessary to be determined the type of organization from the point of view of inclination to accomplishing one or another strategy. In this regard it is advised to be taken into account one of the two models, which are totally opposed – American or Japanese model, after which can be built the own model of insolvency strategy in organization.

On the other hand, the contemporary corporative management is often based on the principles of the method of projects management. The managing against insolvency is a component part of corporative management, this is why in its organization it is necessary to be followed the principles of projects management.

In the present moment in Romania it is accepted an ideology of program managing, meaning the forming process of some sets of programs. In the same time some problems that appear in the process of drawing the curriculum remain still opened. This is related by the difficulty of forecasting the development of economy. Generally, it is established the organizational mechanism of managing the programs. From this point of view, the methodology and technique of projects management is more used and solicited in the conditions of market economy. The methods of projects management can and must be an effective source of accomplishing the reforms both at state and regional level but also at a level of an average element of management.

The experience of Japan, SUA, Korea and other developed countries denotes that the management of projects is a means of going out of economic insolvency and a method of solving major scientific, production and social problems. This method is a way of managing, in condition of transition, the systems in development, in conditions of instability and uncontrolled increase of prices and the deficit of resources, the refuse of state to manage directly the economic activity of the production of enterprise and in the condition of appearance of the owners of investments, projects, unstable fiscal system, etc.

The management of projects is a synthetic discipline that gathers both special and professional knowledge (Paton, & McCalman, 2008). The special knowledge reflects the specific at a certain activity domain at which the projects refer (construction, innovational, ecological, organizing, etc.). The management of projects became an absolute discipline due to the knowledge required as a result of studying the general rules, of their existence in the projects from all the domains of activity, as well as the efficient use of the methods and means used in the different projects (Pettigrew, Woodman & Cameron, 2001).

The groups of processes are similar by the results produced: the results of a process are the entries for the following process (Brown, & Harvey, 2006). Also, the groups of processes of the management of projects do not consist in discrete and homogenous events, they are works that are intersected and manifested with different degrees of intensity within each stage of the projects. The interaction of the groups of processes are intersected with the stages so that, the end of a stage offers entry data for the initiating of the next one. For instance, the closing of the projecting stage requires the receiving from the client of the projecting documents. In the same time the projecting documents serve as description of the product for the execution stage.

The repeating of the initiating processes at the beginning of each stage helps at focusing the project upon the specified necessities in order to satisfy those for whom it was conceived. The management of projects includes all the aspects of the activities of organization and has a big number of subsystems of management. The subsystems of management of the projects are formed depending on the managing domains and elements, quite independent within the projects. They could be: durations, resources of labor forces, expenses, acquisitions and deliveries, information and communication, the risks of the project, etc.

For the accomplishing of the enterprise's program against insolvency it is necessary to act according to a plan previously established and thought which is based on scientific-theoretical resources and applicative practice studies from the domain of management, marketing, personnel management and financial management. Based on the existent performances a plan of managing the enterprise in situation de insolvency or about to enter the insolvency must be drawn by whose application to be solved the internal problems of the enterprises, efficient handling of external unfavorable factors and the use with maximum efficiency of the possibilities offered by the macro-environment of the enterprise.

In the initial stage must be determined the correct strategy of the enterprise that can allow the efficient competing and surviving on the market (Burnes, 2004). This is possible only after a rigorous managerial investigation of the enterprise and making the SWOT analysis (analysis of weak and strong points, risks and possibilities). Further, it must be drawn an efficient instrumentation for executing the strategy, including in it the basis set of forms and means oriented towards the fundamental directions of the activity of the enterprise, focusing the efforts upon one or more of them, according to the situations.

Each enterprise is in continuous change of the factors of internal and external environment (Mikalef, & Pateli, 2017). Taking decisions of „filling in the lacks", (when the management of the enterprise solves only the current business and the problems already appeared), transferring the little resources in areas, where metaphorically speaking it is already fire, is inefficient and fatal for the company (Harari,1999). In most of the situations the main cause of the severe condition of the native enterprises is the managerial ignorance and the reduced capacity of strategic thinking and planning.

The strategic directions drawn within the first mission determine all the basic principles of the functioning of the enterprise, including the type of activity, the resources used, its strategic potential, etc. Making modifications in the functioning of the enterprise means changing its profile and increasing the risk of appearance of some specific consequences. This is why the continuity period of the existence of the enterprise within the first mission is the continuity period of existence not affected by insolvency, characterized by the competitive privilege which will support it. Nevertheless, some managers do not take into account the choice and formulation of the mission of the enterprises. They often do not imagine what it means and what is good for. Sometimes, the mission represents the purpose of obtaining the profit. But it is known that choosing the profit as general mission of the enterprise is incorrect, as the profit represents the problem of internal order of the enterprise. In the same time the enterprise is an open system, it can survive only if it satisfies a necessity which refers to it. This is why the mission of the enterprise is to be established depending on the correlation with the ambient environment.

After choosing the strategy and drawing the adequate plan the management should take a rigorous control of the organizational structure for determining the capacity of achieving the objectives. The strategy established the structure and the structure at its turn always reflects the strategy. Thus, there isn't a certain method to be used at forming the organizational structure. The structure of the enterprise will be one that corresponds to dynamic, complexity and personnel. Once the enterprise develops and its objectives show an evolution the strategies and plans are modified. The same thing happens with its structures. There is a dynamic correlation among strategy, structure and environment in which the enterprise activates. Many enterprises make a big mistake which consists in the fact that they impose new strategies to the existent structures of the enterprises that are not modified when essential changes of the existent environment take place. Such situations shouldn't exist. The structure depends on strategy, and the stage of forming the structure within the process of planning represents the important stage in achieving successfully the strategic plan. Drawing the strategy is a complex stage. The incapacity or the lack of tendency to recognize the importance of the structure within the process of planning determined the failure of many well though and efficient strategies.

Although the purpose of the organizational structure consists in the necessity of assuring the achievement of the suggested objectives, the planning of the structure must relate to the strategic planning of the enterprise. Some authors consider that choosing the general structure of organization represents the decision further to the strategic planning, as it determines the way in which the enterprise will use the efforts in order to achieve its basic goals (Antoni, 2004; Fenton, & Pettigrew, 2000; McCune, 1999; Sementelli, 2016; Mikalef, & Pateli, 2017). In our opinion the activity of the enterprise is another position.

We think that it is based on the strategy of the enterprise but it is not the strategy itself. On the contrary the strategy determines the structure. This means that the structure of the enterprise should be structured in such a manner so that it could assure the execution of the strategy. As strategies are modified, in time there will be necessary the adequate changes in the structure of the enterprise.

According to the classic theory, the organizational structure must be drawn vertically from up to down (Chandler, 1994). No wonder that the succession of the drawing of organizational structure coincides with the succession of the elements of the planning process. At the beginning the managers should make the division of the enterprise on large domains of activity, then to establish actual objectives, as in case of the planning when at the beginning are formulated the general objectives and then are established the actual rules. It is important to understand that the organizational structure appeared in the result of drawing is not a rigid form, resembling the skeleton of the building as the organizational structures are based on plans and any essential modifications in plans may require essential modification in structure. In conclusion the existent enterprises should pay a special attention to the process of modification of the organizational structure as in the case of reorganizational process as this process like all the functions of the enterprises, is infinite.

SOLUTIONS AND RECOMMENDATIONS

An important aspect underlined in the analysis is that of the cycles of development of economy on market which is the main cause of appearance of insolvency situations in enterprises as a result of non-coincidence of economic development in general and of the cycle of life of enterprises in particular. The coordinates of the cycle of life of the enterprise under curve on incomes- losses of the enterprise on a period of time, offers the possibility of building a curve of the cycle of life based on real data and to use this curve as an instrument of strategic management.

The characteristics of the three stages of stages of aggravation of insolvency (presented in this chapter) in case of autonomous stage directions and commercial companies of public administration denote the fact that they go non-uniformly, getting deeper with each stage, and the more profound the process is, the more difficult to reestablish the business will be.

It is remarkable the general solution suggested, namely the improving of managerial quality. The most important thing in the insolvency management is the assuring of necessary resources when the financial difficulties do not have a permanent, stable character. In other words, it must be drawn a certain mechanism of management, that would allow the solving of the problems at the highest level of management of the economic agent, until they will have a severe character. From this kind of approaching of the insolvency management it may be found its purpose– assuring a rigid position on the market and assuring the financial stability of the company regardless the economic, political and social metamorphoses from the country.

Very important is the determination of the functional diagram of insolvency management and the description of the four stages suggested: managing the enterprise when there is no insolvency, detecting the insolvency and the managing in the period of entering in insolvency, managing of enterprise in the period of insolvency and managing the enterprise for coming out of insolvency. It must be emphasized that the stages form a close cycle of management of the organization, in this regard being made the principles of continuity and systematicity of the insolvency management.

FUTURE RESEARCH DIRECTIONS

It was underlined that insolvency reflect the developing rhythms of each organization that sometimes do not coincide with the rhythms of social developing or the developing of other organizations. Each organization has its own developing potential and conditions of accomplishment, subsequently being submitted to the rules of cyclic development of the entire social-economic system. That is why upon the public organization act permanently both external factors, determined by the impact of general economic cycles and the internal ones that depend on their own cycles and by the evolution of insolvency.

It was shown that in order to have the possibility to launch the insolvency management programs, the management of local public administration should know the factors, symptoms and causes of the insolvency. In this regard it is remarked the idea that the symptoms are shown in indicators and, which is not less important, in the tendencies and modifications that reflect the functioning and developing of the public organization. Thus, the management of public administration analyzing the indicators regarding the productivity of work, efficiency of activity, yield of funds, financial condition or factors such as fluctuation of personnel, discipline, satisfaction at work, conflict condition etc. of economic agents from the economic domain from the public administration can characterize the condition of organizing the production based on the appearance of insolvency

CONCLUSION

The instability of the situation of industrial enterprise in insolvency conditions are emphasized on the necessity of processing the prognoses on long term regarding the development of the activity and drawing the decisions of stability of the situation (Parveen, & Noor Ismawati, 2015). This leads to insolvency strategies and mechanism that allow the assurance of balance in the organizations that are in insolvency.

It is analyzed the strategic attitude in insolvency situations. Under the conditions of organizational stress it is required from the top-management of the industrial enterprise an increased ingeniousness and flexibility in the application of different strategies that have as purpose the drawing of the enterprise out of insolvency. There were pointed out the types of strategy that must be applied in the actual situation of the enterprise: growth, stability, coming out.

In this regard the insolvency strategy must have an assembly of formulas (approaches, mechanisms), of the managers ‘decisions taken in different situations that could allow the fast accomplishment of his positions. It is noted that such an approach allows the highlighting of the company’s strategy on a longer or shorter period of time. The main advantage of the strategic management – speed of receiving the decisions at the inferior level of management, being avoided the superior links (except for the procedures coordinated on a long duration). This property of the strategy is mostly applied in the insolvency management, as in the conditions of a changeable environment the decisions must immediately reach the different hierarchic levels.

The aspects presented allowed the approach of insolvency management in a greater extent within the strategic management rather than the operative management (which corresponds more to the technologies of accomplishing the strategic plans).

In drawing the management plan of the enterprise in insolvency or about to enter the insolvency is suggested the use of the management of projects at drawing the concept of the insolvency management of project.

This means first establishing the mission, the objectives and strategic alternatives of the insolvency management. Further it is presented an efficient instrumentation for drawing the strategy, including in it the basis set of forms and means oriented towards the fundamental directions of the activity of the enterprise, focusing the efforts upon one or more of them, according to the actual situation. Based on the real situation, there were pointed out the following main instruments that any enterprise that is in economic recession can use: organizational structure and distributing the positions; management of personnel; optimization of cash flows.

Referring to the organizational structure it is pointed out that its purpose consists in the necessity of assuring the achievement of the suggested objectives of the enterprise, the planning of the structure must relate to the strategic planning of the enterprise. In our opinion the choice of the general structure of organization is based on the strategy of the enterprise but it isn't the strategy itself. On the contrary the strategy determines the structure. This means that the structure of the enterprise should be structured in such a manner so that it could assure the implementation of the strategy. As strategies are modified, in time there will be necessary the adequate changes in the structure of the enterprise.

In case of reorganization of an enterprise which is in insolvency, those who take the decisions regarding the component parts of the insolvency programs should take a series of practical measures regarding the management of the personnel such as: reducing the levels within the organizational structure of the administration and not the reduction of the jobs; correlation of structural subdivisions correlation of structural subdivisions of the organizational structure and taking some measures of maintaining the stability of the new organizational structure, as well as psychological support of the personnel.

Referring to the optimization of the cash flows there are suggested some financial strategies among which can be reminded: strategy of increase of liquidity of assets; strategy of the optimization of the structure of the capital; strategy of improving the quality of the system of registration and control of losses; strategy of optimization the profit; strategy of optimization the financial liabilities.

REFERENCES

Antoni, C. (2004). A motivational perspective on change processes and outcomes. *European Journal of Work and Organizational Psychology, 13*(2), 197–216. doi:10.1080/13594320444000065

Bloodgood, J. M., & Morrow, J. L., Jr. (2000). Strategic organizational change within an institutional framework. *Journal of Managerial Issues, Pittsburgh Summer, 12* (2), 208-226.

Bolman, L. G., & Deal, T. E. (1999). 4 Steps to keeping change efforts heading in the right direction. *Journal for Quality and Participation, 22*(3), 6–11.

Brown, D. R., & Harvey, D. (2006). *An Experimental approach to Organization development. Hoboken, NJ*: Pearson Education.

Buchanan, D. A., & Boddy, D. (1992). *The Expertise of the Change Agent.* London, UK: Prentice Hall.

Burnes, B. (2004). *Managing Change: A Strategic Approach to Organisational Dynamics.* Harlow, UK: Prentice Hall.

Chandler, A. D., Jr. (1994). The history of Business Change. In the Change Management Handbook: A Road Map to Corporate Transformation. Sikora, & Berger. New York, NY: McGraw-Hill.

Day, G. S. (1999). The Market Driven Organization. The Free Press DuPont, GE, Pfizer, and Rubbermaid. New York, NY: Harper Business.

Fenton, E. M., & Pettigrew, A. M. (2000). *Theoretical Perspectives on New Forms of Organizing*. London, UK: Sage. doi:10.4135/9781446219379.n1

Frahm, J., & Brown, K. (2007). First steps: Linking change communication to change receptivity. *Journal of Organizational Change, 20*(3), 370–387. doi:10.1108/09534810710740191

Harari, O. (1999). Why Do Leaders Avoid Change? *Management Review, 88*(3).

Kets de Vries, M. (2003). *Organizations on the couch: A Clinical Perspective on Organizational Dynamics*. UK: John Wiley & Sons.

Kets de Vries, M., & Miller, D. (1984). *The Neurotic Organization: Diagnosing and Changing Counterproductive Styles of Management*. San Francisco, CA: Jossey-Bass.

Latham, G. P., & Pinder, C. C. (2005). Work motivation theory and research at the dawn of the twenty-first century. *Annual Review of Psychology, 56*(1), 485–516. doi:10.1146/annurev.psych.55.090902.142105 PMID:15709944

Levy, A., & Merry, U. (1986). *Organizational Transformation: Approaches, Strategies, Theories*. New York, NY: Praeger.

Lichtenstein, B. B. (2000). Self-Organized Transitions: A Pattern amid the Chaos of Transformative Change. *The Academy of Management Executive, 14*(4).

McCune, J. C. (1999). The Change Makers: Regardless of the obstacles placed in their paths, these agents of change get the job done. *Management Review*, 16.

Munro, I. (2014). Organizational ethics and foucault's 'art of living': Lessons from social movement organizations. *Organization Studies, 35*(8), 1127–1148. doi:10.1177/0170840614530915

Paton, R. A., & McCalman, J. (2008). *Change Management: A Guide to Effective Implementation*. London, UK: Sage.

Peters, T. J. (1998). *The Circle of Innovation: You Can't Shrink Your Way to Greatness*. London, UK: Coronet.

Pettigrew, A. M., Woodman, R. W., & Cameron, K. S. (2001). Studying organizational change and development: Challenges for future research. *Academy of Management Journal, 44*(4), 697–713.

Pfeffer, J., & DeVoe, S. E. (2012). The economic evaluation of time: Organizational causes and individual consequences. *Research in Organizational Behavior, 32*, 1–15. doi:10.1016/j.riob.2012.11.001

Piderit, S. K. (2000). Rethinking Resistance and Recognizing Ambivalence: A Multidimensional View of Attitudes toward an Organizational Change. *Academy of Management Review, 25*(4), 783–794. doi:10.5465/amr.2000.3707722

Sementelli, J. (2016). OD, change management, and the a priori: Introducing parrhesia. *Journal of Organizational Change Management, 29*(7), 1083–1096. doi:10.1108/JOCM-12-2015-0234

Weiss, J. W. (2001). *Organizational Behaviour and Change: Managing Diversity, Cross-Cultural Dynamics and Ethics*. UK: South-Western Thomson Learning.

Witherspoon, P. D., & Wohlert, K. L. (1996). An Approach to Developing Communication Strategies for Enhancing Organizational Diversity. *Journal of Business Communication*, *33*(4), 375–399. doi:10.1177/002194369603300402

ADDITIONAL READING

Mikalef, P., & Pateli, A. (2017). Information technology-enabled dynamic capabilities and their indirect effect on competitive performance: Findings from PLS-SEM and fsQCA. *Journal of Business Research*, *70*, 1–16. doi:10.1016/j.jbusres.2016.09.004

Parveen, F., & Noor Ismawati, J. (2015). Social media usage and organizational performance: Reflections of Malaysian social media managers. *Telematics and Informatics*, *32*(1), 67–78. doi:10.1016/j.tele.2014.03.001

Rojon, C., McDowall, A., & Saunders, M. N. K. (2015). The Relationships between Traditional Selection Assessments and Workplace Performance Criteria Specificity: A Comparative Meta-Analysis. *Human Performance*, *28*(1), 1–25. doi:10.1080/08959285.2014.974757

Wong, K. K.-K. (2013). Partial least squares structural equation modelling (PLS-SEM) techniques using SmartPLS. *Marketing Bulletin*, *24*(1), 1–32.

KEY TERMS AND DEFINITIONS

Environmental Characteristics: The external factors that may limit or support a company's activities.

Managerial Characteristics: Properties of managers who make business decisions.

Organisational Characteristics: An organization's demographic features, such as size, financial revenue, technological expertise and location.

Organisational Performance: elements affecting company performance such as financial and marketing factors, return on sales, return on investment, etc.

Chapter 9
Sustainable Economic Intelligence:
A New Dimension of Information Provided by Non-Financial Indicators

Ionescu Constantin Aurelian
Hyperion University of Bucharest, Romania

Mihaela Denisa Coman
Valahia University of Targoviste, Romania

Liliana Paschia
Hyperion University of Bucharest, Romania

Nicoleta Luminita Gudanescu Nicolau
Institute of National Economy, Romania

Sorina Geanina Stanescu
Valahia University of Targoviste, Romania

ABSTRACT

Sustainable economic intelligence, as a form of superior manifestation of an economy based on knowledge and innovation requires the management, quantification, monitoring, and reporting of non-financial information by economic entities (environmental issues, social and personnel aspects, respect the human rights and combating corruption) defined in relation to the average number of employees, total balance sheet, and net turnover. These elements, combined in the non-financial statements of economic entities, are decisive in achieving the transition to a sustainable global economy, combining profitability with social responsibility and environmental protection. The purpose of this scientific research is to achieve a systematization of the main non-financial performance indicators relevant to the activity of economic entities in Romania in order to favor sustainable economic growth and ensure transparency for stakeholders.

DOI: 10.4018/978-1-7998-1005-6.ch009

INTRODUCTION

Industry, the indispensable engine of economic growth, for its products, a true foundation of contemporary living standards, uses natural resources along the entire value chain, from raw material extraction and exploitation, to product transformation, energy consumption, generation of waste and the use and disposal of products by consumers (Institute for Economics and Peace, 2015). Globally, in order to ensure sustainable development, an astringent need to reorganize industries is identified to address today's society's needs without compromising the ability of future generations to meet their own needs (World Commission on Environment and Development, 1987). Thus, encourages industry and industrial operations to streamline their resource consumption, minimize the amount of waste generated and reduce pollution. At the same time, it is recommended to increase the use of renewable resources to minimize adverse effects on the environment and human health (AlphaBeta, 2017; Schmidt-Traub, 2015).

The European Union promotes resource efficiency and environmental impact reduction through the transition to a circular economy where the value of products, materials and resources is maintained in the economy for as long as possible and pollution and waste generation are minimized (European Commission, 2018). The European Strategy for Bio-Economy supports the modernization and consolidation of the industry by creating cost-effective and ecological industrial chains and processes (European Commission, 2018). The European Commission defines the social responsibility of economic entities as a voluntary way of integrating social, environmental, human and consumer protection concerns into their economic activities, strategies and interactions with stakeholders (European Commission, 2001b). The European Parliament has confirmed the importance of the publication by economic entities of information on sustainability, namely social and environmental factors, in order to quantify the sustainability risks. In this context, the presentation of non-financial information (environmental, social and personnel aspects, respect for human rights and the fight against corruption and bribery) contributes to measuring, monitoring and managing the performance of economic entities and their impact on society (European Parliament, 2014).

Integrating environmental information into industrial planning and decision-making leads to real-time resource and energy consumption evidence, ensuring future resource efficiency, waste reduction, recycling and resource reuse (Ellen Macarthur Foundation, 2015). Economic entities play a key role in the transition to sustainable development (Dvořáková, & Zborková, 2014), integrating in their mission and strategy an essential element, namely social and environmental responsibility, as long-term responsible behavior can contribute to profit growth to the emergence of new market opportunities (European Commission, 2019). Sustainable consumption and production aim to reduce the environmental footprint and involve changing the way economic entities produce, distribute and consume goods and resources (B&S Development Commission, 2017). In order to create a social climate leading to smart growth and social governance, efforts need to be multilaterally concentrated at all macro and micro levels on social responsibility standards, the use of information provided by non-financial indicators thus contributing favorably to the development of sustainable economic intelligence in the economic entities in particular and at the socio-economic level in general (Panayiotou, Aravossis, & Moschou, 2009; Târțiu, Ștefănescu, Petrache, & Gurau, 2019).

In general, the meaning attributed to the domain of economic intelligence in the specialized work involves identifying, searching, collecting, treating, disseminating and exploiting information useful for substantiating decisions at an economic entity level. The definitions given by the specialists reflect the different opinions expressed by them: economic intelligence "represents a set of coordinated actions of research, processing and dissemination of information useful to economic actors" (Martre, 1994). Useful information is needed by the different levels of decision-making in the economic entity to elaborate and implement in a coherent manner the strategy and tactics necessary to achieve the objectives defined by the enterprise in order to improve its position in its competitive environment; economic intelligence is seen as "the systematic research and interpretation of information accessible to all, in order to decrypt the intentions of various actors in economic life" (Harbulot, 2007). This action includes all competition surveillance activities and differs from traditional information through: the nature of its field of application, since it addresses the field of open information, requiring respect for credible deontology, the identity of its actors, to the extent that all staff participate in the construction of collective culture of information, cultural specificity, since each national economy produces an original model of economic intelligence whose impact on commercial and industrial strategies varies from country to country.

The whole process of sustainable economic intelligence translates into actions that integrate into the following coordinates (Haydaroglu, 2015; Nicolau, 2010): defining the information needs according to the strategy of the economic entity concerned, in order to identify the priorities and to fix, consequently, guidance on information gathering; classifying the "wealth" of the information available in the enterprise, which it is not always aware of; collecting open information using appropriate research tools that will allow only the relevant information to be retained; taking into account informal information, which often offers the greatest added value for the enterprise; ranking and processing of information gathered, using information processing tools and consulting experts in the field; disseminating the information to the right people at the right time and in an appropriate form, putting into operation an information flow and implementing an exchange culture within the economic entity that allows for loss prevention and isolation of information; protecting sensitive data, knowledge and all strategic assets, using appropriate IT, organizational, human and legal measures. By achieving all the adhesion and putting into operation of the devices that allow the sharing of information inside the economic entity, according to a vertical hierarchical axis but also transversal, the sustainable economic intelligence represents from this point of view a vector of the organizational culture (Gloaguen, 2012).

Increasing the awareness of the need to conserve resources for future generations and assessing companies' performance not only in terms of their basic level but also their overall impact on the environment and the community has led to an increased commitment at global level towards sustainability programs and increasing demand for formal reporting. However, reporting on the sustainability of most economic entities is currently carried out on the basis of independent reports. Economic entities implementing sustainability programs are expected to get significant benefits from their investments (James, 2015). Reporting on sustainability activities indicates responsible behavior and can lead to increased third-party interest in the company, while generating increased investors' goodwill and willingness to provide capital loyalty, respectively employees and customers (Dhaliwal, Li, Tsang, & Yang, 2011). The purpose of this scientific research is to achieve a systematization of the main non-financial performance indicators relevant to the activity of economic entities in Romania in order to foster sustainable economic growth and to ensure transparency for stakeholders.

BACKGROUND

In the current context of extending the responsibility from the economic sphere to the social and environmental aspects, it is necessary for the reporting model to extend beyond the traditional model of financial reporting. Non-financial reporting describes how key information is managed that can have a significant impact on economic activity, financial, social and environmental information. Growth and increasing interest in reporting sustainability has led to numerous studies and reports among foreign researchers. The latest research in this field has focused on the quality of social responsibility reports (Wolniak, & Hąbek, 2016), the credibility of these reports (Lock, & Seele, 2016), but also the relationship between managerial practices and the quality of CSR reports (Hąbek, & Wolniak, 2016). At the same time, the interest of researchers at the international and national level was increased for the correlation of social responsibility elements with new concepts such as green economy (Ciocoiu, 2011; Cucui, Ionescu, Goldbach, Coman, & Moiceanu, 2018; Lavrinenko, Ohotina, Ignatjeva, Rybalkin, & Lazdans, 2019; Topor, & Capusneanu, 2017), respectively circular economy (Coman, Ionescu, & Lixandru, 2019; Ellen Macarthur Foundation, 2015; Oncioiu et al., 2018).

Studies on the main ways of publishing and reporting non-financial information are also relevant, such as the application of the Global Reporting Initiative guidelines (Fuente, García-Sánchez, & Lozano, 2017), (Michelon, Pilonato, & Ricceri, 2015), or the implementation of Triple bottom line reporting (Husillos, González, & Álvarez Gil, 2011). However, most research is based on CSR reporting (Fifka, 2013; Koerber, 2010; Marimon, Alonso-Almeida, Rodríguez, & Cortez Alejandro, 2012). Sustainable or non-financial reporting is an extension of reporting to corporate reporting, involving the presentation of financial and non-financial information to a broad stakeholder group.

Non-financial reporting is one of the most widely used ways of presenting information on social responsibility and sustainable development. For the submission of this non-financial information, organizations have the opportunity to produce sustainability reports or annual CSR reports. These reports are standardized computerized means of communication (Milne, & Gray, 2013; Schaltegger, Bennett, & Burritt, 2006), combining financial, social and environmental information (Daub, 2007). World Business Council for Sustainable Development (WBCSD) has defined the Sustainability Report as the public internal and external stakeholder report that presents an image of corporate position, economic, social and environmental activities (Heemskerk, Group, Stmicroelectronics, & Scicluna, 2002). Market interest in non-financial information is on the rise, leading to an increase in the number of organizations publishing sustainability reports. Non-financial reporting originally emerged in the late 1990s, when only brief information on social and environmental policies was included in the annual reports (Buhr, 2002). Over time, these reports have included much more complex and relevant information on the impact of economic activity on the environment (Margarit, Bran, Ionescu, & Boca, 2012), on intangible and non-financial aspects (Palenberg, Reinicke, & Witte, 2006) that contribute to solving issues related to organizational legitimacy (Neu, Warsame, & Pedwell, 1998) and facilitates corporate planning (Adams, & McNicholas, 2007) and decisions making (Albareda, Lozano, & Ysa, 2007).

LEGISLATIVE REGULATIONS ON NON - FINANCIAL REPORTING

Evolution of Existing International Regulations

In recent years, many laws and norms have been issued for sustainable development and social responsibility, and the information needs of investors, creditors, business partners on social and environmental issues have greatly increased, so both accounting normalization bodies and other organizations have addressed these issues. Financial statements may be affected by some non-financial aspects that require their consideration, such as:

- Adopting environmental laws and regulations can lead to a depreciation of assets and consequently will reduce their book value.
- Failure to comply with legal provisions on the environment, such as emissions to air, water, soil may require some remediation costs.
- Some economic entities, such as those in the extractive industry (gas, oil, mining), chemical, petrochemical or recycling industries, have environmental obligations as a direct consequence of their activities.
- Implicit obligations that are generated by a voluntary initiative to remedy some environmental problems, for example, an entity may have identified soil contamination and, without being under any obligation, may decide to remedy this.
- Presentation of eventual liabilities in the financial statements if the expenses for the removal of some aspects of the pollution cannot reasonably be estimated.
- Non-compliance with environmental laws and regulations may affect the continuity of an entity's business and as a result of the continuity of business, it may affect the disclosure of information and the basis for preparing the financial statements (International Auditing Practice Statements (IAPS), 2010).

Over the years, several regulations have been adopted at European Union level on the reporting of non-financial information. Thus, in 1997, the Working Group of Experts in International Accounting Standards published "Environmental Financial Accounting and Reporting at the Corporate Level", which defines environmental expenditures, environmental liabilities, eventual liabilities, environmental issues to be presented in the annual reports (United Nations, 1997). The European Accounting Experts' Federation on „Global Accounting Rules on Green Issues – Review of International Accounting Standards for Environmental Issues" addresses the issues of environmental costs and liabilities, the criteria for recording environmental expenditures on fixed assets, environmental provisions, risk information and environmental uncertainties (Accountancy Europe, 1999). European Commission Recommendation 2001/453 / EU „On the Recognition, Measurement and Disclosure of Environmental Issues in the Annual Accounts and Annual Reports of Companies" requires the submission of comparable and pertinent information on environmental issues. The European Commission recognizes the need to harmonize the information presented in the financial statements and aims to clarify the existing rules and to establish a specific framework for accounting, assessment and presentation of environmental aspects in the annual reports (European Commission, 2001a). Currently, Directive 2014/95 / EU regulates non-financial reporting for entities in the European Union. The rules of this Directive apply to large economic entities with more than 500 employees, except for traded companies, banking companies, authorized insurances and companies carrying on insurance market activity (European Parliament, 2014).

The importance of non-financial information has led many national and international bodies to issue standards, regulations and guidelines on the accounting treatment applied to them. We can now identify three types of financial standards that influence how the accounting system addresses non-financial information within an economic entity: national standards, supranational standards (European directives), and international standards (Schaltegger, & Burrit, 2005). The presentation of non-financial information in the financial statements is required either by the national public authority or by different normalization bodies. For example, the IAS/IFRS General Framework recommends that an environmental report or management report be drawn up to capture the main performance features and uncertainties faced by the entity. In fact, economic entities that have adopted IAS/IFRS have an obligation to provide much more detailed and more environmental information in the explanatory notes to the annual financial statements. The IAS/IFRS general framework encourages the submission of additional statements if the information has a significant impact, such as an environmental report or a management report showing the main performance characteristics and uncertainties faced by the enterprise (Istrate, Robu, Păvăloaia, & Herghiligiu, 2017).

Legislative Regulations on Existing Non-Financial Reporting in Romania

The 2014/95/EU Directive adopted at European level is transposed at national level through OMFP 1938/2016 which includes the accounting rules for individual and consolidated annual financial statements. The main legislative provisions of this order refer to non-financial information and diversity information for large economic entities. Thus, starting in 2018, entities that exceed the average number of 500 employees should include in the administrators' report a non-financial statement that includes, besides financial information on performance, position and impact of the business, and non-financial information on, at least, and human rights, respect for human rights, fight against corruption and bribery. The non-financial statement briefly describes the business model used by the entity, the policies developed and applied within the entity, as well as the results obtained by applying it, the breakdown of risks arising from the entity's operations and the main solutions for managing those risks, identifying key non-financial key performance indicators. Where appropriate the non-financial statement may contain additional references and explanations on the amounts reported in the annual financial statements.

Environmental non-financial information to be presented in the non-financial statement shall include the current or future impacts of the entity's activity on the environment, information on health and food safety, renewable energy sources, the impact of greenhouse gas emissions, used water, climate change and atmospheric pollution. As far as social and personnel aspects are concerned, they should contain information on equal opportunities, gender equality, respect for the rights of all employees through optimal working conditions. With regard to human rights, the fight against corruption and bribery, the non-financial declaration may include information on the prevention of human rights abuses and / or on instruments put in place to combat corruption and bribery. In the case of economic entities that separately publish a sustainability report, they are exempted from the preparation of the non-financial statement, provided that this report is published together with the Directors' report, be available to the public within a maximum of 6 months from the balance sheet date. For small and medium-sized economic entities in our country, legislation does not oblige the disclosure of non-financial information in annual reports. The publication of this information is left to the discretion of voluntary leadership at least at this time. This can be done by writing and publishing a sustainability report.

NON-FINANCIAL REPORTING

Traditional financial accounting and published annual reports pay more attention to financial results. According to this model, the annual financial statements reflect the value of the assets and liabilities, the value of the shares, the profit and the evolution of the financial position of the economic entity during the period considered, usually ignoring non-financial information. Currently, users of financial statements have become interested in information on the impact of risks and expenses on the situation of an economic entity, how to approach non-financial information, and assessing overall performance. Effective leadership depends on access to as relevant, good quality information as possible to monitor performance and opens up the prospect of new forms of stakeholder engagement. The publication of non-financial information in the annual reports is of particular importance to users, who are informed about the potential social risks or environmental costs that the entity is likely to employ. Under these conditions, full reporting is required to capture aspects of an entity's economic, social and environmental activities (Arnaud, 2003). An important part of the global impetus towards sustainability practices implies the need to report and present information on sustainable activity.

Non-financial reporting helps to improve management's ability to assess the entity's contribution to human, natural and social capital helps highlight the entity's social and environmental contributions may reduce stock price instability and uncertainty for listed entities and may reduce capital costs. A sustainability report or a non-financial statement must provide environmental, social and economic information and data, the main challenges of sustainable development and a clear sustainable development strategy for the entity (Bachelerie, & Boillet-Mongodin, 1993), the cycle of non-financial reporting being highlighted according to Figure 1. Non-financial reporting can help organizations measure, understand and communicate information on economic, social and environmental performance. The non-financial reporting process is similar to all performance-based management processes. The non-financial reporting

Figure 1. Non-financial reporting cycle
Source: author's own processing

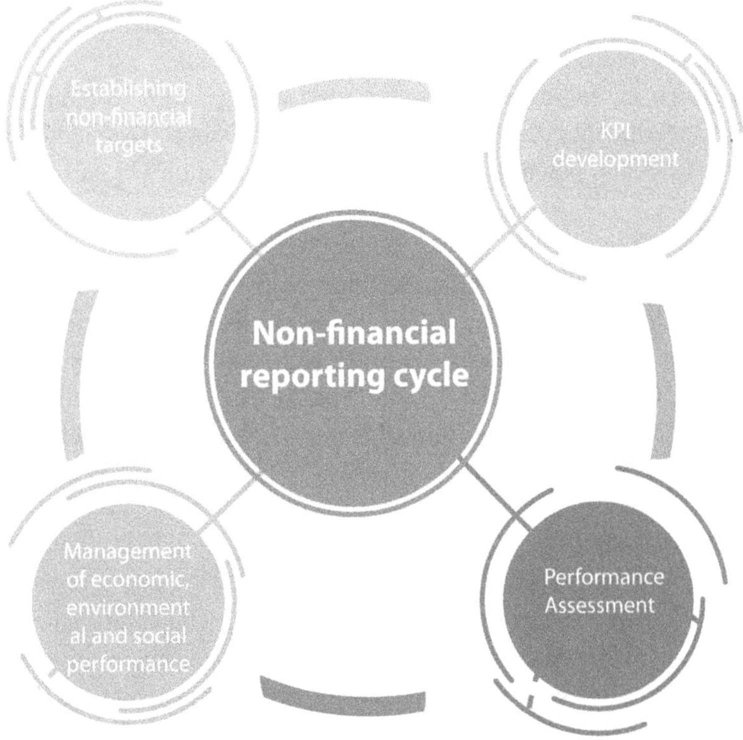

process can be considered a circular process that is based on the definition of performance objectives and values, followed by measurement, evaluation and performance management.

Non-financial information becomes important for an increasing number of entities and may, in some circumstances, have a significant impact on their financial statements. These issues are of great interest to users of financial statements. The recognition, assessment and presentation of these issues is the responsibility of the management. Environmental issues may be complex and may therefore require some additional consideration in the annual financial statements. Environmental financial information is either imposed by the authorities or voluntarily presented by organizations. Environmental information is addressed by international accounting standards IAS/IFRS, like (Istrate, Georgescu, Carp, Robu, & Pavaloaia, 2015):

- IFRS 6 „Exploration and evaluation of mineral resources" applied by entities exploring and exploiting mineral resources when obtaining legal exploration rights. The fundamental objective is to specify how financial reporting is to be used for the exploration and evaluation of mineral resources. Mineral resources include minerals, gas, oil and other non-renewable resources. IFRS 6 does not provide for the estimation of reserves.
- IFRIC 1 "Changes in existing debt due to liquidation, restoration and similar nature" - addresses how to account for the effect of events that alter debt for environmental rehabilitation.
- IFRIC 5 "Rights to funds from liquidation, restoration and environmental rehabilitation funds" – treats the funds created for the purpose of winding up, restoring or rehabilitating the environment and similar expenditures, namely the way of registering the participation in a fund and the reflection of the obligation to make additional contributions in case of bankruptcy of another participant.
- IFRIC 6 "Liabilities arising from participation in a specific market - waste electrical and electronic equipment" provides guidance for the recognition in the financial statements of producers of debt for the management of historical waste from households.
- Environmental issues are addressed in other norms, such as: IAS 16 "Tangible assets", IAS 20 "Accounting for Government Grants", IAS 38 "Intangible assets", IAS 36 "Impairment of assets", IAS 37 "Provisions, debts, potential assets", IAS 41 "Agriculture" (Barbu, Feleaga, & Feleaga, 2011).

Given the increasing interest in assessing companies' contribution to sustainable development and fostering social responsibility, it was necessary to develop non-financial indicators whose primary objective is to reflect the non-financial performance of the economic entity. Thus, mechanisms have been proposed at national and international level to provide a balance between environmental information and the entity's economic performance, such as: Global Reporting Initiative Guidelines and Triple Bottom Line Reporting (Ienciu, 2009).

Triple Bottom Line Reporting

Triple Bottom Line (TBL) also known as the sustainable reporting of the entity is based on addressing the three characteristics of sustainable development: economic, social and environmental. TBL is a philosophy that guides corporate performance, but also a tactic of measuring, managing and reporting business performance, beyond the financial dimension and from the perspective of an integrated vision of the entity, with clear evidence of the economic, social and environmental impact. TBL designates a notion designed to enhance the non-financial and difficult dimensions of an entity's performance and accountability. The strict sense of TBL is used as a framework for measuring and reporting the performance of an entity in three dimensions: social, environmental and economic (Caraiani, Lungu, & Colceag, 2010).

The economic dimension includes traditional accounting reports, which are considered the most important part of TBL reporting. However, financial and accounting reporting does not provide a number of information related in particular to evaluation, so more increasingly consideration is being given to integrating environmental information into traditional financial statements. The environmental dimension has over the past been more than the social dimension. Information on the environmental impact of the economic entity's activity should be included in the financial and non-financial reporting. The reports must therefore contain comparative data to provide the public with relevant information on the legislative requirements and the environments achieved by the industry. Social coordinate is the impact on employees and on the local economy. Social reporting is done by presenting employee information (gender, address, salary received, holiday pay, dividends or other economic benefits offered to them).

Indicators used in TBL reporting can be classified into system indicators and integrated indicators. Systematic indicators show the activity of the economic entity in close connection with the economic, environmental and social systems to which it belongs. An enterprise can assess its environmental performance in line with international standards, for example the percentage rate of total occupational accidents in a sector over a given period. Absolute systemic indicators describe the environmental performance in relation to the maximum allowable limit, the total amount admitted by a public authority in a given region for a given substance. In general, systemic indicators allow understanding of how an organization's performance can influence the performance of a larger system. Integrated indicators make a direct link between two or more dimensions of economic, environmental and social performance. An example of integrated indicators is represented by all the activities undertaken to stimulate eco-efficiency (the amount of emissions per unit of product or per unit of turnover). Integrated indicators effectively demonstrate the magnitude of the negative or positive impact of each change produced in a variable.

Global Reporting Initiatives Sustainability Reporting Guidelines (GRI Guidelines)

Issued by the World Commission on Environment and Development, Global Reporting Initiatives (GRI) is generally accepted as one of the best practices in terms of sustainable social and environmental reporting. The GRI reporting framework is a generally accepted framework for reporting economic, environmental and social performance. It is designed to be used by any enterprise, regardless of size, activity or location. GRI provides a series of information on the performance of sustainable reporting (principles that define the content of reports and that provide the quality of reported information) along with performance indicators within a generally applicable framework. GRI benefits from the active participation of business, accounting, investment, human rights, environmental, research, labor, and global business representatives and aims to ensure the quality of the reports in order to ensure the comparability, reliability and verifiability of the information presented. Adoption of GRI is the result of a voluntary approach, and there is no provision obliging it to apply it (Quairel, 2004). Several versions of the guide have been issued over the years: the first version was released in 2000, the second in 2002, the third version in 2006, the fourth version was published in March 2011, and in 2013, the new Global Reporting Initiative G4 Guidelines on Sustainability Reporting (Global Reporting Initiative, 2014) was adopted.

A sustainability report should provide a balanced and reasonable representation of the organization's sustainable performance, including positive and negative aspects of the impact economic, environmental and social considerations. Sustainability reports based on the GRI Reporting Framework present the results achieved during the reporting period, taking into account the engagement, strategy and management of the organization. These reports can be used to demonstrate the organization's commitment to sustainable development, to compare and evaluate its performance, taking into account existing legislation, norms, voluntary standards and initiatives, and to make comparisons with other organizations and to analyze developments over time. In October 2016, GRI launched the first reporting standards on social responsibility. At present, GRI standards are considered to be the most effective regulations for public reporting that provide economic, social and environmental information. Non-financial reporting based on GRI standards presents the organization's positive and negative aspects for sustainable development (Global Reporting Initiative, n.d.).

NON-FINANCIAL INDICATORS

For the achievement of non-financial reporting, a set of performance indicators has been developed to be used to measure progress towards social responsibility objectives. These indicators are generally referred to as sustainable development indicators or social responsibility indicators. Initially, these indicators were used for external financial communication, later being taken over by organizations management as a result of the need to measure, pilot, verify and report on social and environmental performance (Epstein, & Manzoni, 1997). Non-financial indicators can be defined as measures and data, both quantitative and qualitative, providing information about organizations on the basis of the three axes of sustainable development. GRI has developed a set of key performance dimensions applicable to all entities, sets of specific measures for certain types of economic entities, and a uniform format for reporting information on an entity's economic, environmental and social performance. GRI structures performance metrics in a certain hierarchy, by category, layout, and indicator (Figure 2).

Figure 2. Categories and aspects for GRI Guidelines
Source: author's own processing

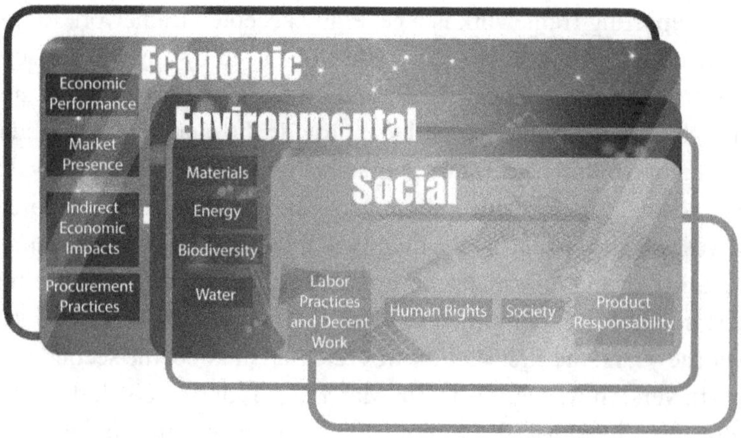

The GRI indicators provide information on economic, environmental and social performance. GRI has set nine indicators for economic performance, 34 for environmental performance and 48 for social performance (divided into four groups: 16 for work practices, 12 for human rights, 11 for company and nine for product warranties) (*Interpretations on the G4 Guidelines*, n.d.).

Economic Indicators

Economic performance indicators present the entity's impact on the local, national and global economic system. Economic indicators illustrate the flow of capital between different categories of users and the entity's economic impact on the company in which they operate. The economic analysis allows managers of economic entities, but also internal and external partners to deepen and appreciate aspects such as: the degree of consistency between the level of activity, the result obtained and the means allocated; the ability of the economic entity to deliver results and to self-finance; the capacity to ensure financial equilibrium and to create economic value. At the same time, in order to be consistent with the alert evolution of the need of information of the various partners of the entity, the analysis should provide pertinent conclusions regarding: the performances achieved and their perspective; the financial situation and its evolution; resource management and management results, the ability of the entity to generate cash or cash equivalents (Niculescu, 2005). Simultaneously, financial analysis is an indispensable tool that ensures: identifying development opportunities and strategies; identifying the different types of risk and the factors likely to create long-term value. The complexity of the phenomena and economic processes in which the activity of different economic entities takes place contributes to the proliferation of financial indicators and by quantifying them contributes to a recurring success that contributes to sustainable development. The performance indicators in the GRI view are presented in Table 1.

Table 1. Indicators of economic performance according to GRI

	Economic Performance
EC1.	Generated and distributed direct economic value, including revenue, operating expenses, employee compensation, donations and other community investment, retained earnings, payments to capital providers and governance
EC2.	Financial implications and other risks and opportunities regarding the entity's activities and climate change
EC3.	Obligations of the entity regarding benefit plans
EC4.	Financial assistance received from the Government
	Market Presence
EC5.	Ratios of standard entry level wage by gender compared to local minimum wage at significant locations of operation
EC6.	Proportion of senior management hired from the local community at significant locations of operation
	Indirect Economic Impacts
EC7.	Development and impact of infrastructure investments and services supported
EC8.	Significant indirect economic impacts, including the extent of impacts
	Procurement Practices
EC9.	Proportion of spending on local suppliers at significant locations of operation

Source: (GRI 4, 2013)

Environmental Indicators

The environmental performance indicators proposed by the guide cover input performance (material, energy, water) and outputs (emissions, waste). In addition, it covers biodiversity performance, compliance with environmental regulations and other relevant information such as environmental spending, environmental impact of products and services. GRI provides a general framework of indicators for all environmental domains that may be affected by the impact of economic activities (Table 2). Depending on the activities and the affected areas, the entities have to select those relevant indicators for determining the environmental performance. Recommendation 2014/95 /EC sets out certain criteria in selecting the appropriate indicators for performance calculation:

- Indicators must ensure accurate assessment of the environmental performance of the economic entity.
- Indicators should be clear and unambiguous in order to provide credibility.
- Indicators should allow for the comparison of environmental performance values from year to year or from one period to the next.
- Indicators should allow comparison of the environmental performance of an economic entity with others in the same sector at national or regional level.
- the Indicators must allow for identification of compliance with the requirements imposed by the regulations in force (European Parliament, 2014).

Environmental indicators are quantitative measures to communicate the complex environmental phenomena that have taken place or the environmental impact of an activity (Wolters, 2000). At an international level, since 1990, specialists from the Organization for Economic Cooperation and Development (OECD) have been concerned with the development of environmental indicators. In the literature, environmental indicators are classified by their nature, by form or by recipients. Qualitative environmental indicators describe environmental actions. The environmental indicators quantified in monetary units include the costs of environmental investments, start up and maintenance costs of environmental management systems, etc. At the European Union level, the European Environment Agency published in 2014 a report outlining 137 non-financial indicators on the environment grouped into 13 categories (European Environment Agency, 2014) (Figure 3).

Among the non-financial indicators in the transport category, the most used are: transport emissions of greenhouse gases, transport emissions of air pollutants, passenger transport demand, energy efficiency and specific CO2 emissions. Another category debated at European level is climate change. EEA has listed 46 indicators in this category, such as: production and consumption of ozone depleting substances, greenhouse gas emissions trends, global warming, global precipitation, precipitation extremes. As any performance indicator, environmental indicators essentially have the role of aggregating environmental data. For example, environmental indicators have the role of controlling a company's "green development" in relation to strategic objectives resulting from environmental concerns. Also with the help of environmental indicators, the company's environmental performance is communicated to stakeholders and new opportunities for improving environmental performance have been identified. Information on efforts to limit the negative impact of economic activity on the environment, monitoring environmental responsibilities and assessing the company's efforts to comply with environmental policies are also provided.

Table 2. Indicators of environmental performance according to GRI

Materials	
EN1.	Using materials by weight and volume
EN2.	Percentage of used materials that are recycled
Energy	
EN3.	Energy consumption within the organization
EN4.	Energy consumption outside of the organization
EN5.	Energy intensity
EN6.	Reduction of energy consumption
EN7.	Reductions in energy requirements of products and services
Water	
EN8.	Total water withdrawal by source
EN9.	Water sources significantly affected by withdrawal of water
EN10.	Percentage and total volume of water recycled and reused
Biodiversity	
EN11.	Operational sites owned, leased, managed in, or adjacent to, protected areas and areas of high biodiversity value outside protected areas
EN12.	Description of significant impacts of activities, products, and services on biodiversity in protected areas and areas of high biodiversity value outside protected areas
EN13.	Habitats protected or restored
EN14.	Total number of IUCN red list species and national conservation list species with habitats in areas affected by operations, by level of extinction risk
Emissions	
EN15.	Direct greenhouse gas (GHG) emissions
EN16.	Energy indirect greenhouse gas (GHG) emissions
EN17.	Other indirect greenhouse gas (GHG) emissions
EN18.	Greenhouse gas (GHG) emissions intensity
EN19.	Reduction of greenhouse gas (GHG) emissions
EN20.	Emissions of ozone-depleting substances (ODS)
EN21.	NO_X, SO_X, and other significant air emissions
Effluents and Waste	
EN22.	Total water discharge by quality and destination
EN23.	Total weight of waste by type and disposal method
EN24.	Total number and volume of significant spills
EN25.	Weight of transported, imported, exported, or treated waste deemed hazardous under the terms of the Basel convention 2 Annex i, ii, iii, and viii, and percentage of transported waste shipped internationally
EN26.	Identity, size, protected status, and biodiversity value of water bodies and related habitats significantly affected by the organization's discharges of water and runoff
Products and Services	
EN27.	Extent of impact mitigation of environmental impacts of products and services
EN28.	Percentage of products sold and their packaging materials that are reclaimed by category

continued on following page

Table 2. Continued

Compliance	
EN29.	Monetary value of significant fines and total number of non-monetary sanctions for non-compliance with environmental laws and regulations
Transport	
EN30.	Significant environmental impacts of transporting products and other goods and materials for the organization's operations, and transporting members of the workforce
Overall	
EN31.	Total environmental protection expenditures and investments by type
Supplier Environmental Assessment	
EN32.	Percentage of new suppliers that were screened using environmental criteria
EN33.	Significant actual and potential negative environmental impacts in the supply chain and actions taken
Environmental Grievance Mechanisms	
EN34.	Number of grievances about environmental impacts filed, addressed, and resolved through formal grievance mechanisms

Source: (GRI 4, 2013)

Figure 3. Non-financial indicators by categories
Source: (European Environment Agency, 2014)

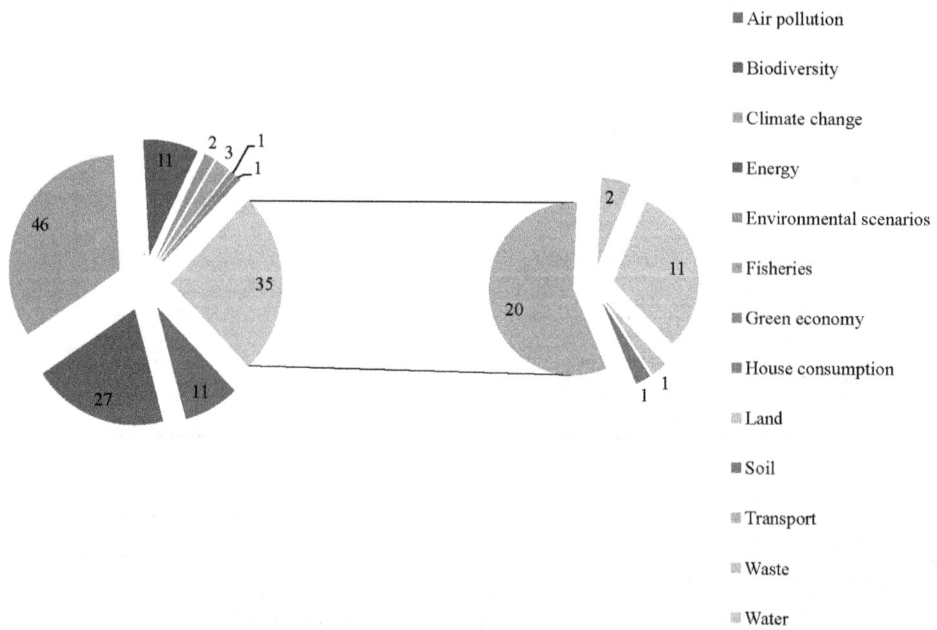

Social Indicators

Social indicators are the third set of sustainable development indicators (Table 3). For a very long time, these indicators have not been detailed, being integrated only in the practices of human resources departments. The need that has led to the development of social indicator systems has been to monitor and report

Table 3. Indicators of social performance - the "Working practices" category according to GRI

Labor Practices and Decent Work	
Employment	
LA1.	Total number and rates of new employee hires and employee turnover by age group, gender and region
LA2.	Benefits provided to full-time employees that are not provided to temporary or part-time employees, by significant locations of operation
LA3	Return to work and retention rates after parental leave, by gender
Labor/Management Relations	
LA4.	Minimum notice periods regarding operational changes, including whether these are specified in collective agreements
Occupational Health and Safety	
LA5.	Percentage of total workforce represented in formal joint management–worker health and safety committees that help monitor and advise on occupational health and safety programs
LA6.	Type of injury and rates of injury, occupational diseases, lost days, and absenteeism, and total number of work-related fatalities, by region and by gender
LA7.	Workers with high incidence or high risk of diseases related to their occupation
LA8.	Health and safety topics covered in formal agreements with trade unions
Training and Education	
LA9.	Average hours of training per year per employee by gender, and by employee category
LA10.	Programs for skills management and lifelong learning that support the continued employability of employees and assist them in managing career endings
LA11.	Percentage of employees receiving regular performance and career development reviews, by gender and by employee category
Diversity and Equal Opportunity	
LA12.	Composition of governance bodies and breakdown of employees per employee category according to gender, age group, minority group membership, and other indicators of diversity
Equal Remuneration for Women and Men	
LA13.	Ratio of basic salary and remuneration of women to men by employee category, by significant locations of operation
Supplier Assessment for Labor Practices	
LA14.	Percentage of new suppliers that were screened using labor practices criteria
LA15.	Significant actual and potential negative impacts for labor practices in the supply chain and actions taken
Labor Practices Grievance Mechanisms	
LA16.	Number of grievances about labor practices filed, addressed, and resolved through formal grievance mechanisms

Source: (GRI 4, 2013)

more adequately the social conditions and processes, the need to develop methods for quantification of these phenomena and to increase the capacity to collect and store data (Gârboan, 2007). In the scientific literature (Khan, Majid, Yasir, & Arshad, 2013; Spataru, Sasu, & Juravle, 2015) the distinction between the social dimensions of CSR refers to:

- Internal dimension refers to activities targeting the internal stakeholders of the economic entity (main indicators: human resource management, health and safety at work, business ethics, adaptation to change, organizational culture).

- Local external dimension, involving local stakeholders outside the organization (customers, local authorities, shareholders, investors, community, local NGOs).
- Global external dimension: human rights, global environmental concerns, security and health in the supply chain, global corporate citizenship, expressing the belief that it is not enough for economic entities to make social commitments only in relation to stakeholders, but they are becoming stakeholders with government and civil society.

Social indicators according to GRI refer to work-related practices (working conditions, personnel policy, managerial relations - employees, occupational health and safety, education and training, diversity and equal opportunities) (Table 3), human rights practices, freedom of association and collective bargaining, child labor, forced labor, community, corruption, etc. (Table 4).

Table 4. Indicators of social performance category "Human rights" according to GRI

Human Rights	
Investment	
HR1.	Total number and percentage of significant investment agreements and contracts that include human rights clauses or that underwent human rights screening
HR2.	Total hours of employee training on human rights policies or procedures concerning aspects of human rights that are relevant to operations, including the percentage of employees trained
Non-discrimination	
HR3.	Total number of incidents of discrimination and corrective actions taken
Freedom of Association and Collective Bargaining	
HR4.	Operations and suppliers identified in which the right to exercise freedom of association and collective bargaining may be violated or at significant risk, and measures taken to support these rights
Child Labor	
HR5.	Operations and suppliers identified as having significant risk for incidents of child labor, and measures taken to contribute to the effective abolition of child labor
Forced or Compulsory Labor	
HR6.	Operations and suppliers identified as having significant risk for incidents of forced or compulsory labor, and measures to contribute to the elimination of all forms of forced or compulsory labor
Security Practices	
HR7.	Percentage of security personnel trained in the organization's human rights policies or procedures that are relevant to operations
Indigenous Rights	
HR8.	Total number of incidents of violations involving rights of indigenous peoples and actions taken
Assessment	
HR9.	Total number and percentage of operations that have been subject to human rights reviews or impact assessments
Supplier Human Rights Assessment	
HR10.	Percentage of new suppliers that were screened using human rights criteria
HR11.	Significant actual and potential negative human rights impacts in the supply chain and actions taken
Human Rights Grievance Mechanisms	
HR12.	Number of grievances about human rights impacts filed, addressed, and resolved through formal grievance mechanisms

Source: (GRI 4, 2013)

Within the EU, fundamental human rights have become increasingly important and valuable, both for national and international governmental institutions and for the private environment, becoming "a hard core of defining features in which every Union citizen can recognize himself, regardless of the political and cultural differences related to national identity" (Commission of the European Communities, 2013). The main social performance indicators on human rights are presented in Table 4, grouped by reference categories (Investment, Non-discrimination, Child Labor, Forced or Compulsory Labor, Security Practices, Indigenous Rights, Assessment, Supplier Human Rights Assessment and Human Rights Grievance Mechanisms).

The benefits of social performance indicators on "human rights" come mainly from the potential for standardization, aggregation and comparability (in time and between companies) of human rights information. Quantification and presentation of viable indicators for business and for human rights could be useful for: economic entities wishing to manage their human rights risks and track their progress in implementing social responsibility standards; auditors who are required to verify the accuracy of human rights policies and diligence processes; governments willing to adopt evidence-based protection measures; local communities that are concerned with the human rights footprint of economic entities operating in their environment; human rights advocates who monitor the impact of human rights on corporative actors; researchers who are interested in exploring the influence factors of responsible corporate behavior (de Felice, 2015).

Table 5. Indicators of social performance category "Society" according to GRI

Society	
Local Communities	
SO1.	Percentage of operations with implemented local community engagement, impact assessments, and development programs
SO2.	Operations with significant actual and potential negative impacts on local communities
Anti-corruption	
SO3.	Total number and percentage of operations assessed for risks related to corruption and the significant risks identified
SO4.	Communication and training on anti-corruption policies and procedures
SO5.	Confirmed incidents of corruption and actions taken
Public Policy	
SO6.	Total value of political contributions by country and recipient/beneficiary
SO7.	Total number of legal actions for anti-competitive behavior, anti-trust, and monopoly practices and their outcomes
Compliance	
SO8.	Monetary value of significant fines and total number of non-monetary sanctions for non-compliance with laws and regulations
Supplier Assessment for Impacts on Society	
SO9.	Percentage of new suppliers that were screened using criteria for impacts on society
SO10.	Significant actual and potential negative impacts on society in the supply chain and actions taken
Grievance Mechanisms for Impacts on Society	
SO11.	Number of grievances about impacts on society filed, addressed, and resolved through formal grievance mechanisms

Source: (GRI 4, 2013)

Corporate reporting on human rights can be conducted by the entity's internal control system as it is clearly best placed to identify the entity's real human rights situation, the information being easily accessible and the figures generally standardized and can be aggregated for comparability.

More and more companies support their community through their donations. These direct contributions can make a significant contribution, for example, to the sustainable development of local infrastructures, such as schools and hospitals, as well as to help with natural disasters. They can help to comply with anti-corruption laws and relevant international standards, taking care not to participate in corruption. The basic measure to be measured in this respect is the number of law violations committed by a corporation because of corruption. This indicator can provide useful information to stakeholders on legal obligations and on internal control issues of the company that require attention.

Product safety is the responsibility of the economic entity that manufactures them, so products do not endanger the health or property of consumers. Product safety is regulated at the legislative level for certain product groups or general consumer safety legislation and can be demonstrated using tests and test results in accordance with standards published in the Official Journal of the European Union. Key factors in ensuring product safety are the transparency and traceability of raw materials and products in the procurement chain and the safety and quality criteria of products. Product´s specific risk assessments according to regulations and own quality control as well as any product-specific risks to obtain additional test and purchase information (Finnish Textile & Fashion, 2016) must be performed at the level of the economic entity. The social performance indicators in the "Product responsibility" category according to GRI are detailed in Table 6.

Table 6. Indicators of social performance category "Product responsibility" according to GRI

Product Responsibility	
Customer Health and Safety	
PR1.	Percentage of significant product and service categories for which health and safety impacts are assessed for improvement
PR2.	Total number of incidents of non-compliance with regulations and voluntary codes concerning the health and safety impacts of products and services during their life cycle, by type of outcomes
Product and Service Labeling	
PR3.	Type of product and service information required by the organization's procedures for product and service information and labeling, and percentage of significant product and service categories subject to such information requirements
PR4.	Total number of incidents of non-compliance with regulations and voluntary codes concerning product and service information and labeling, by type of outcomes
PR5.	Results of surveys measuring customer satisfaction
Marketing Communications	
PR6.	Sale of banned or disputed products
PR7.	Total number of incidents of non-compliance with regulations and voluntary codes concerning marketing communications, including advertising, promotion, and sponsorship, by type of outcomes
Customer Privacy	
PR8.	Total number of substantiated complaints regarding breaches of customer privacy and losses of customer data
Compliance	
PR9.	Monetary value of significant fines for non-compliance with laws and regulations concerning the provision and use of products and services

Source: (GRI 4, 2013)

The assessment of social and environmental performance provides at least the following benefits to economic entities: encourages entities to improve their social performance management; promotes transparency of social performance and social risks related to the activities carried out; provides a basis for making comparisons with other economic entities in the sector or international standards or legal regulations (where applicable); provides relevant information through social reporting to the various categories of stakeholders; attracts and promotes investments in economic entities with increased social performance.

SUSTAINABLE ECONOMIC INTELLIGENCE

The management of any economic entity needs reports on performance indicators, and their complexity increases with the size of the entity. Any economic entity that has a business volume that can not only be managed with the human factor is in the position to implement a computerized management system for critical activities (financial accounting, customer management, etc.) (Stefan, Duica, Coman, & Radu, 2010). Although the majority of economic operators do not usually ask their question whether computer systems can contribute to the sustainable performance of an economic entity, anyone can see that it favors efficiency and performance, all the more if integrated into the system financial and accounting information of the economic entity, and the integration of a sustainable information system at every entity will bring many future benefits. The key issue is the finality of these investments, which often do not generate value for many reasons: the lack of IT specialists, the lack of IT projects, the failure of developing IT budgets, the lack of interest of entities in organizing the IT function. Entities should invest more in integrated solutions, increase IT budget, and pay more attention to investing in Business Intelligence applications that enable the entity to respond to business requirements and act intelligently (D. M. Coman, & Coman, 2016). Fortunately, more and more economic entities are aware of the essentiality of sustainability for prosperity and their long-term survival, even if sustainability is a major challenge in overcoming boundaries and improving social, environmental, and economic aspects at both ICT and at the level of human activity (Bakshi, & Fiksel, 2003). When considering the sustainability of an economic entity, the following three dimensions must be taken into account: social, environmental and economic aspects (Figure 4). The integration of non-financial indicators into the entity's sustainability information system contributes both to the sustainable development of the entity and to the overall community in which it operates.

The digital era, in constant refinement, brings new impetus for healthy sustainable development and produces permanent changes in organizing and communicating sustainability reports. Worldwide, more and more IT developers have focused their attention on producing new certified software and tools to help customers gather and report on sustainable performance information. On the other hand, the interest of economic entities for such instruments is also increased, since the creation of these sustainable performance reports becomes important not only for reporting to state-owned institutions, but also for future business partners, suppliers or potential customers. There are already a multitude of software options on the global market for economic entities seeking sustainability reports.

The progress of on-line formats, the construction of new software for data collection and digital reporting contribute significantly to increasing the sustainable performance of economic entities. GRI has already launched its 2009 Certified Software and Tools Program to meet the needs of the interested economic entities. According to an international survey announced by GRI in January 2011, the number

Figure 4. Dimensions of the sustainable information system
Source: author's own processing

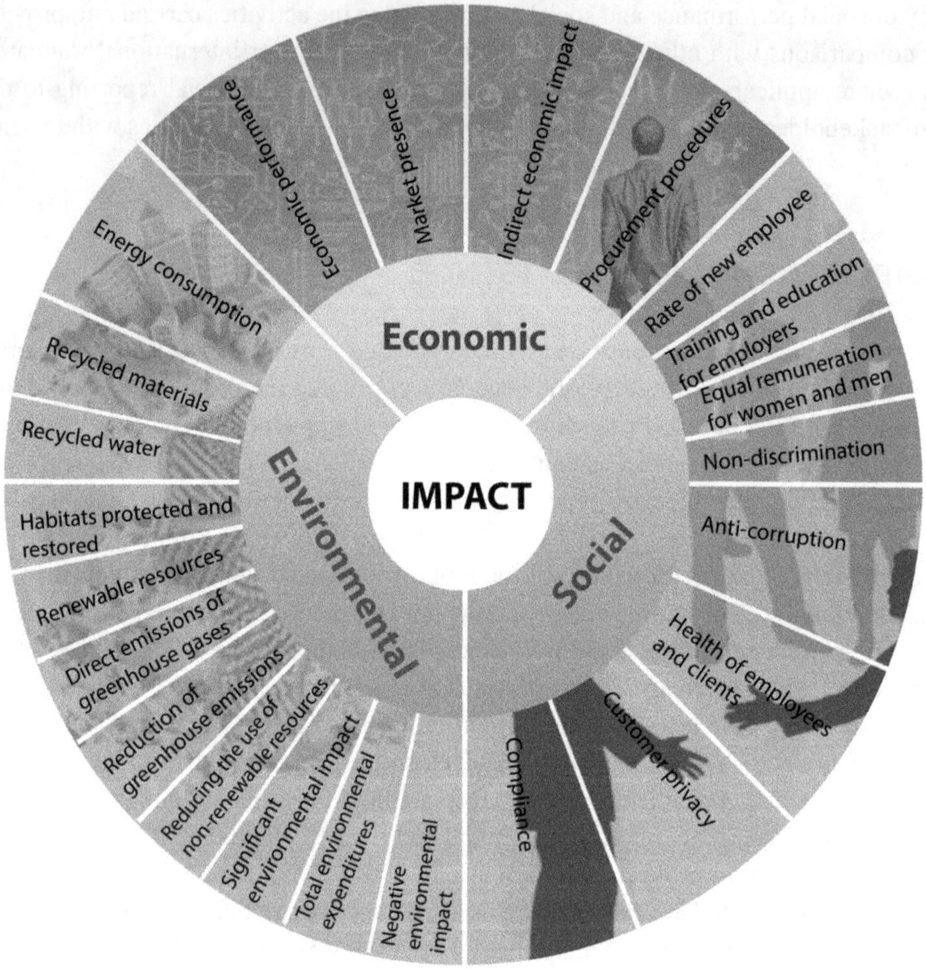

of economic entities using software to monitor sustainable performance increased by about 50% between 2006 and 2011(Global Reporting Initiative, 2010). In a sustainable smart economy, the following statements are considered to be valid: sustainability must be an integral part of the business strategy of any economic entity; sustainable performance management is integrated into the management system of any entity; the sustainable information system includes the three sustainable (economic, social and environmental) dimensions; sustainability information is an integral part of the economic entity.

CONCLUSION

While social responsibility issues are increasingly used at economic entity level and stakeholders are asking for more and more non-financial information, clear, concrete and concise guidelines for sustainability information are at the beginning. Non-financial information provides shareholders and other stakeholders with a more complete picture of the operations and business outcomes. Social responsibility reports are designed to understand the sustainable actions of the economic entity and the quality of its management. Transparency facilitates the adoption of investment decisions and generally allows governments and other actors to assess the contribution of an entity to economic and social development. If the requested additional information on social responsibility is more precise and concrete, the priority is to present relevant and comparable sustainable / non-financial reports.

Non-financial indicators have the role of measuring the level of production quality of an economic entity; the satisfaction of clients or employees; to assess the motivation of employees (strategic indicators). Strategic indicators help managers implement and manage specific medium-term strategies, while operational non-financial indicators, such as waste recycling rates or weekly promotional investment in an organic sales service, highlight day-to-day management. Non-financial indicators are supposed to reflect the company's strategy and performance axes that are recommended to work: customers, internal processes, or human resources. They are non-financial because they do not directly express the financial objective of the entity, as can be the case for profitability indicators, based on the result or turnover. Awareness of non-financial aspects, and in particular their link to economic growth and financial performance, is not a simple trend, but a profound change of paradigm, beginning in the years 1972 when the process of sustainable development is laid. Subsequently, in 2014, the European Parliament adopted a directive on the publication of non-financial information by large enterprises, which was transposed into the legislation of all EU Member States.

Most economic entities are aware of the need for accurate analysis of the potential for long-term value creation, backed by a relevant analysis of intangible assets management, risks and opportunities related to CSR policies and their potential environmental impact. Business model should provide greater consistency in their appreciation of the value of a company. Thus, identifying the risks and opportunities arising from social and social responsibility and the clear vision of investments made for the preservation and development of intangible assets prove to be the structural elements of trust that a business plan can give. Thus, combining financial and non-financial aspects within the same analysis can be fruitful to better assess the viability of a company. The difference between the two analyzes should gradually fade in favor of a more global vision of the determinants of performance. In the same way that integrated reporting aims at understanding the value-creation process in all its dimensions to the best, it is hoped that in the long run, the assessment of an economic entity will also be based on an integrated analysis.

REFERENCES

Accountancy Europe. (1999). *Review of International Accounting Standards for Environmental Issues.* Retrieved from https://www.accountancyeurope.eu/publications/review-of-international-accounting-standards-for-environmental-issues/

Adams, C. A., & McNicholas, P. (2007). Making a difference. *Accounting, Auditing & Accountability Journal, 20*(3), 382–402. doi:10.1108/09513570710748553

Albareda, L., Lozano, J. M., & Ysa, T. (2007). Public Policies on Corporate Social Responsibility: The Role of Governments in Europe. *Journal of Business Ethics, 74*(4), 391–407. doi:10.100710551-007-9514-1

AlphaBeta. (2017). *Valuing the SDG prize unlocking business opportunities to accelerate sustainable and inclusive growth a paper from AlphaBeta commissioned by the Business and Sustainable Development Commission*. Retrieved from http://s3.amazonaws.com/aws-bsdc/Valuing-the-SDG-Prize.pdf

Arnaud, P. (2003). L'information environnementale: Un enjeu à moyen terme pour toutes les entreprises. *Revue Francaise de Comptabilité, 356*, 32.

Bachelerie, V., & Boillet-Mongodin, J. (1993). Le traitement de l'environnement dans les rapport annuels. *Revue Francaise de Compatabilité, 246*, 79–85.

Bakshi, B., & Fiksel, J. (2003). The Quest for Sustainability: Challenges for Process Systems Engineering. *AIChE Journal. American Institute of Chemical Engineers, 49*(6), 1350–1358. Retrieved from http://eco-nomics.com/images/Quest_for_Sustainability.pdf. doi:10.1002/aic.690490602

Barbu, E., Feleaga, N., & Feleaga, L. (2011). Quelles norms IAS/IFRS utiliser pour le reporting environnementale? *Revue Francaise de Comptabilité, 440*, 24–27. Retrieved from http://www.bibliobaseonline.com/notice.php?NUMERO=107993&OLD=96279%7C98765%7C71417

Bartolomeo, M., Bennett, M., Bouma, J. J., Heydkamp, P., James, P., & Wolters, T. (2000). Environmental management accounting in Europe: current practice and future potential. *European Accounting Review,* 9(1), 31-52.

B&S Development Commission. (2017). *Better Business Better World, The report of the Business & Sustainable Development Commission*. Retrieved from http://report.businesscommission.org/uploads/BetterBiz-BetterWorld_170215_012417.pdf

Caraiani, C., Lungu, C. I., & Colceag, F. (2010). *Contabilitatea verde: strategii transdisciplinare către contabilitatea socială şi de mediu: studii şi cercetări*. Editura A.S.E. Retrieved from https://books.google.ro/books/about/Contabilitatea_verde.html?id=0vTCrQEACAAJ&redir_esc=y

Ciocoiu, C. N. (2011). Integrating Digital Economy and Green Economy: opportunities for sustainable development. *Theoretical and Empirical Researches in Urban Management, 6*(1). Retrieved from http://um.ase.ro/no61/3.pdf

Coman, D. M., & Coman, M. D. (2016). The impact of Information Technology on the Company's Financial-Accounting System. *Valahian Journal of Economic Studies, 7*(21), 65–70. Retrieved from https://search.proquest.com/docview/1950619900/fulltextPDF/C16423FE01D2401FPQ/1?accountid=17263

Coman, M. D., Ionescu, C. A., & Lixandru, M. (2019). Romanian Economy between Linearity and Circularity. A Bioeconomic Perspective. In *Communicative Action & Trandisciplinarity in the Ethical Society* (pp. 59–72). LUMEN.

Commission of the European Communities. (2013). *Communication from the Commission to the Council and the European Parliament on Article 7 of the Treaty on European Union. Respect for and promotion of the values on which the union is based.* Brussels, Belgium. Retrieved from http://ec.europa.eu/transparency/regdoc/rep/1/2003/EN/1-2003-606-EN-F1-1.Pdf

Cucui, G., Ionescu, C., Goldbach, I., Coman, M., & Marin, , E. (2018). Quantifying the Economic Effects of Biogas Installations for Organic Waste from Agro-Industrial Sector. *Sustainability*, *10*(7), 2582. doi:10.3390u10072582

Daub, C.-H. (2007). Assessing the quality of sustainability reporting: An alternative methodological approach. *Journal of Cleaner Production*, *15*(1), 75–85. doi:10.1016/j.jclepro.2005.08.013

de Felice, D. (2015). Challenges and opportunities in the production of business and human rights indicators to measure the corporate responsibility to respect. *Human Rights Quarterly*, *37*(2). Retrieved from https://kopernio.com/viewer?doi=10.1353/hrq.2015.0031&route=7. doi:10.1353/hrq.2015.0031

Dhaliwal, D. S., Li, O. Z., Tsang, A., & Yang, Y. G. (2011). Voluntary Nonfinancial Disclosure and the Cost of Equity Capital: The Initiation of Corporate Social Responsibility Reporting We appreciate the valuable comments from. *The Accounting Review*, *86*(1), 59–100. doi:10.2308/accr.00000005

Dvořáková, L., & Zborková, J. (2014). Integration of Sustainable Development at Enterprise Level. *Proceedia Engineering*, *69*, 686–695. Retrieved from https://kopernio.com/viewer?doi=10.1016/j.proeng.2014.03.043&route=6

Ellen Macarthur Foundation. (2015). *Growth within: a circular economy vision for a competitive Europe*. Retrieved from https://www.ellenmacarthurfoundation.org/assets/downloads/publications/EllenMacArthurFoundation_Growth-Within_July15.pdf

Epstein, M. J., & Manzoni, J.-F. (1997). The Balanced Scorecard and Tableau de Bord: Translating strategy into action. *Management Accounting*, *79*(2), 28–37.

European Commission. (2001a). *Commission Recommendation of 30 May 2001 on the recognition, measurement and disclosure of environmental issues in the annual accounts and annual reports of companies, 2001/453/EC*. Retrieved from https://eur-lex.europa.eu/LexUriServ/LexUriServ.do?uri=OJ:L:2001:156:0033:0042:EN:PDF

European Commission. (2001b). *GREEN PAPER Promoting a European framework for Corporate Social Responsibility*. Retrieved from http://ec.europa.eu/transparency/regdoc/rep/1/2001/EN/1-2001-366-EN-1-0.Pdf

European Commission. (2018). *A sustainable Bioeconomy for Europe: strengthening the connection between economy, society and the environment Updated Bioeconomy Strategy*. Brussels, Belgium.

European Commission. (2018). *A Clean Planet for all A European strategic long-term vision for a prosperous, modern, competitive and climate neutral economy*. Retrieved from https://ec.europa.eu/clima/sites/clima/files/docs/pages/com_2018_733_en.pdf

European Commission. (2019). *Towards a sustainable Europe by 2030*. Retrieved from https://ec.europa.eu/commission/sites/beta-political/files/rp_sustainable_europe_30-01_en_web.pdf

European Environment Agency. (2014). Digest of EEA indicators 2014. Copenhagen, Denmark.

European Parliament. (2014). Directive 2014/95/EU of the European Parliament and the Council of 22 October 2014 - amending Directive 2013/34/EU as regards disclosure of non-financial and diversity information by certain large undertakings and groups. *Official Journal of the European Union, L, 330.* Retrieved from https://eur-lex.europa.eu/legal-content/EN/TXT/PDF/?uri=CELEX:32014L0095&from=EN

Fifka, M. S. (2013). Corporate Responsibility Reporting and its Determinants in Comparative Perspective - a Review of the Empirical Literature and a Meta-analysis. *Business Strategy and the Environment, 22*(1), 1–35. doi:10.1002/bse.729

Finnish Textile & Fashion. (2016). *Guidelines and insight for corporate responsibility work Responsible management Putting principles into practice Corporate responsibility manual.* Helsinki, Finland. Retrieved from https://s3-eu-west-1.amazonaws.com/stjm/uploads/20160622103146/STJM_Corporate_responsibility_manual.pdf

Fuente, J. A., García-Sánchez, I. M., & Lozano, M. B. (2017). The role of the board of directors in the adoption of GRI guidelines for the disclosure of CSR information. *Journal of Cleaner Production, 141*, 737–750. doi:10.1016/j.jclepro.2016.09.155

Gârboan, R. (2007). Indicatori utilizaţi în evaluare şi monitorizare: Indicatorii sociali. *Transylvanian Review of Administrative Sciences, 19*, 34–42. Retrieved from http://www.rtsa.ro/rtsa/index.php/rtsa/article/view/158

Gloaguen, P. (2012). *Le guide de l'intelligence économique.* Retrieved from http://www.eure.gouv.fr/content/download/5022/30562/file/Le guide du routard - Intelligence Economique - 2012.pdf

Global Reporting Initiative. (2010). *A new phase: the growth of sustainability reporting.* Amsterdam, The Netherlands. Retrieved from www.globalreporting.org

Global Reporting Initiative. (2014). *G4 Sector Disclosures: Event organizers.* Retrieved from https://www.globalreporting.org/information/sector-guidance/Pages/default.aspx

Global Reporting Initiative. (n.d.). GRI Standards Download Center. Retrieved from https://www.globalreporting.org/standards/gri-standards-download-center/

Hąbek, P., & Wolniak, R. (2016). Relationship between Management Practices and Quality of CSR Reports. *Procedia: Social and Behavioral Sciences, 220*, 115–123. doi:10.1016/j.sbspro.2016.05.475

Harbulot, C. (2007). *La main invisible des puissances.* Paris, France: Ellipses.

Haydaroglu, C. (2015). Final version of capitalism: Economic intelligence in Knowledge Economy. *Journal of Economics, Finance and Accounting, 2*(1), 89–106.

Heemskerk, B., Group, R., Stmicroelectronics, P. P., & Scicluna, M. (2002). *Striking the balance Sustainable development reporting.* Retrieved from https://docs.wbcsd.org/2002/12/SustainableDevReporting-StrikingTheBalance.pdf

Husillos, J., González, C. L., & Álvarez, G, M. J. (2011). The emergence of triple bottom line reporting in Spain. *Revista Española de Financiación y Contabilidad, XI*(150), 195–219. Retrieved from https://kopernio.com/viewer?doi=10.1080/02102412.2011.10779701&route=7. doi:10.1080/02102412.2011.10779701

Ienciu, I. A. (2009). *Implicaţiile problemelor de mediu în contabilitatea şi auditul situaţiilor financiare.* Cluj Napoca: Risoprint. Retrieved from https://scholar.google.com/scholar?hl=en&as_sdt=0%2C5&q=Ionel+Ienciu+%282009%29+Implicaţiile+problemelor+de+mediu+în+contabilitatea+şi+auditul+situaţiilor+financiare.+Cluj+Napoca%3A+Risoprint.&btnG=

Institute for Economics and Peace. (2015). *Global peace index 2015, Measuring peace, its causes and its economic value.* Retrieved from http://economicsandpeace.org/wp-content/uploads/2015/06/Global-Peace-Index-Report-2015_0.pdf

International Auditing Practice Statements (IAPS). (2010). *The Consideration of Environmental Matters in the Audit of Financial Statements.* Retrieved from http://www.ifac.org/system/files/downloads/b007-2010-iaasb-handbook-iaps-1010.pdf

Interpretations on the G4 Guidelines. (n.d.). Retrieved from https://www.globalreporting.org/resourcelibrary/grig4-part1-reporting-principles-and-standard-disclosures.pdf

Istrate, C., Georgescu, I. E., Carp, M., Robu, I. B., & Pavaloaia, L. (2015). Accruals Earnings Management in Emerging Markets under the Transition to IFRS: The Case of Romanian Listed Companies. *Transformations in Business & Economics, 14*(2A), 393–411. Retrieved from https://www.researchgate.net/profile/Ioan-Bogdan_Robu/publication/290820080_Accruals_earnings_management_in_emerging_markets_under_the_transition_to_IFRS_The_case_of_Romanian_listed_companies/links/569bfd7708aea147695466b8.pdf

Istrate, C., Robu, I.-B., Păvăloaia, L., & Herghiligiu, I. V. (2017). Analysis of companies sustainability under the influence of environmental information disclosure. *Environmental Engineering and Management Journal, 16*(4), 957–967. doi:10.30638/eemj.2017.097

James, M. L. (2015). The benefits of sustainability and integrated reporting: an investigation of accounting majors' perceptions. *Journal of Legal, Ethical and Regulatory Issues, 18*(1), 1–20. Retrieved from https://search.proquest.com/docview/1693348218/fulltextPDF/443A5B498B0480EPQ/1?accountid=17263

Khan, M., Majid, A., Yasir, M., & Arshad, M. (2013). Corporate social responsibility and corporate reputation: A case of cement industry in Pakistan. *Interdisciplinary Journal of Contemporary Research in Business, 5*(1), 843–857. Retrieved from https://www.researchgate.net/publication/318359266

Koerber, C. P. (2010). Corporate Responsibility Standards: Current Implications and Future Possibilities for Peace Through Commerce. *Journal of Business Ethics, 89*(S4), 461–480. doi:10.100710551-010-0397-1

Lavrinenko, O., Ohotina, A., Ignatjeva, S., Rybalkin, O., & Lazdans, D. (2019). Entrepreneurship and sustainability issues the role of green economy in sustainable development (case study: the EU states). *Entrepreneurship and Sustainability, 6*(3), 1113–1126.

Lock, I., & Seele, P. (2016). The credibility of CSR (corporate social responsibility) reports in Europe. Evidence from a quantitative content analysis in 11 countries. *Journal of Cleaner Production, 122*, 186–200. doi:10.1016/j.jclepro.2016.02.060

Margarit, S. G., Bran, S., Ionescu, E., & Boca, R. (2012). Coverage of environmental information in annual financial statements in a responsible manner. *Procedia-Social and Behavioral Sciences, 62*, 526–530.

Marimon, F., del Mar Alonso-Almeida, M., del Pilar Rodríguez, M., & Alejandro, K. A. C. (2012). The worldwide diffusion of the global reporting initiative: what is the point? *Journal of Cleaner Production, 33*, 132–144.

Martre, H. (1994). *Intelligence économique et strategie des entreprises*. Retrieved from http://www.bdc.aege.fr

Michelon, G., Pilonato, S., & Ricceri, F. (2015). CSR reporting practices and the quality of disclosure: An empirical analysis. *Critical Perspectives on Accounting, 33*, 59–78. doi:10.1016/j.cpa.2014.10.003

Milne, M. J., & Gray, R. (2013). W(h)ither Ecology? The Triple Bottom Line, the Global Reporting Initiative, and Corporate Sustainability Reporting. *Journal of Business Ethics, 118*(1), 13–29. doi:10.100710551-012-1543-8

Neu, D., Warsame, H., & Pedwell, K. (1998). Managing public impressions: Environmental disclosures in annual reports. *Accounting, Organizations and Society, 23*(3), 265–282. Retrieved from https://www.sciencedirect.com/science/article/pii/S0361368297000081. doi:10.1016/S0361-3682(97)00008-1

Nicolau, C. M. (2010). Operaţionalizare şi delimitare conceptuală a inteligenţei economice. *Studia Universitatis Vasile Goldiş. Arad-Seria Ştiinţe Economice, 20*(1), 436–444.

Niculescu, M. (2005). *Diagnostic financiar*. Bucuresti, Romania: Editura Economica.

Oncioiu, I., Căpuşneanu, S., Türkeş, M., Topor, D., Constantin, D.-M., & Marin-Pantelescu, A. … Ştefan Hint, M. (2018). The Sustainability of Romanian SMEs and Their Involvement in the Circular Economy. *Sustainability, 10*(8), 2761.

Palenberg, M., Reinicke, W., & Witte, J. M. (2006). *Trends in non-financial reporting*. Retrieved from www.gppi.net

Panayiotou, N. A., Aravossis, K. G., & Moschou, P. (2009). A New Methodology Approach for Measuring Corporate Social Responsibility Performance. *Water Air and Soil Pollution Focus, 9*(1-2), 129–138. doi:10.100711267-008-9204-8

Quairel, F. (2004). Responsable mais pas comptable: analyse de la normalisation des rapports environnementaux et sociaux. *Comptabilité - Contrôle - Audit, 10*(1), 7.

Schaltegger, S., Bennett, M., & Burritt, R. (2006). Sustainability Accounting and Reporting: Development, Linkages and Reflection. An Introduction. In *Sustainability Accounting and Reporting* (pp. 1–33). The Netherlands: Springer.

Schaltegger, S., & Burrit, R. (2005). *Contemporary Environmental Accounting: Issues, Concepts and Practice*. Austin, TX: Greenleaf Publishing.

Schmidt-Traub, G. (2015). *Investment Needs to Achieve the Sustainable Development Goals Understanding the Billions and Trillions*. Retrieved from http://unsdsn.org/resources/publications/sdg-investment-needs/.1

Spataru, G. C., Sasu, C., & Juravle, A. I. (2015). Occupational safety and health-vector of corporate social responsibility in Romanian companies Empirical study. *Management Intercultural,* 34, 383–390. Retrieved from http://www.who.int

Stefan, V., Duica, M., Coman, M., & Radu, V. (2010). Enterprise Performance Management with Business Intelligence Solution. In *Proc. 4th WSEAS International Conference on BUSINESS ADMINISTRATION (ICBA'10)* (pp. 244–250). World Scientific and Engineering Academy and Society. Retrieved from http://bit.ly/adIRl0

Târțiu, V. E., Ștefănescu, M., Petrache, A.-M., & Gurau, C. R. (2019). *Tranziția către o economie circulară. De la managementul deșeurilor la o economie verde în România Autori*. (Institutul European din România, Ed.). Bucharest, Romania. Retrieved from www.ier.gov.ro

Topor, D., Capusneanu, S., & Tamas, A. S. (2017). Efficient Green Control (Egc) Encouraging Environmental Investment And Profitability. *Journal of Environmental Protection and Ecology, 18*(1), 191–201. Retrieved from https://www.researchgate.net/profile/Sorinel_Capusneanu/project/Green-controlling/attachment/592c1d6b82999cd4856f3382/AS:499339991502848@1496063339417/download/Articol_4_JEPE_En.pdf?context=projectUpdateDetail

United Nations. (1997). *Environmental Financial Accounting and Reporting at the Corporate Level.* Retrieved from https://unctad.org/en/docs/isa15d2.pdf

Wolniak, R., & Hąbek, P. (2016). Quality Assessment of CSR Reports – Factor Analysis. *Procedia: Social and Behavioral Sciences, 220,* 541–547. doi:10.1016/j.sbspro.2016.05.530

World Commission on Environment and Development. (1987). *Report of the World Commission on Environment and Development: Our Common Future* (Transmitted to the General Assembly as an Annex to document A/42/427 - Development and International Co-operation: Environment).

Chapter 10
The Aspects of Leadership Development in the Digital Economy

Lavinia Essen
University of Lapland, Finland

ABSTRACT

The economic environment of the Digital Age, characterized by the acceleration of technology innovation, fierce competition in gaining competitive advantage, increasing consumer expectations, and emerging market pressure, leads leadership to adapt Vision and Entity Strategy to new performance standards. Thereby, Leadership is the key active force that motivates and coordinates an organization to accomplish its objectives. A leader creates a vision for the others and then directs them towards achieving that vision. To be a leader, you must have followers who have confidence in you and who give you their support and commitment to a goal. The objective of this chapter is to demonstrate the role of contemporary leader in the digital economy.

INTRODUCTION

Numerous people think that leadership and management have the same meaning, but in fact they are different (Lazear, Saiz-Alvarez, Coduras, & Cuervo-Arango, 2013). Leadership is the key active force that motivates and coordinates an organization to accomplish its objectives (Sarasvathy, 2001). A leader creates a vision for the others and then directs them towards achieving that vision. To be a leader you must have followers who have confidence in you and who give you their support and commitment to a goal (Alvarez, & Barney, 2005). On the other hand, management is the process of getting things done, effectively and efficiently, through and with other people (Douglas, & Shepherd, 1997).

Managers deal with difficulty through planning and budgeting (Gaglio, & Katz, 2001). They put goals, determine how to meet those goals and gather resources to meet those goals. Leaders start with the vision and put strategies to meet this vision (Saiz-Alvarez, 2015). Managers organize and staff their employees to meet their goals. They create jobs to achieve the requirement of plans. Leaders try to recruit

DOI: 10.4018/978-1-7998-1005-6.ch010

and keep the employees who participate their vision. Finally, managers control the employees' behaviour to ensure that employees meet the goals (Baron, 2007).

Some contemporary motivation issues facing today's leaders include motivating a diversified workforce, pay for performance programs, motivating minimum wage employees, motivating professional and technical employees, and flexible work schedule options (Saiz-Alvarez, 2018).

Management needs to think in terms of flexibility to motivate a diversified workforce. For instance, studies tell us that men place considerably more importance on autonomy in their jobs than do women (Anna, Chandler, Jansen, & Mero, 2000; Johnson, 1990). In contrast, the opportunity to learn, good interpersonal relations, and convenient work hours are more important to women than to men. Managers need to recognize that the motivation of a single mother with two dependent children, who are working full time to support her family, may be quite different from the needs of a young, single part time worker or the needs of the older employee who is working to supplement his or her pension income. Employees have different personal needs and goals that they're hoping to satisfy through their jobs (Audretsch, 2003).

However, it is also important to look at the fact that doing a job that is the same day in and day out can become quite boring (Silva, 2007). When employees are given a job with different tasks and ability to grow, they tend to stay more motivated. Unfortunately, many workers are unused and do not get challenged or the ability to show their creativity to its potential. Leaders can motivate their work force by improving design of jobs, empowerment, assess fairness through the implementation of the equity theory and finally by implementing a quality of work life by providing safe and healthy environment and fair treatment of their workforce and designing a psychological contract that is used in exchange for the employees' contributions (Wagner, 2003).

This chapter discusses the coordination and motivational aspects of leadership. Two research questions have been selected: What are the coordination aspects of leadership development? and What are the motivational aspects of contemporary leadership development?

BACKGROUND

A review of the leadership literature shows an evolving sequence of schools of thought from Great Man and Trait theories to "Transformational" leadership (Barnes, Dang, Leavitt, Guarana, & Uhlmann, 2018). Although early theories focused on the characteristics and behaviors of successful leaders, later theories begin to consider the role of followers and the related nature of leadership (Drucker,1985; Gnyawali, & Fogel, 1994).

One of the first studies of leadership behaviour explore three leadership styles: autocratic, democratic, and laissez-faire (Schumpeter, 1942; Schumpeter, 1934; Kirzner, 1979).

Autocratic style where a leader has centralized authority, state work methods, makes independent decisions, and puts limit on employee's participation.

Democratic style where the leader involves his employees in the decision making, share his authority with employees, and share the decision making with his subordinates. Democratic style is divided into two other styles, consultative and participative.

Laissez-faire style where the leader gives complete freedom to his employees to do their job and make decisions. Laissez-faire leader basically provide material to employees and answer questions only.

On the other hand, to promote empowerment, leaders must create an environment in which employees feel that they have influence over performance and effective in the areas of their responsibility (Thorton,

& Yang, 2012). By empowering employees, leaders should expect some problems, at least in the short term because of the change and change takes time for employees to adopt to the new roles (Shane, & Venkataraman, 2000). People might make mistakes at first, because of lack of training and more training is needed, the cost are going to be higher because higher skills employees make great contribution to the organization and demand higher wages (Schultz, 1980). Table 1 will illustrate the leadership theories in order (Bula, 2012).

Three contemporary approaches have been emerged lately: charismatic leadership, visionary leadership, and entrepreneurial leadership (Saiz-Alvarez, Coduras, & Cuervo-Arango, 2014; Velilla, Molina, & Ortega, 2018).

A Charismatic leader is one who provides an environment full of energy and positive reinforcement. Charismatic leaders encourage others and inspire them to be their best. Group members and employees want to impress a charismatic leader, so they work hard and strive to succeed. Under charismatic leadership, group members may view success in relation to their leaders. A group success tends to center on the leader that is a major problem with charismatic leadership. The charismatic leader is the glue that holds a group together. So, what happens if the leader should have to step down or transfer? Normally, the group dynamic will fizzle and individual members will lose enthusiasm.

Visionary leadership is the ability to create and articulate a realistic, credible attractive vision of the future for an organization or organizational unit that grows out of an improves on the present. Visionary leaders characterized by his ability to clarify his vision in term of actions and goals verbally. Second is

Table 1. Leadership theories and the main subject of each theory

Leadership Theory(ies)	Main Subject
Great man Theories	Based on the belief that leaders are extraordinary people, born with great qualities and destined to lead. The use of this term 'Man' was intentional since until the later part of the twentieth century leadership was thought of as a concept which is primarily male, military and western. This led to the next school of trait theory
Trait Theories	The list of traits qualities associated with leadership exists in abundance and continues to be produced. They draw on virtually all the adjectives in the dictionary which describes some positive or virtuous human attribute, from ambition to zest for life
Behaviourist Theories	These concentrate on what leaders actually do rather than on their qualities, different patterns of behaviour are observed and categorised as styles of leadership. This theory attracted most attention from practising managers
Situational Leadership	This approach sees leadership as specific to the situation in which it is being exercised. For example, whilst some situations may require an autocratic style, others may need a more participative approach. It also proposes that there may be differences in leadership styles at different levels in the same organisation
Contingency Theory	This is a refinement of the situational viewpoint and focuses on identifying the situational variables which best predict the most appropriate or effective leadership style to fit the circumstances
Transactional theory	This approach emphasises the importance of the relationship between leader and follower, focusing on the mutual benefits derived from a form of 'contract' through which the leader delivers such things as rewards or recognition in return for the commitment or loyalty of the followers
Transformational theory	The concept here is change and the role of leadership in envisioning and implementing the transformation of organisational performance

the ability to express his vision through his behavior. Finally, the ability to extend his vision to different leadership context.

Entrepreneurial leadership the entrepreneur has certain leadership responsibility in the organization (Stephan, Uhlaner, & Stride, 2015). Today's successful entrepreneur must be like the leader of a jazz ensemble that excels in improvisation, innovation, and creativity. Drawing out the best of other individuals even given the unpredictability of the situation (Agboli & Ukaegbu, 2006).

Later studies of leadership styles showed mixed results (Saiz-Alvarez, 2018; Velilla, Molina, & Ortega, 2018). For example, democratic style sometimes created higher performance level than autocratic style of leadership, but at other times they created group performance that was lower than or equal to that of autocratic style.

IMPLICATIONS OF GLOBAL PERSPECTIVE OF ENTREPRENEURSHIP

Fundamental to the achievement of entrepreneurial success, in the view of the author of this chapter, is the technological idea, closely related to its degree of commercial innovation. The degree of innovation is closely correlated with the size of the profit this entrepreneur can get it. Thus, it can be assumed that an entrepreneur who purchases the factors of production on the market, including the technological idea, will obtain a profit that can not exceed the natural rate of profit in that economy. The most researchers also fall into one of the common mistakes made by theoreticians in social sciences, namely to make a parallel between social and biological processes (Saiz-Alvarez, Muñiz, & Huezo, 2016; Aldrich, 2011; Ireland, Hitt, & Sirmon, 2003).

The essence of entrepreneurial spirit is the speculative nature of the extent to which the action of the human individual, in a broader sense, by bearing present costs, aims at satisfying future desires as the most intense (Cuervo et al., 2007). The temporal element necessary for human action and the implicit risk of action in time disappears from models that consider economics in a state of equilibrium, and consequently the role of the entrepreneur is not visible: entrepreneurial judgments are the substitute in the world real forecasts by producers in static equilibrium models (Frese, & Gielnik, 2014).

Gaglio's (1997) approach seeks to identify a set of environmental factors that correlate with a set of human factors to explain where complex contracts depending on a set of events subsequent to their signing are onerous to be negotiated, applied. In the face of these difficulties, the firm may decide to avoid the market and make use of the internal arrangements for the transaction. But this analysis, although seemingly rational, frizzes a functionalist and behavioral approach to human behavior which, under the same conditions, is supposed to have the same reaction. Objectives and subjective judgments of value of individuals and entrepreneurs do not take place in such an analysis but in terms of their rationality.

The idea that companies spend all the resources by ignoring the relative structure of prices on the market is completely erroneous or can only be valid for some entrepreneurs who do not aim to obtain the profit from the activity they are doing (Ahmad, & Seymour, 2008). Equally ignorant of the market prices may be an individual who initiates a market transaction.

First, any business is subject to the final profit test. If the shooter receives a financial loss, it is obvious that the allocation of resources was wrong. If the result is positive, it appears that the allocation of resources by the entrepreneur was more efficient than other entrepreneurs than the relative structure of the prices of all inputs and outputs on the market. This structure, however, always the term of comparison and the way of establishing the profits of entrepreneurship.

Entrepreneurial action always requires an innovative technological idea and the degree of innovation can be defined in a broad sense (Shepherd, & Patzelt, 2011). If this is not the case, it is likely that the profit margin would not be higher than the normal profit in the economy or the extraordinary profit would be in the short term. The entrepreneur who buys all the inputs on the market does not make any contribution to the combination of these resources, at least technologically, is likely to get in just the natural rate of interest. Getting a higher profit than this natural rate of interest implies a new technological idea, which may well be those who view this activity as an arbitrary allocation of resources.

An entrepreneur who sells his services is not an entrepreneur in the sense used by Knight but is a manager (Feeser, & Dugan, 1989). The entrepreneur becomes in this case the one who buys the services of that entrepreneur. Secondly, those employees who are paid a fraction of the profits become entrepreneurs in the broad sense because the rewarding of the production factor that they have the labor is no longer realized by present salary goods but by the side of uncertain future profit. These employees bring their own professional skills to their business and are rewarded with a share of profit. If the profit is 0, it is obvious that they will not be rewarded and will even bear losses that are of an entrepreneurial nature.

Thus, Kirzner (1979) offers an argument that will later see a significant development in company growth theory. Companies grow when entrepreneurs internalize previously traded transactions through the market and decrease when outsourcers outsource transactions that they previously coordinated within firms. Thus, by hierarchically allocating resources within the firm, the entrepreneurs manage to save existing trading costs due to the operation of those transactions through the market. The saving of these transaction costs is the main motivation to extend the limits of organizations to the detriment of market trades.

Another perspective opened by Coase later developed into what is called the theory of incomplete contracts (Stevenson, & Jarillo, 1990). Observing that the more a contract for the supply of products or services over a longer period of time is, the less likely and less desirable, to specify what is expected of at the time of signing the contract. Thus, the two parties may agree only to broadly specify their obligations, and then to set out in more detail what is expected of each. To the extent that the behavior of one of the parties is influenced / directed by the other, the inclination for integration and hence the exercise of control is obvious. Given that short-term market-specific short-term contracts are insufficient, a form of integration is more likely.

Perhaps the most revolutionary view in Schumpter's writings is the idea that one did not need to be rich in order to have the opportunity to start as an entrepreneur/innovator (Scheinberg, & McMillan, 1988). Schumpter (1911, 1997) stated that someone else's could equally support by his own wealth as well as an entrepreneur. If they are supported by their own wealth, then the entrepreneur actually fulfills two jobs: he is the banker and the entrepreneur at the same time. In any event, it is the banker not the entrepreneur, whether the two are the same or not, who truly bears the fruit of the financial risk pertaining to any innovation. Schumpter's theory was the first to treat innovation as an ingenious process. He turned down the predominant paradigm of an entrepreneur as a manager of the firm and replaced it with the alternative that the entrepreneur is the leader and innovator, or what Schumpter called the "primary mover of the economic system." Schumpter integrated the dynamics of technology into the business process when he defined the entrepreneur as an innovator. Schumpter's main contribution was a word picture that he offered in the above-mentioned book where he contrasted two worlds. The first was a world without the entrepreneur and with the circular flow of processes and technologies. In this picture Schumpter painted a static, repetitive process where everyday was the same as the one before and every firm in an industry was like the next one.

The second world was one where the entrepreneur entered the stage (Hébert, & Link, 1989). By seeking an opportunity for profit, the entrepreneur introduces new economic combinations or innovations to reach his goal. This innovative capacity of the entrepreneur was seen as the prime endogenous cause of change or "the development of new economic systems." New combinations destroy the equilibrium of the economy (the circular flow) and create a new equilibrium. Continuous innovation therefore implies permanent change and permanent equilibrium readjustment. Perhaps more so than any other economist, Schumpter realized there was an age to come where the only constant would be constant discontent of the economic process.

Schumpter (1942) does not necessarily view the entrepreneur as the director or independent owner of a business. An entrepreneur can be any person who carries out a new economic combination and tries out new possibilities in order to achieve innovation. In most cases, the one who ends up producing these new combinations does not necessarily carry them out. Often the people who are already engaged in the production process have a natural tendency to fight innovation because innovation typically destroys their equilibrium process.

The complex task of forecasting and providing direction and control to the factors of production at the same time is concentrated on a narrow class of economic agents: the entrepreneurs (Carroll, & Khessina, (2005). In a sense, business decisions are never concrete calculated probabilities. With time and experience, the entrepreneur will specialize in directing, controlling, and bearing uncertainty while locating other economic agents to furnish him with the necessary productive services needed in exchange for a fixed fee. In that sense, other economic agents will not bear any of the uncertainty (changing technology, changing consumer preferences, or changing purchasing power) since the entrepreneur bears it all.

In Silva's view, the other major contribution by the entrepreneur is overall economic progress. In pursuing his/her goals, the entrepreneur will invariably improve the existing technologies and business organizations. In that context, entrepreneurs are the bottlenecks of economic growth: they determine the rate at which the economy grows and the new technologies that evolve. In addition, the entrepreneur is responsible for guaranteeing the pre-agreed remuneration to all interested parties in the firm (Silva, 2007).

The Austrian view of the world economy differs significantly from the standard view of the economist (Woo, Cooper, & Dunkelberg, 1988). The neo-classical economist views the worldwide economic system in a general equilibrium, while the neo-Austrian economists see the world economy from a "dynamics of discovery" point of view. That is, the world economy is almost never at an equilibrium position since it is in a constant dynamism with constant changes. This, in their view, gives rise to constant opportunities for making pure profit. Omitting such opportunities arises only from what neo-Austrian economists coined "utter ignorance:" an unawareness of basic economic information.

Regarding the Chicago and Austrian traditions, Lazear (2004) also notes the mistaken use of political and military terminology in politics: if this idiom would be just an innocent metaphor, it would not need his criticism. But he is the source of serious errors that play a sinister role in contemporary doctrines. The economic calculation specific to the entrepreneurial action does not require the establishment of a hierarchy to be put into practice. The entrepreneur will carry out his work according to the economic calculation he will translate into the transactions he runs through the market. It is obvious that all the exchanges in the market where an entrepreneur engages are made after a certain plan and they all compete for the achievement of a certain objective. The idea that only in a hierarchy can be organized production is free and is such a parallel wrong with military and political activity.

Discovery of profit-making opportunities is not accidental, but is stimulated by the prospect of personal reward. Therefore, the entrepreneur is either by nature (intrinsic motivation) or profit incentive the most alert member of the economic society. This view of entrepreneurship underpins theories and policies of economic development that include location theory, human resource development, and financing. Once outside of the interlocking modern theory of the firm, economic development makes great use of entrepreneurial decision-making. Much of this depends upon the sociological aspects of entrepreneurship.

Moreover, another tool of economic analysis, much used by some economists, is that of game theory (Astebro, & Thompson, 2009; Sijbom, Janssen, & Van Yperen, 2015). However, the parallel between human and game behavior is absolutely simplistic, deterministic and reductive, creating at the same time the impression of a closed system in which, ex ante, the decision tree is given.

However, the concept of information asymmetry starts with a hypothesis that strikes a balance: the idea that between all operators on the market there must be an informational parity, that is, each of the same information, indifferent of its quality. Thus, both insiders and outsiders should have the same information at all times (Islam, 2015).

The information asymmetry exists, according to Mariotti and Glackin (2010), when the true circumstances characterizing a transaction or set of transactions are known by one or more parties but can not be obtained or identified by others at no cost. The information asymmetry, in its view, makes the transactions on the market subject to the risk, to favor the emergence of opportunistic behavior, see below - from those who have access to this information. In this sense, information asymmetry as limited rationality is tautological and can only be the basis of a circular argument. They are essentially the attributes of a normal state, which can not in itself constitute a scientific argument.

In the digital economy, both information asymmetry and limited rationality were the arguments used by some economists to try to explain the behavior of certain economic actors whose actions could not be explained by the mainstream analysis models (Nair, & Saiz-Alvarez, 2019). In this respect, one of the topics in which these arguments were used is that of capital market investors, where even irrational investors have spoken. This perspective on economic behavior is also scientific: the irrational individuals do not operate in the economic sphere and the less can be done. What seems irrational to the outside observer is, however, perfectly rational for the individual who, according to the praxeological theory, uses his limited resources (including his or her own information and abilities) to pursue goals subjectively formulated by him. Some investors, for various reasons (such as the cost of information, the lack of analytical means, trust in others' abilities, etc.), can perfectly duplicate the trading strategy of other investors who have a good reputation and have registered in the past performance superior to the market. This strategy, which can be an observer of a tournament spirit, is as rational as to ignore the whole of the flock, considering that it possesses superior analytical and prognostic skills, adopt a contrarian strategy (opposed, in essence, to market movements).

SOLUTIONS AND RECOMMENDATIONS

As demonstrated above, entrepreneurship has many dimensions ranging from individual risk-taking to collective action and from economic theory to social development. The qualities and characteristics associated with each of these dimensions differ. On this basis, we now shall have a historical view on entrepreneurship theory. The intent was to illustrate the relations and significant differences within the literature of entrepreneurship, thus providing a framework to explain its diffusion.

Also, it is relevant to point out the mistake of many to personify the organisation: seeing the firm as a set of contractual relationships between individuals helps us to clarify that the personalization of the firm involved in formulating such questions as: What should be the company's objective function? or Does the company have a social responsibility? Is totally misleading and confusing.

FUTURE RESEARCH DIRECTIONS

The paradox of planning an economy is that the inputs of this process are purely arbitrary and have no economic significance. Thus, the paradox of economic activity is that anarchic production on the free market is the only one that allows individuals to assess their economic situation according to the realities of free prices, give an idea of the amount of capital they have at their disposal, and thus try to make as much information as possible on the evolution of consumer wishes.

For the future research directions, it is relevant to distinguish between those things that are within the firm. There is, in a very real sense, a multitude of complex (contractual) relationships between the legal fiction (the company) and the owners of the production factors (labor, raw materials, capital) and the consumers of the products made.

CONCLUSION

Companies are having a high level of business growth and motivation, influence positively on the formation of new business ideas. It is therefore essential that emotional characteristics close to the ability to work and enthusiasm must be developed to take forward the company. Without passion, mainly in start-ups, it is impossible for firms to survive in the global market.

Business success is positively related to the level of training, participation in previous projects, business experience, and the number of founders. These factors, however, can change by other endogenous variables, such as debt, product prices, stakeholders' attitudes and investments, purchases, rotation sales, and wages, and exogenous factors, such as energy prices, external shocks, and country risk, among others.

REFERENCES

Agboli, M., & Ukaegbu, C. C. (2006). Business environment and entrepreneurial activity in Nigeria: Implications for industrial development. *The Journal of Modern African Studies*, *44*(1), 1–30. doi:10.1017/S0022278X05001394

Ahmad, N., & Seymour, R. G. (2008). Defining Entrepreneurial Activity: Definitions Supporting Frameworks for Data Collection, *OECD Statistics Working Papers*, 1, Paris (France): OECD Publishing.

Aldrich, H. E. (2011). *An Evolutionary Approach to Entrepreneurship: Selected Essays by Howard E. Aldrich*. Cheltenham, UK: Edward Elgar.

Alvarez, S. A., & Barney, J. B. (2005). How Do Entrepreneurs Organize Under Conditions of Uncertainty? *Journal of Management*, *31*(5), 776–793. doi:10.1177/0149206305279486

Anna, A. L., Chandler, G. N., Jansen, E., & Mero, N. P. (2000). Women business owners in traditional and non-traditional industries. *Journal of Business Venturing, 15*(3), 279–303. doi:10.1016/S0883-9026(98)00012-3

Astebro, T., & Thompson, P. (2009). Entrepreneurs: Jacks of All Trades or Hobos? *Economics Research Working Paper Series*, 48, Miami, FL.: Florida International University.

Audretsch, D. B. (2003). *Entrepreneurship. A Survey of the Literature, Enterprise Papers, 14*. Brussels, Belgium: European Commission.

Baron, R. A. (2007). Entrepreneurship: A Process Perspective. In J. R. Baum, M. Frese, & R. A. Baron (Eds.), *The Psychology of Entrepreneurship* (pp. 19–39). Mahwah, NJ: Erlbaum.

Bula, H. O. (2012). Evolution and Theories of Entrepreneurship: A Critical Review on the Kenyan Perspective. *International Journal of Business and Commerce, 1*(11), 81–96.

Carroll, G. R., & Khessina, O. M. (2005). The Ecology of Entrepreneurship. In S. A. Alvarez, R. Agarwal, & O. Sorenson (Eds.), Handbook of Entrepreneurship Research: Disciplinary Perspectives (pp. 167–200). New York, NY: Springer. doi:10.1007/0-387-23622-8_9

Cuervo, A., Ribeiro, D., & Roig, S. (Eds.) (2007). Entrepreneurship: Concepts, Theory, and Perspective. New York, NY: Springer.

Douglas, E. J., & Shepherd, D. (1997). *Why entrepreneurs create businesses: a utility maximizing response. Frontiers of Entrepreneurship Research* (pp. 185–186). Wellesley, MA.: Babson College.

Drucker, P. F. (1985). *Innovation and Entrepreneurship: Practice and Principles*. New York, NY: Harper Business.

Dubini, P. (1988). *Motivational and environmental influences on business start-ups: some hints for public policies. Frontiers of Entrepreneurship Research* (pp. 31–45). Wellesley, MA.: Babson College.

Feeser, H. R., & Dugan, K. W. (1989). *Entrepreneurial motivation: a comparison of high and low growth high tech founders. Frontiers of Entrepreneurship Research* (pp. 13–27). Wellesley, Mass.: Babson College.

Frese, M., & Gielnik, M. M. (2014). The Psychology of Entrepreneurship. *Annual Review of Organizational Psychology and Organizational Behavior, 1*(1), 413–438. doi:10.1146/annurev-orgpsych-031413-091326

Gaglio, C., & Katz, J. (2001). The Psychological Basis of Opportunity Identification: Entrepreneurial Alertness. *Small Business Economics, 16*(2), 95–111. doi:10.1023/A:1011132102464

Gaglio, C. M. (1997). Opportunity recognition: review, critique, and suggested research directions. In J. Katz (Ed.), *Advances in Entrepreneurship, Firm Emergence and Growth* (pp. 139–202). Greenwich, CT: JAI Press.

Gnyawali, D., & Fogel, D. (1994). Environments for entrepreneurship development: Key dimensions and research implications. *Entrepreneurship Theory and Practice, 18*(4), 43–62. doi:10.1177/104225879401800403

Hébert, R. F., & Link, A. N. (1989). In Search of the Meaning of Entrepreneurship. *Small Business Economics, 1*, 39–49. doi:10.1007/BF00389915

Ireland, R. D., Hitt, M. A., & Sirmon, D. G. (2003). A Model of Strategic Entrepreneurship: The Construct and its Dimensions. *Journal of Management*, *29*(6), 963–989. doi:10.1016/S0149-2063(03)00086-2

Islam, A. (2015). Entrepreneurship and the Allocation of Government Spending Under Imperfect Markets. *World Development*, *70*, 108–121. doi:10.1016/j.worlddev.2015.01.002

Johnson, B. R. (1990). Toward a multidimensional model of entrepreneurship: The case of achievement motivation and the entrepreneur. *Entrepreneurship Theory and Practice*, *14*(3), 39–48. doi:10.1177/104225879001400306

Kirzner, I. M. (1979). *Perception, Opportunity, and Profit: Studies in the Theory of Entrepreneurship*. Chicago, IL: The University of Chicago Press.

Lazear, E. P. (2004). Balanced Skills and Entrepreneurship. *The American Economic Review*, *94*(2), 208–211. doi:10.1257/0002828041301425

Lazear, E. P. (2005). Entrepreneurship. *Journal of Labor Economics*, *23*(4), 649–680. doi:10.1086/491605

Mariotti, S., & Glackin, C. (2010). *Entrepreneurship*. Upper Saddle River, NJ: Prentice Hall.

Saiz-Alvarez, J. M. (2015). Solidarity Entrepreneurship in the European Knowledge Economies: Keys for a New Paradigm to Be Applied into Developing Nations. In N. Baporikar (Ed.), Entrepreneurship in the Contemporary Knowledge-based Global Economy, Hershey, PA: IGI Global, pp. 163-188.

Saiz-Alvarez, J. M. (2018). *Business Strategies and Advanced Techniques for Entrepreneurship 4.0*. Hershey, PA: IGI Global. doi:10.4018/978-1-5225-4978-9

Saiz-Alvarez, J. M., Coduras, A., & Cuervo-Arango, C. (2013). Entrepreneurial Strategy, Innovation, and Cognitive Capabilities. What Role for Intuitive SMEs? *Journal of Small Business Strategy*, *21*(2), 25–35.

Saiz-Alvarez, J. M., Coduras, A., & Cuervo-Arango, C. (2014). An Entrepreneurial Well-being Model based on GEM Data for Spain. *International Journal of Interactive Multimedia and Artificial Intelligence*, *2*(5), 38–47. doi:10.9781/ijimai.2014.255

Sarasvathy, S. D. (2001). Effectuation. Elements of Entrepreneurial Expertise. Cheltenham, UK: Edward Elgar.

Scheinberg, S., & McMillan, I. C. (1988). *An all country study of motivations to start a business. Frontiers of Entrepreneurship Research* (pp. 669–687). Wellesley, MA.: Babson College.

Schultz, T. W. (1980). Investment in Entrepreneurial Ability. *The Scandinavian Journal of Economics*, *82*(4), 437–448. doi:10.2307/3439676

Schumpeter, J. A. (1934). *The Theory of Economic Development: An Inquiry into Profits, Capital, Credit, Interest, and the Business Cycle*. Cambridge, MA: Harvard University Press.

Schumpeter, J. A. (1977). Capitalism, Socialism, and Democracy. New York, NY: Harper Collins Publishers. (Original work published 1942)

Schumpeter, J. A. (1997). *Theorie der wirtschaftlichen Entwicklung: Eine Untersuchung über Unternehmergewinn, Kapital, Kredit, Zins und den Konjunkturzyklus*. Berlin, Germany: Duncker Humblot. (Original work published 1911) doi:10.3790/978-3-428-07725-0

Shane, S., & Venkataraman, S. (2000). The Promise of Entrepreneurship as a Field of Research. *Academy of Management Review*, *25*(1), 217–226.

Shepherd, D. A., & Patzelt, H. (2011). The New Field of Sustainable Entrepreneurship: Studying Entrepreneurial Action Linking "What Is To Be Sustained" with "What Is To Be Developed?". *Entrepreneurship Theory and Practice*, *35*(1), 137–163. doi:10.1111/j.1540-6520.2010.00426.x

Sijbom, R. B. L., Janssen, O., & Van Yperen, N. W. (2015). Leaders' Receptivity to Subordinates' Creative Input: The Role of Achievement Goals and Composition of Creative Input. *European Journal of Work and Organizational Psychology*, *24*(3), 462–478. doi:10.1080/1359432X.2014.964215

Silva, O. (2007). The Jack-of-All-Trades entrepreneur: Innate talent or acquired skill? *Economics Letters*, *97*(2), 118–123. doi:10.1016/j.econlet.2007.02.027

Stephan, U., Uhlaner, L. M., & Stride, C. (2015). Institutions and Social Entrepreneurship: The Role of Institutional Voids, Institutional Support, and Institutional Configurations. *Journal of International Business Studies*, *46*(3), 308–331. doi:10.1057/jibs.2014.38

Stevenson, H. H., & Jarillo, J. C. (1990). A Paradigm of Entrepreneurship: Entrepreneurial Management. *Strategic Management Journal*, *11*, 17–27.

Thorton, P. H., & Yang, L. (2012). *Entrepreneurship*. Oxford, UK: Oxford University Press.

Velilla, J., Molina, J. A., & Ortega, R. (2018). Why Older Workers Become Entrepreneurs? International Evidence Using Fuzzy Set Methods. *The Journal of the Economics of Ageing*, *12*, 88–95. doi:10.1016/j.jeoa.2018.03.004

Wagner, J. (2003). Testing Lazear's jack-of-all-trades view of entrepreneurship with German micro data. *Applied Economics Letters*, *10*(11), 687–689. doi:10.1080/1350485032000133273

Woo, C. Y., Cooper, A. C., & Dunkelberg, W. C. (1988). *Entrepreneurial typologies: definitions and implications. Frontiers of Entrepreneurship Research* (pp. 165–176). Wellesley, MA: Babson College.

ADDITIONAL READING

Barnes, C. M., Dang, C., Leavitt, K., Guarana, C., & Uhlmann, E. L. (2018). Archival data in micro organizational research: A toolkit for moving to a broader set of topics. *Journal of Management*, *44*(4), 1453–1478. doi:10.1177/0149206315604188

Nair, S., & Saiz-Alvarez, J. M. (2019) (Eds.). Ethics, Entrepreneurship, and Governance in Higher Education, Hershey, PA (EE.UU.): Information Science Reference (IGI Global), in press.

Saiz-Alvarez, J. M., Muñiz, E., & Huezo, L. (2016). Informational Competencies, Entrepreneurship, and Integral Values in Higher Education. In Baporikar, N. (Ed.): Innovation and Shifting Perspectives in Management Education, Hershey, PA (EE.UU.): Information Science Reference (IGI Global), pp. 79-100.

KEY TERMS AND DEFINITIONS

Entrepreneur: Individual who starts a new business or adopt new business strategies in existing organizations.

Entrepreneurship: Business strategy focused on the creation of jobs, social wealth, and profit by optimizing the use of productive and commercial resources.

Chapter 11
Management Accounting in the Digital Economy:
Evolution and Perspectives

Sorinel Căpușneanu
https://orcid.org/0000-0003-3799-3993
Titu Maiorescu University, Romania

Dan Ioan Topor
1 Decembrie 1918 University, Romania

Dana Maria (Oprea) Constantin
The University of Bucharest, Romania

Andreea Marin-Pantelescu
The Bucharest University of Economic Studies, Romania

ABSTRACT

This chapter presents the evolution and perspectives of management accounting in the digital economy. The main objectives of this chapter are to present the different conceptual approaches of the digital economy and Industry 4.0, the B20 pillars and their impact on the management accounting, the role of management accounting and of the management accountant in the new economy, forecasts and solutions regarding the adaptation of the management accounting to the digital economy, and cost management of the implementation of innovative information technology. All aspects presented are based on national and international professional studies and attempt to present the current state of the themes addressed. The chapter ends with the author's conclusions regarding management accounting in the digital economy. Through the authors' contribution, the chapter offers perspectives and solutions to increase knowledge to implement information technologies and adapt accounting management to these innovative waves.

DOI: 10.4018/978-1-7998-1005-6.ch011

INTRODUCTION

The implementation by companies of innovative digital technologies contributes to the expansion of social and organizational effects, affecting to a certain extent the operational and managerial economic processes within them. The impact of digitization also has consequences on the behavior and actions of company staff. This impact is also felt on the information and staff dealing with a company's accounting. Management accounting follows an entire process of redefining the shape taking into account the technical, behavioral and organizational dimensions (Bhimani, 2003). The expansion of the IT industry has led to increased organizational and environmental changes. This has created an intense relationship between management accounting, strategic management, performance management and information technology. Management strategies and management accounting innovations are key success stories and decisions are based on economic and social gains and losses (Oncioiu et al., 2017).

The main objectives of this chapter are: (1) *presenting the conceptual approaches of the digital economy and Industry 4.0*, (2) *presenting the impact produced by Industry 4.0 and the digital economy on management accounting, including proposals for possible solutions*; (3) *the role of management accounting and the role of the management accountant in the digital economy;* (4) *cost management and digital economy, and* (5) *predictions about major trends in management accounting.*

BACKGROUND

Digital Economy: Conceptual Approaches

IT technology has now become the cheapest, easiest, fastest, broadest and most impacting on a company's business, taking into account the very agitated business environment that characterizes contemporary society. Due to its major presence in all branches of the economy, it has been called a digital economy or a global knowledge economy that is based on short cycles of innovation and digital information stored on networks (Tapscott, 1996).

In other words, the digital economy is an internet-based network economy that consists in increasing cycles of innovation of technologies, internet applications, or business models that connect users, thus generating a critical mass of participants in a network common collective interests. This implies gaining some advantages by some sellers to the detriment of the losses suffered by other sellers or business participants, while the direct and indirect effects of the network lead to a continuous increase in efficacy (Arthur, 1996). The direct influences of the (social or business) network generated by interoperability and standardization depend to a large extent on the value of using applications or computer products. Thus, some specialists studied the effects of blocking effects due to network effects and switching costs (Shapiro, & Varian, 1999), while other specialists studied the relationship between the participants and the value of the network highlighted by Metcalfe's Law (Zerdick et al., 2001) with positive feedbacks. The basis of new applications is technology, business models and transformation of social behavior and the rules of the digital economy represent the background of the strategic management of applied business models.

The concept of digital economy describes the microeconomic processes of the transition of the industrial society to the information society. As it is well known, the structures of ever-changing economic and social systems contribute to these transformations, especially through technical innovations that drive further technical, economic and social developments. These changes are based on the stimulation of the performance of information and communication technologies and of the resulting digital networks (Zerdick, et al., 2001), which are only possible due to adaptation of behavior in society (Stähler, 2002). The use of the concept of digital economy also took into account the description of the transformations in agriculture and the production of physical goods directed towards economically based information with an emphasis on intangible assets (Bhimani, 2003). In the information era, knowledge, communication and information have become the main production factors and markets have been dominated by the service sector (Hartmann, & Vaassen, 2003).

Other specialists have emphasized the technological side of the digital economy, such as: "the widespread use of information technology (hardware, software, applications and telecommunications) in all aspects of the economy, including the internal operations of non-profit organizations and transactions between individuals, acting both as consumers and citizens and organizations "(Atkinson, & McKay, 2007). Although it is not easy to predict the results, there are still many possibilities to use current technologies (Beaubien, 2013), especially since all the activities of a modern company are affected to a certain degree by digitization (Bhimani, & Willcocks, 2014). Digital culture can influence the decision by changing the way knowledge and actions are taken, with technology and algorithms that eliminate people in production processes and knowledge certification and decision-making as in high-frequency trading (MacKenzie, 2014). Contemporary businesses are visibly affected by major technologies such as Big Data, mobile and cloud services, social media offering to the companies new and flexible ways to store, use and share low-cost resources (Bhimani, & Willcocks, 2014). All these aspects of digitization affect modern business while creating new challenges and opportunities for company management, accounting and control of their administration.

Industry 4.0 and Digital Economy

The way in which society, companies and governments of countries work and communicate in day-to-day activities can be found in the concepts of the Digital Economy and Industry 4.0. Country decision makers should create the environment necessary for digitization development or digital economy that is capable of generating economic growth and improving the social wellbeing of the entire society. In this respect, the B20 calls on governments to use global policies and regulatory frameworks based on the 7 key pillars of digital and industry transformation 4.0: digital skills, industry 4.0, global connectivity, SMSEs (micro and small and medium-sized enterprises) digital and data streams, financial technologies and digital security (B20, 2012).

But who are B20s? As they describe themselves, B20 or Business 20 represents the voice of the private sector of the G20 community and addresses the global challenges and priorities defined by the G20 countries by building a solid consensus among business leaders, international organizations and civil society on how they should be addressed (B20, 2012). B20 provides practical insights into the interests of the G20 private sector, contributing to sustainable development by generating new ideas for issues such as education and employment, trade and investment, increased funding, innovation, infrastructure, and so on. At B20, working groups of around 100 G20 representatives from all over the world are included in the invited countries, and then recommendations are prepared for G20 policy leaders. Returning to the 7 key pillars of B20, they can be described as such:

Digital Skills

Regardless the position held within a company or the nature and volume of data required at the workplace, the staff employed must have a certain level of digital competence. To ensure that it is necessary for governments to promote digital skills by collaborating with all interested companies to assess and eliminate existing differences. This can be put into practice by developing educational, gender-friendly programs to promote digital competences and digital technical skills, ensuring that they are an integral part of the curriculum of staff employed and contributing to human development. In other words, investment in human capital and education is essential at this stage in the development of human society, which through digitization, automation and other technologies will fundamentally change the nature of work.

Industry 4.0

By using digital technologies, production processes become more flexible and more efficient resulting in high-quality products obtained at low cost. These new Industry 4.0 technologies such as robotics, Big Data Analytics, cloud or additive manufacturing, which allow for the collection and analysis of a very large volume of data and in a relatively short timeframe, must be promoted, financially sprinkled and encouraged by government actions, the ultimate goal of which is to develop technological innovation with positive aspects on business and civil society as well as cooperation between public and private institutions. Aligning all stakeholders, creating and bringing together, is a matter for governments and they will require some degree of integration between existing internal and external systems by developing standards for international cooperation.

Global Connectivity

Facilitating and encouraging private investment in infrastructure should be the main tasks of governments in encouraging the development of digitization, knowing that the degree of connectivity has a direct influence on a country's GDP. Expanding consumer connectivity and quick access to the data and services provided will make a decisive contribution to a nation's well-being and measuring company performance in the era of digitization.

Micro and SMEs (MSMEs)

The digitization of SMEs that hold two-thirds of all enterprises worldwide should also be a priority of the governments of their countries. There are a number of barriers that hinder SMEs in adopting Industry 4.0's innovative technologies such as: ignorance of the existence of such technologies, their implementation, or lack of knowledge of the underlying economic fundamentals needed to apply them. All governments in the countries are responsible for informing SMEs about the existence and benefits of implementing new technologies, contributing to making collaborations between them and large businesses. Expansion of communication between them is also achieved through discussion forums or conferences and periodic meetings between businessmen.

Digital Trade and Data Flows

Another equally important task of government in digitalizing the economy is the cross-border e-commerce policy, which is the main driver of growth for any company regardless of its size. To ensure the promotion and encouragement of electronic data commerce, governments need to be involved in avoiding the location of data transfer and effective mechanisms for transferring data. It can also encourage cross-border payment systems, data security, consumer protection and authentication.

Financial Technologies

In view of expanding the digitization of the economy and stimulating innovation, G20 members should propose the adoption of a legislative framework enabling the provision of financial technology services by actors in different sectors of activity, thereby promoting competition at all levels of the value chain of financial services. The elimination of the technological breakthroughs between developed and developing countries is the main goal of financial inclusion with positive effects on population and GDP welfare.

Digital Securing

As computer digitization evolved, cybercrime has also increased and has had a negative impact on the economies of developed countries in general. An essential role in halting threats and reducing economic cybercrime is played by both governments and the business community that need to collaborate and engage directly and unconditionally in ensuring cyber security risk management. It becomes impetuous and necessary to create a trans-sectoral and cross-border collaboration environment that would allow the sharing of information and the protection of valuable data against malicious economic actors or cyber attackers.

Impact of Industry 4.0 and the Digital Economy on Management Accounting: Possible Solutions for the Future

In the context of globalization, entities within a company are determined to make some adjustments or changes that contribute to business performance and success. These entities include: financial accounting, internal audit, taxation, costing, etc. which contributes significantly by providing management accounting and controlling information in order to formulate decisions that are grounded in the management of the company. In this sense, management accounting, which was considered to be just a process of creating and using cost, quality and time-based information within an organization to make effective decisions (O'Mahon, & Doran, 2008), is also given other roles, taking into account the large amount of information provided through information technology.

Thus, management accounting has to integrate different entities of a company to ensure that the set goals are achieved. As it is known, management accounting includes: strategic management, performance management and risk management (Garg et al., 2003). Strategic management considers staff in management accounting as a strategic entity within the company. Performance management takes into account the development of decision-making practice. Performance management along with risk management refers to the practices and frameworks used to measure, identify and report the risks that contribute to achieving a company's goals.

With the digital growth of the economy, including Industry 4.0's impact on managerial accounting, it brings a number of implications with long-term effects. These include: (1) changing the role of an administrative accountant in the company, (2) the influence of advanced technology on management accounting, (3) opportunity by change, (4) pre-investment thinking (5) cloudiness and mobility of Cloud technology, (6) the challenges of new technology, (7) the technological future places its mark on managerial accounting.

Changing the Role of an Administrative Accountant in the Company

The strategies of the digital economy and of the global economy are based on the opportunities and challenges of the influences of time and space of communication, on the rapidity of electronic transactions that take place in all areas of activity of an economy. Such a challenge has also been encountered by administrative accountants in their activities, regardless of the size of the companies they operate in. The role of accountants changes radically, and they are also involved in assessing investments, making decisions about making or buying or measuring a company's performance, apart from simply monitoring and reporting their performance. In this context, distancing them from accounting and managing data and providing information is imminent as they become strategic business partners along with leadership. However, with no decision-making power, accountants become the key element in strategically integrating decisions and actions taken by a company's management, especially on the background of adapting to the digital economy and the global economy. Within contemporary companies, the role of accountants is a difficult and extremely relevant one, especially in developing appropriate reporting platforms or performance measurement systems. Aligning managerial decisions with current organizational actions is done through the financial information obtained as a result of the interdependence of the strategic and technological elements. Managerial information can no longer be of a financial nature only, since strategic intentions and technological options are seen as distinct, separate elements. In other words, the composition of managerial information needs to be rethought and re-examined in the light of these new elements of digitization.

Influence of Advanced Technology on Managerial Accounting

The storage and processing capacity of accounting data has increased with the introduction of new cloud and Big Data Analytics technologies affecting not only administrative accountants but also companies on the whole. Customers give great importance to the technological power that changes unit costs and future product prices.

Opportunity Through Change

Access to Cloud-Based SAAS (Software As A Service) technology allows access to individual applications with low installation costs, improved deployment speeds. Cloud technology is just as safe, offering some benefits such as updates and permanent changes. Along with these changes emerged the opportunities offered by the new technologies that financial staff enjoy such as: producing/creating/maintaining value, shaping the way it is realized and presenting its evolution.

Think Before Investing

In view of the investment in new technologies, accountants should meditate on how it strategically affects the company's business by analyzing its value, the (financial and human) resources needed to implement it. Successful implementation of the new technology must be achieved by to a project team that deals both with the conceptual part and with the applicative part of it, proposing optimal solutions for its accomplishment. Most often, the technical side is well received by management, but staff perceive the implementation of new technology as a barrier that can destroy their workplace.

Tangibility and Mobility of Cloud Technology

The advantage of accessing data with Cloud technology has completely changed the way companies operate. Thus, accountants can quickly generate various reports using the form desired by end-users, including the use of non-financial information. Providing and interpreting financial and non-financial information will be done in a very short time generating major decision-making and competitive advantages for a company's managers.

The Challenges of New Technology

The challenges of new technologies include: data security, staff training, time and trust. Data security aims to protect software, storage devices and data. An overwhelming role is played by the staff that must be trained to adapt to new technologies, and this requires a certain amount of time to accommodate, test and use. Not always staff are convinced of the benefits of new technologies and have a certain lack of trust starting from the testing phase to final clarification that new technologies can be of benefit to them and to the company they are part of.

The Technological Future Puts Its Mark on Managerial Accounting

This revolutionary technological wave must not be ignored by accountants and managerial accounting. Although it looks worrying at first sight, it is still inevitable and useful in the future. The administrative accountants thinking needs to be changed by adapting to the novelty and accustoming with the changes it produces. The accountant's workplace will not be removed as there will always be people who will check the information produced by the technology and validate or invalidate it. The final decision belongs entirely to the administrative accountant, over the computer or technology.

According to the experts' opinions, along with the digital economy, the wave of innovative information technologies offered companies some positive aspects such as: (1) a great impact on business processes and their economic activities, obliging companies to integrate them into their decision-making process (Bhimani, & Bromwich, 2009), being no border between technological, operational activities and strategic decisions; (2) new ways of organizing decision-making and management control systems (Granlund et al., 2013); (3) changes that influenced information collection and management control analysis (Bhimani, & Willcocks, 2014).

Regarding the negative aspects brought by the technological information wave, some specialists become very fierce critics, emphasizing: (1) rising costs related to the functioning of information systems, coordination structures and virtual flow mechanisms, transforming the company into a "virtual enterprise" and declining possibilities of reducing the cost of physical products (Bhimani, & Bromwich, 2009); (2) the inefficiency of IT usage due to the fact that most companies acquire new software packages instead of using, developing and adapting existing and functional needs (Granlund, 2011); (3) the human illusion of technology in terms of lack of control of digital information and its interpretation due to the huge amount of data received (Quattrone, 2016).

One of the solutions proposed by specialists to update management control and decision-making processes is the Enterprise Resourse Planning (ERP) system (Kallunki et al., 2011). According to their views, the ERP system can be defined as follows: (1) the integrated software package that coordinates the entire staff, materials, money, and information flows of a company (Granlund, & Malmi, 2002); (2) collecting all the data of an organization in a single central database that is made available to all users regardless of their position or role within the organization (Dechow, & Mouritsen, 2005); (3) a software program that is used by different business units within an organization to integrate and coordinate information (Monk, & Wagner, 2013).

Among the advantages of ERP systems we can mention: (1) rapidity in solving problems due to the fact that the data are centralized and accessible whenever and by anyone when needed (Granlund, & Malmi, 2002); (2) creating competitive advantages by maintaining contact with their activities and customers (Granlund, & Mouritsen, 2003) or improvements in production and quality in key business areas such as product reliability, knowledge management, client services (Hunton et al., 2003) (3) it forces users to think about problems and then create solutions to solve them, and management control practices are more visible and more acceptable within the organization (Dechow, & Mouritsen, 2005); (4) the existence of operational efficiency in case of ERP implementation (Kallunki et al., 2011); (5) activating the strategic vision; (6) ensuring transparency in the subsidiaries' control; (7) implementation of standards at company and global level (Teittinen et al., 2013).

Like any system and ERP, there are some inadequacies such as: (1) ERP implementation may require some undesirable changes in the company process structure (Granlund, & Malmi, 2004), as it is a standard software that offers the same solutions for any company (Teittinen et al ., 2013); (2) ERP implementation requires time, staff training (Granlund, & Malmi, 2004) and large investments (Dechow, & Mouritsen, 2005), which are expensive especially for SMEs, require ongoing maintenance and updating of the changes and the results are achieved in the long run (Teittinen et al., 2013); (3) Configuration of the ERP system is achieved with some problems but can not cover the complexity of management control issues (Dechow, & Mouritsen, 2005; Topor et al., 2017), situations where the personnel using it can be lead into mistakes (Teittinen et al., 2013) or do not take into account the perspective of customers in gaining competitive advantages (Davenport, 1998).

The Role of Management Accounting and the Role of the Management Accountant in the Digital Economy

The objective of managerial accounting is to transform it from an accounting information provider into a guidance, consultation tool in establishing internal and external actions, procedures, and strategic decisions for any company. The role of the management accountant is to provide an informational feed-back on how operations and activities are conducted according to plans, identify those activities that require corrective action (Volkán, & Pete, 2009). Management accounting should provide economic feedback to managers to help them control costs and improve the efficiency and effectiveness of operations (Drury, 2001). Management accounting should also ensure that there is efficiency in strategic planning, formulation of short-term operational plans, financial control, internal audit (Sangster, 1994). The implementation of a strategy recommends that managers be constantly minded about the change of initiatives and targeted goals. Once established, a company's strategy is translated into specific objectives and initiatives included in a strategic plan. During the implementation of the strategy, managers monitor this process and learn from internal results and external data about competitors and the business environment if the chosen strategy is correct or incorrect. These steps have also been described by Kaplan & Norton (2008), as follows: (1) developing the strategy; (2) translation of the strategy; (3) operational plans; (4) monitoring and learning; (5) testing and adaptation of the strategy.

Over the last 30 years, the studies of the specialists regarding the digital economy and its impact on managerial accounting have intensified, taking into account the uncertain and turbulent conditions in the business environment and have helped to change the competitive circumstances of the companies on the market (Johnson, & Kaplan, 1987; Duberley et al., 2000; Williams, & Seaman, 2002; Baines, & Smith, 2003). All these have led to a radical change of strategies adopted by companies that some of them have been able to anticipate and others do not, leading to a new strategic formulation and adaptation of methods and techniques to these strategies (Laitinen, 2003; Johnny, & Gani, 2004). These economic transformations produced in the structure, functions and roles of an economy were called the new economy (Bhimani, 2003).

The new economy or the digital economy has significantly influenced the role of managerial accounting by creating a complex business environment (Szychta, 2002) which takes into account innovative ideas and technologies, risks, uncertainties and constant changes within it. In this respect, managerial accounting evolves with these changes, adapting and maintaining the means of communication with society, making them more efficient and flexible. The major economic changes (globalization, technological progress and deregulation) involved computer-based information exchanges, but also changes in the nature and functioning of the economy, and related processes and social structures (Bhimani, 2003).

Progress in technology and telecommunication along with the phenomenon of globalization represent the most powerful force which has effect on the business environment (Yip, 2000). The interconnection of political, economic, cultural and social events has a major impact in a globalized world (Baylis, & Smith, 1997). As a result, access to some markets has become easier, dynamic, a transfer of options from sellers to buyers has taken place, the economic dictionary has been enriched with new terms resulting from these phenomena (Wit, & Meyer, 1994) to which have been added the benefits of the digital economy such as high-speed communication, computerized trading, high volume of cross-border entry-exit operations at significant speeds.

Deregulation is considered by specialists as a weakening of government control over economic activities and the accentuation of this phenomenon is due to the fact that private sectors are more efficient in creating economic value than public and bureaucratic organizations. The public sector has been dominated by many problems due to management changes especially in recent years (Broadbent et al., 1996) and the most important issue of developed and developing countries was the privatization of state-owned enterprises (Saygili, & Taymaz, 2001). These aspects have led to some positive effects such as: increasing competition, creating new markets and opportunities for meeting demand and supply.

Flexible companies can react quickly to regulatory changes, but also to technological changes regarding the hardware, software or communication. This new technology or digital economy opens up new channels of communication and distribution (Nixon, 1995), trying to bring new enthusiasts to the edge of other competitors by designing products and providing services that are rapidly adapted to customer requirements. These new technologies include: Computer-Aided-Manufacturing (CAM), computer-aided design (CAD), computer simulations, and so on, which helps smaller companies to gain access to new markets, to compete with other competitors.

According to a study, there are a number of discontinuities that underlie the modeling of the new economy or the digital economy: globalization, deregulation and privatization, eco-sensitivity, disintermediation, standardization, volatility, convergence and undefined industrial boundaries (Prahalad, 1998). Managing these discontinuities automatically enters into the tasks of administrative accountants that can achieve them by integrating existing knowledge flows across companies. As business sizes have undergone important changes, the information provided by accounting administration systems has become irrelevant and distorted in managers' decision-making (Maskell, 1991). In the future, the role of managerial accounting will change, moving from systems like ABC, TQM and others to ABM, BSC, environmental accounting, efficient data exploitation, data channel integration, 3D business models running without budgets, this being a constraint of development (Jenkins, 1998). Also, the role of managerial accounting will increase, while the number of accountants will fall on the background of adapting to the digital economy (Cooper, 1996) being at higher levels (Anastas, 1997).

Changing roles in the accounting profession began in 1980 when the globalization process was at the heart of each country's economy, and the flow of information (Ahid, & Augustine, 2012) went beyond the borders of the countries. On the background of globalization, management accounting was the center of managers' attention being the only one able to bring new responses to the challenges of the business environment. Globalization has led to increased competition and the emergence of advanced innovative technologies, which is why companies need large amounts of information to remain competitive in the markets. Thus, management accounting plays a critical role in the acquisition and provision of company information, being critical in the decision-making process by company managers (Garg et al., 2003). In this context, management accounting became resource-oriented using a variety of process analysis tools such as Activity-Based Costing, Life Cycle Costing and other cost management techniques such as opportunity cost analysis (Hansen et al., 2006).

In a globalized economy, management accounting needs to change its role of providing information only internally to company management; it also has to provide information to the external environment, informing the company's leadership and decision-makers about the external parameters that could affect the company, competition, threats and changes in the business environment (O 'Mahon, & Doran, 2008). Management accounting helps to translate this information into formulating policies and strategic plans for the company's business. Management accounting plays a critical role (Garrison et al., 2006) providing the input needed to formulate strategic business decisions (Garg et al., 2003) and contributing to the completion of the decision-making process, either internally or at external level (Kidane, 2012). In this sense, management accounting contributes to: selection of the most important clients, elimination of unprofitable products on the market, establishment of critical capacities, establishment of the necessary funds for the investments. The management accounting is also the one that creates and adds value to a business by managing material resources, human resources, and activities to achieve the set goals (Bamber et al., 2008). It is the manager who must assume this role through planning, leadership, control and decision-making activities (Shah, 2009).

Among the tasks of the management accounting department are performance tracking through quality, cost, efficiency, time and innovation, including customers (Hansen et al., 2006). Tracking the customer performance can be resolved by benchmarking, alerting managers to the possible changes that customers see and evaluate (Seal et al., 2006). Management accountability plays an important role in the development and implementation of fraud prevention and internal control systems by providing reports on: fraud, causes and mode of fraud, risk management, fraud prevention, fraud detection, measures to be taken to avoid fraud (Ahid, & Augustine, 2012).

Therefore, the roles performed by management accounting vary from company to company based on business size, type of activity, industry or operational niche, culture, and other factors (Hansen et al., 2006) such as globalization. The management accounting roles have not changed significantly, but only the roles execution (Kidane, 2012), especially in the context of globalization and innovative technologies brought by Industry 4.0.

Administrative accountants will become internal consultants who will need to find new ways for a company to remain profitable and competitive (Jenkins, 1998). Starting from the schematization of the role of the administrative accountant between 1999 and 2010 carried out by Jenkins (1998), we want to expand this frame in Table 1.

The characteristics of the digital economy to which management accounting has to adapt are: speed of change, very high competition, virtual organizations, e-commerce, intellectual capital dependence for competitive advantage, alliance dependence and various collaborations for risk management, acquisition of technologies and services, access on the markets (Nixon et al., 2002). Any of these features can be handled with a certain difficulty, but survival in the new digital economy requires that all these forces be managed simultaneously (Abobaker Efkirin, 2014).

Cost Management and Digital Economy

To assess managers' business decisions, administrative accountants used the cost analysis that was considered the most relevant and accurate in providing information. This information was incomplete because managers wanted to know the financial consequences of the *make or buy* actions of a secondary or tertiary component of an existing product. Each company proceeds to an analysis of the costs and benefits derived

Table 1. The role of the management accountant between 1999 and 2019

Criteria	1999	2019
Type of approach type to management accounting issues	Functional	Holistic
Type of guidance on the use of data/ information	Looking inside the company	Look outside the company
The time horizon used for data analysis and processing	Past	Future
Overall vision	National	Global
Type of attributions (duties)	Simple and accurate (Accounting records, financial statements preparation, data analysis and comparison, cost calculation)	Extending of duties Planning and performance, reporting and control, technology and analytics, business acumen and operations, leadership, professional ethics and value
Mode of departmental structure	Separate department of indirect costs	Integrated specialists
Ability to use information technology/ digitization	Technological slaves	Masters in technology

Source: Authors processing

from the internal manufacture of the products, the executed works or the rendered services and their outsourcing, which implies complex and relatively quick managerial decisions (Speklé, 2001, Dekker, 2004, Callioni et al., 2005). In the studies of specialists there is an indicative leap in the collaboration between companies, moving the organizational acquisition from the relationship-oriented transaction to a process of relationship with suppliers (Sheth, & Sharma, 1997). This method of collaboration and relationship is a form of quasi-vertical integration (Tomkins, 2001; Das, & Teng, 2000), which has gained momentum among companies as well as in specialists' studies (Leiblein, & Miller, 2003; Liker, & Choi, 2004; Sako, 2008) trying to determine some aspects related to: (1) the implications of control over collaborative relationships (Anderson, & Sedatole, 2003, Hakansson, & Lind, 2007; Kamminga, & Van der Meer-Kooistra, 2007); (2) the relevance of strategic and contractual issues between buyers and sellers in the context of new product development (Gadde, & Snehota, 2000; Narayanan, & Raman, 2004). Implications for cost management are expanded in terms of product development contribution, price reductions, post-sale warranties, supplier inspection policies, and IT integration (Bhimani, 2012).

Collaborative relationships imply trust-based reciprocal relationships and solid principles with regard to long-term trading through informal channels established by either functional managers or departments within connected companies. These relationships of mutual collaboration set out a series of characteristics related to: the quantities delivered, the time of delivery, the product specifications, the price of the products traded etc. There are a number of factors that can influence mutual collaboration and trading relationships between companies, such as: assessing non-financial consequences, operational flexibility, product lifecycle, additional costs, knowledge transfer. Only the creation of strong, solid alliances will lead to the possibility of expansion and rapid growth in unanticipated ways from the beginning (Child et al., 2005). Depending on the portfolio mix, some companies have different trading options: either they engage in transactions based on collaborative relationships or resort to pure transactions (Axelsson et al., 2000).

Many companies are currently turning to outsourcing of production or services because their only function is to coordinate activities, connect inputs and outputs and orchestrate movements between entities in a resource-efficient manner (Bhimani, 2012). Thus, a company can hold virtual control while maintaining the direction, intensity and nature of the electronic interfaces, becoming what is called the "virtual company". This is created by selecting the organizational resources of several companies and synthesizing them into a single electronic business entity (Nagel, & Dove, 1991). Due to the interconnections between companies who are born with collaborative relationships come also some threats and risks and their impact on costs must be made known to the parties involved. There are some factors that contribute to managing the costs of a virtual company: (1) verification of exits by suppliers and the extent to which they meet the required specifications and standards; (2) verifying the implementation of risk management strategies (systemic risks) through compliance with standards between companies and their IT systems.

A strong collaboration alliance can bring benefits such as: (1) the ability to change product specifications during production flow, depending on market volatility or competitive action (also applicable to virtual companies by continually redefining quantities of processing established at the contractual level); (2) the possibility of altering the volume of unplanned acquisitions or temporary suspension may take place throughout the purchase relationship; (3) cost-cutting opportunities as a result of a partnership with subcomponent suppliers. A strong alliance between companies, even virtual companies, requires a viable infrastructure, sharing operational and accounting information, and they go in the long run and require some financial and human resources.

Gary Cokins Predictions About Major Trends in Management Accounting

Starting from what has been said about the evolution of digital economy and management accounting, our focus has been on the 7 major trends management accounting foreseen by Gary Cokins. Thus, the author highlighted the following major trends in management accounting: "(1) expanding from product to distribution channel and analyzing customer profitability; (2) expanding the role of EPM (Enterprise Performance Management) management accounting; (3) transition to predictive accounting (Cokins et al., 2012); (4) business analysis embedded in EPM methods; (5) the coexistence and improvement of management accounting methods; (6) management of information technology and services shared as a business; (7) Need for better skills and competence in cost management behavior "(Cokins, 2016).

In the following, we will focus on analyzing the sixth trend related to the management of information technology and services shared as a business. In the past decades, IT has evolved from a simple back-office support function to a critical strategic function for any company. Along with the evolution of IT, users' demands for diversified information and quick responses to substantiate decisions have grown, which has inevitably led to an increase in the cost of IT equipment and its maintenance.

The most common questions that arise in these conditions of increasing IT costs are: *How will these costs be charged to staff using them?* and *How will these costs be managed?* The answers to the two questions are also offered by Cokins. Thus, companies use ABC/ABM cost management systems and IT capability reporting systems that develop cost information for both cost management and performance management improvement (Cokins, 2016).

It is very important for any company to develop an internal IT market that becomes a link between suppliers and internal customers by establishing a certain level of service, and at the same time billing these data so that both sides can benefit from it. An important role in this direction is the Chief Information Officer (CIO), who has to demonstrate a certain maturity and experience in IT performance and financial management and how IT contributes to the overall performance of the company (Cokins, 2016).

SOLUTIONS AND RECOMMENDATIONS

Taking into consideration the issues addressed in this chapter, we propose to the specialists and to all those interested the following solutions for improvement:

- Improvement of regulatory infrastructures such as: Electronic Commerce Law, Information Security Law, Digital Signatures Act, Electronic Communications Law, Intellectual Property Rights Law, etc.
- Developing the digital economy ecosystem based on the following pillars: e-Connectivity/e-Infrastructure, e-Security/e-Privacy, e-Skills/e-Literacy;
- Adopting and implementing information technology (IT) such as Big Data Analytics, Cloud Computing, Internet of Things, etc. or software packages dedicated to management accounting methods such as: Activity-Based Costing/Activity-Based Management (ABC/ABM), Target Costing (Anghelache et al., 2019, Capuşneanu et al., 2019, Constantin et al.), Economic Resourse Planning (ERP), etc.
- The development of digitization through the following pillars: (1) empowering employees, (2) engaging customers, (3) optimizing operations, and (4) transforming products and business models

and addressing the related accounting problems: valuation of intangible assets, assets and liabilities embedded, etc.

Based on the concepts discussed in the international literature, we recommend to specialists and to all those interested in deepening the mysteries of the digital economy the following issues:

- Careful analysis of drivers and barriers in implementing Industry 4.0 (Türkeş et al., 2019) and the digital economy at company level.
- Research of specialized literature on the successful adoption and implementation of new innovative technologies alongside other established management accounting methods such as ABC/M, Target Costing, ERP, etc.). Setting up teams for analysis and implementation would be one of the solutions indicated in such cases.
- Research on the national and global level of the impact of new innovative technologies on the circular economy, both at the level of large entities and at the level of SMEs (Oncioiu et al., 2018).
- Adapting and expanding accountant culture in the use of new innovative technologies, including staff within a company's targeted departments.
- The expansion of information technology culture in companies that have adopted or want to adopt software packages dedicated to management accounting and performance improvement. An effective solution in this regard would be to organize training and information courses by specialists on the use of new innovative technologies of the digital economy.

FUTURE RESEARCH DIRECTIONS

The study objectives set at the beginning of the chapter as well as the target segment we have addressed (business environment and academic environment) have been reached. The themes are topical and interesting. The amount of information presented covering a vast area of international literature dedicated to the digital economy, Industry 4.0 and management accounting was synthesized in an attempt to present segments with real future research directions. By doing so, we suggest to the specialists and to all those interested the following research directions:

- Analyzing the possibilities of adapting and implementing new innovative technologies to other existing management accounting methods, existing or mixed methods.
- Analyzing the position of administrative accountants and managerial accounting within a company when adopting new innovative technologies.
- Analyzing the impact of managerial decisions resulting from adapting or implementing new innovative technologies to other management accounting methods as well as the impact on cost management.

CONCLUSION

Through its structure, this chapter covers some segments aiming at the conceptual approaches of the digital economy and Industry 4.0, as well as their impact on managerial accounting and administrative accountants. There are also some predictions about management accounting against the backdrop of the digital economy. The strengths of this chapter are as follows:

- Complements some gaps in managerial accounting and the application of new innovative technologies within companies (large and SMEs) precisely through interpretations of the conceptual approaches debated, including their advantages;
- Analyzes some hypotheses of the change of managerial accounting and the role of the accountant under the conditions of applying new innovative technologies within a company;
- Presents some solutions for adapting to the digital economy and some predictions of specialists that can be the starting points in the future analysis of the researches undertaken.

By contributing to the realization of these chapters, we are sure that we have reached subjects of real and current interest in both the business and the academic environment, prompting new challenges in adopting or implementing new innovative technologies and opening up new research directions. The involvement of specialists regardless of their provenance will contribute to expanding knowledge about the digital economy, the fourth industrial wave and the evolving trends of management accounting. We believe that this chapter will remain open as long as the economy evolves and along with it evolve its other components that have global ties. Only through cooperation and understanding, the current state of knowledge will be permanently enriched, identifying new viable and successful solutions to adapting managerial accounting to new innovative technologies regardless of the branch of the economy in which companies carry out their activities.

REFERENCES

B20.. 2012). *B20 Global Business Leaders Announce Their Prioritized Recommendations for Global Economic Recovery and Growth*, May 2012.

Abobaker Efkirin, A. E. A. (2014). Management Accounting in the New Economy. *University Bulletin*, *16*(2), 131–150.

Réka, V. I., & Ştefan, P. (2009). Adopting Information Technology (IT) in Management Accounting in Order to Achieve IT-Business Alignment, *Analele Universităţii din Oradea*, 18, 1207–1211.

Ahid, M., & Augustine, A. (2012). The Roles and Responsibilities of Management Accountants in the Era of Globalization. *Global Journal of Management and Business Research*, *12*(15).

Anastas, M. (1997). The Changing World of Management Accounting and Financial Accounting (pp. 48–51). Management Accounting (USA), 79(4), 48-51.

Anderson, S. W., & Sedatole, K. (2003). Management Accounting for the Extended Enterprise: Performance Management for Strategic Alliances and Networked Partners. In: A. Bhimani (Ed.), Management Accounting in the Digital Economy, Oxford University Press.

Arthur, W. B. (1996). Increasing Returns and the New World of Business. *Harvard Business Review*, *74*(4), 100–109. PMID:10158472

Atkinson, R., & McKay, A. (2007). *Digital Prosperity: Understanding the economic benefits of the IT revolution*. Washington, DC: ITI Foundation.

Axelsson, B., Van Weele, A., & Wynstra, F. (2000). Driving and enabling factors for purchasing involvement in product development. *European Journal of Purchasing and Supply Management*, *6*(2), 129–141. doi:10.1016/S0969-7012(00)00002-2

Baines, A., & Smith, K. (2003). Antecedents to Management Accounting Changes: A structural equation approach. *Accounting, Organizations and Society*, *28*(7-8), 675–698. doi:10.1016/S0361-3682(02)00102-2

Bamber, L., Broun, K., & Harrison, T. W. (2008). Managerial accounting (1st ed.). Upper Saddle River, NJ: Prentice Hall.

Baylis, J., & Smith, S. (1997). The Globalization of World Politics: An Introduction to International Relations. Oxford, UK: Oxford University Press.

Beaubien, L. (2013). Technology, change, and management control: A temporal perspective. *Accounting, Auditing & Accountability Journal*, *26*(1), 48–74. doi:10.1108/09513571311285612

Bhimani, A. (2003). Management Accounting in the Digital Economy (1st ed.). Oxford, UK: Oxford University Press. doi:10.1093/0199260389.001.0001

Bhimani, A. (2012). Cost management in the digital age. In F. Mitchell, H. Nørreklit, & M. Jakobsen (Eds.), *The Routledge Companion to Cost Management. Routledge companions in business, management and accounting* (pp. 381–388). London, UK: Routledge.

Bhimani, A., & Bromwich, M. (2009). Management Accounting in a Digital and Global Economy: The Interface of Strategy, Technology and Cost Information. In C. S. Chapman, D. J. Cooper, & P. Miller (Eds.), *Accounting, Organizations and Institutions: Essays in Honour of Anthony Hopwood* (pp. 85–111). Oxford, UK: Oxford University Press. doi:10.1093/acprof:oso/9780199546350.003.0005

Bhimani, A., & Willcocks, L. (2014). Digitisation, 'Big Data' and the transformation of accounting information. *Accounting and Business Research*, *44*(4), 469–49. doi:10.1080/00014788.2014.910051

Broadbent, J., Dietrich, M., & Laughlin, R. (1996). The Development of Principal-Agent Contracting and Accountability Relationships in the Public Sector: Conceptual and Cultural Problems. *Critical Perspectives on Accounting*, 7.

Callioni, G., Montgros, X., Slagmulder, R., Wassenhowe, L., & Wright, L. (2005). Inventory-Driven Costs. *Harvard Business Review*, (March): 271–282. PMID:15768682

Child, J., Faulkner, D., & Tallman, S. (2005). Cooperative Strategy. Managing Alliances, Networks, and Joint Ventures (2nd ed.). Oxford, UK: Oxford University Press. doi:10.1093/acprof:oso/9780199266241.001.0001

Cokins, G. (2016). The Top Seven Trends in Management Accounting. *The EDP Audit, Control, and Security Newsletter*, *53*(4), 1–7.

Cooper, R. (1996). *Look out, Management Accountants, Management Accounting* (pp. 35–41). US: May-June.

Das, T. K., & Teng, B. (2000). Instabilities of Strategic Alliances: An Internal tensions perspective. *Organization Science*, *11*(1), 77–101. doi:10.1287/orsc.11.1.77.12570

Davenport, T. H. (1998). Putting the Enterprise into the Enterprise System. *Harvard Business Review*, *76*(4), 121–131. PMID:10181586

Dechow, N., & Mouritsen, J. (2005). Enterprise resource planning systems, management control and the quest for integration. *Accounting, Organizations and Society*, *30*(7-8), 691–733. doi:10.1016/j.aos.2004.11.004

Dekker, H. C. (2004). Control of inter-organizational relationships: Evidence on appropriate concerns and coordination requirements. *Accounting, Organizations and Society*, *29*(1), 27–49. doi:10.1016/S0361-3682(02)00056-9

Drury, C. (2001). *Management Accounting for Business Decisions* (2nd ed.). Thompson Learning.

Duberley, J., Johnson, P., Cassell, C., & Close, P. (2000). Manufacturing Change: The Role of Performance Evaluation and Control Systems. *International Journal of Operations & Production Management*, *20*(4), 427–440. doi:10.1108/01443570010314773

Gadde, L.-E., & Snehota, I. (2000). Making the Most of Supplier Relationships. *Industrial Marketing Management*, *29*(4), 305–316. doi:10.1016/S0019-8501(00)00109-7

Garg, A., Ghosh, D., Hudick, J., & Nowacki, C. (2003). Roles and practices in management accounting today. *Strategic Finance*, *85*(1), 30–65.

Garrison, R., Noreen, E., & Brewer, P. (2006). Managerial Accounting (11th ed.). New York, NY: McGraw-Hill, Irwin.

Granlund, M. (2011). Extending AIS research to management accounting and control issues: A research note. *International Journal of Accounting Information Systems*, *12*(1), 3–19. doi:10.1016/j.accinf.2010.11.001

Granlund, M., & Malmi, T. (2002). Moderate impact of ERPS on management accounting: A lag or permanent outcome. *Management Accounting Research*, *13*(3), 200–321. doi:10.1006/mare.2002.0189

Granlund, M., & Malmi, T. (2004). *Tietotekniikan mahdollisuudet taloushallinnon kehittämisessä/ The potential of information technology in financial management development*. Jyväskylä: Gummerus Kirjapaino Oy.

Granlund, M., & Mouritsen, J. (2003). Introduction: Problematizing the relationship between management control and information technology. *European Accounting Review*, *12*(1), 77–83. doi:10.1080/0963818031000087925

Granlund, M., Mouritsen, J., & Vaassen, E. (2013). On the relations between modern information technology, decision making and management control. *International Journal of Accounting Information Systems*, *14*(4), 275–277. doi:10.1016/j.accinf.2013.10.001

Hakansson, H., & Lind, J. (2007). Accounting in an Interorganizational Setting. In C. Chapman, A. Hopwood, & M. Shields (Eds.), Handbook of Management Accounting Research, 885-902. Amsterdam, The Netherlands: Elsevier.

Hansen, Don R., & Mowen, M. M. (2006). *Cost Management: Accounting and Control*, Cincinnati, OH: South-Western/Thomson Learning.

Hartmann, F. G. H., & Vaassen, E. H. J. (2003). The Changing Role of Management Accounting and Control Systems. In A. Bhimani (Ed.), *Management accounting in the digital economy* (1st ed.). Oxford, UK: Oxford University Press.

Hunton, J. E., Lippincott, B., & Reck, J. L. (2003). Enterprise resource planning systems: Comparing firm performance of adopters and nonadopters. *International Journal of Accounting Information Systems*, *4*(3), 165–184. doi:10.1016/S1467-0895(03)00008-3

Ionica, O., & Alina, S. (2017). The Impact of Management Accounting Innovations on Millennials Business. Ovidius University Annals, Economic Sciences Series, 17(1), 568-572.

Jenkins, M. (1998). *Change in Management Accounting, Handbook of Management Accounting*. CIMA-Publication.

Johnny, J., & Gani, L. (2004). Integrating Business Strategy, Organizational Configurations and Management Accounting Systems with Business Unit Effectiveness: A Fitness Landscape Approach. *Management Accounting Research*, *15*(2), 179–200. doi:10.1016/j.mar.2004.03.002

Johnson, H., & Kaplan, K. (1987). *Relevance Lost, the Rise and Fall of Management Accounting*. Boston, MA: Harvard Business School Press.

Kallunki, J. P., Laitinen, E., & Silvola, H. (2011). Impact of enterprise resource planning systems on management control systems and firm performance. *International Journal of Accounting Information Systems*, *12*(1), 20–39. doi:10.1016/j.accinf.2010.02.001

Kamminga, P. E., & Van der Meer-Kooistra, J. (2007). Management Control Patterns in Joint Venture Relationships: A model and an Exploratory Study. *Accounting, Organizations and Society*, *32*(1-2), 131–154. doi:10.1016/j.aos.2006.03.002

Kaplan, R., & Norton, D. (2008). Mastering the Management System, *Harward Business Review*, January, 63-77.

Kidane, F. (2012). Decision Making and the Role of Management Accounting Function – a Review of Empirical Literature, *Radix International Journal of Banking, Finance and Accounting*, *1*(4), 77–97.

Laitinen, E. (2003). Future-based Management Accounting: A New Approach with Survey Evidence. *Critical Perspectives on Accounting*, 14.

Leiblein, M. J., & Miller, D. J. (2003). An Empirical Examination of Transation and Firm Level Influences on the Vertical Boundaries of the Firm. *Strategic Management Journal*, *24*(9), 839–859. doi:10.1002mj.340

Liker, J. K., & Choi, T. Y. (2004). Building Deep Supplier Relationships. *Harvard Business Review* (Dec.), 29-38.

MacKenzie, D. (2014). *A Sociology of Algorithms: High–Frequency Trading and the Shaping of Markets*. Working paper.

Maskell, B. (1991). *Performance Measurement for World Class Manufacturing: a Model for American Companies*. Cambridge, MA: Productivity Press.

Monk, E., & Wagner, B. (2013). *Concepts in Enterprise Resource Planning* (4th ed.). Boston, MA: Course Technology Cengage Learning.

Nagel, R. N., & Dove, R. (1991). 21st Century Manufacturing Enterprise Strategy: An Industry led View. Collingdale, PA: Diane Publishing.

Narayanan, V. G., & Raman, A. (2004). Aligning Incentives in Supply Chains. *Harvard Business Review*, *82*(11), 94–102. PMID:15559449

Nixon, W. A. J. (1995). Technology Investment and Management Accounting Practice. *British Journal of Management*, *6*(4), 271–288. doi:10.1111/j.1467-8551.1995.tb00100.x

Nixon, W. A. J., Laitinen, E., & Wingren, T. (2002). Implication of the 'New Economy' for Control Systems, *3rd Conference on New Directions in Management Accounting: Innovations in Practice and Research*, Brussels, Belgium.

O' Mahon, A., & Doran, J. (2008). The changing role of management accountants; evidence from the implementation of ERP systems in large organizations. *International Journal of Business and Management*, *3*(8), 109–115.

Prahalad, C. (1998). Managing Discontinuities: The Emerging Challenges. *Research Technology Management*, *4*(3), 14–22. doi:10.1080/08956308.1998.11671205

Quattrone, P. (2016). Management accounting goes digital: Will the move make it wiser? *Management Accounting Research*, *31*, 118–122. doi:10.1016/j.mar.2016.01.003

Sako, M. (2008). *Shifting Boundaries of the Firm*. Oxford, UK: Oxford University Press.

Sangster, A. (1994). The adoption of IT in management accounting: The expert systems experience. *Journal of Information Technology*, *9*(2), 159–169. doi:10.1177/026839629400900207

Saygili, S., & Taymaz, E. (2001). Privatization, Ownership and Technical Efficiency, A Study of the Turkish Cement Industry. *Annals of Public and Cooperative Economics*, *74*(4), 581–605. doi:10.1111/1467-8292.00182

Seal, W., Garrison, R. H., & Noreen, E. W. (2006). *Management Accounting* (2nd ed.). Singapore: McGraw Hill.

Shah, P. (2009). *Management Accounting*. New Delhi, India: Oxford University Press.

Shapiro, C., & Varian, H. R. (1999). *Information Rules: A Strategic Guide to the Network Economy*. Boston, MA: Harvard Business School Press.

Sheth, J. N., & Sharma, A. (1997). Supplier Relationships – Emerging Issues and Challenges. *Industrial Marketing Management*, *26*(2), 91–100. doi:10.1016/S0019-8501(96)00153-8

Speklé, R. F. (2001). Explaining management control structure variety: A transaction cost economics perspective. *Accounting, Organizations and Society*, *3*(4), 141–167.

Stähler, P. (2002). *Geschäftsmodelle in der digitalen Ökonomie-Merkmale, Strategien und Auswirkungen* (2. Ausg.). Lohmar Köln: Josef Eul Verlag.

Szychta, A. (2002). The Scope of Application of Management Accounting Methods in Polish Enterprises. *Management Accounting Research, 13*(4), 401–418. doi:10.1006/mare.2002.0198

Tapscott, D. (1996). *Die digitale Revolution: Verheißungen einer vernetzten Welt – die Folgen für Wirtschaft, Management und Gesellschaft*. Wiesbaden: Gabler. doi:10.1007/978-3-322-82739-5

Teittinen, H., Pellinen, J., & Järvenpää, M. (2013). ERP in action. Challenges and benefits for management control in SME context. *International Journal of Accounting Information Systems, 14*(4), 278–296. doi:10.1016/j.accinf.2012.03.004

Tomkins, C. (2001). Interdependencies, trust and information in relationships, alliances and networks. *Accounting, Organizations and Society, 26*(2), 161–191. doi:10.1016/S0361-3682(00)00018-0

Williams, J., & Seaman, A. (2002). Management Accounting Systems Change and Departmental Performance: The Influence of Managerial Information and Task Uncertainty. *Management Accounting Research, 13*(4), 419–445. doi:10.1006/mare.2002.0199

Wit, B., & Meyer, R. (1994). Strategy: Process, Content, Context, An International Perspective. Eagan, MN: West Publishing Company.

Yip, G. (2000). Global Strategy in the Internet Era. *Business Strategy Review, 11*(4), 1–14. doi:10.1111/1467-8616.00152

Zerdick, A., Schrape, K., Artope, A., Goldhammer, K., Heger, D. K., Lange, U., . . . Silverstone, R. (2001). Die Internet-Okonomie: Strategien für die digitale Wirtschaft (European Communication Council Report) (3. Ausg.). Berlin, Germany: Springer-Verlag. doi:10.1007/978-3-642-56418-5

ADDITIONAL READING

Anghelache, C., Căpuşneanu, S., Topor, D. I., & Marin-Pantelescu, A. (2019). Target Costing and Its Impact on Business Strategy: Computer Program for Cost Accounting and Administration. In I. Oncioiu (Ed.), *Network Security and Its Impact on Business Strategy*, (pp. 20–43). Hershey, PA: IGI Global. doi:10.4018/978-1-5225-8455-1.ch002

Căpuşneanu, S., Topor, D. I., Türkeş, M. C., & Rakoş, I.-S. (2019). Throughput Accounting: Decisional Informational Support for Optimizing Entity's Profit. In I. Oncioiu (Ed.), *Throughput Accounting in a Hyperconnected World*, (pp. 27–56). Hershey, PA: IGI Global. doi:10.4018/978-1-5225-7712-6.ch002

Cokins, G., Căpuşneanu, S., & Briciu, S. (2012). Accounting's shift to decision-based costing. *Theoretical and Applied Economics, 11*, 31–44.

Constantin, D. M., Topor, D. I., Căpuşneanu, S., Türkeş, M. C., & Anghel, M.-G. (2019). Green Reporting and Its Impact on Business Strategy: Computer Program for Evidence and Green Reporting. In I. Oncioiu (Ed.), *Network Security and Its Impact on Business Strategy,* (pp. 91–109). Hershey, PA: IGI Global. doi:10.4018/978-1-5225-8455-1.ch006

Oncioiu, I., Căpuşneanu, S., Türkeş, M., Topor, D., Constantin, D. M., Marin-Pantelescu, A., & Ştefan Hint, M. (2018). The Sustainability of Romanian SME's and their Involvement in Circular Economy. *Sustainability, 10*(8), 2761. doi:10.3390u10082761

Topor, D. I., Căpuşneanu, S., & Tamaş, A. S. (2017). An efficient green control (EGC) encouraging environmental investment and profitability. *Journal of Environmental Protection and Ecology, 18*(1), 191–201.

Türkeş, M. C., Oncioiu, I., Aslam, H. D., Marin-Pantelescu, A., Topor, D. I., & Căpuşneanu, S. (2019). Drivers and Barriers in Using Industry 4.0: A Perspective of SMEs in Romania. *Processes, 7*(3), 153. doi:10.3390/pr7030153

KEY TERMS AND DEFINITIONS

Activity-Based Costing (ABC): An accounting method that identifies the costs of (indirect) activities and then allocates these costs to the products. Allocation of product costs to products is done through cost drivers.

B20: The voice of the private sector of the G20 community and addresses the challenges and global priorities defined by the G20 countries by building a solid consensus among business leaders, international organizations and civil society on how they should be addressed.

Digital Security: How to protect information from the Internet and computer files against intrusion by external and unauthorized users.

Digitization: The process of converting information into a digital format where information is organized in bits whose final result consists of representing an object, image, sound, document or signal by generating a series of numbers describing a discrete set of points or samples.

Industry 4.0: Also called the 4th Industrial Revolution, Industry 4.0 is the trend of automation and data exchange in today's manufacturing technology, including: cyber-physical systems, the Internet of Things, cloud computing, and cognitive computation.

Management Accounting: The process of cost and business analysis for preparing internal financial reports to provide the necessary information to managers in making appeals and achieving business objectives.

Chapter 12
Benchmarking:
A Method to Improve the Entity's Performance and Change Process

Ana Maria Ifrim
Titu Maiorescu University, Romania

Alina Stanciu
1 Decembrie 1918 University, Romania

Monika Brigitte Sürgün
Valahia University, Romania

Hrisanta Cristina Ungureanu
Valahia University, Romania

ABSTRACT

Benchmarking is the process of comparing your own organization, operations, or processes with other organizations in the same industry or a wider market. This chapter intends to analyze the perspective of benchmarking in Romanian SMEs from the perspective of quality, cost, effectiveness, and customer satisfaction. The results show that for many Romanian organizations, benchmarking is still a little overlooked, on the one hand because of the lack of necessary financial resources, on the other hand, of a poor awareness of the importance of these investments in the medium and long term.

INTRODUCTION

Today, organizational culture is one of the concepts of widespread use in practice and in management theory, benefiting from continuous development (Barnes, Dang, Leavitt, Guarana, & Uhlmann, 2018; Cameron, & Quinn, 2011). Specialists are currently trying to explain and demonstrate the role of organizational culture in increasing the efficiency, performance and competitiveness of the firm (Barney, 1986; Lim, 1995; Denison, 1990; Hartnell, Ou, & Kinicki, 2011; Schneider, & Somers, 2006; Tong, & Arvey, 2015).

DOI: 10.4018/978-1-7998-1005-6.ch012

Leaders' decision to apply Benchmarking to their entity can be taken as a result of the desire to continuously improve performance as a result of preventing threats that may arise or as a result of capitalizing on the external or internal environment (Hurley, 2002; Becker, & Huselid, 1998).

Applying the Benchmarking method involves passing it through a complex process of performance comparison, a process that will take place within a predetermined time, and on which it is imperative to establish stages to justify its deployment at the end and to ensure the efficiency reflected in the synchronization of the vision leader with increasing entity performance (Alstete, & Beutell, 2018; Kaplan, & Norton, 2006; Galbraith, & Lawler, 1993).

Foreign managers present in Romania appreciate the good professional training of Romanians, innovation, creativity, sociability, ability to engage in solving situations, the ability to learn quickly and to adopt everything that is Western, but disapprove of the inappropriate use of time, the tendency to solve the tasks at the last moment, the work in jumps, the impression that they can do anything and they are good at everything. It has been found that Romanians are particularly motivated by rewards, and especially by the material ones. Also, Romania's economic situation, the level of inflation, the devaluation of the national currency, the standard of living directly and indirectly affects the components of organizational culture: the aspirations of employees, their expectations, beliefs, behaviors.

In Romanian companies it is necessary to create a model of values compatible with the basic rules of the market economy, to form and consolidate a strong managerial organizational culture. In an organization characterized by such an organizational culture, the values must not only be declared but supported by concrete actions.

The experience of competitive Western firms shows that sometimes the values of organizational culture conflict with the system of objectives. Surviving through a strong organizational culture requires attachment to values, even with the sacrifice of short-term financial interests.

Most initiatives of benchmarking across an entity have pursued competitive advantage through time, quality, cost, effectiveness, and customer satisfaction. The motivation to apply benchmarking by the leader of an entity suggests that it wants one of the processes within the entity to be consolidated.

The current paper intends to identify and analyze the perspective of benchmarking in Romanian SMEs from the perspective of quality, cost, effectiveness, and customer satisfaction.

BACKGROUND

Benchmarking in today's volatile, uncertain, complex, and ambiguous economic environment is the key to controlling entities that have understood and accepted that in order to remain on the market, it is necessary, regardless of the field of activity, to consider Vision Pillar - Innovation as essential. Against the backdrop of rising generations, scarcity of resources, the rate of change is known to continue to accelerate. New social, technological, environmental, political trends converge to create disruptive and disturbing forces, remodeling consumers' behaviors and preferences, going in-depth and responding to how / when / where?

On the other hand, the managers are an element that profoundly marks organizational culture (Amagoh, 2008). The special qualities of the managers, their professional and managerial training, and the specific capacities directly influence the organizational culture. Of course, the highest influence is given by top level managers, then middle managers (Ashkanasy, 2011). They can adopt a simple strategy that moves in the middle of employees to communicate with them and to sensitize them to the values they would like them to adhere to.

Many managers develop and report on their subordinates to communicate their organization's values and objectives. Other times, video cassettes are distributed to employees to highlight the role of each in achieving the company's goals. Each manager is concerned with communicating the values of the organization and integrating these values into their own actions (Rowland, & Hall, 2014).

In Romania we identify mainly two types of organizational cultures: bureaucratic culture and entrepreneurial culture.

Bureaucratic culture is the one that characterizes state-owned enterprises, educational and health institutions belonging to the state, military institutions. This culture is arrogant, focused on the inside of the system and highly politicized. An adaptation of this culture to the environment is difficult because there is no strategic thinking and knowledge of performance management issues. Within these organizations, hostile relationships between employees, between employees and managers are distinguished, and work results are not considered important.

Entrepreneurial culture can be distinguished mostly within private organizations, characterized by greater power of adaptation to the environment and by greater openness to new values and strategies that lead to positive results. Employees are given a set of values, rules that lead to the creation of a relaxed and professional environment: respect and respect for the client, employees and community, creativity, involvement, courage and attachment to the organization.

Successful companies increasingly manifest themselves as true open systems, whose position in the market depends not only on their internal resources, but also their relations with configuration and external entities with complementary skills. External network of the company is basically an extension of the internal borders between the two types of networks becoming increasingly difficult to identify.

External networks of companies, based mainly on cooperation, may develop spontaneously with operators working in the same territory, usually in close proximity and belonging or industry, or suppliers, specialized service providers, distributors etc. to rationalize the various phases of production and distribution of goods. Integration into external networks such synergistic effects materialized in generating competitive advantages for its members.

The managerial vision implies both a good knowledge of the past and the present, as well as ability to make attractive and practical reflections for the future that resonate with the soul and mind of the members of the organization (Tajeddini, 2015). Realistically, the second level prepares the guidelines that the organization must follow to succeed.

Benchmarking as the management tool and the leader's vision is outlined. Some entities, by applying this method, have even changed and improved the field in which they operate, raising it to a different level, shaping new horizons, and even becoming themselves Benchmark / standards of excellence, used in the process of measuring practices, performances an entity, markets, industries. Regardless of the motivation, cultivating an external view of industry and competitors must be a priority to manage the business carried out in this economic vortex (Fisher, 2010).

In terms of its definition, several directions can be identified as shown in Table 1.

In addition, specialist literature brings attention to several variants whereby an entity may decide to apply the Benchmarking method to improve its performance (Arsenault, & Faerman, 2014; Ahearne et al., 2010; Delaney, & Huselid, 1996). It may mean applying:

Table 1. Review of literature to define benchmarking

Reference	Definition
Allan (1993)	a continuous process of performance evaluation ... probably the only way to stay long on the wave, among the best
	a learning tool on how to improve your work, processes, and management
	a process of assessing and applying best practices that improve quality
	an information system that allows an enterprise to map its development strategy
Henczel (2002).	is a way of identifying potential improvements in efficiency and effectiveness, current operations and strategy, by comparing the performance of the firm with the performance of others
Deutsch & Silcox (2003)	a technique for determining competitive advantages and learning about products, services, own operations, by comparing with the best

- Strategic Benchmarking - Used when the organization wishes to improve its overall performance by examining strategies and approaches that have made it possible to achieve high performance "by certain entities.
- Process Benchmarking - is used when trying to improve processes and critical operations in generating organizational performance.
- Competitive Benchmarking - Enhanced performance of the entity by benchmarking of key product and service characteristics obtained by competitors.
- Functional Benchmarking - the entity's performance is analyzed in comparison with other selected entities in different sectors of activity. The purpose of this type of analysis is to improve the performance of similar functions to other entities.
- Internal Benchmarking - Improves the performance of a department of an entity (eg "business unit") as compared to another department within the same entity.
- External Benchmarking - the entity's performances are analyzed against the "best in class" of the market.
- International Benchmarking - An entity's performance analysis is performed by comparison with the performance of other entities on a particular international market.

The classic Benchmarking method requires that complex performance benchmarking and process compiling go through several stages (Lin, Peng & Kao, 2008):

- Planning phase, which involves: Identifying the area of the subject being treated by benchmarking / Defining the objectives and criteria that will be used to assess the performance of the entity / Selecting the benchmarking type / Identifying the competitors / Producing an action plan / Developing a communication strategy / Allocation of resources and selecting the project team / Obtaining the leader's agreement.
- Data and information gathering, seeks: Gathering performance information / Selecting and contacting competitors / Developing together with competitors a mutual understanding of the procedures to be followed / Preparing the questions, agreeing on the terminology and performance indicators that will be Use / Gather information using the chosen method, questionnaires, interviews, visits, telephone, fax, email / Examining and comparing the results for analysis.

- Analyzing the results: Identifying performance differences between the entity being analyzed and competitors / Explaining these performance differences / Ensuring that these comparisons are relevant and credible / identifying opportunities to improve performance.
- Recommendations: Examine the feasibility of measures to improve performance according to the entity's own conditions / agree on performance improvement measures / Produce a report on the benchmarking project, report containing proposed recommendations / obtaining stakeholder support for action corresponding to the recommendations.
- Implementation of recommendations: Implementation of action plans / Performance monitoring / informing stakeholder.
- Monitoring and review: Evaluation of the benchmarking process and results related to performance objectives and criteria as well as overall efficiency / Periodic reassessment of performance benchmarks.

Among the advantages that turn benchmarking into a strategic tool include: helps identify opportunities for improvement, is the source of creativity and change; generates potential improvements in efficiency and effectiveness, both in current operations and strategy; helps establish internal priorities, align with strategy and customer expectations; supports improving productivity strategies (Behery, Jabeen, & Parakandi, 2014); provide qualitative and quantitative information; helps to know your own activity and to appreciate all dimensions of performance; is a tool that links the organization (Akgün, Keskin & Byrne, 2009); people need to cooperate and learn how they work and how others think; this generates interdepartmental knowledge; is an effective tool for planning and implementing the change process that leads to improvement when knowledge is converted into action plans that lead to competitive advantages; increases the company's understanding of its forces and weaknesses towards competitors and signals the existence of competitive disadvantages; sets pragmatic goals based on an external vision (Chan, Shaffer, & Snape, 2004).

A too high rate of personnel change within the organization may have many negative aspects. Among these, the most important is the cost of staff change. Business organizations will scale up their initial staff costs as well as the costs associated with their change so that the profitability targets are not compromised (Fan, Li, & Zheng, 2016).

The change of staff, however necessary, will cause changes in the organizational structure (Bartoli, & Blatrix, 2015). Employees have to work in addition to being a substitute for the vacancy. Many plans can be or need to be reconsidered, and teamwork may no longer be possible when one of the participants is no longer present. If the employee in the organization was popular and loved by others, this change may be due to a general morale, which negatively affects motivation.

The employee's decision to stay or to be the organization is one that can be analyzed with the tools specific to the theory of economics, as we would expect the organization to do when calculating it. Profitability of the workforce flow. In the case of the employee, the cost-benefit analysis can be applied to explain his decision to the organization; the determining factor is mainly the incentive system that characterizes the organizational environment.

Although all these advantages recommend it as a strategic tool that leads to improved performance, there are also critics, circumspect in terms of its usefulness. In this respect, through a review of literature, Longbottom identifies three trends in the literature (Agha, Alrubaiee, & Jamhour, 2012):

- **Traditionalists**: Who explain how Benchmarking works and insist on its major long-term advantage.
- **Criticism:** Shows that rapid changes in the environment alter the importance of change through Benchmarking, so it generates slow and significant improvements. They are the followers of radical improvement through business process reengineering.
- **Modernists**: Argue for the use of global (integrated) models. They accept that Benchmarking is often perceived as an act of imitation or copying, but it shows that it actually supports more innovation than imitation.

In this context, what the leader can do is build, orientate managerial culture, and provide a logical and credible view of where the business should go and what performance is required of its members (Cocca, & Alberti, 2010). Leaders must therefore ensure that they have created the right organizational framework for company employees to showcase their skills and initiative, to capitalize on their knowledge at the highest levels without the need to build sophisticated or inflexible control systems.

BENCHMARKING AND PERFORMANCE: BETWEEN QUESTIONS AND ANSWERS

Various methods and tools have been designed and used over time to assess organizational phenomena, culture and organizational performance respectively (de Waal, & Kourtit, 2013; Taticchi, Tonelli, & Cagnazzo, 2010). One of the questions frequently raised by management specialists relates to what is important for the organization to be assessed: the organizational climate or organizational performance of the firm?

In-depth analysis of organizational performance research requires the consideration of both quantitative and qualitative research (Yadav, & Sagar, 2013). Qualitative research involves an interpretative approach to the subject under study by using and collecting empirical materials (case studies, observation, visual materials, interviews, human stories) describing common and special moments in the lives of individuals and organizations. Among the methods used by a series of sciences, applicable to organizational culture research, the most important are: observation method, experiment method, method of conversation, psychological investigation method, biographical method, modeling and simulation method, psychometric test method, monograph method.

The method of observation lies in the intentional pursuit and accurate recording of the various behavioral manifestations of the members of the organization (Anand, & Kodali, 2010). In essence, the method involves observing conduct, verbal expressions, physical products (uniforms, offices and outward appearance), interpersonal relationships, cultural norms and values, attitudes and beliefs, habits and work processes. The observation allows the direct knowledge of reality, identifying both the material elements of the organizational performance and some behavioral manifestations of the organization's members, negative or positive.

Applying this research method also involves a number of disadvantages, such as the fact that it is not economic, having to passively anticipate the behavior; unintentional changes can be made to the facts studied; the factors involved can not be tracked simultaneously; the information is often very rich, but not all of the same importance.

The psychological investigation method allows us to obtain information about the psychic life of a group of individuals by using oral or written questions (Alhyari et al., 2013). Researchers use two forms of this survey: based on an interview when questions are asked orally and based on a questionnaire when questions are written.

The information resulting from organizational performance research must be processed and presented in an accessible, synthetic and relevant form. Thus, statistical and mathematical methods and graphical methods are used in practice, such as: prediction tests, group conversations, in-depth conversations, motivational study, factorial, multidimensional analysis, etc.

In many cases, the employee's lack of satisfaction (material and professional) contributes decisively to the decision to resign. It may simply fail to find interest in the job, when the task becomes overly monotonous or boring, or it is possible that it does not use its knowledge or skill in its execution. Not knowing about wages and other material benefits, working hours or job security are also a powerful incentive to change the job. The organization, however, has much more control over the elements that affect the resignation of employees, these being related to the personnel policy adopted in the field of work or the decisions taken by the governing body.

Sometimes employees are very happy with the work they do, but they have problems with the company itself. The work environment is a tool and they can not do anything about creating better working conditions. Employees who are not happy with the working conditions will give their superiors or colleagues negative feelings about the organization and its rules, the opportunities it offers, and the chances of the organization and organization become bigger.

This method is used both to create a clearer picture of the company's cultural profile and to provide a database for further interventions. Based on other methods of identifying organizational culture, S.W.O.T. aims to rearrange the elements of the cultural profile corresponding to the following categories: Strengths, Weaknesses, Opportunities and Threats. Based on the Benchmarking, the strengths and weaknesses, the causes that generated them and their implications for the performance of the organization will be analyzed and presented.

Morphological analysis is a way to analyze and predict the components of organizational performance. This allows the decomposition of performance into component elements and their analysis in the context of profound changes in organizational culture in response to changes in the company's external environment.

Value analysis is another technique of organizing and processing the values of individuals and organizational performance (Andriole, 2010). This method provides information about what people value more or less, about what they value as desirable in correspondence with certain intentions, expectations and ideals. In organizations where employees are more concerned with meeting the basic, elementary needs, their behavioral choices are restricted, which leads to a decrease in their contribution to increasing the efficiency of their work. In strong economic firms, employees have higher aspirations, both spiritually and materially, which leads to their participation in organizational performance.

Impact analysis helps to get insight into the interaction between organizational performance and the external environment (Becker, & Huselid, 2006). This type of method provides the possibility to anticipate the possible consequences of managerial decisions as a result of the impact of different environmental changes on the organizational performance in order to guide and control the development of the firm.

As a major difference, this method analyzes managerial performance by trying to assess its context, connect it to the performance of the organization, and discover ways to change it.

Critical Incident Technique Classification as a qualitative method is due to the possibility of a profound approach to the subject, of obtaining a rich material of high authenticity and allowing individuals to clarify the meanings they associate with certain organizational components (Olson et al., 2005).

The use of the method aims at identifying common themes and perceptions and on this basis identifies predominant behavioral patterns of the members of the community in certain circumstances.

Method OCTAVE (Operationally Critical Threat, Asset and Vulnerability Evaluation - Evaluation Threats, Assets and Organizational Vulnerability Critical) based on the definition of complex, systematic and contextual essential components of an information system, using a three-stage organization to determine the risks associated with privacy, integrity and availability of information assets critical to the proper performance of the organization considered. Measuring losses or impact severity level of risk can be both qualitative and quantitative, depending on available resources collective organizational and risk management information security system. Determination of information security risks is generally difficult because information about threats and asset values are generally more difficult to obtain and quantify and risk factors are constantly changing. OCTAVE risk analysis based on the methodology involves the use of risk scenarios associated with each critical asset of the organization.

Regardless of the method used, of a qualitative or quantitative nature, it is important for the initiators of the audit of organizational performance and / or management performance to consider establishing conclusions that provide generally valid information in the context of the diversity of values, beliefs, opinions and attitudes of individuals of an organization.

Studies based on ethnographic analysis require a great involvement of researchers in the life of the organization so that they perceive the whole social construction of the organization, but within it, and even experimenting with these elements themselves (Chen, & Fu, 2008; Rowland, & Hall, 2014; Homburg, & Pflesser, 2000). Therefore researchers must observe the daily activities of the organization, study ceremonies and rituals, to understand the significance given various artefacts, study verbal and nonverbal languages used to capture existing stories and myths etc.

The analysis of organizational evolution can be an information base for the analysis of organizational performance. It is advisable, however, to treat information sources carefully since much of the documents in which these reports are presented are likely to appeal to the general public and are therefore often 'cosmetized'. For this reason, the analysis of organizational evolution is usually associated with other methods of investigation and analysis of organizational performance.

Today's world differs, through a series of essential aspects, from what we have been used to for a long time. The value and performance are the successful formula for effective and modern management of companies. "Measuring performance means appreciating value, and knowing value, means" to translate 'performance'.

Traditional entity operations are now disruptive by new technologies that remove barriers to entry for agile players. Challenged by the evolution of a fragmented market, the pragmatic adoption of new technologies represents new opportunities for new market players to innovate and develop business models that generate profit. Even powerful leadership entities have difficulty finding and finding anchorages in this new economic environment that will keep their competitive advantage and face the new threats to remain performing. The impact of Internet of Things (IoT), Cloud Computing, Distributed Intelligence, and Robotics on entities in 2020-2030 will be very strong. Only a thorough knowledge of the entity and the operations, transparency of management processes and financial knowledge of the external environment especially threats innovation in order to increase product and service quality, diversification and creation of internal mechanisms to respond to forces disruptive together with a managerial culture in which the leader has the force to influence from almost to the world, ensures that he remains in the market.

As one of the most studied subjects in the management, the integrated systems of performance indicators and their influence in the ascension of an organization are today the ground for the assertion of many ideas, much of them controversial, a state determined by the various ways of approaching its problem, which led to the shaping of major research directions.

Acceptance and assumption by top managers not only of their formal role within an entity but also of the informal one contributes to building a strong managerial performance. Involving managers in setting the mission and objectives of the entity in defining policies and action strategies that only make operational the stakeholder's vision make the managerial culture of an entity the link between all the elements that can ensure organizational performance.

SOLUTIONS AND RECOMMENDATIONS

In this Digital Age, performing entities play their best cards for three stakes: the first is sustainable performance, second finding and retaining talent, the quality of the human resource contributing to differentiation in a global and aggressive competitive market, and the third is research and innovation.

In order for this approach to take shape, specialized practice recommends an integrated approach to internal and external resources and greater attention to the implementation of the concepts of knowledge management, supply chain management, knowledge-sharing, open innovation, enterprise resource planning (ERP), enterprise interoperability. In addition to this integrated resource approach, the theoreticians recommend that the entity's leadership develop and apply the linear performance concept step by step, precisely to reduce the rate of change the entity faces in the turbulent environment in order to get closer to the real competitors.

FUTURE RESEARCH DIRECTIONS

The implementation of performance management within an entity meets multiple requirements directly related to the level of achievement of the set goals. A first requirement refers to the need for leadership to evaluate and manage a low level of performance relative to objectives, which has other implications: focusing on the entity's strategic objectives, aligning resources with activities, feedback and future development directions. 2030 represents the new time horizon that has prompted entities to shape their vision, strategy and performance objectives as clearly and convincingly as possible. Although it seems remote as a time horizon, an in-depth knowledge of the resources of each entity with a potential to increase performance includes the management system as a whole, along with the methods and techniques implemented to define performance indicators.

CONCLUSION

For many Romanian organizations, Benchmarking is still a little overlooked, on the one hand because of the lack of necessary financial resources, on the other hand, of a poor awareness of the importance of these investments in the medium and long term.

From the point of view of the improvement of the organizational performance, the following proposals can be recommended:

- In a world where competition is fierce, a leader can no longer meet his responsibilities without having managerial skills and knowledge. It is proposed that the managers go through specialization courses to help them successfully solve the problems, which are becoming more and more complex.
- The impact of Benchmarking on company performance is obvious and does not require much demonstration. The increase in performance gives the firm greater opportunities to adapt to the market, greater flexibility and chances of success compared with competition, and seek to improve financial results.
- The development of Benchmarking can offer the creation and observance of ethical codes that guide their activity and eliminate as far as possible the adoption of unethical behaviors with negative impact on the image of the company on the market.
- The initiation of partnerships, mergers, takeovers that will lead to the reinvigoration of the firm's activity becomes possible by taking into account the organizational element that influences the result of the company.

For the time being, the only alternatives for developing small and medium-sized businesses in Romania are: the ability to create new products and services, the ability to improve internal and external relationships so as to favor the creation of competitive advantages that will ensure success in the market.

REFERENCES

Agha, S., Alrubaiee, L., & Jamhour, M. (2012). Effect of core competence on competitive advantage and organizational performance. *International Journal of Business and Management*, *7*(1), 192–204.

Ahearne, M., Lam, S. K., Mathieu, J. E., & Bolander, W. (2010). Why are some sales people better at adapting to organizational change? *Journal of Marketing*, *74*(3), 65–79. doi:10.1509/jmkg.74.3.065

Akgün, A. E., Keskin, H., & Byrne, J. (2009). Organizational emotional capability, product and process innovation, and firm performance: An empirical analysis. *Journal of Engineering and Technology Management*, *26*(3), 103–130. doi:10.1016/j.jengtecman.2009.06.008

Alhyari, S., Alazab, M., Venkatraman, S., Alazab, M., & Alazab, A. (2013). Performance evaluation of e-government services using balanced scorecard. *Benchmarking: An International Journal*, *20*(4), 512–536. doi:10.1108/BIJ-08-2011-0063

Allan, F. (1993). Benchmarking: Practical aspects for information professionals. *Special Libraries*, *84*(3), 123–130.

Alstete, J. W., & Beutell, N. J. (2018). Designing learning spaces for management education: A mixed methods research approach. *Journal of Management Development*, *37*(2), 201–211. doi:10.1108/JMD-08-2017-0247

Amagoh, F. (2008). Perspectives on organizational change: Systems and complexity theories. *The Innovation Journal*, *13*(3), 1–14.

Anand, G., & Kodali, R. (2010). A mathematical model for the evaluation of roles and responsibilities of human resources in a lean manufacturing environment. *International Journal of Human Resources Development and Management*, *10*(1), 63–100. doi:10.1504/IJHRDM.2010.029447

Andriole, S. J. (2010). Business impact of Web 2.0 Technologies. *Communications of the ACM*, *53*(12), 67–79. doi:10.1145/1859204.1859225

Arsenault, P., & Faerman, S. R. (2014). Embracing paradox in management: The value of the competing values framework. *Organizational Management Journal*, *11*(3), 147–158. doi:10.1080/15416518.2014.949614

Ashkanasy, N. (2011). International happiness; a multilevel perspective. *The Academy of Management Perspectives*, (February): 23–29.

Barney, J. B. (1986). Organizational culture: Can it be a source of sustained competitive advantage. *Academy of Management Review*, *11*(3), 656–665. doi:10.5465/amr.1986.4306261

Becker, B. E., & Huselid, M. A. (1998). High performance work systems and firm performance: A synthesis of research and managerial implications. *Research in Personnel and Human Resources Management*, *16*, 53–101.

Becker, B. E., & Huselid, M. A. (2006). Strategic human resources management: Where do we go from here? *Journal of Management*, *32*(6), 898–925. doi:10.1177/0149206306293668

Behery, M., Jabeen, F., & Parakandi, M. (2014). Adopting a contemporary performance management system. *International Journal of Productivity and Performance Management*, *63*(1), 22–43. doi:10.1108/IJPPM-07-2012-0076

Cameron, K. S., & Quinn, R. E. (2011). *Diagnosing and Changing Organizational Culture: Based on the Competing Values Framework*. San Francisco, CA: Jossey-Bass.

Chan, L. L., Shaffer, M. A., & Snape, E. (2004). In search of sustained competitive advantage: The impact of organizational culture, competitive strategy and human resource management practices on firm performance. *International Journal of Human Resource Management*, *15*(1), 17–35. doi:10.1080/0958519032000157320

Chen, H. M., & Fu, P. C. (2008). A systematic framework for performance appraisal and compensation strategy. *Human Systems Management*, *27*, 161–175.

Cocca, P., & Alberti, M. (2010). A framework to assess performance measurement in SMEs. *International Journal of Productivity and Performance Management*, *59*(2), 186–200. doi:10.1108/17410401011014258

Davila, A. (2012). New trends in performance measurement and management control. In *Performance Measurement and Management Control: Global Issues* (pp. 65–87). Bingley, UK: Emerald Group Publishing Limited.

de Waal, A. A., & Kourtit, K. (2013). Performance measurement and management in practice. *International Journal of Productivity and Performance Management, 62*(5), 446–473. doi:10.1108/IJPPM-10-2012-0118

Delaney, J. T., & Huselid, M. A. (1996). The impact of human resource management practices on perceptions of organizational performance. *Academy of Management Journal, 39*, 949–969.

Denison, D. R. (1990). *Corporate Culture and Organizational Effectiveness*. New York, NY: Wiley.

Deutsch, P., & Silcox, B. (2003). Learning from other libraries: Benchmarking to assess library performance. *Information Outlook, 7*(7), 18–25.

Fisher, C. D. (2010). Happiness at Work. *International Journal of Management Reviews, 12*(4), 384–412. doi:10.1111/j.1468-2370.2009.00270.x

Galbraith, J. R., & Lawler, E. E. (1993). *Organizing for the Future: The New Logic for Managing Complex Organizations*. San Francisco, CA: Jossey-Bass.

Hartnell, C. A., Ou, A. Y., & Kinicki, A. (2011). Organizational culture and organizational effectiveness: A meta-analytic investigation of the competing values framework's theoretical suppositions. *The Journal of Applied Psychology, 96*(4), 677–694. doi:10.1037/a0021987 PMID:21244127

Henczel, S. (2002). Benchmarking – measuring and comparing for continuous improvement. *Information Outlook, 6*(7), 12–20.

Homburg, C., & Pflesser, C. (2000). A Multiple Layer Model of Market-Oriented Organizational Culture: Measurement Issues and Performance Outcomes. *Journal of Marketing Research, 37*(4), 449–462. doi:10.1509/jmkr.37.4.449.18786

Hurley, R. F. (2002). Putting people back into organizational learning. *Journal of Business and Industrial Marketing, 17*(4), 270–281. doi:10.1108/08858620210431679

Kaplan, R. S., & Norton, D. P. (2006). How to implement a new strategy without disrupting your organization. *Harvard Business Review, 84*(3), 100. PMID:16515159

Lim, B. (1995). Examining the organizational culture and organizational performance link. *Leadership and Organization Development Journal, 16*(5), 16–21. doi:10.1108/01437739510088491

Lin, C. H., Peng, C. H., & Kao, D. T. (2008). The innovativeness effect of market orientation and learning orientation on business performance. *International Journal of Manpower, 29*(8), 752–772. doi:10.1108/01437720810919332

Olson, E. M., Slater, S. F., Tomas, G., & Hult, M. (2005). The performance implications of fit among business strategy, marketing organization structure, and strategic behavior. *Journal of Marketing, 69*(3), 49–65. doi:10.1509/jmkg.69.3.49.66362

Rowland, C., & Hall, R. (2014). Management learning, performance and reward: Theory and practice revisited. *Journal of Management Development, 33*(4), 342–356. doi:10.1108/JMD-08-2012-0110

Schneider, M., & Somers, M. (2006). Organizations as complex adaptive systems: Implications of complexity theory for leadership research. *The Leadership Quarterly*, *17*(4), 351–365. doi:10.1016/j.leaqua.2006.04.006

Tajeddini, K. (2015). Exploring the antecedents of effectiveness and efficiency. *International Journal of Hospitality Management*, *49*(7), 125–135. doi:10.1016/j.ijhm.2015.06.007

Taticchi, P., Tonelli, F., & Cagnazzo, L. (2010). Performance measurement and management: A literature review and a research agenda. *Measuring Business Excellence*, *14*(1), 4–18. doi:10.1108/13683041011027418

Tong, Y. K., & Arvey, R. D. (2015). Managing complexity via the Competing Values Framework. *Journal of Management Development*, *34*(6), 653–673. doi:10.1108/JMD-04-2014-0029

Yadav, N., & Sagar, M. (2013). Performance measurement and management frameworks. *Business Process Management Journal*, *19*(6), 947–971. doi:10.1108/BPMJ-01-2013-0003

ADDITIONAL READING

Barnes, C. M., Dang, C., Leavitt, K., Guarana, C., & Uhlmann, E. L. (2018). Archival data in micro organizational research: A toolkit for moving to a broader set of topics. *Journal of Management*, *44*(4), 1453–1478. doi:10.1177/0149206315604188

Bartoli, A., & Blatrix, C. (2015). Management dans les orgaisations publiques - 4eme edition (Management in Public Organization - 4th edition), Dunod, Paris.

Fan, J. P. H., Li, J., & Zheng, G. (2016). Revisiting the bright and dark sides of capital flows in business groups. *Journal of Business Ethics*, *134*(4), 509–528. doi:10.100710551-014-2382-6

KEY TERMS AND DEFINITIONS

Cost: the money form of all material and labor expenses made by the company to produce and market material goods, execution works and service works.

Economic Management: The achievement of the budget objectives with minimum costs so that when the activity is completed the revenue exceeds the costs, namely there is a profit that ensures a level of profitability as high as possible both at general level and by product, department or service performed.

Financial Management: A tool in the decision-making relating to the collection and analysis of information in order to increase the performance level of the economic entity.

Integrity: The prohibition amendment - by deleting or adding - or the unauthorized destruction of information; integrity refers to confidence in the data and resources of a system by which to manage information.

Chapter 13
Digital Divide and Its Socio-Psychological Implications on Rural Dwellers in Nigeria

Afolayan Oluyinka Titilope
University of Ilorin, Nigeria

ABSTRACT

Unprecedented growth in the use of ICTs has contributed to digital divide in Nigeria. Despite global efforts in bridging the digital divide in developed and developing nations, digital equality is yet to be achieved in nations. Government's effort in bridging the digital divide in Nigeria has become a daunting task due to several barriers hindering the use of ICTs by the rural dwellers such as low income, low deployment of telecommunication infrastructure, lack of skills, access, language and cultural challenges, among others. In view of this, the aim of this paper is to unravel the socio-psychological consequences of the digital divide on rural dwellers in Nigeria. This paper further discussed dimensions and perspectives to the digital divide, causes of digital divide, global efforts in bridging the digital divide, barriers militating against digital divide, and social psychological consequences of the digital divide on rural dwellers. Policy recommendations were made towards addressing the socio-psychological implications of digital divide on rural dwellers in Nigeria.

INTRODUCTION

The unprecedented growth in the uptake of Information Communication Technologies (ICTs) such as computers, mobile phones, broadband, internet among others have contributed immensely to the economy of both developed and developing nations in numerous ways such as sharing of global knowledge and expertise across nations, better communication with trading partners through e-commerce, marketing tourism and participating in trade opportunities (Cullen, 2002; Callegati, Giallorenzo, Melis, & Prandini, 2018). However, the use of ICTs have continued to widen the gap between the developed and developing nations across countries, states, races, ethnic groups, urban and rural areas respectively. For instance, Samuelson (2002) pinpointed that the growth of the internet is unevenly distributed, it reaches fewer

DOI: 10.4018/978-1-7998-1005-6.ch013

than 7% of the world population; it tends to reach the wealthier and educated elites who appreciate the usefulness and relevance of ICT tools. These inequalities created through the use and non-use of ICTs has been widely referred to as "digital divide" around the globe- internationally, nationally and at local levels.

Digital divide can simply be defined as the gap between the "information – haves and have-not" that is, those who use or have access to telecommunication and information technologies such as computers, internet cable, telephone, satellite, wireless among others and those who do not or have limited access (Lennard, & Angela, 2013). In another sense, digital divide is the disparity between the technology rich and the technology poor or have- not. For instance, PC ownership levels differ dramatically and numerically between developed and developing nations. In South Asia, for example, 4 persons per 1000 own a PC compared to 585 per 1000 in the United States. These figures depict a high level of inequality across nations in their internet usage and PC ownership. Apart from the internet and PC ownership, levels of disparities have been found in the use of other types of ICTs across nations such as broad brand deployment, mobile phones and other telecommunications infrastructure (Lennard, & Angela, 2013). Global initiatives such as UNICT task force, G8 Digital Opportunity Taskforce (DOT) among others have been embarked upon to bridge the digital divide taking into consideration specific groups of people that are marginalized in the uptake of ICTs across nations.

Specifically, in a country like Nigeria, digital divide also cuts across different categories of people both in the urban and rural communities respectively. These categories of people are digitally divided along the lines of gender, age, class, socioeconomic status, disability among others in varying proportions. Rural people are those living in the remotest areas such as villages where the basic amenities of life are lacking such as pipe borne water, electricity and facilities such as hospitals, information centres, cybercafés etc. According to the literature, rural people have demonstrated a low uptake of ICTs due to reasons of low income, low education, health status, cultural differences, and lack of telecommunication infrastructure among others (Caspary, & O'Connor, 2003; Gbenga-Ilori, & Ibiyemi, 2010). Rural population are digitally excluded from the rest of world in the use of ICTs due to their backwardness and high level of illiteracy which account for lack of skills and inability to use information for their personal and collective advantage. Chowdhury (2000) identified a number of factors that characterized the rural people such as lack of access to accurate information, lack of telecommunication infrastructure and appropriate skills which accounted for the gap in technology use.

Coming down to the African Continent, high level of poverty and low level of education are prevalent factors responsible for low internet usage among the rural poor, with a resultant high level of digital divide across nations (Joseph, & Hollifield, 2003; Akanbi, & Akanbi, 2012). Similarly, Fong (2007) also found a significant relationship between GNI per capita and adoption of ICTs such as mobile phones, personal computers and telephone. This implies that majority of rural poor are low income earners and as such, accessing and procuring ICTs for use appears challenging. Amidst such challenges, the rural poor first considers his immediate needs- food, shelter and clothing before he/she engages in the utilization of ICTs. Therefore, in making the benefits of ICTs realizable, rural people need to be aware of the usefulness and relevance of ICTs to their development and the various ways it can contribute to meeting the Millennium Development Goals (MDG).

In `the context of Nigeria, the situation experienced by the rural people are not totally different from the experiences of rural dwellers in other parts of the world; except that the government of some of these countries have enacted digital inclusive programmes and policies for the rural poor to promote ICT use for development. A low level of ICT use is still apparent in rural communities in Nigeria due to socio-economic factors that have been identified in the literature, therefore, widening the digital divide. Rural communities in Nigeria suffer from marginalization due to illiteracy and lack of access to the many opportunities that ICTs offer (Gbenge-Ilori, & Ibiyemi, 2010). Despite the efforts of the Nigerian government in bridging the digital divide through several initiatives and collaboration with International bodies and private investors, the drive towards bridging the gap in rural areas have not been very productive, rather, the evolvement of new ICTs have continue to widen the gap between the rural and urban people. It may be appropriate to say that government must develop a strategic plan to bridge digital divide in urban and rural communities, therefore, combating digital inequality.

Digital divide has its attendant problems if not tackled successfully by the government, thereby affecting negatively rural dwellers socially and psychologically due to their lack of preparedness, lack of readiness to embrace technologies, ineptitude, low confidence, and backwardness. In view of this, the aim of this paper is to examine the socio- psychological implications of digital divide on the rural dwellers in Nigeria. This paper will further delve on the causes of global digital divide, the barriers and challenges of digital divide in the rural areas, policy interventions in bridging the digital divide in rural areas and lastly, recommendations will be made towards positive measures that can be undertaken by the government in combating the digital divide in rural areas.

DIMENSIONS AND PERSPECTIVES TO DIGITAL DIVIDE

The term "digital divide" is a global concept that has been examined widely by different authors, International bodies from varying dimensions and perspectives across nations, within racial and ethnic groups and among marginalized groups such as women, girl child, elderly people and the rural people among others. In spite of the various definitions of digital divide in the literature, it gives one the impression of a gulf, dichotomy or separation between two entities (Sahmim, & Gharsellaoui, 2017).

Norris (2001) in her book on "Digital Divide" highlighted the multi- dimensional perspectives of digital divide which constitute: (a) Global divide – divergence of internet access between industrialized and developing nations; (b) Social and economic divide constituting the gap between the information rich and information poor within a nation; (c) Democratic divide depicts the difference between those who use ICT to engage, mobilize and participate in political life and those who do not and cannot. DiMaggio and Hargittai (2001) also perceived digital divide as beyond the question of inequality in the use and non-use of the internet, instead they defined digital divide as the inequalities in access to the internet, extent of use, knowledge of search strategies, quality of technical connections, evaluating information and knowledge transmitted through the technology. In other words, digital divide is connected to the differences in computer skills needed to search for information, evaluating and use of information. In essence, rural people that are not able to read and write cannot possess the information searching and evaluating skills, therefore computer literacy is sine qua non to bridging digital divide in rural areas.

In the same vein, Sahmim and Gharsellaoui (2017) analyzed digital divide from 12 perspectives along the views of various professionals in the use and non-use of technology such as demographers, geographers, engineers and political scientists, economists, sociologist and many others. For instance, demographers view digital divide in terms of population count or census of internet users versus non- internet users; while geographers perceive digital divide in terms of space and location, that is the developed north and west are referred to as digital-haves; while the underdeveloped south are the digital have not.

In spite of the different angles to defining digital divide, the most popularly adopted definition in the literature is a one-dimensional approach to the digital divide (Wresch, 1996). The one-dimensional approach therefore, differentiates between the digital haves and digital haves- not or the technology rich and the technology poor in the areas such as usage level, access, skill level, ownership among others. The rural dwellers fall in the category of the digital haves-not due to the low level of penetration and use of technology for developmental purposes.

CAUSES OF DIGITAL DIVIDE

Global digital divide is referred to the International differences in the use and diffusion of information and communication technology across countries (Menzie, & Robert, 2004). In other words, there is high level of inequality and disparity in the area of access to ICTs across countries to aid information distribution and timely usage for development. Studies from the literature have identified determinants of global digital divide among countries which include differential income, human capital, policy regulatory effectiveness and telecommunications infrastructure (Dasgupta, Somnik, & David, 2001; Wallsten, 2003; Yucen, Wei, Wei, Delicato, Pires, & Zomaya, 2018).

Besides, Pohjola (2003) observed investment in information and communication technologies in 49 countries from 1993-2000. Findings from the study revealed differential investment in ICTs across these countries due to factors such as income per capita, relative price of ICT equipment, human capital measures, the share of agriculture and openness to international trade. Similarly, Kilsko and Pohjola (2001) examined internet penetration, that is, internet host per 1000 across a total of sixty OECD and developing countries. Variables such as income per capita, telephone access cost and average year of schools accounted for differential usage of the internet. Differential Income per capita is a key variable that was ranked high in other studies and is important in explaining the global digital divide across the countries understudied.

Menzie and Robert (2004) also examined cross country analysis of PC ownership and internet penetration on a larger sample comprising 161 countries from 1999- 2001 period. Findings revealed that sets of variables were statistically significant in relation to computer ownership with the exception of trade openness and telecomm pricing measures. These variables were categorized as: Economic variables (income per capita, years of schooling, illiteracy and trade openness), Demographic variables (youth and aged dependency ratios, urbanization rate) Infrastructure indicators (telephone density, electricity consumption) telecommunication pricing measures and regulatory quality. A similar trend holds true for internet use except telephone density and aged dependency. It was concluded that public investment in human capital, telecommunication and regulatory infrastructure can mitigate the digital divide in PC and internet use across countries. Furthermore, independent results from different countries using microdata have concluded that income and education are strong determinant of computer ownership and internet use (OECD, 2001 for several countries).

Based on the foregoing, the determinants of digital divide across countries include per capital income, education, differences in ICT investment, prices of ICT equipment, regulatory and telecommunication infrastructure among others. These numerous factors are predictive of the digital divide in the Nigerian environment, especially in the rural areas where most of the inhabitants are poor, low income earners and illiterates, thereby, hindering their ICT skill acquisition, access and use of these technologies.

GLOBAL EFFORTS IN BRIDGING THE DIGITAL DIVIDE

Multiple initiatives, however, have been implemented through international agencies, private investors and individual countries across the globe in addressing the barriers hindering efforts in bridging the digital divide, most importantly in the rural areas. Success stories have been recorded so far in some countries such as United States, Thailand, China, India among others in their efforts in bridging the digital divide. For instance, Indian government embarked on various IT projects to ensure the accessibility and availability of information to the rural population. One of the successful projects called Gyandoot project designed for the rural information network in the Dhar district of Madya Pradesh. Gyandoot literally means knowledge messenger, and it aided local farmers to get better yields through appropriate information dissemination channels. Also e-voice and e-chat mechanisms brought farmers to solve problems in agriculture and farming (Singh, 2007)

Similarly, China invested heavily in the creation of telecommunications infrastructure in rural and remote areas to bridge the widening internet connection between the rural and urban areas. China embarked on specific projects for the rural areas tagged "Every Village has a Phone", and "Gold Farm Engineering project" which promoted telephone access and internet applications in rural areas. Furthermore, China initiated the online and enterprise programme in the 1990's to facilitate information access at all levels of government. E-government programmes gave the citizens the opportunity of accessing or obtaining government information on policies, regulations law and enterprise services (en.wikipedia.org/wiki/)

In the case of Nigeria, deliberate efforts have also been made towards bridging the digital divide among its citizenry at all levels of government. Akanbi and Akanbi (2012) identified some of the initiatives implemented by the Nigerian government in collaboration with the international Community and private investors to address digital divide in rural areas. For instance the Universal Service Provision Fund (USPF) was established by the Nigeria Communications Agency in 2003 to provide ICT access by rural and urban population. Other projects include Community Communication Centre, Schools, Universities access programme (SUAP), Rural broadband Internet (RUBI) and Access, Accelerated mobile Phone Expansion (AMPE) among others. Apart from these initiatives, policies of liberalization, deregulation and privatization of the telecomm sector and regulatory bodies have succeeded in bridging the digital divide in the urban cities and rural areas in several states in Nigeria to a certain extent considerably (Akanbi, & Akanbi, 2012). For instance the privatization of the telecommunications sector have given the internet service providers ((ISPs) a leverage to operate in the Nigerian market. As a result, Mobile phones have been widely embraced in both urban and rural areas due to reason of affordability and accessibility, reduced cost of line, service charges and improved interoperability. In spite of this milestone achievements, Nigeria as a developing nation is still grabbling with problems associated with` ICT diffusion in the area of access, skill access, disparity in telecommunications facilities between the rural and urban areas (Akanbi, & Akanbi, 2012).

BARRIERS AND CHALLENGES IN BRIDGING THE DIGITAL DIVIDE IN RURAL COMMUNITIES IN NIGERIA

Digital divide occurs when there are disparities in skills and access in the use of information communication technologies between two or more groups of people As identified in the literature, Crosby, (1997) mentioned some barriers hindering the use of ICTs among rural dwellers which include lack of knowledge and awareness, lack of infrastructure, lack of access, complexity in the use of new technologies and cost in the area of access, learning, training and development. Nigeria as a developing country is still experiencing these aforementioned barriers affecting ICT diffusion and use in rural areas most especially.

Several challenges militating against the realization of digital equality in rural areas are mentioned below, though in varying degrees. These are: (i) Infrastructural barriers which is as a result of lack of robust infrastructure with sufficient and reliable bandwidth for internet connection. Apart from telecommunications infrastructure, lack of stable supply of electricity has been hindering the effective use of ICTs in both urban and rural areas, therefore, constituting a divide between the "digital haves" and "digital haves-not".

(ii) Lack of literacy and access skills have also affected the use of ICTs in the rural areas where majority are not able to read and write coupled with the lack of knowledge in the use of ICT tools such as computer, internet among others. Inequality in literacy and skill levels has continued to widen the digital gap between the haves and haves-not among the different categories of people in the rural and urban areas.

(iii) Language and cultural barrier also constitute a big hindrance in bridging the digital divide among the rural people in Nigeria due to lack of local contents on the internet. Most of the contents on the internet and other ICT tools are in foreign language, therefore causing the problem of access and use of such information for the people whose primary language is not English. This means the contents are not indigenous in nature, therefore hindering the use and application of such knowledge to their day to day living. Unless the language barrier is adequately tackled, rural people will continue to be digitally divided and left behind.

(iv)Economic barrier is another factor that hinders the rural people from accessing information and procuring ICT tools due to lack of financial resources. The rural people, being economically disadvantaged cannot afford the use of ICTs due to high cost of access and service charges.

(v) Attitudinal barriers which connote cultural and behavioural inclinations have negatively affected the use of ICTs among rural dwellers. Rural dwellers have wrong and erroneous beliefs about the use of technologies, they believe it is meant for the elitist group and not for people like them that are illiterates, backward, and lacks knowledge in the use of technologies.

Therefore, unless these barriers militating against the use of ICTs among rural dwellers are adequately tackled, it would continue to widen the digital divide in the area of access, skills and usage. Apart from this, digital divide has its negative consequences socially, economically and psychologically on the rural people (Parker, Husson, Dillman, Strover, & Williams, 1992; Lennard, & Angela, 2013).

SOCIO- PSYCHOLOGICAL CONSEQUENCES OF THE DIGITAL DIVIDE ON RURAL COMMUNITIES IN NIGERIA

Technology use has its social consequences on the society, groups and individual person. It is believed that technology users are engaged in social relations as they interact and communicate with one another (Sahmim, & Gharsellaoui, 2017). At the same time, non use of technology has its social and psychological implications that maybe negatively inclined. Therefore, non- accessibility and availability of appropriate ICTs are responsible for the social psychological problems experienced by the rural people. However, the social psychological implications of the digital divide cannot be undermined, but government must painstakingly address these issues. These include:

(i) Lack of development and empowerment due to non access to information and technologies. Access to relevant information is a key to development and vice versa. Therefore, rural people need relevant information to meet specific MDG goals. However, non-access to information widens the gap between the digital haves and digital haves-not. If the digital divide is left unaddressed, rural communities remain backward socially, attitudinally and are totally isolated from the rest of the world. This is in line with Parker et al., (1992) who pinpointed that the lack of information and communication technologies in rural communities will result in their lagging behind in development with growing gaps socially, economically and welfare.

(ii) Rural urban migration is another negative consequence of the digital divide especially for the youths in those communities. There will be a drift from the rural to urban life which may lead to the urban areas being over populated. The youths in the rural communities will be attracted to the urban life where they are better informed, empowered and educated, thereby making those communities desolated and under developed.

(iii) Fourthly, there will be rise in the Poverty level due to lack of access to relevant information that will improve their standard of living. The rural dwellers are affected negatively, and as such cannot contribute positively to the development of their local communities. The rural people will end up living a life of impoverishment with no hope for the future.

(iv) Another socio psychological consequence is that rural dwellers will exhibit low self-esteem, inferiority complex due to inability to compete favourably with urban dwellers. Rural dwellers may feel socially excluded from the rest of the world due to their inability to access and use ICT tools.

(v). Rural people may also experience technophobia due to anxiety and their non-familiarization with ICT tools, therefore, widening the digital divide There is the need to enlighten rural people on the usefulness and relevance of ICTs to their local development. This can be accomplished through community training, awareness programmes that will repose their confidence in the use of ICTs.

POLICY INTERVENTIONS IN BRIDGING THE DIGITAL DIVIDE IN RURAL COMMUNITIES

In bridging the digital divide, speedy interventions is necessary in ameliorating the effect of the divide on rural dwellers, through the enactment of appropriate policies that will address the digital divide in rural communities. To this end, Nigeria must embrace an all inclusive ICT policy for the rural population that will specifically address the needs of marginalized groups such as women, girl child, elderly people and the disabled. These Policy issues will invariably address these following areas:

(i) Basic literacy and IT literacy programmes for rural communities especially for women, girl child and elderly people that cannot afford the cost of procuring ICT tools for their use. These literacy programmes will afford them the opportunity of reading and writing and being skilled in the use of ICT tools due to the high level of illiteracy.

(ii) Development of local content in the language of the rural communities is a key issue in promoting the use and access to these technologies. Policies must drive the development of local contents in order to improve accessibility and usability of indigenous knowledge such as agricultural information for local farmers.

(iii) The role of the library cannot be undermined in bridging the digital divide in rural communities. Policy must drive the setting up of libraries in rural communities with the aim of promoting lifelong learning and continuous access to evolving ICTs. The library will be a one stop point for the rural dwellers in the area of access to ICTs such as internet, computer among others, and also other programmes such as community centres for training, awareness creation, enlightenment and the maintenance of communities' cultural values and heritage.

(iv)Government must budget substantial amount of money for the procurement and installation of ICT infrastructure in the rural communities as a way of bridging digital divide. Several initiatives through the collaboration and support of private investors will go a long way in reducing cost of procuring the equipment. Efforts must be geared towards measuring the project outcomes and following it to a logical conclusion.

SOLUTIONS AND RECOMMENDATIONS

Bridging the digital divide in rural communities remain a daunting task for government, nevertheless, digital divide and its attendant problems cannot be overlooked due to its adverse effect on rural dwellers. Some of these problems emanating from the digital divide in rural communities include social isolation inferiority complex, lack of development and empowerment, increase in poverty level, rural urban drift and technophobia resulting from fear and anxiety to use ICTs.

In view of the above, the following recommendations are made in addressing the socio-psychological consequences of the digital divide on the rural dwellers in Nigeria.

CONCLUSION

Government should continually exercise effort in bridging the digital divide by increasing the penetration and usage levels of specific ICT tools in rural communities such as computers, internet, mobile phones, and broad band among others. Also, government should collaborate through partnership with external bodies such as World Bank, International community or donor organizations in seeking for funds to facilitate evenly distribution and diffusion of ICT tools in rural communities. In essence, if the digital divide is successfully bridged, its socio-psychological effects are adequately combated. Furthermore, challenges peculiar to rural areas such as low education, low earning capacity among others must be addressed in bridging the digital divide in rural communities.

In conclusion, the evolvement of new ICTs in this technological age will continue to widen the digital divide in Nigeria; therefore, government should be relentless in her efforts toward bridging the existing disparities in access, skills and use of ICT tools through appropriate training programmes and implementation of the digital inclusive policy for the rural dwellers.

REFERENCES

Akanbi, B. E., & Akanbi, C. O. (2012). Bridging the Digital Divide and the impact on Poverty in Nigeria. *Computing Information Systems and Development Informatics*, *3*(4), 1–12.

Callegati, F., Giallorenzo, S., Melis, A., & Prandini, M. (2018). Cloud-of-Things meets Mobility-as-a-Service: An insider threat perspective. *Computers & Security*, *74*, 277–295. doi:10.1016/j.cose.2017.10.006

Caspary, G., & O'Connor, D. (2003). *Providing Low-Cost Information Technology Access to Rural Communities in Developing Countries: What works? What pay?* (Working paper No. 229), OECD Development Centre.

Chowdhury, N. (2000). *Information and Communications Technologies and IFPRI's Mandate: A Conceptual Framework.* Retrieved from http://www.ifpri.org/divs/cd/dp/ictdp01.pdf

Crosby, E. M. (1997). Connecting with Country People. Armidale, New South Wales, AU: The Rural Development Centre. University of New England.

Cullen, R. (2002). *Addressing the Digital Divide.* Presented at the School of Information Management, University of Wellington, New Zealand.

Dasgupta, S., Somik, L., & David, W. (2001). *Policy Reform, Economic Growth and the Digital Divide: An Econometric analysis.* World Bank Working Paper No. 2567 (March).

DiMaggio, P., & Hargittai, E. (2001). *From the 'Digital Divide' to 'Digital Inequality': Studying Internet Use as Penetration Increases.* Princeton, NJ: Center for Arts and Cultural Policy Studies, Woodrow Wilson School, Princeton University.

Fong, M. (2009). *Digital Divide: Reaping the Benefits of ICT. Europe's productivity Challenge.* Report Sponsored by Microsoft Euro Monitor International, GMI Database. Retrieved from http://graphics.eiu.com/files/ad_pdfs/MICROSOFT_FINAL.pdf

Gbenga-Ilori, A. O., & Ibiyemi, T. S. (2010). Directing the Digital Divide towards Bridging the Digital Divide in Nigeria. *European Journal of Scientific Research*, *45*(1), 79–88.

Joseph, F. D., & Hollifield, C. A. (2003). Digital Divide Evidence in Four Rural Towns. *IT & Society*, *1*(4), 107–117.

Kiiski, S., & Pohjola, M. (2001). *Cross-country diffusion of the internet.* WIDER Discussion Paper No. 2001/11. Helsinki, Finland: World Institute for Development Economics Research.

Lennard, G. K., & Angele A. G. (2013). *Broadband Internet Access and the Digital Divide: Federal Assistance Programs.* A Report delivered at Congressional Research Service.

Menzie, D. C., & Robert, W. F. (2004). *The Determinants of the Global Digital Divide: A Cross-Country Analysis of Computer and Internet penetration.* Working Paper Presented at the National Bureau of Economic Research, Cambridge, MA.

Norris, P. (2001). *Digital Divide: Civic Engagement, Information Poverty, and the Internet Worldwide.* New York, NY: Cambridge University Press. doi:10.1017/CBO9781139164887

OECD. (2001). *Understanding the Digital Divide.* Paris, France: Organization for Economic Cooperation and Development.

Pohjola, M. (2003). *The Adoption and Diffusion of ICT across Countries: Patterns and Determinants. The New Economy Handbook.* Academic Press.

Primrose, J. (2003). *2001 Census: Computer and Internet Use. Census Paper No. 03/03.* Australian Bureau of Statistics.

Sahmim, S., & Gharsellaoui, H. (2017). Privacy and Security in Internet-based Computing: Cloud Computing, Internet of Things, Cloud of Things: A review. *Procedia Computer Science*, *112*, 1516–1522. doi:10.1016/j.procs.2017.08.050

Samuelson, R. J. (2002). Debunking the Digital Divide. *Newsweek, 139*, 22-40.

Singh, N. (2007). Bridging the Digital Divide in India: Some Challenges and Opportunities. *World Libraries*, *17*(1), 32–51.

Wallsten, S. (2003). Regulation and Internet Use in Developing Countries, *AEI-Brookings* Brookings Institution, May.

Wresch, W. (1996). *Disconnected: Haves and Have-Nots in the Information Age.* New Brunswick, NJ: Rutgers University Press.

Yucen, N., Wei, L., Wei, B., Delicato, F. C., Pires, P. F., & Zomaya, A. Y. (2018). A dynamic tradeoff data processing framework for delay-sensitive applications in Cloud of Things systems. *Journal of Parallel and Distributed Computing*, *112*(1), 53–66.

Chapter 14
Uncommon Sources of Finance and Sustainability, Growth and Development of Small Medium-Scale Enterprises in Nigeria

Abraham Oketooyin Gbadebo
Osun State University, Niger

ABSTRACT

This chapter presents uncommon sources of financing SMEs. Finance is indispensable factor for development and growth of SMEs everywhere in the world. However, few people are acquainted to alternative sources of financing SMEs other than the traditional mediums. In Nigeria, lack of knowledge on non-traditional sources of funding has either contributed to the death or slow pace of development of SMEs. Some of the uncommon sources are crowdfunding, merchant cash advance, elusive business grant, and small business administration. In the chapter, the author exposes these sources as well as present guidelines on how they could be accessed.

INTRODUCTION

The idea of Small and Medium Enterprises (SMEs) was introduced into the development landscape as early as the late 1940s (OECD, 2004). The prime goal of SMEs has encouraged countries all over the world to improve trade and industrialization. The definitions of SME are usually derived in each country, based on the role of SME in such an economy, policies and programmes designed by particular agencies or institutions empowered to develop SMEs. In case of a small business in the developed economy like Japan, Germany or United States of America (USA), be described as a medium or large-scale business in a developing nation like Nigeria.

The definition of SME varies over time from one agency or developing institution to another, contingent on its policy focus. The above variation notwithstanding, SME can be defined quantitatively and qualitatively. According to Filion, (1990), SMEs can be quantitatively defined based on certain criteria

DOI: 10.4018/978-1-7998-1005-6.ch014

such as turnover, the number of employees, profit, capital employed, available finance, market share and relative size within the industry. As an example the 1975 Companies Act in the United Kingdom stated that an enterprise with a turnover of less than one million, four hundred thousand pounds (£1,400,000) was small, those with turnover between one million four hundred thousand pounds (£1,400,000) and five million, seven hundred pounds (£5,700,000) were medium, while those enterprises having turnover above five million, seven hundred pounds (£5,700,000) were described as large. It also went further to classify the enterprises based on a number of employees: those with fewer than fifty (50) workers being small, between fifty (50) and two hundred and fifty (250) workforces being medium and businesses that employ above two hundred and fifty (250) employees were considered as large. Similarly, the European Union (EU) in 1995, defined SME as any enterprise employing less than 250 employees, went further to break down the SME into micro (less than ten (10) employees, small (from ten (10) to forty nine (49) employees and medium (between fifty (50) and two hundred and forty nine (249) employees.

In Nigeria, the National Council of Industry, 2003 categorized SMEs as Micro, Small and Medium. A Microenterprise is a business with between one (1) and ten (10) staff strength with a total cost of less than one million (N1, 000,000) including working capital but excluding land. A small size business is the one with a workforce of between workers of eleven (11) and thirty-five (35) with total assets of a minimum of one million (N1, 000,000) and less than forty million (N40, 000,000) including working capital but excluding land. A medium scale enterprise is a business with thirty-six (36) and one hundred (100) employees and asset base of a minimum of forty million (N40, 000,000) and less than two hundred million N200, 000, 000) including working capital but excluding land. On the other hand, the qualitative methods are independent ownership and independent capital (Recklies, 2001), entities not publicly traded (Osteryoung, & Newman 1993). In addition, IFRS IASB (2003) defined SME as an entity that does not have public accountability and publishes general purpose financial statements for external users it also classified it as enterprises by their nature.

According to Lawson (2007) access to finance has been identified to be one of the crucial factors militating against the survival and growth of Small Medium Enterprises especially in emerging economies like Nigeria. Abereijo and Fayomi (2005) noted that majority of loans offered by Deposit Money Banks to SMEs are usually for a short period and grossly inadequate for initial capital of a sizeable business let alone their expansion purposes.

Other essential factors hindering the survival and growth of SMEs in Nigeria are erratic power supply, poor management, corruption, lack of training and experience, poor infrastructure, insufficient profits, and low demand for product and services incompetence of the entrepreneur, incessant changes in government policies, multiple taxation, and lack of tax holiday for infant enterprises; high interest rate on lending, inflation rate and exchange rate (Essien, 2014). According to Ossai (2017), the challenges enumerated do not prevent the prospects of SMEs in Nigeria which include: Employment Generation, Wealth Creation, and Poverty Reduction, Promotion of Local Entrepreneurship and Indigenous Technology Development, Mitigation of Rural-Urban Drift, Income Redistribution and Industrial Dispersal and Export Promotion.

However, SMEs have been regarded as the bedrock for employment generation and technological development not just in Nigeria but all over the world. On the crucial problem of finance on SMEs, some scholars: Ubesie, Onuaguluchi, and Mbah, (2017) examined the effect of deposit money banks' credit on small and medium scale enterprises growth in Nigeria; Abdulsaleh and Worthington (2013), identified sources of finance for SMEs to range from original private sources of the owner and manager's savings and retained earnings. Other sources included financial support from family and associates, trade credit, venture capital, and angel investor. Lastly, Gbandi and Amissah (2014) considered the business financing of SMEs in Nigeria, and viewed the importance of microfinance banks, cooperatives, and commercial banks as major sources in Nigeria. Other sources of investment finance for SMEs in Nigeria included proprietor's savings, moneylenders, and local authorities.

This chapter intends to contribute to the ongoing debate on the sources of finance especially on how to grow SMEs in Nigeria. The objectives of this chapter are to: identify and discuss uncommon sources of financing for SMEs in Nigeria; examine the arguments of scholars on the sources of financing SMEs in Nigeria

The chapter will be of use to all stakeholders in the SMEs management, especially the managers, entrepreneurs, account officers who will be exposed to various forms of uncommon sources of financing businesses hence grow their business potentials, researchers who want to add to the existing body of knowledge will see the chapter useful, students who want to use the contents of this chapter as their reading materials and government who formulates relevant policies and interventions that will enhance survival and growth of SMEs and consequently facilitate economic growth and development in Nigeria. The panache of this chapter will course its contents to be simple to comprehend hence can be used for pertinent professional examinations

The uncommon sources of finance can be classified into four main groups according to the providers of the funds viz: individuals, corporate organization, non-governmental organization and Government.

BACKGROUND

Traditional methods of financing SMEs in Nigeria were examined by some scholars among which are Gbandi and Amissah (2014), who examined the business financing of SMEs in Nigeria, taking into consideration the importance of microfinance banks, cooperatives, and commercial banks in Nigeria. The sources of investment finance for SMEs in Nigeria included proprietor's savings, moneylenders, and local authorities. The formal investment sector included equity financing through Venture Capital and business angels (Gbandi, & Amissah, 2014).

Financing for SMEs usually comes from individual savings, family, and associates, while credits from banks and other commercial institutions hardly occur (Gulani, & Usman, 2013; Ilegbinosa, & Jumbo, 2015).

Kishor and Dereje (2018) examined Financial Sustainability of SMEs by injecting Debt Finance The analysis reveals that the debt finance exerts positive influence on both short term and long-term financial performance of SMEs. Debt finance does not influence the asset turnovers as well as the current profitability of SMEs. Since the financial performance of SMEs can be measured by short term and long-term financial position, the influence of debt finance over short term as well as long term financial position implies that debt finance exerts positive influence on financial performance of SMEs. The financial sustainability of SMEs depends on long term financial position which is an important indicator of financial performance. Therefore, debt finance influences significantly the financial sustainability of SMEs

Taiwo, Yewande, Edwin, and Benson (2016) explored the roles of microfinance banks on SMEs and the benefit derived from the credit scheme of microfinance banks. They interviewed 15 SMEs leaders across Lagos state in Nigeria. Their findings revealed that recapitalization of microfinance banks in Nigeria would improve the capacity to granting credit to SME for growth and development. They recommended that the government of Nigeria should encourage microfinance banks and other monetary institutions to support the SMEs in Nigeria

Financing for SMEs is crucial to the economic growth of Nigeria (Ilegbinosa, & Jumbo, 2015; Gbandi, & Amissah, 2014). SMEs in Nigeria face difficulty in accessing bank credits and other commercial agencies (Gulani, & Usman, 2013; Ilegbinosa, & Jumbo, 2015). Banks found it harder to deal with SMEs in comparison to other clients because of the high risks and lack of information associated with SMEs. Access to operational funds such as credit finance, labor, and technology were significant problems faced by SMEs (Gulani et al, 2013). Financing for SMEs usually comes from individual savings, family, and associates, while credits from banks and other commercial institutions hardly occur (Gulani et al, 2013; Ilegbinosa et.al 2015)

Gbandi and Amissah (2014) examined business financing of SMEs in Nigeria, taking into consideration the importance of microfinance banks, cooperatives, and commercial banks in Nigeria. The sources of investment finance for SMEs in Nigeria included proprietor's savings, moneylenders, and local authorities. The formal investment sector included equity financing through Venture Capital and business angels (Gbandi et al, 2014). The informal finance sector (IFS) provided more than 70% of the funds needed by SMEs (Gbandi, & Amissah, 2014).

Tende (2014) examined government strategies and programs encouraging entrepreneurship and investments in new businesses. Governments in developing countries introduced some strategies and interventions intended to promote entrepreneurship through SMEs expansion programs (Adedayo et al., 2016; Tan, & Tan, 2014; Tende, 2014). Tende used a random sample of 1,159 beneficiaries of Entrepreneurship Development Programmes (EDP) and National Directorate of Employment (NDE) programs to obtain information for 10years, between 2001 and 2010. Successive Nigerian government established various agencies and policies, which included credit guidelines for credits and loans for banks to make available credits to Nigerian SMEs (Abdulazeez Suleiman, & Yahaya, 2016; Adedayo Ojo, & Toluwalope, 2016; Tende, 2014).

The government credit policies had no significant effect on the development of 34 entrepreneurial activities in the country (Tende, 2014). The EDP and NDE beneficiaries did not achieve maximum benefit from government programs and policies (Tende, 2014) The successive government in Nigeria, over the years, established various financing institutions, structured to provide assistance to SMEs to help in the development and growth of the SME sector (Afolabi, 2015; Obaji, & Olugu, 2014). The institutions included the Nigerian Industrial Development Bank (NIDB), the Nigerian Bank of Commerce and Industry (NBCI), National Economic Reconstruction Fund (NERFUND), Nigerian Export-Import Bank (NEXIM), and the Peoples Bank of Nigeria (Afolabi, 2015; Obaji et al 2014). Other institutions included National Directorate of Employment (NDE), Industrial Development Coordinating Centre (IDCC), Community Banks, Family Economic Advancement Program (FEAP), and State Ministries of Industry SME schemes, the Nigerian Agricultural, and Cooperative Development Bank (NACDB), and Bank of Industry (BOI). However, the innovative success of developing nations depended on the financial policy behaviour of government (Tan et al 2014; Obaji et al, 2014).

Evbuomwan, Ikpi, Okoruwa, and Akinyosoye, (2013) examined the sources of finance for micro, small and medium enterprises in Nigeria claimed that among the constraints to effective development of MSMEs in Nigeria is the limited access of the investors to long term credit. The study also averred that various credit initiatives have been instituted in the past to improve the access of MSMEs to long term funds. The study showed that commercial banks loans constituted over 90 percent of sources of funds to MSMEs in Nigeria and their loans and advances to agriculture and manufacturing sectors combined (where the MSMEs are dominant) grew from N83.40 million in 1970 to N1,129,158.30 million in 2009 and averaged N149,106.08 million per annum thereby constituting 17.81% of total commercial banks loans and advances to the Nigerian economy on the average between 1970 and 2009, whereas the MSMEs currently contribute about 50% to the nation's Gross Domestic Product. The study further observed that MSME operators still do not have enough funds for their operations as a frequency analysis indicated that inadequate fund/working capital was the most mentioned problem with a percentage share of 60.7%. In view of the assured role of MSMEs in economic development and poverty alleviation they recommended that all the funding apparatus directed at the MSMEs in Nigeria, be sustained and intensified.

INDIVIDUALS FUNDING SCHEMES

Crowdfunding is the process of mobilizing of small amounts of capital from a large number of individuals to finance a new business venture. Crowdfunding makes use of the easy accessibility of vast networks of people through social media and crowdfunding websites to bring investors and entrepreneurs together, and has the potential to increase entrepreneurship by expanding the pool of investors from whom funds can be raised beyond the traditional circle of owners, relatives and venture capitalists. Investors buy securities in a fund which makes the loans to individual borrowers or bundles of borrowers. Investors generate returns from interest on the unsecured loans; the system operators derived their income through charging of a certain percentage of the loan and a loan service charge (Golić, 2014). On the other hand, borrowers apply for the funds online which does not attract any fee. On receipt of their applications they reviewed and verified by an automated system, which also determines the borrower's credit risk and interest rate.

Crowdfunding can be used for motion picture promotion, free software development, inventions development, scientific research and civic projects. There are four major methods of crowd funding: debt-based, rewards-based, equity-based, and charity-based.

Debt-based crowdfunding also known as Peer-to-Peer (P2P) lending allows a business to gain access to funds from an online platform that has a pool of investors ready to invest in a particular business. Investors lend a fixed sum of money over a period of time to the business and they earn interest. Ideally, debt crowdfunding is great for a single purpose over a select period of time, such as entry to a new market. If the business has been in existence for a couple of years, and it has assets and enough cash flow to make repayments, debt crowdfunding could be a good option. Characteristics of Debt-based crowdfunding are: most startup businesses fail hence it may lead to loss of capital invested; investing in startup businesses should only be done as part of a diversified portfolio; tax relief depends on an individual's circumstances that may be subjected to changes in the future; tax reliefs are not guaranteed, as it depend on qualifying status of the entities invested; past performance is not a reliable indicator of future performance.

Rewards-based crowdfunding is the process where the receiver of the funds needs not to pay the money back; but agree to give the backers something in return for the money released. Characteristics of rewards-based crowdfunding: it does not rely on location: This implies that the distance between the creators and benefactors is irrelevant; funding for the projects is distributed unevenly, with a few projects accounting for the majority of overall funding; funding increases as a project nears its completion thereby encourage "herding behavior"; funders are often too hopeful about project returns and must revise expectations when returns are not met.

Equity-based crowdfunding is the collective effort of individuals to support efforts initiated by other people or organizations through the provision of finance in the form of equity in exchange for share(s) of a firm or business. Characteristics of equity crowdfunding are: it contains heightened "information asymmetries" hence the creator must not only produce the product for which it has raised capital, but also create equity to represent the finance it has received; it involves the offer of securities which include the potential for a return on investment; syndicates, which involve many investors following the strategy of a single lead investor, can be effective in reducing information asymmetry and in avoiding the outcome of market failure associated with equity crowdfunding.

Charity/Donation - based crowdfunding is a way to source money for a project by asking a large number of contributors to individually donate a small amount to it. In return, the backers may receive token rewards that increase in prestige as the size of the donation increases. For the smallest sums, however, the funder may receive nothing at all. Charities might look at crowdfunding as a means to gather support for relief efforts or causes an organization is championing. For example, disaster relief charities may seek funds to aid in the search, rescue, recovery, and treatment of individuals affected by devastating storms or earthquakes. There may be campaigns for specific needs such as funding the transport of food and clothing to the disaster area. The donations may be sought to support the construction of temporary shelters or the procurement of medical supplies. Crowdfunding might also be used to pay for reconstruction of infrastructure and utilities that would not otherwise be covered by government disaster funds.

The requirements of securing money are not as stringent as using a financial institution and the amount of funding being sought may be smaller than the minimum loan or credit amount that is available from a bank or traditional investors. It is possible for the final amount realized from such a source to far exceed the initial amount that was targeted.

ANGEL INVESTORS FOR EQUITY FINANCING

Angel investors can provide second-tier financing to businesses. They constitute wealthy individuals or groups who are looking for a high return on investment and are very stringent about the businesses in which they invest. Some Angel groups, such as Southern California's Tech Coast Angels, have over 300 investors that actively seek early-stage companies for investment, and also provide technical and operational knowledge to startup ventures (Dije, 2017).

Founded by Mr. Tony Elumelu, the successful Nigerian entrepreneur and philanthropist, the fund seeks to identify and support 1,000 entrepreneurs from across the continent each year over the next decade. It is an annual program of training, funding and mentoring, designed to empower the next generation of African entrepreneurs. Each successful participant in the program gets an initial seed investment of $5,000 after a 12-week mentoring program. Another $5,000, structured as equity or an affordable loan, is also given to participants who meet certain milestones. Over the next 10 years, the fund expects to support 10,000 start-ups and young businesses selected from across Africa who will ultimately create one million new jobs and add $10 billion in annual revenues to Africa's economy. The TEEP Fund focuses on citizens and legal residents of all 54 African countries. Applications can be made by any for-profit business based in Africa in existence for less than three years, including new business ideas.

CORPORATE ORGANIZATION FUNDING SCHEMES

Merchant Cash Advances is an advance against future earnings. In this instance a lender grants sum cash advance to a business for a startup and begins to recouping the advance (plus interest) as a percentage of business daily sales. This implies that the amount the business pays daily fluctuate with sales. It has a factor-rate fee structure, and can be a lot more expensive than a regular bank loan. There is no specific set deadline to repay a Merchant Cash Advances the MCA company will just keep collecting an agreed percentage of business daily sales until the advances is fully repaid. Merchant Cash Advances are one of the few sources of financing available to brand-new enterprises, bad-credit, or otherwise struggling businesses that are excluded from the traditional lending market. Borrower should ensure that the company granting the advance does not practice double-dipping (charging compounding interest) and use a merchant cash advance calculator to determine the business approximate daily payment and approximate number of days for repayment (Dije, 2017).

Invoice factoring is a type of financing that frees up cash from outstanding invoices. The invoice factoring company or "factor" will purchase the business unpaid invoices and pay the entity between 85% and 95% of the value of the invoice. The factor then collects payment from your principal debtor and pays the creditor (the business) the balance of the invoice, less a 1–5% representing factoring fee. Factoring fee is determined, in part, by the period of time it takes debtor to pay. This type of financing is appropriate for businesses that frequently have unpaid invoices and have cash flow problems. This type of financing option is available to both new and old businesses (Dije, 2017).

GroFin is a pioneering private development finance institution specialized in financing and supporting small and growing businesses (SGBs) across Africa and the Middle East by combining medium term loan capital and value-added business support. It generates employment, strengthens value chains and builds markets, the investments bring about inclusive economic growth and improved living conditions in the low- and middle-income countries where the scheme operates (Dije, 2017).

GroFin is a pioneering private development finance institution specialized in financing and supporting small and growing businesses (SGBs) across Africa and the Middle East by combining medium term loan capital and value-added business support. It generates employment, strengthens value chains and builds markets, the investments bring about inclusive economic growth and improved living conditions in the low- and middle-income countries where the scheme operates (Dije, 2017).

It is a trusted partner with more than 30 international development finance institutions, development organizations and other private funders, we have raised cumulative funds worth US$ 500M towards the ten funds and programs managed by GroFin. Since the inception in 2004, it has invested in 700 SMEs and sustained 89,740 jobs across a wide spectrum of business activities within 14 countries in Africa and Middle East with its headquarters in Mauritius.

It is widely accepted that the private sector is the key driver of sustainable economic development in emerging economies. Small and medium sized enterprises typically make up 80-90% of the economy in developing countries and create as well as sustain employment at scale. Small and growing businesses (SGBs) at the base of the SME pyramid thus constitute a vital link in the development chain.

However, despite the SME sector's capacity to provide employment at scale and support multiple livelihoods, it is prone to high failure rates as many as 70% to 90% of SMEs do not survive past their fifth year of operations. Banks and other institutional investors are normally reluctant to invest in these businesses, dooming SGBs to the so-called 'missing middle', where they are considered too large for micro-finance, too small for traditional private equity and too risky for traditional security-based lenders. The GroFin model fills this gap.

The GroFin model has its origins in entrepreneurship. Founded by an African serial entrepreneur around the needs of fellow emerging market entrepreneurs, a deep understanding of the factors that drive SME success is central to GroFin's model, as is the steadfast belief that SME success leads to impact success. GroFin's approach from the start was to develop a scalable institutional model to deliver an integrated solution of finance and business support to SGBs to de-risk the asset class, and, in parallel, to develop befitting funding structures that address the need for skills and knowledge development as well as provision of affordable, medium-term capital. The GroFin's SME development model has gained international recognition and several awards (the 2017 SME Social Impact Finance award for Africa by CFI.co, the 2013 SME Finance Solution Award, the 2010 World Business and Development Award and the Africa Investor Award for 2007 and 2008) and represents a unique approach to providing SMEs with risk capital, access to markets, skills and the ability to grow.

Seedstars Africa is a member of Seedstars Group, a Swiss-based venture builder that is active and invests in over 35 countries around the world especially in emerging markets in Asia, South America, The Middle East and Africa. Through Seedstars World, its popular, highly competitive and exclusive startup competition for startups in emerging markets, the company is able to identify promising companies to support with capital and technical help. In 2014, Seedstars invested $330,000 in SimplePay, a young Nigerian third-party payment processing company that created a solution to disrupt payment services in Nigeria and Africa (Dije, 2017).

Commonwealth Development Corporation (CDC) is the UK's Development Finance Institution (DFI) was founded in 1948. It is wholly owned by the UK Government's Department for International Development (DFID). It is the world's oldest DFI with a history of making successful investments in businesses which have become industry leaders. CDC actively supports businesses throughout Africa and South Asia, and its portfolio of investments is valued at over £2.5bn (year end 2013). In November 2013, CDC announced a US$18.1m investment into Feronia, an agricultural production and processing business focused on palm oil plantations and arable farming in the Democratic Republic of Congo (DRC).

Based in Sweden, *Investment AB Kinnevik* was founded in 1936 and is one of the largest listed investment companies in Europe with total assets of $7 billion. Over the past few years, the firm has invested significantly in businesses in Africa. Some of its most notable investments on the continent include: Millicom, Tele2, Jumia, MTG, Rocket Internet, Iroko Partners and several others. AB Kinnevik is a major investor in emerging markets. As a result, about 8 percent of its portfolio consists of African businesses. It invests and focuses on entrepreneurs and businesses in the following business segments: Communications, Ecommerce & Marketplaces, Entertainment and Financial Services and Others (Dije, 2017).

Royalty financing is a type of investment where the business gets money based on future revenue (Creators Syndicate, Inc. 2019). It's similar to an advance on a paycheck. The investors get their money back through royalties that are a percentage of the company's revenue. The repayment terms and the total amount repaid are negotiated at the start of the loan. The company's income and revenue determine how long it takes to repay the loan, which in turn affects the final repayment amount. However, a cap will be placed on the repayment amount during the initial negotiations. Royalty financing is usually used for companies with large revenue streams. Less profitable companies wouldn't be able to repay the loan plus pay their business expenses.

The concept of royalty financing began with Bart Goodwin and Ed Mello when they saw a gap in the market for this type of investment opportunity. Their company, Cypress Growth Capital, decided to take a percentage of the borrower's monthly revenue instead of the traditional equity stake. Royalty financing was first popular in industries such as oil and gas, pharmaceuticals, film, and even mining. However, companies like Cypress Growth Capital, Barkerville, Osisko, and Grenville Strategic Royalty Corporation have expanded their investment model into new industries.

Debt financing means getting a traditional loan in which ownership was not given up in the business. Equity financing, on the other hand, requires you to give up stocks in your company to the investors. When the company gives up part of ownership, it risks losing some control over your business and its finances. Royalty financing is a sort of compromise between the two. Investors see greater returns than they would with a traditional loan, and companies don't have to trade equity for financing. When deciding which type of financing is right for you, keep the following facts in mind: Businesses that plan on selling eventually offering an IPO are more likely to attract equity financing. Lines of credit or debt financing is harder to get since the financial crisis in 2008. Debt financing requires fixed payments which might be challenging for companies in the early stages. Royalty Financing is relevant to companies that work seasonally since the revenues vary greatly during the year. Royalty and debt payments typically are tax-deductible while equity financing doesn't affect taxes. Flexibility is highest for royalty financing, while equity is less flexible and debt financing is very limited.

Royalty financing guarantees a faster return unlike initial public offer or other traditional type of loan. In some instances, the investors start receiving return almost immediately. On the other hands, the business must have accrued a certain amount of revenue before the commencement of loan repayment. Therefore, with the other options, it often takes longer than five years for an investor to start getting the return.

The following features of royalty financing also make it more flexible and less risky for businesses: No minimum payments, No personal guarantees, No fixed loan terms, No lump sum payments, No restrictive conditions, Small business loans are cost effective and it easier to attract more investors because the royalty payments do not show up as debt like other interest paying loans.

Royalty financing may be difficult to acquire as the business convince the investor into believing that the product will take off and that the company will earn sufficient revenue to the worth of the investment, It can negatively impact the company's growth because a percentage of revenue goes back to the investor instead of its being reinvested in the company. This type of financing can also make it harder to pay off other debt. If the company has small profit margins, it might not be able to spare money for the loan repayment. The company must repay the investors even where it is profitable. Royalty financing is a loan, and if the company cannot repay the loan, it to may have to dispose the assets to effect repayments.

Businesses need investments for a variety of reasons, and royalty financing may provide the following opportunities: a bridge to the next round of financing or investments; growth capital for business owners who want to keep control and don't want to give investors a board seat; preserved ownership and value for the future sale of the business; it helps in the acquisition capital.

Mezzanine financing is a hybrid between debt and equity. In a multi-tiered financing of an operation, for instances, the sources of money will be senior debt, senior subordinated debt, subordinated debt, mezzanine debt, and finally the owner's own equity.

In other words, the mezzanine lender is very close to being last to get paid if something goes wrong. Mezzanine financing is a loan to the owner with terms that subordinate the loan both to different levels of senior debt as well as to secured junior debt. But the mezzanine lender typically has a warrant (meaning a legal right fixed in writing) enabling him or her to convert the security into equity at a predetermined price per share if the loan is not paid on time or in full. Many variants exist, of course, the most common being that a portion of the money is paid back as equity. Being unsecured and highly subordinated, mezzanine financing is very expensive, with lenders looking for 20 percent returns and up. Unless a market is very flush with money and "irrational exuberance" reigns (to use a phrase coined by the retired chairman of the Federal Reserve, Alan Greenspan), the mezzanine lender will be reluctant to lend unless the company has a high cash flow, a good history of earnings and growth, and stature within its industry. Mezzanine is decidedly not a source of start-up funding. Major sources of mezzanine financing include private investors, insurance companies, mutual funds, pension funds, and banks.

Financing programs or acquisitions by this mechanism typically involve some combination of lending by the source of money and provision of equity by the borrower. The narrowest case is one in which the lender lends cash and gets a warrant to convert the loan, or portions of it, to stock either any time at the lender's option or in the case of partial or complete default. More usually the following conditions prevail: A sum of money changes hands. Most of it is lent to the borrower at an interest rate but a portion of it is in the form of a favorable sale of equity. In addition, there may also be a warrant for the lender and restrictive covenants under which the lender is further protected. The loan will typically fetch an interest rate well above the prime rate and will be for a period of four to eight years. In an ideal case, the mezzanine financier anticipates to earn a high interest on the loan and rapid appreciation of the equity he or she has acquired (or can acquire at a low price with the warrant). Mezzanine financing is typically used in acquisitions based on leveraged buyouts in which all of the investors, not least the mezzanine financier, anticipate cashing out by taking the business public again and refinancing it after the acquisition. Thus, the equity can be turned into cash with a substantial gain on the capital. In the event of a failure, the mezzanine lender has little recourse except to influence the company's turnaround by using its stock acquired by means of the warrant. The borrower turns to mezzanine lenders because he or she cannot acquire capital by other means for lack of collateral or because its finances cannot attract less expensive lending. The price of the money, of course, is high due to high rates of interest, but the owner is betting on being able to repay the loan without yielding too much control.

Advantages of Mezzanine are: the owner rarely loses outright control of the company or its direction. Provided the company continues to grow and prosper, its owners are unlikely to encounter any interference from the mezzanine lender; the method offers a lot of flexibility in shaping amortization schedules and the rules of the borrowing itself, not least specifying special conditions for repayment; lenders willing to enter into the world of mezzanine financing tend to be long-term investors rather than people looking to make a quick killing; mezzanine lenders can provide valuable strategic assistance; mezzanine financing increases the value of stock held by existing shareholders although mezzanine equity will dilute the value of the stock; most importantly, mezzanine financing provides business owners with the capital they need to acquire another business or expand into another production or market area.

Regarding the disadvantages of Mezzanine, we can mention: Mezzanine financing may involve loss of control over the business particularly if projections do not work out as envision or if the equity portion of the borrowing is high enough to give the mezzanine lender a larger share; subordinated debt agreements may include restrictive covenants. Mezzanine lenders frequently insist on restrictive covenants; these may include requirements that the borrower is not to borrow more money, refinance senior debt from traditional loans, or create additional security interests in the company's assets; covenants may also force the borrower to meet certain financial ratios e.g., cash flow to equity; similarly, business owners who agree to mezzanine financing may be forced to accept restrictions in how they spend their money in certain areas, such as compensation of important personnel (in such instances, a business owner may not be able to offer above-market packages to current or prospective employees). In some cases, business owners have even been asked to take pay cuts themselves and/or limit dividend payouts.

NON-GOVERNMENTAL ORGANIZATION FUNDING SCHEMES

Elusive business grants/Free Money. This is probably the most difficult type of business financing to be granted, but if the enterprise thinks it might be eligible, the business should search for the grant options. Most business grants of this nature are government-funded (either at federal, state, or local level), though some NGOs and even privately held businesses also offer small business grants. It is an interest free loan.

SMEFUNDS is an International Non-Governmental Organization (NGO) fighting to end poverty through the promotion of sustainable enterprise development in Africa (Dije, 2017). The platform, SMEFUNDS accelerates the flow of finance to SMEs in Africa using social investments and ethical financial intermediation solutions. Its energy and environmental program promote clean and green energy to support household at the Bottom of the Pyramid (BoP), combats Climate change, and increases Youth employment in Africa. They invest in ethical, green and social enterprises by creating the much-needed platform, linkages and capital to help transform ideas into flourishing businesses that create jobs, improve women livelihood and move the poor out of poverty.

The *Africa's Young Entrepreneurs Empowerment Nigeria* program has over the years provided business mentorship and training across Nigeria in various sectors, the programs mostly include Agriculture and Aquaculture training while the participants are empowered with basics of starting up, sustaining and expanding their business. The mentorship program caters to all business sectors giving guidance, advice and necessary information to young entrepreneurs. Tools are also provided for the grassroots entrepreneurs and artisans to enhance their business productivity. It also finances small business in various sectors of the economy. The business owners and businesses will be duly monitored for a period of one year. The only criteria for the program are that the applicant must be a Nigerian and the business must be located in any of the 36 states of the country (Dije, 2017).

Africa's Young Entrepreneurs (A.Y.E) is committed to empowering young entrepreneurs across Africa by creating platforms that facilitate intra-trade on the continent (Dije, 2017). We are dedicated to developing the next generation of outstanding African entrepreneurs, who will shape the economies and political landscapes of their home countries. The annual Networking with the Giants conference will bring together young entrepreneurs and established business luminaries in one space to network, and to close business deals. We envision new partnerships being formed at the conference that will lead to numerous investments and translate in job creation across the continent. Becoming an affiliate with the Africa's Young Entrepreneurs is the best opportunity to establish most prospective business relationships and further the business growth with this global eager audience. Africa's Young Entrepreneurs has been synonymous with the renaissance of Africa entrepreneurial development. Billions of dollars have been injected into the continent as investors used the support of young and bright entrepreneurs to discover new opportunities in business resources, financial models and business.

The *African Women's Development Fund* is the first pan-African women's grant maker in Africa. Since the start of its operations in 2001, AWDF has provided $17 million in grants to 800 women's organizations in 42 African countries (Dije, 2017). The AWDF is an institutional capacity-building and program development fund, which aims to help build a culture of learning and partnerships within the African women's movement. In addition to raising money and awarding grants, the AWDF attempt to strengthen the organizational capacities of its grantees. The AWDF only awards grants to organizations, not individuals.

Acumen is a charity organization incorporated in 2001 with seed capital from the Rockefeller Foundation, Cisco Systems Foundation and three individual philanthropists. The Acumen Fund invests in entrepreneurs who have the capability to bring sustainable solutions to big problems. In May 2014, The Acumen Fund co-invested $1.5 million in Esoko Networks Limited ("Esoko"), a Ghanaian-built technology platform that connects African farmers to markets via mobile phones. In October 2014, Acumen announced a $1.4 million investment in Solar Now, a company that sells and finances solar home systems in Uganda (Dije, 2017).

88mph is a Seed Fund and Accelerator that started in 2011 and currently operates out of hubs in Nairobi (Kenya), Cape Town (South Africa), and Lagos (Nigeria). It currently has more than $1.5 million in funds for investment in African tech startups. Some of its successful investments include: Baby Group South Africa's first online shop for new parents and their babies, Byte Money – A mobile payment platform for the insurance industry and Ekaya; A service that matches good landlords with good tenants. Its main focus is to attract the best entrepreneurs, invest seed cash, and bring them to a point where their businesses can grow independently, or be adequately evaluated by angels and Venture Capital firms.

GOVERNMENTS AND GOVERNMENT PARASTATALS FUNDING SCHEMES

Small Business Administration (SBA) loans are form of loans that is backed by the US government. They are alternative loans to conventional bank loans most especially if the borrowers do not have much collateral (Osano, & Languitone, 2016). The SBA does not grant loans; instead, it guarantees a portion of a loan granted by a bank, credit union, nonprofit, or other lenders. The guarantee means that, if business default on the loan repayment, the SBA will repay a portion of the remaining debt. Consequently, the bank can offer the borrowers lower interest rates than it is applicable without the SBA's backing. The SBA guarantees a few different loan programs, but the most popular one is the general small business loan. It may take several months to receive SBA loan funds after approval. However, there are online lenders that use technology to speed up and simplify the process of application for an SBA loan, which may result into a borrower accessing loan within few weeks.

The *African Development Foundation* (ADF) is an independent Federal agency of the United States government that was established to support African-led development that grows community enterprises by providing seed capital and technical support (Dije, 2017). The United States African Development Foundation (USADF) connects community enterprises with capital and technical support. It helps organizations and businesses in Africa to create and sustain jobs, improve income levels, achieve greater food security, and address human development needs. In 2014 alone, the USADF gave out 336 grants worth over $50 million and impacted over 1.3 million people in Africa.

TraderMoni is a loan program of the Federal Government of Nigeria, created specifically for petty traders and artisans across the country. It is a part of the Government Enterprise and Empowerment Program (GEEP) scheme of the Federal Government, being executed by the Bank of Industry. With TraderMoni, the borrower can receive interest-free loans starting from N10,000 and growing all the way to N100,000 as the borrower pays back. The first set of loan of N10,000 is granted to the borrower. On repayment of the first loan, it immediately qualifies the beneficiary for a second set of loan of N15,000.

Upon the payback of the second loan, it qualifies the borrower for a N20,000 loan, and later N50,000, and lastly N100,000.

SOLUTIONS AND RECOMMENDATIONS

Empirical evidence shows that SMEs dominate the industrial sector in Nigeria, accounting for about 70% of industrial employment and 10% to 15% of manufacturing output (CBN, 2000). Available information confirms that informal manufacturing enterprises are dominated by small-size operators in Nigeria, in terms of number of people employed with percentage distribution ranging between 92 and 98 across activity sectors. Furthermore, the contribution of the entire informal sector (agricultural sector inclusive) to the GDP was put at 38.7% (Central Bank of Nigeria/National Bureau of Statistics, 2010). They have been very prominent in the manufacture of bakery products, leather products, furniture, textiles and products required for the construction industry. Consequently, the need to explore other sources of SME financing for accessibility to enhance sustainability, growth and development of Nigerian economy.

CONCLUSION

Finance is obviously not the factor militating against SME growth and development in Nigeria it is certainly the most crucial. The chapter presents different definitions of SMEs in quantitative and qualitative terms. It also discusses the uncommon sources of financing SMEs in Nigeria. Finally, this chapter presents arguments of scholars on the sources of financing SMEs in Nigeria. It shows that there is no consensus in the sources of finance identified by the researcher. Also, many of the studies concentrated on traditional sources of financing that are well known. Consequently, there is need for SMEs stakeholders to go beyond the traditional method of financing and explore the possibilities of the uncommon ones discuss in this chapter with a view to getting solution to paucity of funds that has been hindering the steady progress of SMEs in Nigeria.

REFERENCES

Abdulazeez, D. A., Suleiman, O., & Yahaya, A. (2016). Impact of merger and acquisitions on the financial performance of deposit money banks in Nigeria. *Arabian Journal of Business and Management Review*, *6*(4), 1–5.

Abdulsaleh, A. M., & Worthington, A. C. (2013). Small and medium-sized enterprises financing: A review of literature. *International Journal of Business and Management*, *8*(14), 36–54. doi:10.5539/ijbm.v8n14p36

Abereijo, I. O., & Fayomi, A. O. (2005). Innovative approach to SME financing in Nigeria: A review of small and medium industry equity investment scheme (SMEIS). *Journal of Social Science*, *11*(3), 219–227.

Adedayo, O. E., Ojo, A. S., & Toluwalope, O. A. (2016). Banks' Involvement in SMEs: identifying financing gaps in Nigerian banking sector. *International Journal of Banking, Finance, Management, & Development Studies, 17*, 105-118. Retrieved from http://www.ijbssnet.com

Afolabi, A. (2015). The effect of entrepreneurship on economic growth and development in Nigeria. *International Journal of Development and Economic Sustainability, 3*, 49–65. Retrieved from http://www.eajournals.org and http://borrower.prudentialcapitalgroup.com/what-is-mezzanine-financing--content-1411.php

Creators Syndicate, Inc. (2019). Retrieved from https://www.creators.com/read/succeeding-in-your-cbusiness/11/17/royalty-financing-the-new-thing-in-venture-capital

Dije, U. W. (2017). Sources of Financing for Small and Medium Enterprises in Nigeria. (Unpublished Ph.D. Dissertation, Walden University). Retrieved from http://scholarworks.waldenu.edu/dissertations utm_source=scholarworks.waldenu.edu

Essien, B. S. (2014). The Nigerian business environment and growth Constraints of Micro and Small-Scale Manufacturing Industries. *American International Journal of Social Science, 3*(6), 67–76.

Evbuomwan, G. O., Ikpi, A. E., Okoruwa, V. O., & Akinyosoye, V. O. (2013). Sources of Finance b for Micro, Small and Medium Enterprises in Nigeria. In Proceedings of *19th International Farm Management Congress, SGGW,* Warsaw, Poland. Retrieved from www.ifmaonline.org

Filion, L. J. (1990). Free trade: The need for a definition of small business. *Journal of Small Business and Entrepreneurship, 7*(2), 33–46. doi:10.1080/08276331.1990.10600347

Gbandi, E. C., & Amissah, G. (2014). Financing options for small and medium enterprises (SMEs) in Nigeria. *European Scientific Journal, 10*, 327–340.

Gulani, M. G., & Usman, A. (2013). Financing small and medium scale enterprises (SMEs): A challenge for entrepreneurial development in Gombe state. *Asian Journal of Business and Management Sciences, 2*, 17–23.

IASB. (2003). *International Financial Standard for Small and Medium-sized enterprises.* IFRS for SME.

Ilegbinosa, I. A., & Jumbo, E. (2015). Small and medium scale enterprises and economic growth in Nigeria: 1975-2012. *International Journal of Business and Management, 10*(3), 203–215. doi:10.5539/ijbm.v10n3p203

Lawson, B. (2007). *Access to finance for SMEs.* Paper at the Abuja International Conference on Financial System Strategy. Retrieved from http://www.cenbank.org/fss/mon/FSS2020Presentation%20at%20International%20Conference.ppt

Meher, K. C., & Ajibie, D. (2018) Financial Sustainability of SMEs by injecting Debt Finance. *The Management Accountant Journal, 53*(1), 80-87. Retrieved from https://www.researchgate.net/publication/324676445

Mohammed, I., & Ali, I. (2015). The Effect of SMEs' Cost of Capital on their Financial Performance in Nigeria. *Journal of Finance and Accounting, 3*(1), 8–11.

Obaji, N. O., & Olugu, M. U. (2014). The role of government policy in entrepreneurship development. Science. *Journal of Business and Management*, *2*, 109–115.

Organisation for Economic Co-operation Development (OECD). (2004).

Ossai, A. (2017). The Problems and Prospects of Small and Medium Scale Enterprises (SMEs) Growth and Development in Nigeria: A Study of Selected SMEs in Delta State. *International Journal of Scientific Research in Education*, *10*(3), 278–294.

Osteryoung, J. S., & Newman, D. (1993). What is a Small Business? *The Journal of Small Business Finance*, *2*(3), 219–231.

Recklies, D. (2001). *Small Business – Size as a Chance or Handicap.* Retrieved from http://www.the-manager.org/resources/Small%20Business.htm

Subrahmanya, M. H. (2005) SMEs in India: Will they be able to join "Global Chains"? CA J Chart Account (The Institute of Chartered Accountants of India, New Delhi), 54 (3),421–427.

Taiwo, J. N., Yewande, O. A., Edwin, A., & Benson, K. N. (2016). The role of Microfinance Institutions in financing small businesses. *Journal of Internet Banking and Commerce*, *21*(1), 1–20.

Tan, K. G., & Tan, K. Y. (2014). Foreign direct investment (FDI), productivity spillovers and the role of small and medium enterprises (SMEs) financing: An overview. *Journal of International Commerce Economic Policy*, *5*, 1403002–1403006.

Tende, S. B. A. (2014). Government initiatives toward entrepreneurship development in Nigeria. *Global Journal of Business Research*, *8*, 109-120. Retrieved from http://papers.ssrn.com/sol3/JELJOUR_Results.cfm? Journal Browse & journal_id

Ubesie, M. C., Onuaguluchi, I. F., & Mbah, A. M. (2017). Effect of Deposit Bank Credit on Small and Medium Scale Enterprises Growth in Nigeria. *International Journal of Finance and Accounting*, *5*(6), 117–132.

Chapter 15
Importance of Information Security and Strategies to Prevent Data Breaches in Mobile Devices

Maulik Desai
Swinburne University of Technology, Australia

Swati Jaiswal
https://orcid.org/0000-0001-9671-534X
SKNSITS, India

ABSTRACT

Mobile devices have upgraded from normal java-based phones whose basic functionality was calling, messaging, and storing contact information to a more adaptive operating system like Symbian, iOS, and Android, which have smart features like e-mail, audio player, camera, etc. Gradually, everyone started relying more and more on these mobile devices. This led to an increase in the number of cell phone hackers. Common ways that a hacker gets access to your phone is via phishing, shoulder surfing, piggybacking, etc. There are countermeasures to this like bookmarking your most visited sites, using VPN, using encryption algorithms. Data theft and identity theft are a new concern for today's user; this chapter is to educate the end user of different ways in which their privacy can be invaded via a mobile phone. This chapter will help the researchers to know the mindset of a cell phone hacker and what are the potential damages that can be caused by them and strategies to prevent them.

INTRODUCTION

Smartphones have been around for ages now. The best thing about them being the mobility that they offer and how one can use them anywhere that suits them. In 2017 around 1.54 Billion smartphones were sold worldwide this includes, smartphones that had operating system as (Android, Symbian, Windows,

DOI: 10.4018/978-1-7998-1005-6.ch015

iOS, etc.) which is a significant increase in number from last year which was 1.49 Billion smartphones. The smartphone industry is booming like never before to give a frame of reference in 2012 just 5 years before this the number of smartphones sold were 680 million and today the number is almost thrice. Smartphone was helping end users to accomplish complex task at just the reach of their hand but it also came in with an unknowing alarming issue that is data breach and Information leakage. Initially, the hackers were persistent on breaching the data on desktop only but as they found out that more and more users are shifting to the world of smartphone they, started targeting the unknown world of smartphone.

The hackers started finding Breach in the system using third party application. The common thing among all this smartphone is that they have the application store of their own. Hackers can simply add a new application on the application store and once you download and install it the Virus can be multiplied (worm virus). This is happening because smartphone is becoming the most preferred platform for using the Internet medium. As soon as you are connected to an internet source in the form of Wi-Fi or 2g or 3g internet, you are vulnerable. If you are using, public Wi-Fi more than often, than chances are there that your information is already compromised and you can't do anything about it. According to the report created by cheetah, one in every five virus-infected phones is from India. This is an alarming rate at which this is turning out.

As quoted in the Paper "*Emerging security threats for mobile platforms.*"

Smartphones are also vulnerable to malware, which are malicious programs designed to run on infected systems without their owners' awareness. While users are keen on downloading apps from app markets, this provides hackers a convenient way to infect smartphones with malware. For example, they would repackage popular games with malware and distribute them in the app markets. Very often users are attracted to download the infected apps. A recent survey reported that 267,259 malware-infected apps have been found, among which 254,158 reside on the Android platform. It also suggested that the number of malware in apps has increased by 614 percent since 2012. There are also a variety of other ways for mal- ware to infect targets. Some malware is dis-guised as the macros of files. Some are installed through certain known vulnerabilities existing in a network device or mobile platform. Some are installed in victims' smartphones when they click a multimedia messaging service (MMS) message or open an email attachment. In any case, malware can cause serious issues relating to information security and data privacy, with severe repercussions for users and even organizations. In this chapter we first discuss the potential threats to the information security in smartphones. We discuss the way we can prevent them from happening and the techniques that can be used to implement it (Delac G et al., 2011).

Common Types of Malware

- **Expander:** This type of programs is used to make a purchase on the victims' phone bill without him/her knowing about those ill-legal purchase and finally, will come to know about this after the end of their billing cycle.
- **Worm:** This type of virus multiples, itself and spread to the devices that are connected with it. Worms can be harmful because they might be given destructive instructions. They can be transmitted using SMS or MMS, they don't require any action from the user, they are slow and difficult to detect.
- **Trojan:** The require user command to execute itself. They are quick and can cause a serious damage to the mobile OS and even harm some personal data.

Table 1. Comparison of Malware

Name	Speed	Replication	Data Capture	Controlling Remotely
Expander	Moderate	No	No	Yes
Worm	Slow	Yes	Maybe	No
Trojan	Fast	No	Maybe	Yes
Spyware	Fast	No	Yes	Yes

- **Spyware:** As the name suggests, they act like a spy and are difficult to trace in the system because they don't show any abnormality in the system. However, they have the potential to transmit your date over the internet without the knowledge or the permission of the user (Gibbs, 2016).

Notable Smartphone Malignant Malware

- **Cabir:** This was one of the first malware that affected the Symbian OS, It was first found in June of 2004, when the phone has been affected by this virus the message 'Caribe' is displayed and every time the phone is switched on, this message gets displayed.
- **Gingermaster:** One of the first Trojan, developed for Android OS, It had a hidden script in the background which when installed would propagate throughout the system.
- **Ikee:** The first worm known to infect, the iOS platform. The Pre- requisite for this was it required a Jail – Broken iPhone and once the iPhone is infected the wallpaper was changed to a picture of singer Rick Astley to provide and inference to the 'Rickroll' reference.
- **Gunpoder:** This worm file infector virus is the first known virus that officially infected the Google Play Store in few countries.
- **HummingBad** - has infected over 10 million Android operating systems. User details are sold and adverts are tapped on without the user's knowledge thereby generating fraudulent advertising revenue.

Different Data Theft Techniques for Smartphones

Phishing Attack

During, the era of computing, users used to check their e-mails, bank statements or any sensitive information on the computers because of the convince it provides and the mobility that it offered. That's the reason that, this computer's back in the day were more prone to Information security breach. In recent times, this same phenomenon is used in Smartphones, so the attackers have shifted their focus from Personal Computing to Smartphones. Phishing is relatively old technique but till date works really fine. In Phishing the attacker creates a fake webpage and it is as good as the replica of the real one and it might be very hard to identify, the difference between the two webpages (Figure 1 and Figure2).

This images are so, similar that making a difference between them is next to impossible. For someone, who uses the Google mail (G-mail) everyday, even for them it becomes difficult to differentiate between the two.

Figure 1. Authentic web page.

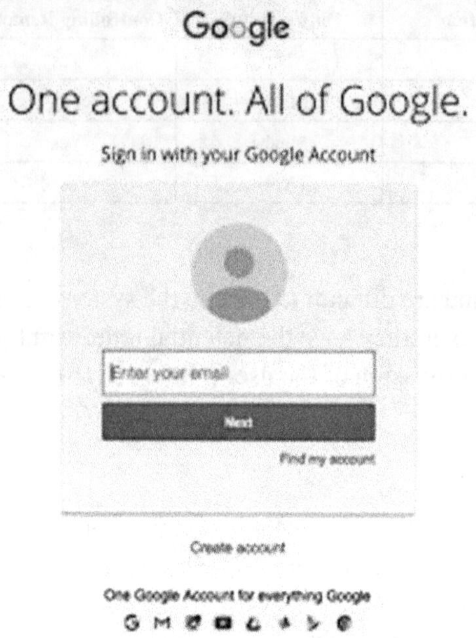

Figure 2. Phished Image.

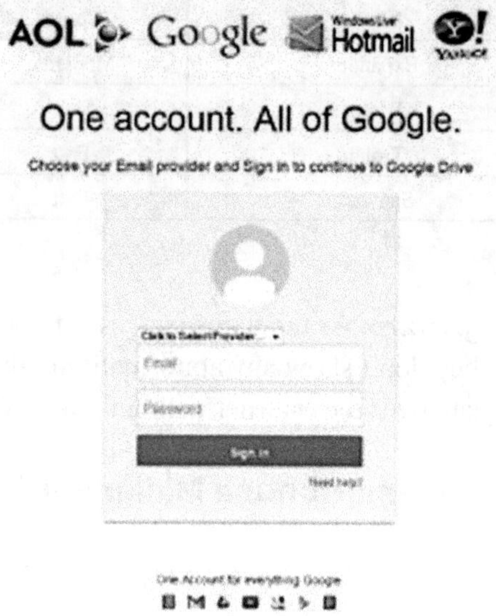

Possible solutions:

- **Bookmark your Most Visited Website:** Suppose, you are accessing G-mail or Facebook or any other website, it is better to Bookmark as this minimize the chances of you being routed to a different URL (infected one) altogether.
- **Always Check Before Proceeding:** If you finding something that is unusual and doesn't match your everyday pattern, stop then and there. Try, to look for the URL and whether it has some discrepancy in it or not.
- **Use a Security Mechanism:** Popular, websites usually offer an alternative method to keep your data safe like in G-mail there is a two – step login mechanism, where you get an OTP on your phone to avoid any malpractices.
- **Block Phishing Sites:** If you find a phishing site block it immediately, if you are not technically well versed then you can contact the admin of the original site and inform them about this and request them to block or bring the site down, so that other users are not affected.

Shoulder Surfing Attack

Smartphones are really helpful because the mobility that they offer but there is also a downside to this. Shoulder surfing attacks raised after the launch of smartphones because it is easier to look into someone's portable device then on their personal computer (Figure 3).

Here the person in Green is the victim and the person in orange is the attacker. He is trying to get information of the pattern lock on the green person's phone. The biggest advantage to the shoulder surfing attacker is that there is no need for him to be technically sound. They, just need to be a good observer for observing the information and recollecting it as and when required.

Figure 3. Shoulder Surfing Attack.

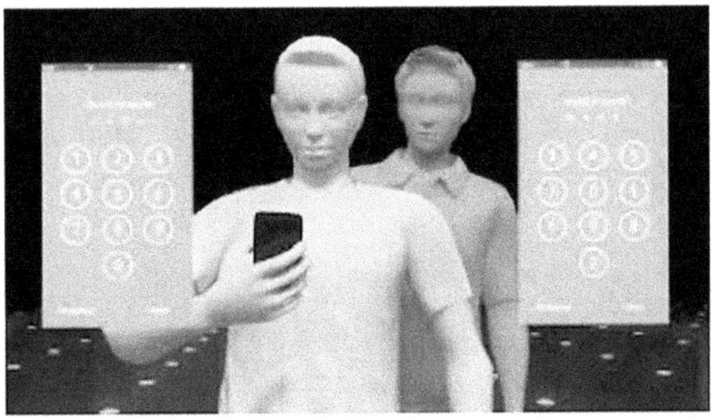

Figure 4. Shoulder surfing attack based on Location, Activity, Time of day and Device.

Code	Count
Location:	**193**
– public transport	130
– theatre hall / lecture hall	13
– at work / university	10
– cafe, restaurant, bar	9
– narrow / crowded places	8
– public open spaces	7
– other	16
Activity:	**189**
– on the way	72
– commuting	69
– working / studying	16
– other	32
Time of day:	**158**
– morning	57
– evening	40
– afternoon	34
– midday	13
– all day	14
Device:	**175**
– smartphone	157
– tablet	8
– laptop	7
– ebook reader	3

The Figure 4 represents the shoulder surfing attack data in everyday life, as one can see shoulder surfing took place in public transport, while the victims were commuting and It majorly involved smartphones, which accounted 157 out of 175 cases that were reported. In other attacks, the attacker needs to have some basic technical knowledge but in this type of attack the attacker, can be anyone and doesn't have to be technically knowledgeable (Kouraogo et al., 2016).

Possible solution:

- **Avoid accessing sensitive data in public places.** While you are traveling or commuting avoid accessing the data that might lead to lose of some personal data, access it in more secure location.
- **Be alert, while accessing value data.** Always have a keen eye before, accessing any important data and look around and if you find someone suspicious or overlooking avoid accessing that data.

- **Change the passwords regularly.** Most people, make this mistake of not changing their password regularly assuming, that it has not been compromised but a recent survey shows that out of 174 people on the survey 168 reported shoulder surfing.
- **Keep a recovery mechanism.** If someone has access to your data and tries to modify it, you should get notified on you alternate number or e-mail address. Most of the banks or the mailing services provide this functionality but users fail to make use of that.

Public Wi-Fi Attacks

This days public Wi-Fi, is available everywhere and users are tempting to use them because that doesn't cost them a penny but in this process they forget an important aspect, that their data might be getting monitored and they might not even be aware about that.

There are common methods to carry on this kind of attacks:

- **Man-in-the-Middle-attack:** Here the attacker intercepts the message from sender to receiver and hence the confidentiality of the message in compromised. Sender is not aware that the confidentiality of the message is compromised, nor is the receiver.

This generally happens because the data that is transmitted from the sender to receiver or client to server is not encrypted and thus, the information transmitting through that Public Wi-Fi can be easily compromised (Figure 5).

- **Fake Wi-Fi Connection**: Another most globally used phenomenon is to set-up a fake public Hotspot near cafes or eateries with the name of that shop or store. User being unaware of whether this is fake or original one will connect to this hotspot and in the end might lose their data or even their bank details (Figure 6).

Here the Wi-Fi hotspot with same two names has been setup, one of them is definitely fake and doesn't belong to the coffee shop. If a user comes across any such situation, then instead of just connecting to one of them, it is better to inform the coffee shop manager or any person in charge of coffee shop. So, they can take the necessary action and damage can be minimal and less users are affected (Hughes E., 2019).

Figure 5. Man-in-the-Middle-attack

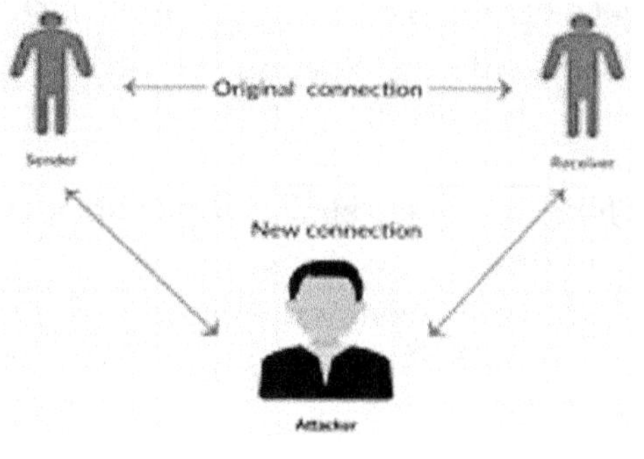

Figure 6. Fake Wi-Fi Hotspot.

Table 2. Comparison between different data theft techniques

Name of Attack	Technical Knowledge Required	Social Engineering Required	Internet Connection Required
Phishing	Yes	No	Yes
Shoulder Surfing	No	Yes	No
Public Wi-Fi attacks	Yes	Maybe	Yes

Possible solutions:

- **Use Virtual Private Network:** Avoid accessing personal data on public Wi-Fi, if it is necessary and you want to do it, better use a virtual private network (VPN).
- **Use SSL Connections:** SSL stands for Secure Socket Layer and IT encrypts the data for the website that you are trying to access. You will know a website has an SSL certificate because it will show "HTTPS" in the URL of the website.
- **Avoid connecting to public Wi-Fi:** Avoid connecting to public Wi-Fi, if your application or your work can be done offline or later on, then prefer the delay over the risk of compromising your data.
- **Limit your browsing experience:** It is okay to use the public Wi-Fi for watching movies or even streaming to any online content but beware of what you are sharing on the public Wi-Fi and If that information is compromised, will it cause any trouble to you or not?

Symptoms That Your Phone Is Infected With Virus

- **Smartphone performance is slow or irregular:** This happens because the virus/malware takes up most of the processing space in the ram and eventually, degrades the performance of your phone but before concluding that your phone is infected, check your ram management and see whether the ram is occupied because of multiple widgets or multiple application running in the background, if that's not the case there is a high chance that your phone is infected.
- **Battery draining faster than usual:** Battery starts draining faster with the same daily usage, this one is difficult to rectify because over time, the battery capacity of the smartphone usually degrades and you can't differentiate whether this is happening because of the old battery or the virus.
- **Unknown application appears:** This one is a bigger red light then it seems, all of a sudden an application pops up, that you have never installed and have never seen before. The notification from this kind off, unknown application keeps on popping up every now and then.
- **Increase in advertisement:** Users, shouldn't be alarmed by this if they have installed third party application (not recommended), If they have don't have third party application and still they get an advertisement, when no application is running on the screen then there might be some malicious activity going on and there is high chance that the users phone might be infected.
- **Un-accounted increase in the phone bills:** Every month have a detailed look of your phones billables, sometimes the virus that has infected your smartphone secretly subscribes you to premium SMS services or MMS services that you didn't opt for. They may also play with user's data, whereby more data is used then the one actually consumed by the user (Ehling, 2019).

Security Measures to Avoid Data Theft on your Smartphone

- **Avoid Installing Third Party Application:** Most of the mobile operating system will have their official application store, try and download from them, this cuts down the risk of user's phone getting infected substantially because before a developer's application gets live on the operating system platform, they have follow certain set of instructions and this helps in prevention of virus entering into user's smartphone.
- **Giving Installation Access that are Necessary for the Application:** This is one of the biggest mistake by the user, even for someone who has basic technical knowledge or who has been using smartphones for ages they tend to forget that, whether an application actually requires all that access (Gates et al., 2014).

Here, the example is of a simple calendar application (Figure 7), why would it require access to your microphone or even your camera, calendar has nothing to do with it. User accept this permission and then are always vulnerable to data theft. Many applications ask for root privileges, don't provide this privileges unless you think that an application requires it and that application is installed from a trustable source.

- **Updating Operating System.** All the smartphone OS developers roll out security patches, application updates and OS updates, this is to keep the user safe from malicious activities. Most, users ignore or delay this updates and that makes you more and more vulnerable or prone to attacks.
- **Investing in an Anti – virus on Smartphones.** Many of the smartphone users, are also users of desktops and laptops, they invest in an anti – virus for desktop OS and laptop OS but forget to invest one for their smartphones, in today's age and world smartphone is more vulnerable to attacks then a desktop because of its mobility and usability throughout the day.

Figure 7. Calendar application image.

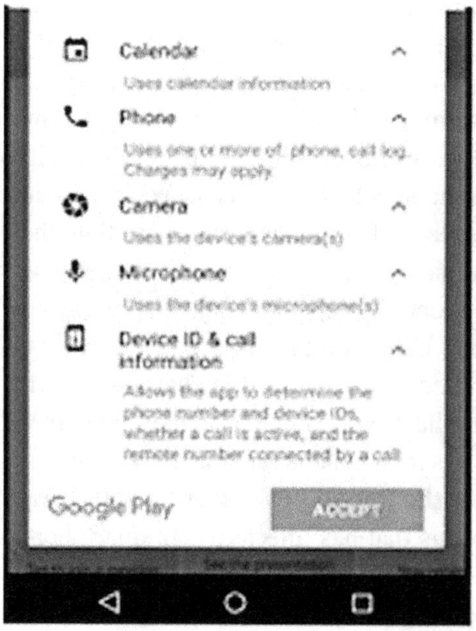

- **Updating the anti – virus on smartphones.** Many users, invest in an anti – virus but don't timely update it. This leads to some serious damage because updates from the anti – virus companies are usually in response to the recent attacks that were monitored by them and is a patch to those viruses or security threats.
- **Activating parental control.** Many operating systems have the option of enabling the parenting control. What it does is, it doesn't allow a child to download unknown application or visit malicious sites, this is important because most infants or teenagers have access to their parent's phone and might unknowing download a corrupted file and that might lead to huge loss in terms of data or identity.
- **Not storing personal passwords on phone.** Users have this habit of storing personal data on the phone but some users take it a notch up and even store their passwords on notes application or something similar, incase if the smartphone is stolen or there is some attack, it becomes easier for the attacker to get access to your personal information and ultimately your personal data.
- **Avoid clicking on tempting messages/e-mails.** Many spam messages or e-mails are sent by the attacker, which are tempting to the victim because it claims that they have won 1000 euros in lottery or something similar and they just have to click on the link provided in the message and they will do this because of the fake monetary benefits (Figure 8).

Figure 8. Spam messages from attacker.

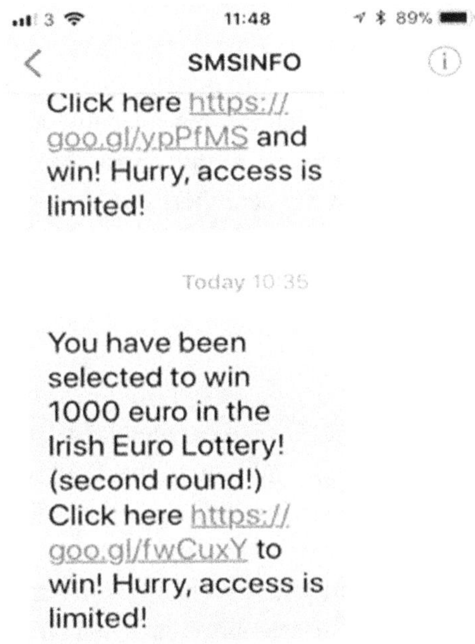

As soon as the user clicks the link either a virus is deployed on their phone or they are re- directed to a phishing web page and when they enter their information, it is noted by the attacker and their data and identity will be compromised. It is simple, if you haven't participated in an event or lucky draw or lottery, you won't be winning one.

- **Use encryption to transmit email or any related document.** Try to transfer e-mails or documents using certain encryption this makes it difficult for the attacker to compromise the confidentiality of the document.

If the users follow the security measures mentioned above there is a high chance that they will be safe from data theft or malicious activities, this is not certain but there is a high chance of not getting victimized.

Challenges

- Everyday a new virus is introduced over and over again, even if there is a secured anti-virus on smartphone, sending updates every time a new virus is discovered is not possible
- When the mobile is stolen there are certain OS that allow to remotely wipe the data but it is easy to recover that data using data retrieval software.
- Social networking sites, where you think your data is safe and won't be shared with anyone but in return there are a few sites who end up selling your data.
- Jail breaking or rooting the device, users root the device to overcome certain restrictions from the smartphone manufactures but in return they are making their phones vulnerable to attacks
- Spam messages sent from the websites that are not traceable and if someone is victim to those message it is difficult to locate the true owner of that spam SMS.
- No source of education, for the user on the data theft and security breaches in the mobile phones (Kouraogo et al., 2016)

CONCLUSION

In the past few years, the has been a raise in the awareness about data theft on the phones and even some sort of education for the user, so that they don't fall prey to this kind of attacks but still there is a major chunk of people who are not aware about this. Smartphone is a great tool and as some people suggest it is a computer in a pocket but with the raise of attacks using various techniques, companies' needs to start building more and more secure smartphones. This chapter will educate companies and organization about potential risk and how they can make better smartphones, which are prone to such attacks and risk.

REFERENCES

Benítez-Mejía, D. G. N., Sánchez-Pérez, G., & Toscano-Medina, L. K. (2016, July). *Android applications and security breach.* Paper presented at the 2016 Third International Conference on Digital Information Processing, Data Mining, and Wireless Communications (DIPDMWC). 10.1109/DIPDMWC.2016.7529383

Delac, G., Silic, M., & Krolo, J. (2011). *Emerging security threats for mobile platforms.* Academic Press.

Ehling, J. (2019). *Hackers set up fake Wi-Fi hotspots to steal your information.* [online] ABC13 Houston. Retrieved from: https://abc13.com/technology/hackers-set-up-fake-wi-fi-hotspots-to-steal-your-information/835223/

Gates, C. S., Chen, J., Li, N., & Proctor, R. W. (2014). Effective Risk Communication for Android Apps. *IEEE Transactions on Dependable and Secure Computing, 11*(3), 252–265. doi:10.1109/TDSC.2013.58

Gibbs, S. (2016). *HummingBad malware infects 10m Android devices.* Retrieved from https://www.theguardian.com/technology/2016/jul/06/hummingbad-malware-infects-10m-android-devices-information-apps-ads

He, D., Chan, S., & Guizani, M. (2015). Mobile application security: Malware threats and defenses. *IEEE Wireless Communications, 22*(1), 138–144. doi:10.1109/MWC.2015.7054729

Hughes, E. (2019). *National Lottery warns public of lotto scam text circulating in Ireland.* Retrieved from https://www.irishmirror.ie/news/irish-news/national-lottery-warns-public-scam-11868654

Kouraogo, Y., Zkik, K., Noreddine, E. J. E. I., & Orhanou, G. (2016). *Attacks on Android banking applications.* Paper presented at the 2016 International Conference on Engineering & MIS (ICEMIS). 10.1109/ICEMIS.2016.7745337

Malin, E., & Mohamed, K. (2017). Understanding Shoulder Surfing in the Wild: Stories from Users and Observers. In *Proceedings of the* 2017 *CHI Conference on Human Factors in Computing Systems* (pp. 4254-4265). Denver, CO: ACM.

Skovoroda, A., & Gamayunov, D. (2015). *Review of the mobile malware detection approaches.* Paper presented at the 2015 23rd Euromicro International Conference on Parallel, Distributed, and Network-Based Processing. 10.1109/PDP.2015.54

Yoon, S., Jeon, Y., & Kim, J. (2015). *Mobile security technology for smart devices.* Paper resented at the 2015 International Conference on Information and Communication Technology Convergence (ICTC). 10.1109/ICTC.2015.7354766

Compilation of References

Abdelkafi, N. B., Blecker, T., & Raasch, C. (2009). From open source in the digital to the physical world: A smooth transfer? *Management Decision*, *47*(10), 1610–1632. doi:10.1108/00251740911004718

Abdulazeez, D. A., Suleiman, O., & Yahaya, A. (2016). Impact of merger and acquisitions on the financial performance of deposit money banks in Nigeria. *Arabian Journal of Business and Management Review*, *6*(4), 1–5.

Abdulsaleh, A. M., & Worthington, A. C. (2013). Small and medium-sized enterprises financing: A review of literature. *International Journal of Business and Management*, *8*(14), 36–54. doi:10.5539/ijbm.v8n14p36

Abereijo, I. O., & Fayomi, A. O. (2005). Innovative approach to SME financing in Nigeria: A review of small and medium industry equity investment scheme (SMEIS). *Journal of Social Science*, *11*(3), 219–227.

Abobaker Efkirin, A. E. A. (2014). Management Accounting in the New Economy. *University Bulletin*, *16*(2), 131–150.

Abrams, R. (2019). USA Today recognizes Tierra Resources in leading the charge to prevent the next Katrina, *Tierra Resources*. Retrieved from https://tierraresourcesllc.com/usa-today-recognizes-tierra-resources-leading-charge-prevent-next-katrina

Accountancy Europe. (1999). *Review of International Accounting Standards for Environmental Issues.* Retrieved from https://www.accountancyeurope.eu/publications/review-of-international-accounting-standards-for-environmental-issues/

Adams, C. A., & McNicholas, P. (2007). Making a difference. *Accounting, Auditing & Accountability Journal*, *20*(3), 382–402. doi:10.1108/09513570710748553

Adedayo, O. E., Ojo, A. S., & Toluwalope, O. A. (2016). Banks' Involvement in SMEs: identifying financing gaps in Nigerian banking sector. *International Journal of Banking, Finance, Management, & Development Studies, 17*, 105-118. Retrieved from http://www.ijbssnet.com

Afolabi, A. (2015). The effect of entrepreneurship on economic growth and development in Nigeria. *International Journal of Development and Economic Sustainability*, *3*, 49–65. Retrieved from http://www.eajournals.org and http://borrower.prudentialcapitalgroup.com/what-is-mezzanine-financing--content-1411.php

Afonso, O., Monteiro, S., & Thompson, M. (2012). A growth model for the quadruple helix. *Journal of Business Economics and Management*, *13*(5), 849–865. doi:10.3846/16111699.2011.626438

Agboli, M., & Ukaegbu, C. C. (2006). Business environment and entrepreneurial activity in Nigeria: Implications for industrial development. *The Journal of Modern African Studies*, *44*(1), 1–30. doi:10.1017/S0022278X05001394

Agha, S., Alrubaiee, L., & Jamhour, M. (2012). Effect of core competence on competitive advantage and organizational performance. *International Journal of Business and Management*, *7*(1), 192–204.

Agrawal, N., & Tapaswi, S. (2017). Defense schemes for variants of distributed denial-of-service (DDoS) attacks in cloud computing: A survey. *Information Security Journal: A Global Perspective, 26*(1), 1-13.

Ahearne, M., Lam, S. K., Mathieu, J. E., & Bolander, W. (2010). Why are some sales people better at adapting to organizational change? *Journal of Marketing, 74*(3), 65–79. doi:10.1509/jmkg.74.3.065

Ahid, M., & Augustine, A. (2012). The Roles and Responsibilities of Management Accountants in the Era of Globalization. *Global Journal of Management and Business Research, 12*(15).

Ahmad, N., & Seymour, R. G. (2008). Defining Entrepreneurial Activity: Definitions Supporting Frameworks for Data Collection, *OECD Statistics Working Papers*, 1, Paris (France): OECD Publishing.

Ahrens, T. (2008). Overcoming the subjective–objective divide in interpretive management accounting research. *Accounting, Organizations and Society, 33*(2), 292-297.

Ajzen, A., & Fishbein, M. (2005). *The Influence of Attitude on Behavior. The handbook of attitudes.* Mahwah, NJ: Erlbaum.

Akanbi, B. E., & Akanbi, C. O. (2012). Bridging the Digital Divide and the impact on Poverty in Nigeria. *Computing Information Systems and Development Informatics, 3*(4), 1–12.

Akgün, A. E., Keskin, H., & Byrne, J. (2009). Organizational emotional capability, product and process innovation, and firm performance: An empirical analysis. *Journal of Engineering and Technology Management, 26*(3), 103–130. doi:10.1016/j.jengtecman.2009.06.008

Albareda, L., Lozano, J. M., & Ysa, T. (2007). Public Policies on Corporate Social Responsibility: The Role of Governments in Europe. *Journal of Business Ethics, 74*(4), 391–407. doi:10.100710551-007-9514-1

Albrecht, W. S. (1991). Fraud in government entities: The perpetrators and the types of fraud. *Government Finance Review, 7*(6), 27–30.

Aldrich, H. E. (2011). *An Evolutionary Approach to Entrepreneurship: Selected Essays by Howard E. Aldrich.* Cheltenham, UK: Edward Elgar.

Alhyari, S., Alazab, M., Venkatraman, S., Alazab, M., & Alazab, A. (2013). Performance evaluation of e-government services using balanced scorecard. *Benchmarking: An International Journal, 20*(4), 512–536. doi:10.1108/BIJ-08-2011-0063

Allan, F. (1993). Benchmarking: Practical aspects for information professionals. *Special Libraries, 84*(3), 123–130.

Allen, A., & Ramanna, K. (2013). Towards an understanding of the role of standard setters in standard setting. *Journal of Accounting and Economics, 55*(1), 1–66. doi:10.1016/j.jacceco.2012.05.003

AlphaBeta. (2017). *Valuing the SDG prize unlocking business opportunities to accelerate sustainable and inclusive growth a paper from AlphaBeta commissioned by the Business and Sustainable Development Commission.* Retrieved from http://s3.amazonaws.com/aws-bsdc/Valuing-the-SDG-Prize.pdf

Alstete, J. W., & Beutell, N. J. (2018). Designing learning spaces for management education: A mixed methods research approach. *Journal of Management Development, 37*(2), 201–211. doi:10.1108/JMD-08-2017-0247

Alvarez, S. A., & Barney, J. B. (2005). How Do Entrepreneurs Organize Under Conditions of Uncertainty? *Journal of Management, 31*(5), 776–793. doi:10.1177/0149206305279486

Alzola, M. A. (2017). Beware of the watchdog: Rethinking the normative justification of gatekeeper liability. *Journal of Business Ethics, 140*(4), 705–721. doi:10.100710551-017-3460-3

Amagoh, F. (2008). Perspectives on organizational change: Systems and complexity theories. *The Innovation Journal, 13*(3), 1–14.

Anand, G., & Kodali, R. (2010). A mathematical model for the evaluation of roles and responsibilities of human resources in a lean manufacturing environment. *International Journal of Human Resources Development and Management, 10*(1), 63–100. doi:10.1504/IJHRDM.2010.029447

Anastas, M. (1997). The Changing World of Management Accounting and Financial Accounting (pp. 48–51). Management Accounting (USA), 79(4), 48-51.

Anderson, S. W., & Sedatole, K. (2003). Management Accounting for the Extended Enterprise: Performance Management for Strategic Alliances and Networked Partners. In: A. Bhimani (Ed.), Management Accounting in the Digital Economy, Oxford University Press.

Andon, P., Baxter, J., & Chua, W. F. (2007). Accounting change as relational drifting: A field study of experiments with performance measurement. *Management Accounting Research, 18*(2), 273–308. doi:10.1016/j.mar.2006.06.007

Andress, A. (2003). *Surviving Security: How to Integrate People, Process, and Technology*. Boca Raton, FL: Auerbach Publications. doi:10.1201/9780203501405

Andriole, S. J. (2010). Business impact of Web 2.0 Technologies. *Communications of the ACM, 53*(12), 67–79. doi:10.1145/1859204.1859225

Angelidou, M. P., Psaltoglou, A., Komninos, N., Kakderi, C., Tsarchopoulos, P., & Panori, A. (2018). Enhancing sustainable urban development through smart city applications. *Journal of Science and Technology Policy Management, 9*(2), 146–169. doi:10.1108/JSTPM-05-2017-0016

ANN7. (2018). *Uber SA launches Incident Response Team.* Retrieved from http://www.aan7.com/uber-sa-launches-incident-response-team/

Anna, A. L., Chandler, G. N., Jansen, E., & Mero, N. P. (2000). Women business owners in traditional and non-traditional industries. *Journal of Business Venturing, 15*(3), 279–303. doi:10.1016/S0883-9026(98)00012-3

Antoni, C. (2004). A motivational perspective on change processes and outcomes. *European Journal of Work and Organizational Psychology, 13*(2), 197–216. doi:10.1080/13594320444000065

AP. (2019). Alligator Program, *Louisiana Wildlife & Fisheries*. Retrieved from http://www.wlf.louisiana.gov/wildlife/alligator-program

Applbaum, A. I. (2000). *Ethics for Adversaries. The Morality of Roles in Public and Professional Life*. Princeton, NJ: Princeton University Press. doi:10.1515/9781400822935

Arakji, R. Y., & Lang, K. R. (2007). Digital consumer networks and producer-consumer collaboration: Innovation and product development in the video game industry. *Journal of Management Information Systems, 24*(2), 195–219. doi:10.2753/MIS0742-1222240208

Armstrong, M. B. (1993). Ethics and Professionalism in Accounting Education: A Sample Course. *Journal of Accounting Education, 11*(1), 77–92. doi:10.1016/0748-5751(93)90019-F

Arnaud, P. (2003). L'information environnementale: Un enjeu à moyen terme pour toutes les entreprises. *Revue Francaise de Comptabilité, 356*, 32.

Arsalidou, D. (2017). Educating Bankers on Law, Ethics and Social Values: A Perspective from the US, the UK and Europe. *European Company and Financial Law Review, 14*(4), 569–608. doi:10.1515/ecfr-2017-0026

Arsenault, P., & Faerman, S. R. (2014). Embracing paradox in management: The value of the competing values framework. *Organizational Management Journal*, *11*(3), 147–158. doi:10.1080/15416518.2014.949614

Arthur, W. B. (1996). Increasing Returns and the New World of Business. *Harvard Business Review*, *74*(4), 100–109. PMID:10158472

Arukonda, S., & Sinha, S. (2015). The innocent perpetrators: Reflectors and reflection attacks. *Advanced Computer Science*, *4*, 94–98.

Asemota, J., & Chahine, T. (2017). Social franchising as an option for scale. *Voluntas*, *28*(6), 2734–2762. doi:10.100711266-016-9763-7

Ashkanasy, N. (2011). International happiness; a multilevel perspective. *The Academy of Management Perspectives*, (February): 23–29.

Ashkanasy, N. M., & Windsor, C. A. (1997). Personal and Organisational Factors Affecting Auditor Independence: Empirical Evidence and Directions for Future Research. *Research on Accounting Ethics*, *3*, 35–48.

Astebro, T., & Thompson, P. (2009). Entrepreneurs: Jacks of All Trades or Hobos? *Economics Research Working Paper Series*, 48, Miami, FL.: Florida International University.

Atkinson, R., & McKay, A. (2007). *Digital Prosperity: Understanding the economic benefits of the IT revolution.* Washington, DC: ITI Foundation.

Audretsch, D. B. (2003). *Entrepreneurship. A Survey of the Literature, Enterprise Papers, 14.* Brussels, Belgium: European Commission.

Austin, R. D., Devin, L., & Sullivan, E. E. (2012). Accidental innovation: Supporting valuable unpredictability in the creative process. *Organization Science*, *23*(5), 1505–1522. doi:10.1287/orsc.1110.0681

Axelsson, B., Van Weele, A., & Wynstra, F. (2000). Driving and enabling factors for purchasing involvement in product development. *European Journal of Purchasing and Supply Management*, *6*(2), 129–141. doi:10.1016/S0969-7012(00)00002-2

B&S Development Commission. (2017). *Better Business Better World, The report of the Business & Sustainable Development Commission*. Retrieved from http://report.businesscommission.org/uploads/BetterBiz-BetterWorld_170215_012417.pdf

B20.. 2012). *B20 Global Business Leaders Announce Their Prioritized Recommendations for Global Economic Recovery and Growth*, May 2012.

Bachelerie, V., & Boillet-Mongodin, J. (1993). Le traitement de l'environnement dans les rapport annuels. *Revue Francaise de Compatabilité*, *246*, 79–85.

Baines, A., & Smith, K. (2003). Antecedents to Management Accounting Changes: A structural equation approach. *Accounting, Organizations and Society*, *28*(7-8), 675–698. doi:10.1016/S0361-3682(02)00102-2

Baker, C., & Bettner, M. (1997). Interpretive and Critical Research in Accounting: A Commentary on its Absence from Mainstream Research||. *Critical Perspectives on Accounting*, *8*(4), 293–310. doi:10.1006/cpac.1996.0116

Bakshi, B., & Fiksel, J. (2003). The Quest for Sustainability: Challenges for Process Systems Engineering. *AIChE Journal. American Institute of Chemical Engineers*, *49*(6), 1350–1358. Retrieved from http://eco-nomics.com/images/Quest_for_Sustainability.pdf. doi:10.1002/aic.690490602

Baldwin, C. V., & von Hippel, E. (2011). Modeling a paradigm shift: From producer innovation to user and open collaborative innovation. *Organization Science*, *22*(6), 1399–1417. doi:10.1287/orsc.1100.0618

Ball, R. (2013). Accounting informs investors and earnings management is rife: Two questionable beliefs. *Accounting Horizons*, *27*(4), 847–853. doi:10.2308/acch-10366

Bamber, L., Broun, K., & Harrison, T. W. (2008). Managerial accounting (1st ed.). Upper Saddle River, NJ: Prentice Hall.

Barbu, E., Feleaga, N., & Feleaga, L. (2011). Quelles norms IAS/IFRS utiliser pour le reporting environnementale? *Revue Francaise de Comptabilité*, *440*, 24–27. Retrieved from http://www.bibliobaseonline.com/notice.php?NUMERO=107993&OLD=96279%7C98765%7C71417

Barney, J. B. (1986). Organizational culture: Can it be a source of sustained competitive advantage. *Academy of Management Review*, *11*(3), 656–665. doi:10.5465/amr.1986.4306261

Barney, J. B. (1991). Firm resources and sustained competitive advantage. *Journal of Management*, *17*(1), 99–120. doi:10.1177/014920639101700108

Baron, R. A. (2007). Entrepreneurship: A Process Perspective. In J. R. Baum, M. Frese, & R. A. Baron (Eds.), *The Psychology of Entrepreneurship* (pp. 19–39). Mahwah, NJ: Erlbaum.

Barrett, M., Oborn, E., & Orlikowski, W. (2016). Creating value in online communities: The sociomaterial configuring of strategy, platform, and stakeholder engagement. *Information Systems Research*, *27*(4), 704–723. doi:10.1287/isre.2016.0648

Barrett, M., Oborn, E., Orlikowski, W., & Yates, J. (2012). Reconfiguring boundary relations: Robotic innovations in pharmacy work. *Organization Science*, *23*(5), 1448–1466. doi:10.1287/orsc.1100.0639

Barth, M. E. (2013). Global comparability in financial reporting: What, why, how, and when? *China Journal of Accounting Studies*, *1*(1), 2–12. doi:10.1080/21697221.2013.781765

Barth, M. E., Landsman, W. R., Young, D., & Zhuang, Z. (2014). Relevance of Differences between Net Income based on IFRS and Domestic Standards for European Firms. *Journal of Business Finance & Accounting*, *41*(3-4), 297–506. doi:10.1111/jbfa.12067

Barth, M., Landsman, W., & Lang, M. (2008). International accounting standards and accounting quality. *Journal of Accounting Research*, *46*(3), 467–498. doi:10.1111/j.1475-679X.2008.00287.x

Bartolomeo, M., Bennett, M., Bouma, J. J., Heydkamp, P., James, P., & Wolters, T. (2000). Environmental management accounting in Europe: current practice and future potential. *European Accounting Review,* 9(1), 31-52.

Bauer, R. M., & Gegenhuber, T. (2015). Crowdsourcing: Global search and the twisted roles of consumers and producers. *Organization*, *22*(5), 661–681. doi:10.1177/1350508415585030 PMID:27524930

Baylis, J., & Smith, S. (1997). The Globalization of World Politics: An Introduction to International Relations. Oxford, UK: Oxford University Press.

Baylis, F., & Downie, J. (1991). Ethics Education for Canadian Medical Students. *Academic Medicine*, *66*(7), 413–414. doi:10.1097/00001888-199107000-00009 PMID:2059268

BBBW. (2019). *Better Business, Better World*. Retrieved from http://report.businesscommission.org

Beaubien, L. (2013). Technology, change, and management control: A temporal perspective. *Accounting, Auditing & Accountability Journal*, *26*(1), 48–74. doi:10.1108/09513571311285612

Becker, B. E., & Huselid, M. A. (1998). High performance work systems and firm performance: A synthesis of research and managerial implications. *Research in Personnel and Human Resources Management*, *16*, 53–101.

Becker, B. E., & Huselid, M. A. (2006). Strategic human resources management: Where do we go from here? *Journal of Management*, *32*(6), 898–925. doi:10.1177/0149206306293668

Behery, M., Jabeen, F., & Parakandi, M. (2014). Adopting a contemporary performance management system. *International Journal of Productivity and Performance Management*, *63*(1), 22–43. doi:10.1108/IJPPM-07-2012-0076

Ben-Asher, N., & Gonzalez, C. (2015). Effects of cyber security knowledge on attack detection. *Computers in Human Behavior*, *48*, 51–61. doi:10.1016/j.chb.2015.01.039

Benghozi, P. J., & Salvador, E. (2016). How and where the R&D takes place in creative industries? Digital investment strategies of the book publishing sector. *Technology Analysis and Strategic Management*, *28*(5), 568–582. doi:10.1080/09537325.2015.1122184

Benítez-Mejía, D. G. N., Sánchez-Pérez, G., & Toscano-Medina, L. K. (2016, July). *Android applications and security breach.* Paper presented at the 2016 Third International Conference on Digital Information Processing, Data Mining, and Wireless Communications (DIPDMWC). 10.1109/DIPDMWC.2016.7529383

Benner, M. J., & Tushman, M. L. (2015). Reflections on the 2013 Decade Award—"Exploitation, exploration, and process management: The productivity dilemma revisited" ten years later. *Academy of Management Review*, *40*(4), 497–514. doi:10.5465/amr.2015.0042

Bettner, M., & Kate, K. (2013). Changes in annual reporting rituals of financial services firms in periods of market crisis. *International Journal of Critical Accounting*, *5*(6), 577–593. doi:10.1504/IJCA.2013.059027

Bhattacharya, A., & Balachandram, M. (2017). *Uber and Ola may soon have a new competitor: the government of India.* Retrieved from https://qz.com/103837/

Bhimani, A. (2003). Management Accounting in the Digital Economy (1st ed.). Oxford, UK: Oxford University Press. doi:10.1093/0199260389.001.0001

Bhimani, A. (2012). Cost management in the digital age. In F. Mitchell, H. Nørreklit, & M. Jakobsen (Eds.), *The Routledge Companion to Cost Management. Routledge companions in business, management and accounting* (pp. 381–388). London, UK: Routledge.

Bhimani, A., & Bromwich, M. (2009). Management Accounting in a Digital and Global Economy: The Interface of Strategy, Technology and Cost Information. In C. S. Chapman, D. J. Cooper, & P. Miller (Eds.), *Accounting, Organizations and Institutions: Essays in Honour of Anthony Hopwood* (pp. 85–111). Oxford, UK: Oxford University Press. doi:10.1093/acprof:oso/9780199546350.003.0005

Bhimani, A., & Willcocks, L. (2014). Digitisation, 'Big Data' and the transformation of accounting information. *Accounting and Business Research*, *44*(4), 469–49. doi:10.1080/00014788.2014.910051

Bloodgood, J. M., & Morrow, J. L., Jr. (2000). Strategic organizational change within an institutional framework. *Journal of Managerial Issues, Pittsburgh Summer, 12* (2), 208-226.

Bogers, M., Chesbrough, H., & Moedas, C. (2018). Open innovation: Research, practices, and policies. *California Management Review*, *60*(22), 5–16. doi:10.1177/0008125617745086

Bogers, M., Hadar, R., & Bilberg, A. (2016). Additive manufacturing for consumer-centric business models: Implications for supply chains in consumer goods manufacturing. *Technological Forecasting and Social Change*, *102*, 225–239. doi:10.1016/j.techfore.2015.07.024

Bogers, M., Zobel, K., Afuah, A., Almirall, E., Brunswicker, S., Dahlander, L., ... Ter Wal, A. L. J. (2017). The open innovation research landscape: Established perspectives and emerging themes across different levels of analysis. *Industry and Innovation, 24*(1), 8–40. doi:10.1080/13662716.2016.1240068

Bohnsack, R. H. (2018). Same, same, but different!? A systematic review of the literature on digital transformation. Academy of Management Proceedings, 2018(1), 16262.

Bolman, L. G., & Deal, T. E. (1999). 4 Steps to keeping change efforts heading in the right direction. *Journal for Quality and Participation, 22*(3), 6–11.

Book, L. (2012). Symposium Introduction: Offshore Accounts, Corporate Income Shifting, and Executive Compensation. *Villanova Law Review, 57*(3), 421–432.

Boudreau, K. J. (2012). Let a thousand flowers bloom? An early look at large number of software app developers and patterns of innovation. *Organization Science, 23*(5), 1409–1427. doi:10.1287/orsc.1110.0678

Boudreau, K. J., & Jeppesen, L. B. (2015). Unpaid crowd complementors: The platform network effect mirage. *Strategic Management Journal, 36*(12), 1761–1777. doi:10.1002mj.2324

Boyack, K. W., & Klavans, R. (2010). Co-citation analysis, bibliographic coupling, and direct citation: Which citation approach represents the research front most accurately? *Journal of the American Society for Information Science and Technology, 61*(12), 2389–2404. doi:10.1002/asi.21419

Brazil, N., & Kirk, D. (2016). *Uber and Metropolitan Traffic Fatalities in the United States.* Retrieved from https://www.researchgate.net/publications/

Broadband. (2006). *Travel pioneer starts online roll-out in SA.* Retrieved from https://broadband.co.za/nephp/4021.html/

Broadband. (2018). *Uber South Africa adds call-back line for safety.* Retrieved from https://broadband.co.za/news/motoring/

Broadbent, A., & Schaffner, C. (2016). Quantum cryptography beyond quantum key distribution. *Designs, Codes and Cryptography, 78*(1), 351–382. doi:10.100710623-015-0157-4

Broadbent, J., Dietrich, M., & Laughlin, R. (1996). The Development of Principal-Agent Contracting and Accountability Relationships in the Public Sector: Conceptual and Cultural Problems. *Critical Perspectives on Accounting*, 7.

Broadus, R. (1987). Toward a definition of "bibliometrics". *Scientometrics, 12*(5-6), 373–379. doi:10.1007/BF02016680

Brown, D. R., & Harvey, D. (2006). *An Experimental approach to Organization development. Hoboken, NJ*: Pearson Education.

Brown, J. (2010). Accounting and visual cultural studies: Potentialities, challenges and prospects. *Accounting, Auditing & Accountability Journal, 23*(4), 482–505. doi:10.1108/09513571011041598

Buchanan, D. A., & Boddy, D. (1992). *The Expertise of the Change Agent.* London, UK: Prentice Hall.

Bula, H. O. (2012). Evolution and Theories of Entrepreneurship: A Critical Review on the Kenyan Perspective. *International Journal of Business and Commerce, 1*(11), 81–96.

Burnes, B. (2004). *Managing Change: A Strategic Approach to Organisational Dynamics.* Harlow, UK: Prentice Hall.

Byard, D., Li, Y., & Yu, Y. (2011). The effect of mandatory IFRS adoption on financial analysts' information environment. *Journal of Accounting Research, 49*(1), 69–96. doi:10.1111/j.1475-679X.2010.00390.x

Cahan, S. F., & Sun, J. (2015). The effect of audit experience on audit fees and audit quality. *Journal of Accounting, Auditing & Finance, 30*(1), 78–100. doi:10.1177/0148558X14544503

Callegati, F., Giallorenzo, S., Melis, A., & Prandini, M. (2018). Cloud-of-Things meets Mobility-as-a-Service: An insider threat perspective. *Computers & Security, 74*, 277–295. doi:10.1016/j.cose.2017.10.006

Callioni, G., Montgros, X., Slagmulder, R., Wassenhowe, L., & Wright, L. (2005). Inventory-Driven Costs. *Harvard Business Review*, (March): 271–282. PMID:15768682

Cameron, K. S., & Quinn, R. E. (2011). *Diagnosing and Changing Organizational Culture: Based on the Competing Values Framework*. San Francisco, CA: Jossey-Bass.

Campbell, D., & Cowton, C. J. (2015). Method issues in business ethics research: Finding credible answers to questions that matter. *Business Ethics (Oxford, England), 24*(S1), S3–S10. doi:10.1111/beer.12093

Caraiani, C., Lungu, C. I., & Colceag, F. (2010). *Contabilitatea verde: strategii transdisciplinare către contabilitatea socială şi de mediu: studii şi cercetări*. Editura A.S.E. Retrieved from https://books.google.ro/books/about/Contabilitatea_verde.html?id=0vTCrQEACAAJ&redir_esc=y

Carayannis, E. G., & Turner, E. (2006). Innovation diffusion and technology acceptance: The case of PKI technology. *Technovation, 26*(7), 847–855. doi:10.1016/j.technovation.2005.06.013

Carroll, G. R., & Khessina, O. M. (2005). The Ecology of Entrepreneurship. In S. A. Alvarez, R. Agarwal, & O. Sorenson (Eds.), Handbook of Entrepreneurship Research: Disciplinary Perspectives (pp. 167–200). New York, NY: Springer. doi:10.1007/0-387-23622-8_9

Caspary, G., & O'Connor, D. (2003). *Providing Low-Cost Information Technology Access to Rural Communities in Developing Countries: What works? What pay?* (Working paper No. 229), OECD Development Centre.

Cassiman, B., Di Guardo, M. C., & Valentini, G. (2009). Organising R&D projects to profit from innovation: Insights from co-opetition. *Long Range Planning, 42*(2), 216–233. doi:10.1016/j.lrp.2009.01.001

Cassiman, B., Di Guardo, M. C., & Valentini, G. (2010). Organizing links with science: Cooperate or contract?: A project-level analysis. *Research Policy, 39*(7), 882–892. doi:10.1016/j.respol.2010.04.009

Cassiman, B., & Valentini, G. (2016). Open innovation: Are inbound and outbound knowledge flows really complementary? *Strategic Management Journal, 37*(6), 1034–1046. doi:10.1002mj.2375

Castriotta, M., & Di Guardo, M. C. (2011). Open innovation and crowdsourcing: the case of mulino bianco. Information Technology and Innovation Trends in Organizations (pp. 407–414). Heidelberg, Germany: Physica-Verlag HD. doi:10.1007/978-3-7908-2632-6_46

Castriotta, M., & Di Guardo, M. C. (2016). Disentangling the automotive technology structure: A patent co-citation analysis. *Scientometrics, 107*(2), 819–837. doi:10.100711192-016-1862-0

Castriotta, M., Loi, M., Marku, E., & Naitana, L. (2019). What's in a name? Exploring the conceptual structure of emerging organizations. *Scientometrics, 118*(2), 407–437. doi:10.100711192-018-2977-2

Caylor, M. L. (2010). Strategic revenue recognition to achieve earnings benchmarks. *Journal of Accounting and Public Policy, 29*(1), 82–95. doi:10.1016/j.jaccpubpol.2009.10.008

CBEEE. (2019). Can't Beat 'Em, Eat 'Em. Retrieved from http://www.cantbeatemeatem.us

CERA. (2019). *Coastal Emergency Risks Assessment*. Retrieved from https://cera.coastalrisk.live

Chandler, A. D., Jr. (1994). The history of Business Change. In the Change Management Handbook: A Road Map to Corporate Transformation. Sikora, & Berger. New York, NY: McGraw-Hill.

Chan, L. L., Shaffer, M. A., & Snape, E. (2004). In search of sustained competitive advantage: The impact of organizational culture, competitive strategy and human resource management practices on firm performance. *International Journal of Human Resource Management, 15*(1), 17–35. doi:10.1080/0958519032000157320

Chen, M. K., Chevalier, J. A., Rossi, P. E., & Oehlsen, E. (2017). *The value of flexible work: Evidence from Uber drivers.* NBER Working Paper Series.

Chen, Y., & Justis, R. T. (2006). Chinese franchise brands going globalization. *1st Annual China Franchise International Summit*, International Franchise Academy, Zhuhai, China.

Chen, Y., Chen, G., & Wu, S. (2006). A Simonian approach to digital business research: A study in netchising. Advanced Topics in Digital business Research: Digital business Innovation and Process Management, Vol. 1.

Chen, Y., Chong, P., & Justis, R. T. (2000a, November). Information technology solutions to increase franchise efficiency and productivity. *Proceedings of the 2000 Franchise China Conference and Exhibition*, Beijing, Guangzhou, and Shanghai, China.

Chen, Y., Lu, B. Z, & Zeng, C.F. (2014). Business analytics in franchising. *Encyclopedia of Information Science and Technology*, Third Edition, July.

Chen, Y., Seidman, W., & Justis, R. T. (2005). Strategy and docility in franchise organizations. In the *Proceedings of: 19th Annual International Society of Franchising Conference*, London, UK.

Chen, Y., Watson, E., & Azevedo, R. F. L. (2011). Soft landings curriculum of U.S.-China entrepreneurship. China Currents, 10(2).

Chen, Y., Watson, E., Liu, C., Cornachione, E., & Wu, S. (2010). Soft landing curriculum of entrepreneurship in emerging markets, *Academy of International Business 2010 Annual Meeting*, Rio de Janeiro, Brazil.

Chen, H. M., & Fu, P. C. (2008). A systematic framework for performance appraisal and compensation strategy. *Human Systems Management*, *27*, 161–175.

Chen, H., Ge, L., & Xie, L. A. (2015). User Authentication Scheme Based on Elliptic Curves Cryptography for Wireless Ad Hoc Networks. *Sensors (Basel, Switzerland)*, *15*(7), 17057–17075. doi:10.3390150717057 PMID:26184224

Chen, H., Tang, Q., Jiang, Y., & Lin, Z. (2010). The role of international financial reporting standards in accounting quality: Evidence from the European Union. *Journal of International Financial Management & Accounting*, *21*(3), 220–278. doi:10.1111/j.1467-646X.2010.01041.x

Chen, M., Qu, X., & Sun, X. (2017). Whose cost of equity capital reduces after IFRS convergence and why? Heterogeneity evidence from Chinese stock market. *China Journal of Accounting Studies*, *5*(1), 1–27. doi:10.1080/21697213.2017.1304539

Chen, Y., Chong, P., & Justis, R. T. (2000b). Franchising knowledge repository: A structure for learning organizations. *Proceedings of the 14th Annual International Society of Franchising Conference*, San Diego, CA.

Chen, Y., Chong, P., & Justis, R. T. (2002). Digital business Strategy in Franchising: A Customer-Service-Life-Cycle Approach. *Proceedings of the 16th Annual International Society of Franchising Conference*, Orlando, FL.

Chen, Y., Ford, C., Justis, R. T., & Chong, P. (2001). Application service providers in franchising: Opportunities and issues. *Proceedings of the 15th Annual International Society of Franchising Conference*, Las Vegas, NV.

Chen, Y., Hammerstein, S., & Justis, R. T. (2002). Knowledge, learning, and capabilities in franchise organizations. *Proceedings of the 3rd European Conference on Organizational Knowledge, Learning, and Capabilities*, Athens, Greece.

Chen, Y., Justis, R. T., & Chong, P. P. (2008). Data mining in franchise organizations. In J. Wang (Ed.), *Data Warehousing and Mining: Concepts, Methodologies, Tools, and Applications* (pp. 2722–2733). doi:10.4018/978-1-59904-951-9.ch169

Chen, Y., Justis, R. T., & Yang, H. L. (2004). Global digital business, international franchising, and theory of netchising: A research alliance of East and West. *Proceedings of the 18th Annual International Society of Franchising Conference*, Las Vegas, NV.

Chen, Y., Justis, R., & Wu, S. (2006). Value networks in franchise organizations: A study in the senior care industry. *Proceedings of the 20th Annual International Society of Franchising Conference*, Palm Springs, CA.

Chen, Y., Watson, E., Cornacchione, E., & Azevedo, R. F. L. (2013). "Flying High, Landing Soft": An innovative entrepreneurial curriculum for Chinese SMEs going abroad. *Journal of Chinese Entrepreneurship*, *5*(2), 122–143. doi:10.1108/JCE-10-2012-0025

Chesbrough, H. W. (2006). Open innovation: The new imperative for creating and profiting from technology. Brighton, MA: Harvard Business Press.

Chesbrough, H., & Bogers, M. (2014). *Explicating Open Innovation: Clarifying an Emerging Paradigm for Understanding Innovation* (Vol. 3). Oxford, UK: Oxford University Press. doi:10.1093/acprof:oso/9780199682461.003.0001

Child, J., Faulkner, D., & Tallman, S. (2005). Cooperative Strategy. Managing Alliances, Networks, and Joint Ventures (2nd ed.). Oxford, UK: Oxford University Press. doi:10.1093/acprof:oso/9780199266241.001.0001

Choi, Y., Lee, D., Kim, J., Jung, J., Nam, J., & Won, D. (2014). Security Enhanced User Authentication Protocol for Wireless Sensor Networks Using Elliptic Curves Cryptography. *Sensors (Basel, Switzerland)*, *14*(6), 10081–10106. doi:10.3390140610081 PMID:24919012

Chowdhury, N. (2000). *Information and Communications Technologies and IFPRI's Mandate: A Conceptual Framework.* Retrieved from http://www.ifpri.org/divs/cd/dp/ictdp01.pdf

Christensen, J. F., Olesen, M. H., & Kjær, J. S. (2005). The industrial dynamics of Open Innovation: Evidence from the transformation of consumer electronics. *Research Policy*, *34*(10), 1533–1549. doi:10.1016/j.respol.2005.07.002

Ciocoiu, C. N. (2011). Integrating Digital Economy and Green Economy: opportunities for sustainable development. *Theoretical and Empirical Researches in Urban Management, 6*(1). Retrieved from http://um.ase.ro/no61/3.pdf

Cocca, P., & Alberti, M. (2010). A framework to assess performance measurement in SMEs. *International Journal of Productivity and Performance Management*, *59*(2), 186–200. doi:10.1108/17410401011014258

Cokins, G. (2016). The Top Seven Trends in Management Accounting. *The EDP Audit, Control, and Security Newsletter*, *53*(4), 1–7.

Collins, S., & McCombie, S. (2012). Stuxnet: The emergence of a new cyber weapon and its implications. *Journal of Policing. Intelligence and Counter Terrorism*, *7*(1), 80–91. doi:10.1080/18335330.2012.653198

Coman, D. M., & Coman, M. D. (2016). The impact of Information Technology on the Company's Financial-Accounting System. *Valahian Journal of Economic Studies, 7*(21), 65–70. Retrieved from https://search.proquest.com/docview/1950619900/fulltextPDF/C16423FE01D2401FPQ/1?accountid=17263

Coman, M. D., Ionescu, C. A., & Lixandru, M. (2019). Romanian Economy between Linearity and Circularity. A Bioeconomic Perspective. In *Communicative Action & Trandisciplinarity in the Ethical Society* (pp. 59–72). LUMEN.

Commission of the European Communities. (2013). *Communication from the Commission to the Council and the European Parliament on Article 7 of the Treaty on European Union. Respect for and promotion of the values on which the union is based.* Brussels, Belgium. Retrieved from http://ec.europa.eu/transparency/regdoc/rep/1/2003/EN/1-2003-606-EN-F1-1.Pdf

Competition Commission. (2015). *Uber: A game-changer in passenger transport in South Africa.* Retrieved from http:/.www.competition.org.za/

Cooper, A. (2016). Staying safe with strangers. Lifetech. *Sunday Independent,* Sept. 18.

Cooper, R. (1996). *Look out, Management Accountants, Management Accounting* (pp. 35–41). US: May-June.

Cowton, C. J., & San-Jose, L. (2016). On the ethics of trade credit: Understanding good payment practice in the supply chain. *Journal of Business Ethics, 140*(4), 673–685. doi:10.100710551-016-3050-9

Cramer, J., & Krueger, A. B. (2016). *Disruptive change in the taxi business: The case of Uber.* NBER Working Paper Series.

CRDS. (2019). *Coastal Resilience Decision-Support.* Retrieved from http://maps.coastalresilience.org/gulfmex/#

Creators Syndicate, Inc. (2019). Retrieved from https://www.creators.com/read/succeeding-in-your-cbusiness/11/17/royalty-financing-the-new-thing-in-venture-capital

Crosby, E. M. (1997). Connecting with Country People. Armidale, New South Wales, AU: The Rural Development Centre. University of New England.

Cucui, G., Ionescu, C., Goldbach, I., Coman, M., & Marin, , E. (2018). Quantifying the Economic Effects of Biogas Installations for Organic Waste from Agro-Industrial Sector. *Sustainability, 10*(7), 2582. doi:10.3390u10072582

Cuervo, A., Ribeiro, D., & Roig, S. (Eds.) (2007). Entrepreneurship: Concepts, Theory, and Perspective. New York, NY: Springer.

Cullen, R. (2002). *Addressing the Digital Divide.* Presented at the School of Information Management, University of Wellington, New Zealand.

Curley, M. S. B. (2013). Open Innovation 2.0: A New Milieu. OISPG Open Innovation 2.0 Year Book 2014, European Commission, 1-14.

Dahlander, L. G., & Gann, D. M. (2010). How open is innovation? *Research Policy, 39*(6), 699–709. doi:10.1016/j.respol.2010.01.013

Damayant, T. (2013). Who is afraid of Qualitative Research? A Compromise Accounting Research Failure in Improving Accounting Practices. *International Journal of Advances in Management and Economics, 2*(2), 89-94.

Dasgupta, S., Somik, L., & David, W. (2001). *Policy Reform, Economic Growth and the Digital Divide: An Econometric analysis.* World Bank Working Paper No. 2567 (March).

Das, T. K., & Teng, B. (2000). Instabilities of Strategic Alliances: An Internal tensions perspective. *Organization Science, 11*(1), 77–101. doi:10.1287/orsc.11.1.77.12570

Daub, C.-H. (2007). Assessing the quality of sustainability reporting: An alternative methodological approach. *Journal of Cleaner Production, 15*(1), 75–85. doi:10.1016/j.jclepro.2005.08.013

Davenport, T. H. (1998). Putting the Enterprise into the Enterprise System. *Harvard Business Review, 76*(4), 121–131. PMID:10181586

David, F. (2017). *Lawsuit spotlights regulation of sharing economy.* Tourism Update. Retrieved from http://www.tourismupdate.co.za/article/118539/

Davila, A. (2012). New trends in performance measurement and management control. In Performance Measurement and Management Control. *Global Issues (Washington, D.C.)*, *25*, 65–87.

Davila, A. (2012). New trends in performance measurement and management control. In *Performance Measurement and Management Control: Global Issues* (pp. 65–87). Bingley, UK: Emerald Group Publishing Limited.

Day, G. S. (1999). The Market Driven Organization. The Free Press DuPont, GE, Pfizer, and Rubbermaid. New York, NY: Harper Business.

de Felice, D. (2015). Challenges and opportunities in the production of business and human rights indicators to measure the corporate responsibility to respect. *Human Rights Quarterly*, *37*(2). Retrieved from https://kopernio.com/viewer?doi=10.1353/hrq.2015.0031&route=7. doi:10.1353/hrq.2015.0031

De Waal, P. (2015). *Technology is reshaping the travel industry.* Tourism Update. Retrieved from http://www.tourismupdate.co.za/artile/29777/Technology/

de Waal, A. A., & Kourtit, K. (2013). Performance measurement and management in practice. *International Journal of Productivity and Performance Management*, *62*(5), 446–473. doi:10.1108/IJPPM-10-2012-0118

Dechow, N., & Mouritsen, J. (2005). Enterprise resource planning systems, management control and the quest for integration. *Accounting, Organizations and Society*, *30*(7-8), 691–733. doi:10.1016/j.aos.2004.11.004

Dechow, P. M., Ge, W., & Schrand, K. M. (2010). Understanding earnings quality: A review of the proxies, their determinants and their consequences. *Journal of Accounting and Economics*, *50*(2-3), 344–401. doi:10.1016/j.jacceco.2010.09.001

Dechow, P., Hutton, A., Kim, J. H., & Sloan, R. G. (2012). Detecting earnings management: A new approach. *Journal of Accounting Research*, *50*(2), 275–334. doi:10.1111/j.1475-679X.2012.00449.x

Dekker, H. C. (2004). Control of inter-organizational relationships: Evidence on appropriate concerns and coordination requirements. *Accounting, Organizations and Society*, *29*(1), 27–49. doi:10.1016/S0361-3682(02)00056-9

Delac, G., Silic, M., & Krolo, J. (2011). *Emerging security threats for mobile platforms.* Academic Press.

Delaney, J. T., & Huselid, M. A. (1996). The impact of human resource management practices on perceptions of organizational performance. *Academy of Management Journal*, *39*, 949–969.

Denison, D. R. (1990). *Corporate Culture and Organizational Effectiveness.* New York, NY: Wiley.

Dennis, I. (2014). *The Nature of Accounting Regulation.* New York, NY: Routledge.

Deutsch, P., & Silcox, B. (2003). Learning from other libraries: Benchmarking to assess library performance. *Information Outlook*, *7*(7), 18–25.

Dhaliwal, D. S., Li, O. Z., Tsang, A., & Yang, Y. G. (2011). Voluntary Nonfinancial Disclosure and the Cost of Equity Capital: The Initiation of Corporate Social Responsibility Reporting We appreciate the valuable comments from. *The Accounting Review*, *86*(1), 59–100. doi:10.2308/accr.00000005

Dholakia, U. M. (2015). Everyone hates Uber's surge pricing-Here's how to fix it. *Harvard Business Review.* Retrieved from https://hbr.org/2015/12/

Di Guardo, M. C., & Harrigan, K. R. (2012). Mapping research on strategic alliances and innovation: A co-citation analysis. *The Journal of Technology Transfer*, *37*(6), 789–811. doi:10.100710961-011-9239-2

Dije, U. W. (2017). Sources of Financing for Small and Medium Enterprises in Nigeria. (Unpublished Ph.D. Dissertation, Walden University). Retrieved from http://scholarworks.waldenu.edu/dissertations utm_source=scholarworks.waldenu.edu

DiMaggio, P., & Hargittai, E. (2001). *From the 'Digital Divide' to 'Digital Inequality': Studying Internet Use as Penetration Increases*. Princeton, NJ: Center for Arts and Cultural Policy Studies, Woodrow Wilson School, Princeton University.

Dipa, K. (2016). Taxify to take on Uber in SA. Retrieved from http://www.iol.co.za/motoring/industry-news/

Dolan, D. (2014). Inside SA's R40bn taxi industry. Retrieved from http://www.moneyweb.co.za/archive/

Douglas, E. J., & Shepherd, D. (1997). *Why entrepreneurs create businesses: a utility maximizing response. Frontiers of Entrepreneurship Research* (pp. 185–186). Wellesley, MA.: Babson College.

Doukakis, L. C. (2014). The effect of mandatory IFRS adoption on real and accrual-based earnings management activities. *Journal of Accounting and Public Policy*, *33*(6), 551–572. doi:10.1016/j.jaccpubpol.2014.08.006

Dow. (2016). Going Back to School: Ambassadors for Science – How Dow is working to increase STEM literacy and prepare tomorrow's workforce to develop the innovative solutions we all need. Retrieved from https://corporate.dow.com/en-us/science-and-sustainability/earth-day/stem-outreach

Drucker, P. F. (1985). *Innovation and Entrepreneurship: Practice and Principles*. New York, NY: Harper Business.

Drury, C. (2001). *Management Accounting for Business Decisions* (2nd ed.). Thompson Learning.

Dube, S. H. (2015). Uber: A game changer in passenger transport in South Africa. Retrieved from https://www.competition.org.za/review/

Duberley, J., Johnson, P., Cassell, C., & Close, P. (2000). Manufacturing Change: The Role of Performance Evaluation and Control Systems. *International Journal of Operations & Production Management*, *20*(4), 427–440. doi:10.1108/01443570010314773

Dubini, P. (1988). *Motivational and environmental influences on business start-ups: some hints for public policies. Frontiers of Entrepreneurship Research* (pp. 31–45). Wellesley, MA.: Babson College.

Dvořáková, L., & Zborková, J. (2014). Integration of Sustainable Development at Enterprise Level. *Proceedia Engineering, 69*, 686–695. Retrieved from https://kopernio.com/viewer?doi=10.1016/j.proeng.2014.03.043&route=6

Eaton, B., Elaluf-Calderwood, S., Sorensen, C., & Yoo, Y. (2015). Distributed tuning of boundary resources: The case of Apple's iOS service system. *MIS Quarterly: Management Information Systems*, *39*(1), 217–243. doi:10.25300/MISQ/2015/39.1.10

ECREA. (2019). *EPA's Climate Resilience Evaluation and Awareness*. Retrieved from https://www.epa.gov/crwu/creat-risk-assessment-application-water-utilities

Eggers, W. D., & Macmillan, P. (2013). The Solution Revolution: How Business, Government, and Social Enterprises Are Teaming Up to Solve Society's Toughest Problems. Brighton, MA: Harvard Business Review Press.

Ehling, J. (2019). *Hackers set up fake Wi-Fi hotspots to steal your information*. [online] ABC13 Houston. Retrieved from: https://abc13.com/technology/hackers-set-up-fake-wi-fi-hotspots-to-steal-your-information/835223/

Ellen Macarthur Foundation. (2015). *Growth within: a circular economy vision for a competitive Europe*. Retrieved from https://www.ellenmacarthurfoundation.org/assets/downloads/publications/EllenMacArthurFoundation_Growth-Within_July15.pdf

Elmquist, M., Fredberg, T., & Ollila, S. (2009). Exploring the field of open innovation. *European Journal of Innovation Management, 12*(3), 326–345. doi:10.1108/14601060910974219

Epstein, M. J., & Manzoni, J.-F. (1997). The Balanced Scorecard and Tableau de Bord: Translating strategy into action. *Management Accounting, 79*(2), 28–37.

Ernkvist, M. (2015). The double knot of technology and business-model innovation in the era of ferment of digital exchanges: The case of OM, a pioneer in electronic options exchanges. *Technological Forecasting and Social Change, 99*, 285–299. doi:10.1016/j.techfore.2015.02.001

Essien, B. S. (2014). The Nigerian business environment and growth Constraints of Micro and Small-Scale Manufacturing Industries. *American International Journal of Social Science, 3*(6), 67–76.

European Commission. (2001a). *Commission Recommendation of 30 May 2001 on the recognition, measurement and disclosure of environmental issues in the annual accounts and annual reports of companies, 2001/453/EC.* Retrieved from https://eur-lex.europa.eu/LexUriServ/LexUriServ.do?uri=OJ:L:2001:156:0033:0042:EN:PDF

European Commission. (2001b). *GREEN PAPER Promoting a European framework for Corporate Social Responsibility.* Retrieved from http://ec.europa.eu/transparency/regdoc/rep/1/2001/EN/1-2001-366-EN-1-0.Pdf

European Commission. (2018). *A Clean Planet for all A European strategic long-term vision for a prosperous, modern, competitive and climate neutral economy.* Retrieved from https://ec.europa.eu/clima/sites/clima/files/docs/pages/com_2018_733_en.pdf

European Commission. (2018). *A sustainable Bioeconomy for Europe: strengthening the connection between economy, society and the environment Updated Bioeconomy Strategy.* Brussels, Belgium.

European Commission. (2019). *Towards a sustainable Europe by 2030.* Retrieved from https://ec.europa.eu/commission/sites/beta-political/files/rp_sustainable_europe_30-01_en_web.pdf

European Environment Agency. (2014). Digest of EEA indicators 2014. Copenhagen, Denmark.

European Parliament. (2014). Directive 2014/95/EU of the European Parliament and the Council of 22 October 2014 - amending Directive 2013/34/EU as regards disclosure of non-financial and diversity information by certain large undertakings and groups. *Official Journal of the European Union, L, 330.* Retrieved from https://eur-lex.europa.eu/legal-content/EN/TXT/PDF/?uri=CELEX:32014L0095&from=EN

Evbuomwan, G. O., Ikpi, A. E., Okoruwa, V. O., & Akinyosoye, V. O. (2013). Sources of Finance b for Micro, Small and Medium Enterprises in Nigeria. In Proceedings of *19th International Farm Management Congress, SGGW,* Warsaw, Poland. Retrieved from www.ifmaonline.org

Fahey, L., & Randall, R. M. (2001). *The Portable MBA in Strategy* (2nd ed.). New York, NY: Wiley & Sons.

Fang, B., Ye, Q., & Law, R. (2016). Effect of sharing economy on tourism industry employment. Research Notes and Report. *Annals of Tourism Research, 57*, 234–278. doi:10.1016/j.annals.2015.11.018

Faraj, S., von Krogh, G., Monteiro, E., & Lakhani, K. R. (2016). Special section introduction—Online community as space for knowledge flows. *Information Systems Research, 27*(4), 668–684. doi:10.1287/isre.2016.0682

Feeser, H. R., & Dugan, K. W. (1989). *Entrepreneurial motivation: a comparison of high and low growth high tech founders. Frontiers of Entrepreneurship Research* (pp. 13–27). Wellesley, Mass.: Babson College.

Fenton, E. M., & Pettigrew, A. M. (2000). *Theoretical Perspectives on New Forms of Organizing.* London, UK: Sage. doi:10.4135/9781446219379.n1

Ferreira, F. A. (2018). Mapping the field of arts-based management: Bibliographic coupling and co-citation analyses. *Journal of Business Research*, *85*, 348–357. doi:10.1016/j.jbusres.2017.03.026

Fifka, M. S. (2013). Corporate Responsibility Reporting and its Determinants in Comparative Perspective - a Review of the Empirical Literature and a Meta-analysis. *Business Strategy and the Environment*, *22*(1), 1–35. doi:10.1002/bse.729

Filion, L. J. (1990). Free trade: The need for a definition of small business. *Journal of Small Business and Entrepreneurship*, *7*(2), 33–46. doi:10.1080/08276331.1990.10600347

Finnish Textile & Fashion. (2016). *Guidelines and insight for corporate responsibility work Responsible management Putting principles into practice Corporate responsibility manual*. Helsinki, Finland. Retrieved from https://s3-eu-west-1.amazonaws.com/stjm/uploads/20160622103146/STJM_Corporate_responsibility_manual.pdf

Fischbacher-Smith, D. (2016). Breaking bad? In search of a (softer) systems view of security ergonomics. *Security Journal*, *29*(1), 5–22. doi:10.1057j.2015.41

Fisher, C. D. (2010). Happiness at Work. *International Journal of Management Reviews*, *12*(4), 384–412. doi:10.1111/j.1468-2370.2009.00270.x

Fitzgerald, M., Kruschwitz, N., Bonnet, D., & Welch, M. (2014). Embracing digital technology: A new strategic imperative. *MIT Sloan Management Review*, 1–12.

Florou, A., & Pope, P. (2012). Mandatory IFRS adoption and institutional investment decisions. *The Accounting Review*, *87*(6), 1993–2025. doi:10.2308/accr-50225

Fong, M. (2009). *Digital Divide: Reaping the Benefits of ICT. Europe's productivity Challenge*. Report Sponsored by Microsoft Euro Monitor International, GMI Database. Retrieved from http://graphics.eiu.com/files/ad_pdfs/MICROSOFT_FINAL.pdf

Force, C. (2014). The Star Factor-Discover What Your Top Performers Do Differently-and Inspire a New Level of Greatness in All. *The Journal of Applied Management and Entrepreneurship*, *19*(1), 127–129. doi:10.9774/GLEAF.3709.2014.ja.00012

Frahm, J., & Brown, K. (2007). First steps: Linking change communication to change receptivity. *Journal of Organizational Change*, *20*(3), 370–387. doi:10.1108/09534810710740191

Frese, M., & Gielnik, M. M. (2014). The Psychology of Entrepreneurship. *Annual Review of Organizational Psychology and Organizational Behavior*, *1*(1), 413–438. doi:10.1146/annurev-orgpsych-031413-091326

Friedberg, I., McLaughlin, K., Smith, P., Laverty, D., & Sezer, S. (2016). STPA-SafeSec: Safety and security analysis for cyber-physical systems. *Journal of Information Security and Applications*, *29*, 1–12.

Fuente, J. A., García-Sánchez, I. M., & Lozano, M. B. (2017). The role of the board of directors in the adoption of GRI guidelines for the disclosure of CSR information. *Journal of Cleaner Production*, *141*, 737–750. doi:10.1016/j.jclepro.2016.09.155

Gabel, D. (2016). Uber and the persistence of market power. *Journal of Economic Issues*, *50*(2), 527–534. doi:10.1080/00213624.2016.1179060

Gadde, L.-E., & Snehota, I. (2000). Making the Most of Supplier Relationships. *Industrial Marketing Management*, *29*(4), 305–316. doi:10.1016/S0019-8501(00)00109-7

Gaglio, C. M. (1997). Opportunity recognition: review, critique, and suggested research directions. In J. Katz (Ed.), *Advances in Entrepreneurship, Firm Emergence and Growth* (pp. 139–202). Greenwich, CT: JAI Press.

Gaglio, C., & Katz, J. (2001). The Psychological Basis of Opportunity Identification: Entrepreneurial Alertness. *Small Business Economics*, *16*(2), 95–111. doi:10.1023/A:1011132102464

Gaidelys, V., & Valodkiene, G. (2011). The Methods of Selecting and Assessing Potential Consumers Used of by Competitive Intelligence. *Inzinerine Ekonomika-Engineering Economics*, *22*(2), 196–202.

Galbraith, J. R., & Lawler, E. E. (1993). *Organizing for the Future: The New Logic for Managing Complex Organizations*. San Francisco, CA: Jossey-Bass.

Gandino, F., Celozzi, C., & Rebaudengo, M. (2017). A Key Management Scheme for Mobile Wireless Sensor Networks. *Applied Sciences*, *7*(5), 490. doi:10.3390/app7050490

Garg, A., Ghosh, D., Hudick, J., & Nowacki, C. (2003). Roles and practices in management accounting today. *Strategic Finance*, *85*(1), 30–65.

Garrison, R., Noreen, E., & Brewer, P. (2006). Managerial Accounting (11th ed.). New York, NY: McGraw-Hill, Irwin.

Gassmann, O. (2006). Opening up the innovation process: Towards an agenda. *R & D Management*, *36*(3), 223–228. doi:10.1111/j.1467-9310.2006.00437.x

Gassmann, O. E. (2010). The future of open innovation. *Research Management*, *40*(3), 213–221.

Gates, B. (1999). Business @ the Speed of Thought: Succeeding in the Digital Economy. New York, NY: Warner Books. doi:10.1111/1467-8616.00097

Gates, C. S., Chen, J., Li, N., & Proctor, R. W. (2014). Effective Risk Communication for Android Apps. *IEEE Transactions on Dependable and Secure Computing*, *11*(3), 252–265. doi:10.1109/TDSC.2013.58

Gawer, A., & Cusumano, M. A. (2014). Industry Platforms and Ecosystem Innovation. *Journal of Product Innovation Management*, *31*(3), 417–433. doi:10.1111/jpim.12105

Gbandi, E. C., & Amissah, G. (2014). Financing options for small and medium enterprises (SMEs) in Nigeria. *European Scientific Journal*, *10*, 327–340.

Gbenga-Ilori, A. O., & Ibiyemi, T. S. (2010). Directing the Digital Divide towards Bridging the Digital Divide in Nigeria. *European Journal of Scientific Research*, *45*(1), 79–88.

Ghazawneh, A. H., & Henfridsson, O. (2015). A paradigmatic analysis of digital application marketplaces. *Journal of Information Technology*, *30*(3), 198–208. doi:10.1057/jit.2015.16

Giacomino, D. E. (1992). Ethical Perceptions of Accounting Majors and Other Business Majors: A 402 Steven Dellaporta Empirical Study. *Accounting Educators' Journal*, *4*(2), 126–132.

Gibbs, S. (2016). *HummingBad malware infects 10m Android devices*. Retrieved from https://www.theguardian.com/technology/2016/jul/06/hummingbad-malware-infects-10m-android-devices-information-apps-ads

Gino, F. (2015). Understanding ordinary unethical behavior: Why people who value morality act immorally. *Current Opinion in Behavioral Sciences*, *3*, 107–111. doi:10.1016/j.cobeha.2015.03.001

Gloaguen, P. (2012). *Le guide de l'intelligence économique*. Retrieved from http://www.eure.gouv.fr/content/download/5022/30562/file/Le guide du routard - Intelligence Economique - 2012.pdf

Global Reporting Initiative. (2010). *A new phase: the growth of sustainability reporting*. Amsterdam, The Netherlands. Retrieved from www.globalreporting.org

Global Reporting Initiative. (2014). *G4 Sector Disclosures: Event organizers*. Retrieved from https://www.globalreporting.org/information/sector-guidance/Pages/default.aspx

Global Reporting Initiative. (n.d.). GRI Standards Download Center. Retrieved from https://www.globalreporting.org/standards/gri-standards-download-center/

Gnyawali, D., & Fogel, D. (1994). Environments for entrepreneurship development: Key dimensions and research implications. *Entrepreneurship Theory and Practice, 18*(4), 43–62. doi:10.1177/104225879401800403

Gobble, M. M. (2018). Digitalization, Digitization, and Innovation. Research-Technology Management. *Research Technology Management, 61*(4), 56–59. doi:10.1080/08956308.2018.1471280

Goodfellas. (2018). Reasons to Join. Retrieved from https://www.gfellas.co.za/index/php?option=com_content&view=article&id=3/

Govender, J. J. (2014). Public transport service quality in South Africa: A case study of bus and mini bus and mini-bus services in Johannesburg. *African Journal of Business Management, 8*(10), 317–326.

Granlund, M. (2011). Extending AIS research to management accounting and control issues: A research note. *International Journal of Accounting Information Systems, 12*(1), 3–19. doi:10.1016/j.accinf.2010.11.001

Granlund, M., & Malmi, T. (2002). Moderate impact of ERPS on management accounting: A lag or permanent outcome. *Management Accounting Research, 13*(3), 200–321. doi:10.1006/mare.2002.0189

Granlund, M., & Malmi, T. (2004). *Tietotekniikan mahdollisuudet taloushallinnon kehittämisessä/The potential of information technology in financial management development*. Jyväskylä: Gummerus Kirjapaino Oy.

Granlund, M., & Mouritsen, J. (2003). Introduction: Problematizing the relationship between management control and information technology. *European Accounting Review, 12*(1), 77–83. doi:10.1080/0963818031000087925

Granlund, M., Mouritsen, J., & Vaassen, E. (2013). On the relations between modern information technology, decision making and management control. *International Journal of Accounting Information Systems, 14*(4), 275–277. doi:10.1016/j.accinf.2013.10.001

Gray, R. H., Bebbington, J., & McPhail, K. J. (1994). Teaching Ethics and the Ethics of Teaching: Educating for Immorality and a Possible Case for Social and Environmental Accounting. *Accounting Education, 3*, 51–75. doi:10.1080/09639289400000005

Greenfield, A. C. Jr, Norman, C. S., & Wier, B. (2008). The effect of ethical orientation and professional commitment on earnings management behavior. *Journal of Business Ethics, 83*(3), 419–434. doi:10.100710551-007-9629-4

Greenstein, S. L., Lerner, J., & Stern, S. (2013). Digitization, innovation, and copyright: What is the agenda? *Strategic Organization, 11*(1), 110–121. doi:10.1177/1476127012460940

Gulani, M. G., & Usman, A. (2013). Financing small and medium scale enterprises (SMEs): A challenge for entrepreneurial development in Gombe state. *Asian Journal of Business and Management Sciences, 2*, 17–23.

Guttentag, D., & Kirk, D. (2016). Uber and Metropolitan Traffic Fatalities in the United States. *American Journal of Epidemiology, 184*(3), 192–198. doi:10.1093/aje/kww062 PMID:27449416

Haas, A., & Bird, J. (2016). *Uber is arriving now: Driving urban mobility in Africa.* Retrieved from http://blogs.lse.ac.uk/africaatlse/

Hąbek, P., & Wolniak, R. (2016). Relationship between Management Practices and Quality of CSR Reports. *Procedia: Social and Behavioral Sciences, 220*, 115–123. doi:10.1016/j.sbspro.2016.05.475

Hadfield, B. (1995). Wealth Within Reach. Tallahassee, FL: Cypress Publishing.

Hadžiosmanović, D., Bolzoni, D., & Hartel, P. H. (2012). A log mining approach for process monitoring in SCADA. *International Journal of Information Security*, *11*(4), 231–251. doi:10.100710207-012-0163-8

Hakansson, H., & Lind, J. (2007). Accounting in an Interorganizational Setting. In C. Chapman, A. Hopwood, & M. Shields (Eds.), Handbook of Management Accounting Research, 885-902. Amsterdam, The Netherlands: Elsevier.

Hall, J. D., Palsson, C., & Prince, J. (2017). *Is Uber a substitute or complement for public transit?* Source Unknown.

Hamari, J., Sjoklint, M., & Ukkonen, A. (2015). The sharing economy: Why people participate in collaborative consumption. Retrieved from http://onlinelibrary.wiley.com/doi/10.1002/asi.23552/abstract/

Hansen, Don R., & Mowen, M. M. (2006). *Cost Management: Accounting and Control*, Cincinnati, OH: South-Western/ Thomson Learning.

Harari, O. (1999). Why Do Leaders Avoid Change? *Management Review*, *88*(3).

Harbulot, C. (2007). *La main invisible des puissances*. Paris, France: Ellipses.

Harding, S., Kandlikar, M., & Gulati, S. (2016). Taxi apps, regulation and the market for taxi journeys. *Transportation Research Part A, Policy and Practice*, *88*, 15–25. doi:10.1016/j.tra.2016.03.009

Harryson, S. J. (2008). Entrepreneurship through relationships–navigating from creativity to commercialisation. *R & D Management*, *38*(3), 290–310. doi:10.1111/j.1467-9310.2008.00516.x

Hartmann, F. G. H., & Vaassen, E. H. J. (2003). The Changing Role of Management Accounting and Control Systems. In A. Bhimani (Ed.), *Management accounting in the digital economy* (1st ed.). Oxford, UK: Oxford University Press.

Hartnell, C. A., Ou, A. Y., & Kinicki, A. (2011). Organizational culture and organizational effectiveness: A meta-analytic investigation of the competing values framework's theoretical suppositions. *The Journal of Applied Psychology*, *96*(4), 677–694. doi:10.1037/a0021987 PMID:21244127

Hassan, M. K. (2005). Management accounting and organizational change: An institutional perspective. *Accounting & Organizational Change*, *1*(2), 125–140. doi:10.1108/18325910510635326

Hawkins, A. J. (2017). *Uber's 'flying cars' could arrive in LA by 2020-and here's what it'll be like to ride one*. Retrieved from https://www.theverge.com/

Haydaroglu, C. (2015). Final version of capitalism: Economic intelligence in Knowledge Economy. *Journal of Economics, Finance and Accounting*, *2*(1), 89–106.

Hébert, R. F., & Link, A. N. (1989). In Search of the Meaning of Entrepreneurship. *Small Business Economics*, *1*, 39–49. doi:10.1007/BF00389915

He, D., Chan, S., & Guizani, M. (2015). Mobile application security: Malware threats and defenses. *IEEE Wireless Communications*, *22*(1), 138–144. doi:10.1109/MWC.2015.7054729

He, D., Chen, C., Chan, S., & Bu, J. (2012). Secure and efficient handover authentication based on bilinear pairing functions. *IEEE Transactions on Wireless Communications*, *11*(1), 48–53. doi:10.1109/TWC.2011.110811.111240

Heemskerk, B., Group, R., Stmicroelectronics, P. P., & Scicluna, M. (2002). *Striking the balance Sustainable development reporting*. Retrieved from https://docs.wbcsd.org/2002/12/SustainableDevReporting-StrikingTheBalance.pdf

He, K., Pan, X., & Tian, G. (2017). Legal liability, government intervention, and auditor behavior: Evidence from structural reform of audit firms in China. *European Accounting Review*, *26*(1), 61–95. doi:10.1080/09638180.2015.1100547

Henama, U. S. (2013). A dream deferred? Santaco Airways, A low cost carrier that never launched in South Africa. *International Journal of Business, Economics and Law*, *2*(2), 60–67.

Henczel, S. (2002). Benchmarking – measuring and comparing for continuous improvement. *Information Outlook*, *6*(7), 12–20.

Henderson, K. (2016). Innovators or Rule Breakers? Regulating Uber, Airbnb & the Sharing Economy. *(Unpublished Dissertation, University of Otago).*

Herndon, N. C. Jr. (1996). A New Context for Ethics. Education Objectives in a College of Business: Ethical Decision-Making Models. *Journal of Business Ethics*, *15*(5), 501–510. doi:10.1007/BF00381926

Hiller, J., & Russel, R. (2013). The challenge and imperative of private sector cybersecurity: An international comparison. *Computer Law & Security Review*, *29*(3), 236–245. doi:10.1016/j.clsr.2013.03.003

Hitt, M. A., Ireland, R. D., Sirmon, D. G., & Trahms, C. A. (2011). Strategic entrepreneurship: Creating value for individuals, organizations, and Society. *The Academy of Management Perspectives*, *25*(2), 57–75.

Hjortdal, M. (2011). China's use of cyber warfare: Espionage meets strategic deterrence. *The Journal of Strategic Studies*, *4*(2), 1–24.

Hoffman, W. M., Brown Kamm, J., Frederick, R. E., & Petry, E. S. (Eds.). (2006). *The Ethics in Accounting & Finance: Trust, Responsibility and Control*. Westport, PA: Quorum Books.

Holmes, T. (2016). Uber cited as example of sharing economy, but its vast resources suggest otherwise. *Mail & Guardian*. Retrieved from https://mg.co.za/article/

Holthausen, R. W., & Watts, R. L. (2001). The relevance of the value-relevance literature for financial accounting standard setting. *Journal of Accounting and Economics*, *31*(1-3), 3–75. doi:10.1016/S0165-4101(01)00029-5

Homburg, C., & Pflesser, C. (2000). A Multiple Layer Model of Market-Oriented Organizational Culture: Measurement Issues and Performance Outcomes. *Journal of Marketing Research*, *37*(4), 449–462. doi:10.1509/jmkr.37.4.449.18786

Hong, J., Kim, J., & Cho, J. (2010). The trend of the security research for the insider cyber threat. *International Journal of Future Generation Communication and Networking*, *3*(2), 31–40.

Ho, S. C., Kauffman, R. J., & Liang, T.-P. (2011). Internet-based selling technology and e-commerce growth: A hybrid growth theory approach with cross-model inference. *Information Technology Management*, *12*(4), 409–429. doi:10.100710799-010-0078-x

Hoşbay, D. (2014). Organizational Misbehavior: A Research about Perceptions of Managers and Employees in Banking Sector. *The WEI International Academic Conference Proceedings*, (pp. 7-20).

Hou, Q., Jin, Q., Yang, R., Yuan, H., & Zhang, G. (2015). Performance commitments of controlling shareholders and earnings management. *Contemporary Accounting Research*, *32*(3), 1099–1127. doi:10.1111/1911-3846.12111

Huet, E. (2017). Uber plans to test flying cars in Dallas and Dubai by 2020. Retrieved from http://www.fin24.com/Tech/Companies/uber/

Hughes, E. (2019). *National Lottery warns public of lotto scam text circulating in Ireland*. Retrieved from https://www.irishmirror.ie/news/irish-news/national-lottery-warns-public-scam-11868654

Hunton, J. E., Lippincott, B., & Reck, J. L. (2003). Enterprise resource planning systems: Comparing firm performance of adopters and nonadopters. *International Journal of Accounting Information Systems*, *4*(3), 165–184. doi:10.1016/S1467-0895(03)00008-3

Hurley, R. F. (2002). Putting people back into organizational learning. *Journal of Business and Industrial Marketing*, *17*(4), 270–281. doi:10.1108/08858620210431679

Husillos, J., González, C. L., & Álvarez, G, M. J. (2011). The emergence of triple bottom line reporting in Spain. *Revista Española de Financiación y Contabilidad*, *XI*(150), 195–219. Retrieved from https://kopernio.com/viewer?doi=10.1080/02102412.2011.10779701&route=7. doi:10.1080/02102412.2011.10779701

IASB. (2003). *International Financial Standard for Small and Medium-sized enterprises*. IFRS for SME.

Ienciu, I. A. (2009). *Implicaţiile problemelor de mediu în contabilitatea şi auditul situaţiilor fnanciare*. Cluj Napoca: Risoprint. Retrieved from https://scholar.google.com/scholar?hl=en&as_sdt=0%2C5&q=Ionel+Ienciu+%282009%29+Implicaţiile+problemelor+de+mediu+în+contabilitatea+şi+auditul+situaţiilor+financiare.+Cluj+Napoca%3A+Risoprint.&btnG=

Ilegbinosa, I. A., & Jumbo, E. (2015). Small and medium scale enterprises and economic growth in Nigeria: 1975-2012. *International Journal of Business and Management*, *10*(3), 203–215. doi:10.5539/ijbm.v10n3p203

IMPACT2030. (2019). *Impact (Sydney)*, *2030*. Retrieved from https://www.impact2030.com

Institute for Economics and Peace. (2015). *Global peace index 2015, Measuring peace, its causes and its economic value*. Retrieved from http://economicsandpeace.org/wp-content/uploads/2015/06/Global-Peace-Index-Report-2015_0.pdf

International Auditing Practice Statements (IAPS). (2010). *The Consideration of Environmental Matters in the Audit of Financial Statements*. Retrieved from http://www.ifac.org/system/files/downloads/b007-2010-iaasb-handbook-iaps-1010.pdf

Interpretations on the G4 Guidelines. (n.d.). Retrieved from https://www.globalreporting.org/resourcelibrary/grig4-part1-reporting-principles-and-standard-disclosures.pdf

IOL. (2018). Uber introduces rider call back line for added safety. *Travel News*. Retrieved from https://www.iol.co.za/travel/travel-news/

Ionica, O., & Alina, S. (2017). The Impact of Management Accounting Innovations on Millennials Business. Ovidius University Annals, Economic Sciences Series, 17(1), 568-572.

Ireland, R. D., Hitt, M. A., & Sirmon, D. G. (2003). A Model of Strategic Entrepreneurship: The Construct and its Dimensions. *Journal of Management*, *29*(6), 963–989. doi:10.1016/S0149-2063(03)00086-2

Islam, A. (2015). Entrepreneurship and the Allocation of Government Spending Under Imperfect Markets. *World Development*, *70*, 108–121. doi:10.1016/j.worlddev.2015.01.002

Istrate, C., Georgescu, I. E., Carp, M., Robu, I. B., & Pavaloaia, L. (2015). Accruals Earnings Management in Emerging Markets under the Transition to IFRS: The Case of Romanian Listed Companies. *Transformations in Business & Economics*, *14*(2A), 393–411. Retrieved from https://www.researchgate.net/profile/Ioan-Bogdan_Robu/publication/290820080_Accruals_earnings_management_in_emerging_markets_under_the_transition_to_IFRS_The_case_of_Romanian_listed_companies/links/569bfd7708aea147695466b8.pdf

Istrate, C., Robu, I.-B., Păvăloaia, L., & Herghiligiu, I. V. (2017). Analysis of companies sustainability under the influence of environmental information disclosure. *Environmental Engineering and Management Journal*, *16*(4), 957–967. doi:10.30638/eemj.2017.097

Ives, B., & Mason, R. O. (1990). Can information technology revitalize your customer service? *The Academy of Management Executive*, *4*(4), 52–69.

Jackson, S. B., & Liu, X. K. (2010). The allowance for uncollectible accounts, conservatism, and earnings management. *Journal of Accounting Research, 48*(3), 565–601. doi:10.1111/j.1475-679X.2009.00364.x

James, M. L. (2015). The benefits of sustainability and integrated reporting: an investigation of accounting majors' perceptions. *Journal of Legal, Ethical and Regulatory Issues, 18*(1), 1–20. Retrieved from https://search.proquest.com/docview/1693348218/fulltextPDF/443A5B498B0480EPQ/1?accountid=17263

Jane, G., & Gravelle, I. (2009). Tax Havens: International Tax Avoidance and Evasion. *National Tax Journal, 62*(4), 727–753. doi:10.17310/ntj.2009.4.07

Jenkins, M. (1998). *Change in Management Accounting, Handbook of Management Accounting*. CIMA- Publication.

Johnny, J., & Gani, L. (2004). Integrating Business Strategy, Organizational Configurations and Management Accounting Systems with Business Unit Effectiveness: A Fitness Landscape Approach. *Management Accounting Research, 15*(2), 179–200. doi:10.1016/j.mar.2004.03.002

Johns, G. (1998). *Organizational behavior*. Bucharest, Romania: Economic Publishing House.

Johnson, B. R. (1990). Toward a multidimensional model of entrepreneurship: The case of achievement motivation and the entrepreneur. *Entrepreneurship Theory and Practice, 14*(3), 39–48. doi:10.1177/104225879001400306

Johnson, E., Fleishman, G., Valentine, S., & Walker, K. (2012). Managers' ethical evaluations of earnings management and its consequences. *Contemporary Accounting Research, 29*(3), 910–927. doi:10.1111/j.1911-3846.2011.01135.x

Johnson, H., & Kaplan, K. (1987). *Relevance Lost, the Rise and Fall of Management Accounting*. Boston, MA: Harvard Business School Press.

Jorgic, D. (2016). Uber seeks to lure cabbies in Africa expansion plan. *Moneyweb.* Retrieved from http://www.moneyweb.co.za/news/tech

Joseph, F. D., & Hollifield, C. A. (2003). Digital Divide Evidence in Four Rural Towns. *IT & Society, 1*(4), 107–117.

Justis, R. T., & Judd, R. J. (2002). *Franchising*. DAME Publishing.

Justis, R. T., & Vincent, W. S. (2001). *Achieving Wealth Through Franchising*. Avon, MA: Adams Media Corporation.

Juul, M. (2015). *The sharing economy and tourism: Tourist accommodation*. European Parliamentary Research Services.

Kallunki, J. P., Laitinen, E., & Silvola, H. (2011). Impact of enterprise resource planning systems on management control systems and firm performance. *International Journal of Accounting Information Systems, 12*(1), 20–39. doi:10.1016/j.accinf.2010.02.001

Kalmbach, Z. (2015). The effect of ridesharing services on drunk driving. *(Undergraduate research thesis, Texas University).*

Kamminga, P. E., & Van der Meer-Kooistra, J. (2007). Management Control Patterns in Joint Venture Relationships: A model and an Exploratory Study. *Accounting, Organizations and Society, 32*(1-2), 131–154. doi:10.1016/j.aos.2006.03.002

Kaplan, R., & Norton, D. (2008). Mastering the Management System, *Harward Business Review*, January, 63-77.

Kaplan, R. S., & Norton, D. P. (2006). How to implement a new strategy without disrupting your organization. *Harvard Business Review, 84*(3), 100. PMID:16515159

Karim, H. V. (2007). Strategic security management: a risk assessment guide for decision makers. Amsterdam, The Netherlands: Elsevier.

Katzenbach, J. R., & Smith, D. K. (2015). *The Wisdom of Teams: Creating the High-Performance Organization*. Boston, MA: Harvard Business Review Press.

Keen, L., & Ligthart, J. E. (2006). Information Sharing and International Taxation: A Primer. *International Tax and Public Finance, 13*(1), 81–110. doi:10.100710797-006-3090-7

Kelly, R. W. (2016). *The Uber Effect. Undergraduate Awards*. Retrieved from http://ir.lib.uwo.ca/undergradawards_2016/8/

Kesan, P. J., & Hayes, M. C. (2012). Mitigative counterstriking: Self-defense and deterrence in cyberspace. *Harvard Journal of Law & Technology, 25*(2), 474–529.

Kessler, M. M. (1963). Bibliographic coupling between scientific papers. *American Documentation, 14*(1), 10–25. doi:10.1002/asi.5090140103

Kets de Vries, M. (2003). *Organizations on the couch: A Clinical Perspective on Organizational Dynamics*. UK: John Wiley & Sons.

Kets de Vries, M., & Miller, D. (1984). *The Neurotic Organization: Diagnosing and Changing Counterproductive Styles of Management*. San Francisco, CA: Jossey-Bass.

Khan, M., Majid, A., Yasir, M., & Arshad, M. (2013). Corporate social responsibility and corporate reputation: A case of cement industry in Pakistan. *Interdisciplinary Journal of Contemporary Research in Business, 5*(1), 843–857. Retrieved from https://www.researchgate.net/publication/318359266

Khan, S., Gani, A., Wahab, A. W. A., Shiraz, M., & Ahmad, I. (2016). Network forensics: Review, taxonomy, and open challenges. *Journal of Network and Computer Applications, 66*, 214–235. doi:10.1016/j.jnca.2016.03.005

Kidane, F. (2012). Decision Making and the Role of Management Accounting Function – a Review of Empirical Literature, *Radix International Journal of Banking, Finance and Accounting, 1*(4), 77–97.

Kiiski, S., & Pohjola, M. (2001). *Cross-country diffusion of the internet*. WIDER Discussion Paper No. 2001/11. Helsinki, Finland: World Institute for Development Economics Research.

King, I., & Newcomer, E. (2018). *Uber spends $10.7bn in 9 years-here's how that stacks up*. Retrieved from https://www.iol.co.za/business-report/

Kirzner, I. M. (1979). *Perception, Opportunity, and Profit: Studies in the Theory of Entrepreneurship*. Chicago, IL: The University of Chicago Press.

Koerber, C. P. (2010). Corporate Responsibility Standards: Current Implications and Future Possibilities for Peace Through Commerce. *Journal of Business Ethics, 89*(S4), 461–480. doi:10.100710551-010-0397-1

Kohler, T. M., Matzler, K., & Füller, J. (2009). Avatar-based innovation: Using virtual worlds for real-world innovation. *Technovation, 29*(6-7), 395–407. doi:10.1016/j.technovation.2008.11.004

Kotler, Ph. T., & Keller, K. L. (2015). *Marketing Management* (15th ed.). USA: Pearson.

Kouraogo, Y., Zkik, K., Noreddine, E. J. E. I., & Orhanou, G. (2016). *Attacks on Android banking applications*. Paper presented at the 2016 International Conference on Engineering & MIS (ICEMIS). 10.1109/ICEMIS.2016.7745337

Kovacs, A., Van Looy, B., & Cassiman, B. (2015). Exploring the scope of open innovation: A bibliometric review of a decade of research. *Scientometrics, 104*(3), 951–983. doi:10.100711192-015-1628-0

Krombholz, K., Hobel, H., Huber, M., & Weippl, E. (2015). Advanced social engineering attacks. *Journal of Information Security and Applications, 22*, 113–122. doi:10.1016/j.jisa.2014.09.005

Kurosawa, K., Ohta, H., & Kakuta, K. (2017). How to make a linear network code (strongly) secure. *Designs, Codes and Cryptography, 82*(3), 559–582. doi:10.100710623-016-0180-0

Kyriakou, H. N., Nickerson, J. V., & Sabnis, G. (2017). Knowledge reuse for customization: Metamodels in an open design community for 3D printing. 2017. *MIS Quarterly, 41*(1), 315–332. doi:10.25300/MISQ/2017/41.1.17

Laengle, S. M., Merigó, J. M., Miranda, J., Słowiński, R., Bomze, I., Borgonovo, E., ... Teunter, R. (2017). Forty years of the European Journal of Operational Research: A bibliometric overview. *European Journal of Operational Research, 262*(3), 803–816. doi:10.1016/j.ejor.2017.04.027

Laitinen, E. (2003). Future-based Management Accounting: A New Approach with Survey Evidence. *Critical Perspectives on Accounting*, 14.

Landoll, D. J. (2010). The security risk assessment handbook: a complete guide for performing security risk assessment. Second Edition. Boca Raton, FL: CRC Press, Taylor & Francis Group.

Latham, G. P., & Pinder, C. C. (2005). Work motivation theory and research at the dawn of the twenty-first century. *Annual Review of Psychology, 56*(1), 485–516. doi:10.1146/annurev.psych.55.090902.142105 PMID:15709944

Laurell, C., & Sandstrom, C. (2016). Analysing Uber in social media-disruptive technology or institutional disruption? *International Journal of Innovation Management, 20*(5), 1–19. doi:10.1142/S1363919616400132

Lavrinenko, O., Ohotina, A., Ignatjeva, S., Rybalkin, O., & Lazdans, D. (2019). Entrepreneurship and sustainability issues the role of green economy in sustainable development (case study: the EU states). *Entrepreneurship and Sustainability, 6*(3), 1113–1126.

Lawson, B. (2007). *Access to finance for SMEs.* Paper at the Abuja International Conference on Financial System Strategy. Retrieved from http://www.cenbank.org/fss/mon/FSS2020Presentation%20at%20International%20Conference.ppt

Lazear, E. P. (2004). Balanced Skills and Entrepreneurship. *The American Economic Review, 94*(2), 208–211. doi:10.1257/0002828041301425

Lazear, E. P. (2005). Entrepreneurship. *Journal of Labor Economics, 23*(4), 649–680. doi:10.1086/491605

Lee, Y. G., Lee, J.-H., Song, Y.-I., & Kim, H.-J. (2008). Technological convergence and open innovation in the mobile telecommunication industry. *Asian Journal of Technology Innovation, 16*(1), 45–62. doi:10.1080/19761597.2008.9668646

Leiblein, M. J., & Miller, D. J. (2003). An Empirical Examination of Transation and Firm Level Influences on the Vertical Boundaries of the Firm. *Strategic Management Journal, 24*(9), 839–859. doi:10.1002mj.340

Lennard, G. K., & Angele A. G. (2013). *Broadband Internet Access and the Digital Divide: Federal Assistance Programs.* A Report delivered at Congressional Research Service.

Levy, A., & Merry, U. (1986). *Organizational Transformation: Approaches, Strategies, Theories.* New York, NY: Praeger.

Lewis, S., & Lallo, E. (2013). *Alligators are helping save Louisiana's coastal wetlands.* Retrieved from http://gulfseafoodnews.com/2013/09/18/the-business-of-alligator-part-four-the-thick-skinned-environmentalists

Leydesdorff, L., & Park, H. W. (2017). Full and fractional counting in bibliometric networks. *Journal of Informetrics, 11*(1), 117–120. doi:10.1016/j.joi.2016.11.007

Liaudanskienel, R., Ustinovicius, L., & Bogdanovicius, A. (2009). Evaluation of Construction Process Safety Solutions Using the TOPSIS Method. *Inzinerine Ekonomika-Engineering Economics, 64*(4), 32–40.

Lichtenstein, B. B. (2000). Self-Organized Transitions: A Pattern amid the Chaos of Transformative Change. *The Academy of Management Executive*, *14*(4).

Lichtenthaler, U. (2011). Open innovation: Past research, current debates, and future directions. *The Academy of Management Perspectives*, *25*(1), 75–93.

Lichtenthaler, U. (2017). Shared value innovation: Linking competitiveness and societal goals in the context of digital transformation. *International Journal of Innovation and Technology Management*, *14*(4), 1–14. doi:10.1142/S0219877017500183

Lien, T. (2017). *As Uber spends big to compete with Lyft, profitability in the U.S. is not in sight.* Retrieved from http://www.latimes.com/business/technology/

Liker, J. K., & Choi, T. Y. (2004). Building Deep Supplier Relationships. *Harvard Business Review* (Dec.), 29-38.

Li, L., Qi, B., Tian, G., & Zhang, G. (2017). The contagion effect of low-quality audits at the level of individual auditors. *The Accounting Review*, *92*(1), 137–163. doi:10.2308/accr-51407

Lim, B. (1995). Examining the organizational culture and organizational performance link. *Leadership and Organization Development Journal*, *16*(5), 16–21. doi:10.1108/01437739510088491

Lin, C. H., Peng, C. H., & Kao, D. T. (2008). The innovativeness effect of market orientation and learning orientation on business performance. *International Journal of Manpower*, *29*(8), 752–772. doi:10.1108/01437720810919332

Lin, Z., Lin, D., & Pei, D. (2017). Practical construction of ring LFSRs and ring FCSRs with low diffusion delay for hardware cryptographic applications. *Cryptography and Communications*, *9*(4), 431–440. doi:10.100712095-016-0183-8

Li, S. (2010). Does mandatory adoption of international accounting standards in the European Union reduce the cost of equity capital? *The Accounting Review*, *85*(2), 607–636. doi:10.2308/accr.2010.85.2.607

Li, Sh., Xu, L. D., & Zhao, S. (2018). 5G Internet of Things: A survey. *Journal of Industrial Information Integration*, *10*, 1–9. doi:10.1016/j.jii.2018.01.005

Liu, W. K. (2008). *KFC in China: Secret Recipe for Success. John Wiley & Sons (Asia).* PTE LTD.

Liu, X. Y. (2010). Weighted hybrid clustering by combining text mining and bibliometrics on a large-scale journal database. *Journal of the American Society for Information Science and Technology*, *61*(6), 1105–1119.

Lock, I., & Seele, P. (2016). The credibility of CSR (corporate social responsibility) reports in Europe. Evidence from a quantitative content analysis in 11 countries. *Journal of Cleaner Production*, *122*, 186–200. doi:10.1016/j.jclepro.2016.02.060

Loeb, S. E. (1988). Teaching Students Accounting Ethics: Some Crucial Issues. *Accounting Education*, *3*, 316–329.

Loi, M., Castriotta, M., & Di Guardo, M. C. (2016). The theoretical foundations of entrepreneurship education: How co-citations are shaping the field. *International Small Business Journal*, *34*(7), 948–971. doi:10.1177/0266242615602322

Lombard, L. (2016). *Alert: Uber changes pick-up regulations at SA international airports.* Retrieved from http://traveller24.news24.com/TravelPlanning/

LS. (2019). *The economy of seafood in Louisiana.* Retrieved from http://www.louisianaseafood.com/industry

Lukka, K. (2010). The roles and effects of paradigms in accounting research. *Management Accounting Research*, *21*(2), 110–115. doi:10.1016/j.mar.2010.02.002

Macchi, M., Rizzo, U., & Ramaciotti, L. (2014). From services dealers to innovation brokers: How open innovation paradigm affects incubator activities. Evidence from Italy. *Journal of Intellectual Capital, 15*(4), 554–575. doi:10.1108/JIC-06-2014-0078

MacKenzie, D. (2014). *A Sociology of Algorithms: High–Frequency Trading and the Shaping of Markets.* Working paper.

Madisha, K. (2018). Uber, Taxify drivers 'at risk'. *Afro Voice. Gauteng News.* May 16.

MAE. (2019). *Microsoft AI for Earth.* Retrieved from https://www.microsoft.com/en-us/aiforearth

Malatras, A., Geneiatakis, D., & Vakalis, I. (2016). On the efficiency of user identification: A system-based approach. *International Journal of Information Security, 15*(1), 1–19.

Malhotra, A. G., Gosain, S., & El Sawy, O. A. (2007). Leveraging standard electronic business interfaces to enable adaptive supply chain partnerships. *Information Systems Research, 18*(3), 260–279. doi:10.1287/isre.1070.0132

Malin, E., & Mohamed, K. (2017). Understanding Shoulder Surfing in the Wild: Stories from Users and Observers. In *Proceedings of the* 2017 *CHI Conference on Human Factors in Computing Systems* (pp. 4254-4265). Denver, CO: ACM.

Manavhela, P., & Henama, U. S. (2018). Surge pricing as a new pricing model for transport services: The case of Uber in South Africa. *Conference proceedings of the 8th AHTMM Conference,* Bangkok, Thailand, (pp. 606-618).

Margarit, S. G., Bran, S., Ionescu, E., & Boca, R. (2012). Coverage of environmental information in annual financial statements in a responsible manner. *Procedia-Social and Behavioral Sciences, 62*, 526–530.

Marimon, F., del Mar Alonso-Almeida, M., del Pilar Rodríguez, M., & Alejandro, K. A. C. (2012). The worldwide diffusion of the global reporting initiative: what is the point? *Journal of Cleaner Production, 33*, 132–144.

Mariotti, S., & Glackin, C. (2010). *Entrepreneurship.* Upper Saddle River, NJ: Prentice Hall.

Marku, E., Castriotta, M., & Di Guardo, M. C. (2017). Disentangling the intellectual structure of innovation and M&A literature. *Technological Innovation Networks: Collaboration and Partnership, 47.*

Marsh, C. (2013). Business executives' perceptions of ethical leadership and its development. *Journal of Business Ethics, 114*(3), 565–582. doi:10.100710551-012-1366-7

Martínez-López, F. J.-F., Merigó, J. M., Valenzuela-Fernández, L., & Nicolás, C. (2018). Fifty years of the European Journal of Marketing: A bibliometric analysis. *European Journal of Marketing, 52*(1/2), 439–468. doi:10.1108/EJM-11-2017-0853

Martínez-Torres, M. R. (n.d.). The role of Internet in the development of future software projects. *Internet Research, 20*(1), 72-86.

Martre, H. (1994). *Intelligence économique et strategie des entreprises.* Retrieved from http://www.bdc.aege.fr

Maskell, B. (1991). *Performance Measurement for World Class Manufacturing: a Model for American Companies.* Cambridge, MA: Productivity Press.

McCuen, R. H. (1994). Constructivist Learning Model for Ethics Education. *Journal of Professional Issues in Engineering Education and Practice, 120*(3), 273–278. doi:10.1061/(ASCE)1052-3928(1994)120:3(273)

McCune, J. C. (1999). The Change Makers: Regardless of the obstacles placed in their paths, these agents of change get the job done. *Management Review*, 16.

McDonald, G. M., & Donleavy, G. D. (1995). Objections to the Teaching of Business Ethics. *Journal of Business Ethics, 14*(10), 839–853. doi:10.1007/BF00872350

McQuade, S. (2006). *Understanding and Managing Cybercrime*. Boston, MA: Allyn & Bacon.

MD. (2019). *Marshdog.com*. Retrieved from http://www.marshdog.com

ME. (2019). Martin ecosystems. Retrieved from http://www.martinecosystems.com

Meher, K. C., & Ajibie, D. (2018) Financial Sustainability of SMEs by injecting Debt Finance. *The Management Accountant Journal, 53*(1), 80-87. Retrieved from https://www.researchgate.net/publication/324676445

Mele, D. (2005). Ethical Education in Accounting: Integrating Rules, Values and Virtues. *Journal of Business Ethics, 57*, 97–109. doi:10.100710551-004-3829-y

Menzie, D. C., & Robert, W. F. (2004). *The Determinants of the Global Digital Divide: A Cross-Country Analysis of Computer and Internet penetration*. Working Paper Presented at the National Bureau of Economic Research, Cambridge, MA.

Michelon, G., Pilonato, S., & Ricceri, F. (2015). CSR reporting practices and the quality of disclosure: An empirical analysis. *Critical Perspectives on Accounting, 33*, 59–78. doi:10.1016/j.cpa.2014.10.003

Michel, S. D., & Rosenbloom, H. D. (2011). Teaching Clinical Ethics as a Professional Skill: Bridging the Gap Between Knowledge About Ethics and its Use in Clinical Practice. *Journal of Medical Ethics, 21*, 97–103. PMID:7608948

Millar, D. (2012). Louisiana alligator industry stages a comeback, thanks to growing demand for skins. *The Times-Picayune*, June 17. Retrieved from https://www.nola.com/business/2012/06/louisianas_alligator_industry.html

Milne, M. J., & Gray, R. (2013). W(h)ither Ecology? The Triple Bottom Line, the Global Reporting Initiative, and Corporate Sustainability Reporting. *Journal of Business Ethics, 118*(1), 13–29. doi:10.100710551-012-1543-8

Mims, C. (2018). *Uber's biggest problem: Its business model*. Source Unknown.

Mittelman, J. H. (2011). Global (in) security: The confluence of intelligence and will. *Global Change, Peace & Security, 23*(2), 135–139. doi:10.1080/14781158.2011.580954

Mohammed, I., & Ali, I. (2015). The Effect of SMEs' Cost of Capital on their Financial Performance in Nigeria. *Journal of Finance and Accounting, 3*(1), 8–11.

Moneyweb. (2017). *Namibia tells Airbnb hosts to register or face jail*. Retrieved from https://www.moneyweb.co.za/news-fast-news/

Monk, E., & Wagner, B. (2013). *Concepts in Enterprise Resource Planning* (4th ed.). Boston, MA: Course Technology Cengage Learning.

Munro, I. (2014). Organizational ethics and foucault's 'art of living': Lessons from social movement organizations. *Organization Studies, 35*(8), 1127–1148. doi:10.1177/0170840614530915

Mwaura, G. (2016). *Uber: The beauty and wrath of disruptive technologies in Africa*. Retrieved from http://www.newtimes.co.rw/section/article/

Nagel, R. N., & Dove, R. (1991). 21st Century Manufacturing Enterprise Strategy: An Industry led View. Collingdale, PA: Diane Publishing.

Naik, S. (2015). *We compare: Uber vs metered taxi*. Retrieved from https://www.iol.co.za/motoring/industry-news/

Nambisan, S. S., Siegel, D., & Kenney, M. (2018). On open innovation, platforms, and entrepreneurship. *Strategic Entrepreneurship Journal, 12*(3), 354–368. doi:10.1002ej.1300

Nambisan, S., Lyytinen, K., Majchrzak, A., & Song, M. (2017). Digital Innovation Management: Reinventing innovation management research in a digital world. *Management Information Systems Quarterly*, *41*(1), 223–238. doi:10.25300/MISQ/2017/41:1.03

Narayanan, V. G., & Raman, A. (2004). Aligning Incentives in Supply Chains. *Harvard Business Review*, *82*(11), 94–102. PMID:15559449

NBIA. (2014). National Business Incubation Association. Retrieved from http://www.nbia.org/member_services/soft_landings

Neu, D., Warsame, H., & Pedwell, K. (1998). Managing public impressions: Environmental disclosures in annual reports. *Accounting, Organizations and Society*, *23*(3), 265–282. Retrieved from https://www.sciencedirect.com/science/article/pii/S0361368297000081. doi:10.1016/S0361-3682(97)00008-1

Newman, M. E., & Girvan, M. (2004). Finding and evaluating community structure in networks. *Physical Review E*, *69*(2), 026113 - 026113/15.

Ngcukana, L. (2017). Uber rival Taxify launches service in Eastern Cape. *City Press,* Nov. 12.

Nicolau, C. M. (2010). Operaţionalizare şi delimitare conceptuală a inteligenţei economice. *Studia Universitatis Vasile Goldiş. Arad-Seria Ştiinţe Economice*, *20*(1), 436–444.

Niculescu, M. (2005). *Diagnostic financiar*. Bucuresti, Romania: Editura Economica.

Nieto, M. J., & Santamaría, L. (2007). The importance of diverse collaborative networks for the novelty of product innovation. *Technovation*, *27*(6-7), 367–377. doi:10.1016/j.technovation.2006.10.001

Nixon, W. A. J. (1995). Technology Investment and Management Accounting Practice. *British Journal of Management*, *6*(4), 271–288. doi:10.1111/j.1467-8551.1995.tb00100.x

Nixon, W. A. J., Laitinen, E., & Wingren, T. (2002). Implication of the 'New Economy' for Control Systems, *3rd Conference on New Directions in Management Accounting: Innovations in Practice and Research*, Brussels, Belgium.

Nkanjeni, U. (2017). *Uber gift cards: A new offering across SA*. Retrieved from http://www.traveller24.com/TravelPlanning/uber-goft-card/

NOGE. (2015). *Making cities resilient: New Orleans / Gothenburg Exchange*. Retrieved from http://sdmi-resilient-cities.com

Norris, P. (2001). *Digital Divide: Civic Engagement, Information Poverty, and the Internet Worldwide*. New York, NY: Cambridge University Press. doi:10.1017/CBO9781139164887

Nosella, A. C., Cantarello, S., & Filippini, R. (2012). The intellectual structure of organizational ambidexterity: A bibliographic investigation into the state of the art. *Strategic Organization*, *10*(4), 450–465. doi:10.1177/1476127012457979

NSLRV. (2019). *NOAA Sea Level Rise Viewer*. Retrieved from https://coast.noaa.gov/slr

Nucciarelli, A. L., Li, F., Fernandes, K. J., Goumagias, N., Cabras, I., Devlin, S., ... Cowling, P. (2017). From value chains to technological platforms: The effects of crowdfunding in the digital game industry. *Journal of Business Research*, *78*, 341–352. doi:10.1016/j.jbusres.2016.12.030

NUTRIA. (2019). *Nutria.com*. Retrieved from https://nutria.com/site.php

Nylén, D. H., & Holmström, J. (2015). Digital innovation strategy: A framework for diagnosing and improving digital product and service innovation. *Business Horizons*, *58*(1), 57–67. doi:10.1016/j.bushor.2014.09.001

O' Mahon, A., & Doran, J. (2008). The changing role of management accountants; evidence from the implementation of ERP systems in large organizations. *International Journal of Business and Management*, *3*(8), 109–115.

O'Toole, J., & Matherne, B. (2017). *Uber: Aggressive management for growth.* Retrieved from https://www.researchgate.net/publications/

Oates, G., & Dias, R. (2016). Including ethics in banking and finance programs: Teaching "we shouldn't win at any cost". *Education + Training*, *58*(1), 94–111. doi:10.1108/ET-12-2014-0148

OB. (2019). *Oyster Bed.* Retrieved from https://theoysterbed.com

OB. (2019). *The Oyster Bed.* Retrieved from https://theoysterbed.com

Obaji, N. O., & Olugu, M. U. (2014). The role of government policy in entrepreneurship development. Science. *Journal of Business and Management*, *2*, 109–115.

Obal, M. L., & Lancioni, R. A. (2013). Maximizing buyer–supplier relationships in the Digital Era: Concept and research agenda. *Industrial Marketing Management*, *42*(6), 851–854. doi:10.1016/j.indmarman.2013.06.002

Ocasio, W. (1997). Towards an attention-based view of the firm. *Strategic Management Journal*, *18*(S1), 187–206. doi:10.1002/(SICI)1097-0266(199707)18:1+<187::AID-SMJ936>3.3.CO;2-B

OECD. (2001). *Understanding the Digital Divide.* Paris, France: Organization for Economic Cooperation and Development.

Okamoto, T., & Takashima, K. (2015). Achieving short ciphertexts or short secret-keys for adaptively secure general inner-product encryption. *Designs, Codes and Cryptography*, *77*(2), 725–771. doi:10.100710623-015-0131-1

Olson, E. M., Slater, S. F., Tomas, G., & Hult, M. (2005). The performance implications of fit among business strategy, marketing organization structure, and strategic behavior. *Journal of Marketing*, *69*(3), 49–65. doi:10.1509/jmkg.69.3.49.66362

ORAE. (2019). *ORA Estuaries.* Retrieved from https://www.oraestuaries.com

Organisation for Economic Co-operation Development (OECD). (2004).

Orzan, G. (2001). *Cybermarketing.* Bucharest, Romania: Uranus Publishing House.

Ossai, A. (2017). The Problems and Prospects of Small and Medium Scale Enterprises (SMEs) Growth and Development in Nigeria: A Study of Selected SMEs in Delta State. *International Journal of Scientific Research in Education*, *10*(3), 278–294.

Osteryoung, J. S., & Newman, D. (1993). What is a Small Business? *The Journal of Small Business Finance*, *2*(3), 219–231.

Overly, S. (2017). Driver tips to change for Uber. *Business Report.* Retrieved from http://www.iol.co.za/business-report/international/

Palenberg, M., Reinicke, W., & Witte, J. M. (2006). *Trends in non-financial reporting.* Retrieved from www.gppi.net

Pallot, M. (2015). Open Innovation 2.0: Living Labs . Open Innovation Ecosystems: A Study on Matchmaking between Living Labs and other Organisations within Horizon 2020 Calls. *Open Innovation YearBook 2015 European Commission.*

Pal, R. (2016). Extended responsibility through servitization in PSS: An exploratory study of used-clothing sector. *Journal of Fashion Marketing and Management: An International Journal*, *20*(4), 453–470. doi:10.1108/JFMM-12-2015-0100

Panayiotou, N. A., Aravossis, K. G., & Moschou, P. (2009). A New Methodology Approach for Measuring Corporate Social Responsibility Performance. *Water Air and Soil Pollution Focus*, *9*(1-2), 129–138. doi:10.100711267-008-9204-8

Parker, A. (2017). *Uber vs. meter taxis: The last of the professional drivers.* Retrieved from http://www.wheels24.co.za/News/Gear_and_Tech/

Parker, N. (2016). After exiting China, Uber shifts focus to Latin Maerica. *CNN Tech.* Retrieved from http://money.cnn.com/2016/12/06/technology/uber-latin-america/

Parker, G. V., Van Alstyne, M., & Jiang, X. (2016). Platform ecosystems: How developers invert the firm. 2017. *Management Information Systems Quarterly, 41*(1), 255–266. doi:10.25300/MISQ/2017/41.1.13

Parker, L. (2012). Qualitative management accounting research: Assessing deliverables and relevance. *Critical Perspectives on Accounting, 23*(1), 54–70. doi:10.1016/j.cpa.2011.06.002

Parmentier, G. M., & Mangematin, V. (2014). Orchestrating innovation with user communities in the creative industries. *Technological Forecasting and Social Change, 83*, 40–53. doi:10.1016/j.techfore.2013.03.007

Paronda, A. G., Regidor, J. R. F., & Gaabucayan-Napalang, S. (2017). *An exploratory study on Uber, GrabCar and Conventional Taxis in Metro Manila.* Conference Paper. Retrieved from http://www.researchgate.net/publication/31895959598/

Parviainen, P., Tihinen, M., Kääriäinen, J., & Teppola, S. (2017). Tackling the digitalization challenge: How to benefit from digitalization in practice. *International Journal of Information Systems and Project Management, 5*(1), 63–77.

Paton, R. A., & McCalman, J. (2008). *Change Management: A Guide to Effective Implementation.* London, UK: Sage.

Pearce, J. A., & Robinson, R. B. Jr. (2007). *Strategic Management: Formulation, Implementation and Control.* Boston, MA: McGraw-Hill.

Peltier, T. R. (2010). Information security risk analysis. Third Edition. Boca Raton, FL: CRC Press, Taylor & Francis Group, Auerbach Publications. doi:10.1201/EBK1439839560

Pera, R. V., & Viglia, G. (2015). Turning ideas into products: Subjective well-being in co-creation. *Service Industries Journal, 35*(7-8), 388–402. doi:10.1080/02642069.2015.1015521

Peters, T. J. (1998). *The Circle of Innovation: You Can't Shrink Your Way to Greatness.* London, UK: Coronet.

Petropoulos, G. (2016). *Uber and the economic impact of sharing economy platforms.* Retrieved from http://bruegel.org/2016/02/02/

Pettigrew, A. M., Woodman, R. W., & Cameron, K. S. (2001). Studying organizational change and development: Challenges for future research. *Academy of Management Journal, 44*(4), 697–713.

Pfeffer, J., & DeVoe, S. E. (2012). The economic evaluation of time: Organizational causes and individual consequences. *Research in Organizational Behavior, 32*, 1–15. doi:10.1016/j.riob.2012.11.001

Phakathi, B. (2006). *Uber to experiment with cash payments.* Retrieved from http://www.bdlive.co.za/business/transport/

Piderit, S. K. (2000). Rethinking Resistance and Recognizing Ambivalence: A Multidimensional View of Attitudes toward an Organizational Change. *Academy of Management Review, 25*(4), 783–794. doi:10.5465/amr.2000.3707722

Pilaj, H. (2015). The choice architecture of sustainable and responsible investment: Nudging investors toward ethical decision making. *Journal of Business Ethics, 140*(4), 609–613.

Pohjola, M. (2003). *The Adoption and Diffusion of ICT across Countries: Patterns and Determinants. The New Economy Handbook.* Academic Press.

Ponemon, L. A. (1995). The Objectivity of Accountants' Litigation Support Judgments. *The Accounting Review, 70*(3), 467–488.

Porter, M. (1985). *Competitive Advantage: Creating and Sustaining Superior Performance*. New York, NY: The Free Press.

Prahalad, C. (1998). Managing Discontinuities: The Emerging Challenges. *Research Technology Management*, *4*(3), 14–22. doi:10.1080/08956308.1998.11671205

Primrose, J. (2003). *2001 Census: Computer and Internet Use. Census Paper No. 03/03*. Australian Bureau of Statistics.

Pritchard, A. (1969). Statistical bibliography or bibliometrics. *The Journal of Documentation*, *25*(4), 348–349.

Propeller. (2016). *Water challenge winner recycles water bottles to protect coasts & reduce pollutants*. March 15, Propeller.com. Retrieved from http://gopropeller.org/news/1583

Quairel, F. (2004). Responsable mais pas comptable: analyse de la normalisation des rapports environnementaux et sociaux. *Comptabilité - Contrôle - Audit*, *10*(1), 7.

Quattrone, P. (2016). Management accounting goes digital: Will the move make it wiser? *Management Accounting Research*, *31*, 118–122. doi:10.1016/j.mar.2016.01.003

Queensland Tourism Industry Council. (2014). *The Sharing Economy: How it will impact the tourism landscape and what businesses can do*. Queensland Tourism Industry Council.

Ramanna, K. (2008). The implications of unverifiable fair-value accounting: Evidence from the political economy of goodwill accounting. *Journal of Accounting and Economics*, *45*(2-3), 253–281. doi:10.1016/j.jacceco.2007.11.006

Randall, K. (2015). Local company helps Louisiana ecosystem with dog treats, The Daily Reveille, Nov 18. Retrieved March 31, 2019 from http://www.lsunow.com/daily/local-company-helps-louisiana-ecosystem-with-dog-treats/article_383e337a-8e48-11e5-b788-3391e5941165.html

Rawlins, L. K. (2015). *Uber stifled by slow regulation*. Retrieved from http://www.itweb.co.za/

Rayle, L., Dai, D., Chan, N., Cervero, R., & Shaheen, S. (2016). Just a better taxi? A survey-based comparison of taxis, transit and ridesourcing services in San Francisco. *Transport Policy*, *45*, 168–178. doi:10.1016/j.tranpol.2015.10.004

Rayna, T., & Striukova, L. (2015). Open innovation 2.0: Is co-creation the ultimate challenge? *International Journal of Technology Management*, *69*(1), 38–53. doi:10.1504/IJTM.2015.071030

Recklies, D. (2001). *Small Business – Size as a Chance or Handicap*. Retrieved from http://www.themanager.org/resources/Small%20Business.htm

Réka, V. I., & Ştefan, P. (2009). Adopting Information Technology (IT) in Management Accounting in Order to Achieve IT-Business Alignment, *Analele Universităţii din Oradea*, 18, 1207–1211.

Reuters. (2017). *Malaysia legalises e-hailing services as Grab, Uber compete*. Retrieved from http://www.reuters.com/article/

RF. (2019). Righteousfur.com. Retrieved from http://www.righteousfur.com

Richardson, A. (2011). Myth, Paradigms and Academic Accounting Research: A Comment on Reading and Understanding Academic Research in Accounting. *Global Perspectives on Accounting Education*, *8*, 67–77.

Rogers, E. M. (1962). *Diffusion of Innovation*. New York, NY: Free Press of Glencoe.

Rowland, C., & Hall, R. (2014). Management learning, performance and reward: Theory and practice revisited. *Journal of Management Development*, *33*(4), 342–356. doi:10.1108/JMD-08-2012-0110

Roxas, M. L., & Stoneback, J. Y. (2004). The importance of gender across cultures in ethical decision-making. *Journal of Business Ethics*, *50*(2), 149–165. doi:10.1023/B:BUSI.0000022127.51047.ef

Roy, B., Mamun, A., & Kuri, B. C. (2015). Sustainable tourism supply chain management for tourism industry in Bangladesh. *Global Journal of Management and Business Research for Real Estate, Event & Tourism Management*, *15*(2), 1–7.

RT. (2019). Louisiana kids help build Floating Islands Restoration Project, *Riding Tide*. Retrieved from https://risingtide.joincca.org/news3

Ruževičius, J., & Gedminaitė, A. (2007). Business Information Quality and its Assessment. *Inzinerine Ekonomika-Engineering Economics*, *52*(2), 18–25.

Sack, K., & Schwartz, J. (2018). The Drowning Coast. *New York Times*. Retrieved from https://www.nytimes.com/interactive/2018/02/24/us/jean-lafitte-floodwaters.html

Sahmim, S., & Gharsellaoui, H. (2017). Privacy and Security in Internet-based Computing: Cloud Computing, Internet of Things, Cloud of Things: A review. *Procedia Computer Science*, *112*, 1516–1522. doi:10.1016/j.procs.2017.08.050

Saiz-Alvarez, J. M. (2015). Solidarity Entrepreneurship in the European Knowledge Economies: Keys for a New Paradigm to Be Applied into Developing Nations. In N. Baporikar (Ed.), Entrepreneurship in the Contemporary Knowledge-based Global Economy, Hershey, PA: IGI Global, pp. 163-188.

Saiz-Alvarez, J. M. (2018). *Business Strategies and Advanced Techniques for Entrepreneurship 4.0*. Hershey, PA: IGI Global. doi:10.4018/978-1-5225-4978-9

Saiz-Alvarez, J. M., Coduras, A., & Cuervo-Arango, C. (2013). Entrepreneurial Strategy, Innovation, and Cognitive Capabilities. What Role for Intuitive SMEs? *Journal of Small Business Strategy*, *21*(2), 25–35.

Saiz-Alvarez, J. M., Coduras, A., & Cuervo-Arango, C. (2014). An Entrepreneurial Well-being Model based on GEM Data for Spain. *International Journal of Interactive Multimedia and Artificial Intelligence*, *2*(5), 38–47. doi:10.9781/ijimai.2014.255

Sako, M. (2008). *Shifting Boundaries of the Firm*. Oxford, UK: Oxford University Press.

Salomon, R. (2016). Why Uber couldn't crack China. *Fortune*. Retrieved from http://fortune.com/uber-china-didi-chuxing/

Samsudin, F., & Wahab, S. A. (2018). Sustainable Development in Franchising: Measuring the Impacts of Strategic Direction in Franchise Organization. Retrieved from https://www.researchgate.net/publication/325816508_SUSTAINABLE_DEVELOPMENT_IN_FRANCHISING_MEASURING_THE_IMPACTS_OF_STRATEGIC_DIRECTION_IN_FRANCHISE_ORGANIZATION

Samuelson, R. J. (2002). Debunking the Digital Divide. *Newsweek*, *139*, 22-40.

Sangster, A. (1994). The adoption of IT in management accounting: The expert systems experience. *Journal of Information Technology*, *9*(2), 159–169. doi:10.1177/026839629400900207

Sanlam. (2017). *Independent contractor or employee-the Uber case*. Cape Town, South Africa: Sanlam.

Sarasvathy, S. D. (2001). Effectuation. Elements of Entrepreneurial Expertise. Cheltenham, UK: Edward Elgar.

Saunders, M. (1995). The Forgotten Curriculum: An Argument for Medical Ethics Education. *Journal of the American Medical Association*, *274*(9), 768–769. doi:10.1001/jama.274.9.768 PMID:7650832

Saygili, S., & Taymaz, E. (2001). Privatization, Ownership and Technical Efficiency, A Study of the Turkish Cement Industry. *Annals of Public and Cooperative Economics*, *74*(4), 581–605. doi:10.1111/1467-8292.00182

SB. (2018). *Trucost's new evaluation tool will help companies align strategy with the SDGs*, Sustainable Brands. Retrieved from https://sustainablebrands.com/read/new-metrics/trucost-s-new-evaluation-tool-will-help-companies-align-strategy-with-the-sdgs

Schaltegger, S., & Burrit, R. (2005). *Contemporary Environmental Accounting: Issues, Concepts and Practice*. Austin, TX: Greenleaf Publishing.

Schaltegger, S., Bennett, M., & Burritt, R. (2006). Sustainability Accounting and Reporting: Development, Linkages and Reflection. An Introduction. In *Sustainability Accounting and Reporting* (pp. 1–33). The Netherlands: Springer.

Scheinberg, S., & McMillan, I. C. (1988). *An all country study of motivations to start a business. Frontiers of Entrepreneurship Research* (pp. 669–687). Wellesley, MA.: Babson College.

Schildt, H. (2017). Big data and organizational design–the brave new world of algorithmic management and computer augmented transparency. *Innovation-Management Policy & Practice*, *19*(1), 23–30. doi:10.1080/14479338.2016.1252043

Schleicher, T., Tahoun, A., & Walker, M. (2010). IFRS adoption in Europe and investment-cash flow sensitivity: Outsider versus insider economies. *The International Journal of Accounting*, *45*(2), 143–168. doi:10.1016/j.intacc.2010.04.007

Schmidt-Traub, G. (2015). *Investment Needs to Achieve the Sustainable Development Goals Understanding the Billions and Trillions*. Retrieved from http://unsdsn.org/resources/publications/sdg-investment-needs/.1

Schneider, M., & Somers, M. (2006). Organizations as complex adaptive systems: Implications of complexity theory for leadership research. *The Leadership Quarterly*, *17*(4), 351–365. doi:10.1016/j.leaqua.2006.04.006

Schreuder, A. N., Krige, L., & Parker, E. (2000). The franchisee lifecycle concept – A new paradigm in managing the franchisee-franchisor relationship. *Proceedings of the 14th annual International Society of Franchising Conference*, San Diego, CA.

Schultz, T. W. (1980). Investment in Entrepreneurial Ability. *The Scandinavian Journal of Economics*, *82*(4), 437–448. doi:10.2307/3439676

Schumpeter, J. A. (1977). Capitalism, Socialism, and Democracy. New York, NY: Harper Collins Publishers. (Original work published 1942)

Schumpeter, J. A. (1934). *The Theory of Economic Development: An Inquiry into Profits, Capital, Credit, Interest, and the Business Cycle*. Cambridge, MA: Harvard University Press.

Schumpeter, J. A. (1997). *Theorie der wirtschaftlichen Entwicklung: Eine Untersuchung über Unternehmergewinn, Kapital, Kredit, Zins und den Konjunkturzyklus*. Berlin, Germany: Duncker Humblot. (Original work published 1911) doi:10.3790/978-3-428-07725-0

Schwab, K. (2019). *Globalization 4.0. A New Architecture for the Fourth Industrial Revolution. A call for engagement.* Geneva, Switzerland: World Economic Forum.

Schwartz, M. (2001). The Nature of the Relationship between Corporate Codes of Ethics and Behaviour. *Journal of Business Ethics*, *32*(3), 247–262. doi:10.1023/A:1010787607771

Scuotto, V., Del Giudice, M., della Peruta, M. R., & Tarba, S. (2017). The performance implications of leveraging internal innovation through social media networks: An empirical verification of the smart fashion industry. *Technological Forecasting and Social Change*, *120*, 184–194. doi:10.1016/j.techfore.2017.03.021

Scuotto, V., Ferraris, A., & Bresciani, S. (2016). Internet of Things: Applications and challenges in smart cities: a case study of IBM smart city projects. *Business Process Management Journal*, *22*(2), 357–367. doi:10.1108/BPMJ-05-2015-0074

Scuotto, V., Santoro, G., Bresciani, S., & Del Giudice, M. (2017). Shifting intra-and inter-organizational innovation processes towards digital business: An empirical analysis of SMEs. *Creativity and Innovation Management*, *26*(3), 247–255. doi:10.1111/caim.12221

Seal, W., Garrison, R. H., & Noreen, E. W. (2006). *Management Accounting* (2nd ed.). Singapore: McGraw Hill.

Secchi, D. (2010). Extendable Rationality: Understanding Decision Making in Organizations. New York, NY: Springer.

Seidman, W., & Grbavac, R. (2013). *The Star Factor: Discover What Your Top Performers Do Differently--and Inspire a New Level of Greatness in All*. AMACOM.

Selander, L. H., Henfridsson, O., & Svahn, F. (2013). Capability search and redeem across digital ecosystems. *Journal of Information Technology*, *28*(3), 183–197. doi:10.1057/jit.2013.14

Sementelli, J. (2016). OD, change management, and the a priori: Introducing parrhesia. *Journal of Organizational Change Management*, *29*(7), 1083–1096. doi:10.1108/JOCM-12-2015-0234

Shane, S., & Venkataraman, S. (2000). The Promise of Entrepreneurship as a Field of Research. *Academy of Management Review*, *25*(1), 217–226.

Shapiro, C., & Varian, H. R. (1999). *Information Rules: A Strategic Guide to the Network Economy*. Boston, MA: Harvard Business School Press.

Shepherd, D. A., & Patzelt, H. (2011). The New Field of Sustainable Entrepreneurship: Studying Entrepreneurial Action Linking "What Is To Be Sustained" with "What Is To Be Developed?". *Entrepreneurship Theory and Practice*, *35*(1), 137–163. doi:10.1111/j.1540-6520.2010.00426.x

Sheth, J. N., & Sharma, A. (1997). Supplier Relationships – Emerging Issues and Challenges. *Industrial Marketing Management*, *26*(2), 91–100. doi:10.1016/S0019-8501(96)00153-8

Sigala, M. (2014). Customer involvement in sustainable supply chain management: A research framework and implications in tourism. *Cornell Hospitality Quarterly*, *55*(1), 76–88. doi:10.1177/1938965513504030

Sijbom, R. B. L., Janssen, O., & Van Yperen, N. W. (2015). Leaders' Receptivity to Subordinates' Creative Input: The Role of Achievement Goals and Composition of Creative Input. *European Journal of Work and Organizational Psychology*, *24*(3), 462–478. doi:10.1080/1359432X.2014.964215

Silva, O. (2007). The Jack-of-All-Trades entrepreneur: Innate talent or acquired skill? *Economics Letters*, *97*(2), 118–123. doi:10.1016/j.econlet.2007.02.027

Simeoni, F., & Cassia, F. (2019). From vehicle suppliers to value co-creators: The evolving role of Italian motorhome manufacturers. *Current Issues in Tourism*, *22*(2), 218–236. doi:10.1080/13683500.2017.1293619

Simon, H. A. (1971). Designing organizations for an information rich world. In M. Greeberger (Ed.), Computers, Communications, and the Public Interest, pp. 38-52. Baltimore, MD: The Johns Hopkins Press.

Simon, H. A. (1993). Altruism and economics. *The American Economic Review*, *83*(2), 156–161.

Singer, W. P., & Friedman, A. (2014). *Cyber Security and Cyber War: What Everyone Needs to Know*. New York, NY: Oxford University Press.

Singh, A., & Fhom, H. C. S. (2017). Restricted usage of anonymous credentials in vehicular ad hoc networks for misbehavior detection. *International Journal of Information Security*, *16*(2), 195–201. doi:10.100710207-016-0328-y

Singh, N. (2007). Bridging the Digital Divide in India: Some Challenges and Opportunities. *World Libraries*, *17*(1), 32–51.

Sirmon, D. G., Hitt, M. A., Ireland, R. D., & Gilbert, B. A. (2011). Resource orchestration to create competitive advantage: Breadth, depth, and life cycle effects. *Journal of Management*, *37*(5), 1390–1412. doi:10.1177/0149206310385695

Sithole, H. (2016). We don't feel safe: Uber drivers. Retrieved from http://www.sabc.co.za/news/a/

Skarzauskiene, A., & Zaitsava, M. (2016). Exploring the Potential of Open Innovation 2.0 and Web 3.0 for SMEs. *3rd European Conference on Social M di R h Media Research EM Normandie*, (p. 369). Caen, France.

Skovoroda, A., & Gamayunov, D. (2015). *Review of the mobile malware detection approaches.* Paper presented at the 2015 23rd Euromicro International Conference on Parallel, Distributed, and Network-Based Processing. 10.1109/PDP.2015.54

SL. (2019). SHORE|LINKS. Retrieved from http://www.shore-links.com

Smith, D. (2005). Dancing with the mysterious forces of chaos: Issues around complexity, knowledge and the management of uncertainty. *Clinician in Management, (3/4)*, 115–123.

Solima, L. D., Della Peruta, M. R., & Maggioni, V. (2016). Managing adaptive orientation systems for museum visitors from an IoT perspective. *Business Process Management Journal*, *22*(2), 285–304. doi:10.1108/BPMJ-08-2015-0115

Soltani, B. (2014). The anatomy of corporate fraud: A comparative analysis of high profile American and European corporate scandals. *Journal of Business Ethics*, *120*(2), 251–274. doi:10.100710551-013-1660-z

Spataru, G. C., Sasu, C., & Juravle, A. I. (2015). Occupational safety and health-vector of corporate social responsibility in Romanian companies Empirical study. *Management Intercultural,* 34, 383–390. Retrieved from http://www.who.int

Speklé, R. F. (2001). Explaining management control structure variety: A transaction cost economics perspective. *Accounting, Organizations and Society*, *3*(4), 141–167.

Stähler, P. (2002). *Geschäftsmodelle in der digitalen Ökonomie-Merkmale, Strategien und Auswirkungen* (2. Ausg.). Lohmar Köln: Josef Eul Verlag.

Stefan, V., Duica, M., Coman, M., & Radu, V. (2010). Enterprise Performance Management with Business Intelligence Solution. In *Proc. 4th WSEAS International Conference on BUSINESS ADMINISTRATION (ICBA'10)* (pp. 244–250). World Scientific and Engineering Academy and Society. Retrieved from http://bit.ly/adIRl0

Stepchenko, D., & Voronova, I. (2015). Assessment of Risk Function Using Analytical Network Process. *Inzinerine Ekonomika-Engineering Economics*, *26*(3), 264–271.

Stephan, U., Uhlaner, L. M., & Stride, C. (2015). Institutions and Social Entrepreneurship: The Role of Institutional Voids, Institutional Support, and Institutional Configurations. *Journal of International Business Studies*, *46*(3), 308–331. doi:10.1057/jibs.2014.38

Stevenson, H. H., & Jarillo, J. C. (1990). A Paradigm of Entrepreneurship: Entrepreneurial Management. *Strategic Management Journal*, *11*, 17–27.

Steyn, L. L. (2017). Travelstart partners with Uber for half-price airport transfers. Retrieved from: http: //www.traveller24.com/TravelPlanning/travelstart

Stuebs, M., & Wilkinson, B. (2010). Ethics and the Tax Profession: Restoring the Public Interest Focus. *Accounting and the Public Interest*, *10*(1), 13–35. doi:10.2308/api.2010.10.1.13

Subrahmanya, M. H. (2005) SMEs in India: Will they be able to join "Global Chains"? CA J Chart Account (The Institute of Chartered Accountants of India, New Delhi), 54 (3),421–427.

Suseno, Y., Laurell, C., & Sick, N. (2018). Assessing value creation in digital innovation ecosystems: A Social Media Analytics approach. *The Journal of Strategic Information Systems*, *27*(4), 335–349. doi:10.1016/j.jsis.2018.09.004

SVIMD. (2019). *Social Vulnerability Index Mapping Dashboard.* Retrieved from https://svi.cdc.gov/map.aspx?txtzipcode=70806&btnzipcode=Submit

Szpilko, D. (2017). Tourism Supply Chain-Overview of Selected Literature. 7th International Conference on Engineering, Project and Production Management. *Procedia Engineering*, *182*, 687–693. doi:10.1016/j.proeng.2017.03.180

Szychta, A. (2002). The Scope of Application of Management Accounting Methods in Polish Enterprises. *Management Accounting Research*, *13*(4), 401–418. doi:10.1006/mare.2002.0198

Taiwo, J. N., Yewande, O. A., Edwin, A., & Benson, K. N. (2016). The role of Microfinance Institutions in financing small businesses. *Journal of Internet Banking and Commerce*, *21*(1), 1–20.

Tajeddini, K. (2015). Exploring the antecedents of effectiveness and efficiency. *International Journal of Hospitality Management*, *49*(7), 125–135. doi:10.1016/j.ijhm.2015.06.007

Tan, K. G., & Tan, K. Y. (2014). Foreign direct investment (FDI), productivity spillovers and the role of small and medium enterprises (SMEs) financing: An overview. *Journal of International Commerce Economic Policy*, *5*, 1403002–1403006.

Tapscott, D. (1996). *Die digitale Revolution: Verheißungen einer vernetzten Welt – die Folgen für Wirtschaft, Management und Gesellschaft.* Wiesbaden: Gabler. doi:10.1007/978-3-322-82739-5

Taticchi, P., Tonelli, F., & Cagnazzo, L. (2010). Performance measurement and management: A literature review and a research agenda. *Measuring Business Excellence*, *14*(1), 4–18. doi:10.1108/13683041011027418

Tau, P. (2017). Uber driver's death raises fears, tensions. *City Press,* July 23.

Täuscher, K. (2017). Leveraging collective intelligence: How to design and manage crowd-based business models. *Business Horizons*, *60*(2), 237–245. doi:10.1016/j.bushor.2016.11.008

TBF. (2019). *Tech Business Franchises.* Retrieved from https://www.entrepreneur.com/franchises/category/tech

Teittinen, H., Pellinen, J., & Järvenpää, M. (2013). ERP in action. Challenges and benefits for management control in SME context. *International Journal of Accounting Information Systems*, *14*(4), 278–296. doi:10.1016/j.accinf.2012.03.004

Tende, S. B. A. (2014). Government initiatives toward entrepreneurship development in Nigeria. *Global Journal of Business Research, 8*, 109-120. Retrieved from http://papers.ssrn.com/sol3/JELJOUR_Results.cfm? Journal Browse & journal_id

Thomas, D., & Seid, M. (2000). Franchising for Dummies. Foster City, CA: IDG Books.

Tiago, O., Manoj, T., & Espadanal, M. (2014). Assessing the determinants of cloud computing adoption: An analysis of the manufacturing and services sectors. *Information & Management*, *51*(5), 497–510. doi:10.1016/j.im.2014.03.006

Tilson, D., Lyytinen, K., & Sørensen, C. (2010). Research commentary—Digital infrastructures: The missing IS research agenda. *Information Systems Research*, *21*(4), 748–759. doi:10.1287/isre.1100.0318

TNCCW. (2019). *The Nature Conservancy Climate Wizard.* Retrieved from http://www.climatewizard.org/index.html

Tomkins, C. (2001). Interdependencies, trust and information in relationships, alliances and networks. *Accounting, Organizations and Society*, *26*(2), 161–191. doi:10.1016/S0361-3682(00)00018-0

Tong, Y. K., & Arvey, R. D. (2015). Managing complexity via the Competing Values Framework. *Journal of Management Development*, *34*(6), 653–673. doi:10.1108/JMD-04-2014-0029

Topor, D., Capusneanu, S., & Tamas, A. S. (2017). Efficient Green Control (Egc) Encouraging Environmental Investment And Profitability. *Journal of Environmental Protection and Ecology, 18*(1), 191–201. Retrieved from https://www.researchgate.net/profile/Sorinel_Capusneanu/project/Green-controlling/attachment/592c1d6b82999cd4856f3382/AS:499339991502848@1496063339417/download/Articol_4_JEPE_En.pdf?context=projectUpdateDetail

TR. (2019). *Tierra Resources.* Retrieved from https://tierraresourcesllc.com

Tralac. (2017). *The sub-Saharan African services economy: Insights and trends.* Retrieved from https://www.tralac.org/news/article/

Trantopoulos, K., von Krogh, G., Wallin, M. W., & Woerter, M. (2017). External knowledge and information technology: Implications for process innovation performance. *Management Information Systems Quarterly, 41*(1), 287–300. doi:10.25300/MISQ/2017/41.1.15

Tropina, T., & Callanan, C. (2015). *Self- and Co-regulation in Cybercrime, Cybersecurity and National Security.* New York, NY: Springer International Publishing. doi:10.1007/978-3-319-16447-2

U.S. Commercial Service. (2007). *China Franchising Industry: Access Dynamics and Emerging Markets*, The JLJ Group, September. Retrieved from http://export.gov/china/build/groups/public/@eg_cn/documents/webcontent/eg_cn_027119.pdf

U.S. Commercial Service. (2008). *China Franchising Industry*, The JLJ Group, April.

U.S. Commercial Service. (2010). *Doing Business in South Africa - 2010 Country Commercial Guide for U.S. Companies.* Retrieved from http://www.franchise.org/uploadedFiles/Franchise_Industry/International_Development/Country_Profiles/South%20Africa_2010.pdf

U.S. Commercial Service. (2018). *Brazil - Services - Franchising.* Retrieved from https://www.export.gov/article?id=Brazil-Services-Franchising

U.S. Commercial Service. (2018). *India - Franchising.* Retrieved from https://www.export.gov/article?id=India-Franchising

U.S. Commercial Service. (2018). *Russia - Franchising Industry.* Retrieved from https://www.export.gov/apex/article2?id=Russia-Franchising-Industry-Sector

Uber. (2018). *How are fares calculated?* Retrieved from https://help.uber.com/

Ubesie, M. C., Onuaguluchi, I. F., & Mbah, A. M. (2017). Effect of Deposit Bank Credit on Small and Medium Scale Enterprises Growth in Nigeria. *International Journal of Finance and Accounting, 5*(6), 117–132.

UNISDR. (2019). *Making cities resilient: My city is getting ready.* United Nations International Strategy for Disaster Reduction. Retrieved from https://www.unisdr.org/campaign/resilientcities

United Nations. (1997). *Environmental Financial Accounting and Reporting at the Corporate Level.* Retrieved from https://unctad.org/en/docs/isa15d2.pdf

UNSDG. (2015). *Sustainable development goals: 17 goals to transform our world.* Retrieved from https://www.un.org/sustainabledevelopment/sustainable-development-goals

Van Eck, N. J., & Waltman, L. (2007). *Advances in data analysis. VOS: A new method for visualizing similarities between objects* (pp. 299–306). Berlin, Germany: Springer. doi:10.1007/978-3-540-70981-7_34

Van Eck, N. J., & Waltman, L. (2017). Citation-based clustering of publications using CitNetExplorer and VOSviewer. *Scientometrics, 111*(2), 1053–1070. doi:10.100711192-017-2300-7 PMID:28490825

Van Eck, N. J., Waltman, L., Dekker, R., & van den Berg, J. (2010). A comparison of two techniques for bibliometric mapping: Multidimensional scaling and VOS. *Journal of the American Society for Information Science and Technology*, *61*(12), 2405–2416. doi:10.1002/asi.21421

Van Eck, N., & Waltman, L. (2009). Software survey: VOSviewer, a computer program for bibliometric mapping. *Scientometrics*, *84*(2), 523–538. doi:10.100711192-009-0146-3 PMID:20585380

van Oorschot, J. A., Hofman, E., & Halman, J. I. (2018). A bibliometric review of the innovation adoption literature. *Technological Forecasting and Social Change*, *134*, 1–21. doi:10.1016/j.techfore.2018.04.032

Van Zyl, G. (2015a). *Cape Town is Airbnb's top African market.* Retrieved from http://www.fin24.com/Tech/Companies/Cape-Town-is-Airbnb's-top-market/

Van Zyl, G. (2015b). *Uber, WesBank in R200 m car rental deal.* Retrieved from http://www.fin24.com/Tech/Companies/uber-wesbank/

Van Zyl, G. (2016a). *Travelstart receives $40m investment boost.* Retrieved from http://www.fin24.com/Tech/Companies/travelstart/

Van Zyl, G. (2016b). *Uber pilots dashcams, panic buttons in SA.* Retrieved from http://www.fin24.com/Tech/Companies/travelstart/

Velilla, J., Molina, J. A., & Ortega, R. (2018). Why Older Workers Become Entrepreneurs? International Evidence Using Fuzzy Set Methods. *The Journal of the Economics of Ageing*, *12*, 88–95. doi:10.1016/j.jeoa.2018.03.004

Vetter, S. (2016). *Uber, digital and disruption: what is happening and why does it work?* Retrieved from https://digital.pwc.co.nz/uber/

Vladu, A. B., Amat, O., & Cuzdriorean, D. D. (2016). Truthfulness in accounting: How to discriminate accounting manipulators from non-manipulators. *Journal of Business Ethics*, *140*(4), 633–648. doi:10.100710551-016-3048-3

Vogel, R., & Güttel, W. H. (2013). The dynamic capability view in strategic management: A bibliometric review. *International Journal of Management Reviews*, *15*(4), 426–446.

von Hippel, E. (2005). *Democratizing Innovation*. Cambridge, MA: MIT Press. doi:10.7551/mitpress/2333.001.0001

Waanabe, C., Naveed, K., Neittaanmaki, P., & Fox, B. (2016). Consolidated challenge to social demand for resilient platforms-lessons from Ube's global expansion. *Technology in Society*. doi:10.1010/J.TECHSOC.2016/10.006

Wagner, J. (2003). Testing Lazear's jack-of-all-trades view of entrepreneurship with German micro data. *Applied Economics Letters*, *10*(11), 687–689. doi:10.1080/1350485032000133273

Wallsten, S. (2003). Regulation and Internet Use in Developing Countries, *AEI-Brookings* Brookings Institution, May.

Wang, W., & Hu, L. (2014). A secure and efficient handover authentication protocol for wireless networks. *Journal of Sensors*, *14*(7), 11379–11394. doi:10.3390140711379 PMID:24971471

Wang, X., He, F., Yang, H., & Gao, H. O. (2016). Pricing strategies for a taxi-hailing platform. *Transportation Research Part E, Logistics and Transportation Review*, *93*, 212–231. doi:10.1016/j.tre.2016.05.011

WBCSD. (2018). *The Chemical Sector SDG Roadmap*, World Business Council for Sustainable Development. Retrieved from https://sdgroadmaps.wbcsd.org/overview

Webb, J. (1996). Inventing the Good: A Prospectus for Clinical Education and the Teaching of Legal Ethics in England. *The Law Teacher*, *30*(3), 270–294. doi:10.1080/03069400.1996.9992956

Weiss, J. W. (2001). *Organizational Behaviour and Change: Managing Diversity, Cross-Cultural Dynamics and Ethics.* UK: South-Western Thomson Learning.

West, J. B., & Bogers, M. (2014). Leveraging external sources of innovation: A review of research on open innovation. *Journal of Product Innovation Management, 31*(4), 814–831. doi:10.1111/jpim.12125

Wheels24. (2016). *Would you tip your Uber driver? More than 6000 South Africans say NO.* Retrieved from http://www.wheels24.co.za/News/

Wilfredo Bohorquez Lopez, V., & Esteves, J. (2013). Acquiring external knowledge to avoid wheel re-invention. *Journal of Knowledge Management, 17*(1), 87-105.

Willems, E. (2011). Cyber-terrorism in the process industry. *Computer Fraud & Security, 3*(3), 16–19. doi:10.1016/S1361-3723(11)70032-X

Williams, J., & Seaman, A. (2002). Management Accounting Systems Change and Departmental Performance: The Influence of Managerial Information and Task Uncertainty. *Management Accounting Research, 13*(4), 419–445. doi:10.1006/mare.2002.0199

Winkler, I. (2010). Justifying IT Security – Managing Risk & Keeping your network Secure. Foster City, CA: Qualys Inc.

Wired Transport. (2017). *Airbus has designed a part-car part-drone to help beat traffic.* Retrieved from http://www.wired.co.uk/article/airbus-flying-car/

Wit, B., & Meyer, R. (1994). Strategy: Process, Content, Context, An International Perspective. Eagan, MN: West Publishing Company.

Witherspoon, P. D., & Wohlert, K. L. (1996). An Approach to Developing Communication Strategies for Enhancing Organizational Diversity. *Journal of Business Communication, 33*(4), 375–399. doi:10.1177/002194369603300402

Wolniak, R., & Hąbek, P. (2016). Quality Assessment of CSR Reports – Factor Analysis. *Procedia: Social and Behavioral Sciences, 220*, 541–547. doi:10.1016/j.sbspro.2016.05.530

Woo, C. Y., Cooper, A. C., & Dunkelberg, W. C. (1988). *Entrepreneurial typologies: definitions and implications. Frontiers of Entrepreneurship Research* (pp. 165–176). Wellesley, MA: Babson College.

World Commission on Environment and Development. (1987). *Report of the World Commission on Environment and Development: Our Common Future* (Transmitted to the General Assembly as an Annex to document A/42/427 - Development and International Co-operation: Environment).

World Economic Forum. (2016). *The regulatory challenges of disruptive companies.* Retrieved from https://www.weforum.org/agenda/

World Economic Forum. (2018). *Globalization 4.0 – What Does It Mean?* Retrieved from https://www.weforum.org/agenda/2018/11/globalization-4-what-does-it-mean-how-it-will-benefit-everyone

World Economic Forum. (2019). *The Global Risks Report 2019.* Retrieved from https://www.weforum.org/reports/the-global-risks-report-2019

Wresch, W. (1996). *Disconnected: Haves and Have-Nots in the Information Age.* New Brunswick, NJ: Rutgers University Press.

Yadav, N., & Sagar, M. (2013). Performance measurement and management frameworks. *Business Process Management Journal, 19*(6), 947–971. doi:10.1108/BPMJ-01-2013-0003

Yang, C. N., Wu, C. C., & Wang, D. S. (2014). A discussion on the relationship between probabilistic visual cryptography and random grid. *Information Sciences*, *278*, 141–173. doi:10.1016/j.ins.2014.03.033

Yar, M. (2006). *Cybercrime and Society*. London, UK: Sage.

Yip, G. (2000). Global Strategy in the Internet Era. *Business Strategy Review*, *11*(4), 1–14. doi:10.1111/1467-8616.00152

Yoon, S., Jeon, Y., & Kim, J. (2015). *Mobile security technology for smart devices.* Paper resented at the 2015 International Conference on Information and Communication Technology Convergence (ICTC). 10.1109/ICTC.2015.7354766

Yoo, Y. B., Boland, R. J. Jr, Lyytinen, K., & Majchrzak, A. (2012). Organizing for innovation in the digitized world. *Organization Science*, *23*(5), 1398–1408. doi:10.1287/orsc.1120.0771

Yucen, N., Wei, L., Wei, B., Delicato, F. C., Pires, P. F., & Zomaya, A. Y. (2018). A dynamic tradeoff data processing framework for delay-sensitive applications in Cloud of Things systems. *Journal of Parallel and Distributed Computing*, *112*(1), 53–66.

Zang, A. Y. (2012). Evidence on the trade-off between real activities manipulation and accrual-based earnings management. *The Accounting Review*, *87*(2), 675–703. doi:10.2308/accr-10196

Zeng, Q., Chen, W., & Huang, L. (2008). Digital business transformation: An analysis framework based on critical organizational dimensions. *Journal of Tsinghua Science and Technology*, *13*(3), 408–413. doi:10.1016/S1007-0214(08)70065-8

Zerdick, A., Schrape, K., Artope, A., Goldhammer, K., Heger, D. K., Lange, U., . . . Silverstone, R. (2001). Die Internet-Okonomie: Strategien für die digitale Wirtschaft (European Communication Council Report) (3. Ausg.). Berlin, Germany: Springer-Verlag. doi:10.1007/978-3-642-56418-5

Zupic, I., & Čater, T. (2015). Bibliometric methods in management and organization. *Organizational Research Methods*, *18*(3), 429–472. doi:10.1177/1094428114562629

About the Contributors

Hakan Altinpulluk is a Research Assistant in Distance Education at the College of Open Education of Anadolu University, Turkey. He undertook undergraduate studies in the field of Computer Education and Instructional Technologies (CEIT) between the years of 2005- 2009 at Anadolu University. Also, he is currently a PhD candidate in the Department of Distance Education at Anadolu University. Hakan Altınpulluk continues to work in the field of Open and Distance Learning, Augmented Reality, Mobile Learning, Massive Open Online Courses, Personal Learning Environments, and E-Learning Systems.

Yayoi Anzai is an Associate Professor at the Innovation Center for Educational Resource at Kyushu University, where she develops Massive Open Online Courses (MOOCs) and teaches English as a Foreign Language. Since she received her Ph.D. at International Christian University in Tokyo, she has been designing, developing and evaluating EFL instruction which integrates ICT. She is very active at both international and domestic conferences. Dr. Anzai's research interests include English education, Open education, MOOCs/OER, mobile learning, and collaborative learning. Currently, she has been doing research on how MOOCs can be used meaningfully in English education, supported by Grants-in-Aid for Scientific Research, JSPS KAKENHI.

Aras Bozkurt is a researcher in the Department of Distance Education at Anadolu University, Turkey. He holds MA and Ph.D. degrees in distance education. He conducts empirical studies on online learning through resorting to critical theories including connectivism, rhizomatic learning, and heutagogy. He is interested in emerging research paradigms including social network analysis, sentiment analysis, and data mining.

Köksal Büyük has been the head of Anadolu University, Open Education Faculty, Learning Technologies Research and Development since July 2015. Büyük also serves as the head of Anadolu University, Strategic Research Center. Büyük holds a bachelor's degree in business administration, a master and doctoral degree in management and organization. His research interests are: Governance, management, administration, strategic management, strategic performance, management of strategic performance, organizational culture, managements in non-governmental organizations, institutional achievement report, open and distance learning, distance education, management of distance education processes.

Inge de Waard (PhD) has an extensive research background in investigating and implementing Innovative Educational Technologies (The Open University, UK, EIT InnoEnergy, EU; Institute of Tropical Medicine – Belgium; Athabasca University - Canada). She has set-up, coordinated and developed several online and mobile learning projects, always with a focus on participation and durability. These projects involved partners and individuals from both the Northern (Canada, United States, Italy, Belgium, Ireland, Germany, UK) and Southern regions (South-Africa, India, Peru, Morocco). She set up the first MOOC on mobile learning, called MobiMOOC (2011 & 2012), enabling learners to realize their own mobile project. As an avid enthusiast of open science, I am an active international speaker giving keynotes and guest lectures, as well as providing knowledge input (and consequently receiving lots of input) at seminars, SIGs and workshops. Her latest research resulted in a conceptual framework describing how adult learners with prior online learning experience self-direct their informal learning using multiple devices as they engage in the social learning MOOC platform of FutureLearn.

Ugur Demiray received his BA in Media Studies from Anadolu University, Eskisehir, Turkey. He also received his Ph.D from Anadolu University's Social Sciences Graduate Institution, Department of Educational Communication. He is currently working for the Anadolu University. His research in distance education is applied at Anadolu University, the Ministry of Education, and by other universities in Turkey. He is interested in changing ethical behaviors around the world by inserting technological developments to the educational field, especially within distance education applications, for 3 years. He is also interested in the profile of DE students and the relationship between graduates and the job market. He has extensive experience in publishing articles on the topic of distance education, including articles within Anadolu University's Turkish Online Journal for Distance Education (TOJDE). He is also an editor, consultant editor reviewer and book reviewer for more than 10 journals which deal with distance education, educational technology and on education fields around the world, such as Quarterly Review of Distance Education (QRDE), Editor, Association for Educational Communication and Technology, Information Age Publishing, Miami, USA; The Turkish Online Journal of Educational Technology (TOJET), Editor, Sakarya Universitesi, Turkey; Universite ve Toplum, Editor, Ankara, Turkey; Open Education-The Journal for Open and Distance Education and Educational Technology, Editor, Hellenic Network of Open and Distance Education, Greece; S n rs z Ö renme Dergisi [Journal of Learning Witout Frontiers], Turkey; The e-Journal of Instructional Science and Technology (e-JIST), Editor, University of Southern Queensland; Studies in Learning, Evaluation, Innovation and Development, Central Queensland University, Australia; The International Journal of Education and Development Using Information and Communication Technology (IJEDICT), The University of the West Indies, West Indies; Malaysian Online Journal of Instructional Technology (MOJIT), Editor, Malaysian Educational Technology Association (META), Malaysia; Anadolu Üniversitesi Sosyal Bilimler Dergisi [Anadolu University Journal of Social Sciences], Anadolu University; EGITIM ARASTIRMALARI DERGISI (Eurasian Journal of Educational Research, EJER), Turkey; Education and Progress eJournal-EPeJ, Associate Editor, http://www.hamdan-edu.com, Syria; Educational Research and Reviews, Associate Editor, http://www.academicjournals.org/ERR; Ilorin Journal of Education, University of Ilorin, Conusulting Editor, http://www.ijeunilorin.net/editorial_board.php. In addition, he has responsibilities on Advisory, Scientific Board and Referee on conferences, symposiums and panels. He has co-authored and individually contributed chapters in some Turkish and international books too.

Gurhan Durak has been working as a lecturer in Computer Education & Instructional Technology department at Balıkesir university since 2006. He received B.S and M.S degree in Computer Education & Instructional Technology Department at Balıkesir university. He has completed his doctoral degree on Distance Education at Anadolu University. He gives lessons about instructional design, technology integration and distance education. He interested in online learning, instructional design, educational social networking sites, computer programming and distance education.

Gülay Ekren has been working as a lecturer at the Department of Computer Technologies of Vocational School of Ayancık, Sinop University since 2009. She has a BA degree from the Computer and Instructional Technologies Department of Ege University, and MA degree from the Management Information Systems Department of Gazi University. She also has an online MA degree from the Distance Education Department of Anadolu University. She is now a Phd student in Department of Management and Information Systems in Sakarya University. Her research interests are open and distance learning, distance education management, mobile learning, quality assurance and accreditation in open and distance learning, management and information systems.

Jonathan Flutey is the Learning and Research Technology Manager for Information Technology Services at Victoria University of Wellington. Jonathan's team was created with the core focus of increasing the digital capability of the institution in technology that directly enhances and supports Learning & Teaching, Research and the students experience on-campus and online. Roles within the team include a digital capability builder, digital learning designers, digital research consultants, eResearch specialists and learning space designers. Jonathan's role developed after 6 years of being an ITS Customer Relationship Co-ordinator and developing an understanding of academic and administrative technology requirements. Working closely with the University's Center for Academic Development, Jonathan has aided in the development of faculty based support for academics and professional staff. This support model is now delivering strategic projects on behalf of the university including a cross disciplinary MOOC programme, convening the regional Research Bazaar conference and developing the designs and capability programmes for new 'scaled-up' active learning spaces. This new model of delivery for a central IT team within a New Zealand higher education institution has been highlighted by winning the Microsoft Innovation Award for Learning, Research and Students in 2014 and 2016.

Michael S. Gallagher is a member of the Centre for Research in Digital Education at the University of Edinburgh and Director of Panoply Digital, a consultancy dedicated to mobile for development (M4D). His research focus is on mapping the effects of mobility and mobile technology on open spaces, built environments, and urban spaces to support practice in the humanities in higher education, particularly in the Asia Pacific region.

Hakan Kilinc is currently working as a research assistant at the Distance Education Department of Anadolu University. He graduated from Computer Education And Instructional Technology Department of Anadolu University. His professional interests include educational technology, distance education technology, leadership in open and distance learning institutions and personalized learning environments.

Serpil Kocdar works as an assistant professor at Open Education Faculty of Anadolu University, Turkey. She is a graduate of Economics and she has a master's degree in Distance Education. She worked in corporate banking sector as a vice manager from 1997 to 2002. She received her Ph.D. in Distance Education from Anadolu University in 2011. She worked in the Assessment Department of Open Education Faculty from 2002 to 2014. Currently, she works for the Quality Office and R&D and Instructional Technologies Department. Her research interests are quality assurance and accreditation, evaluation, assessment, instructional design and new learning technologies in open and distance learning.

Sotco Claudius Komba holds a doctoral (PhD) degree from the University of Dar es Salaam, Tanzania. He also holds a Master of Arts degree in Education and Bachelor of Arts with Education degree, both from the University of Dar es Salaam, Tanzania. Currently, Dr Sotco Claudius Komba is a Senior Lecturer in the College of Social Sciences and Humanities, Sokoine University of Agriculture, Tanzania.

Apostolos Koutropoulos ("AK") is the program manager for the online MA program in Applied Linguistics and a faculty member in the instructional design MEd program at UMass Boston. Over the past few years he has participated in many massive online open courses (MOOCs) and has authored and co-authored research papers on open learning and learning in networked environments. AK holds a BA in Computer Science, an MBA with a focus on Human Resources, an MSc in Information Technology, an MEd in Instructional Design, and an MA in Applied Linguistics. His research interests include knowledge management, educational technology, applied linguistics, and open education.

Alper Tolga Kumtepe earned his BSc degree in Educational Communications in 1995 at Anadolu University. He then completed his MS degree in 2000 and Ph.D. degree in 2005 in the program of Early Childhood Education at the Florida State University with an overseas graduate scholarship by the Turkish Ministry of Education. He worked as a researcher at the Florida Center for Reading Research. He is currently working asfaculty member at the College of Open and Distance Education, Anadolu University, Turkey. His research interests include e-learning, teacher education, quantitative research methods, assesment, and evaluation. He participated in various online learning projects.

Moeketsi Letseka holds a D.Ed. in philosophy of education. He is Editor-in-Chief of Africa Education Review; Consultant Editor of South African Journal of Higher Education; Associate Editor of Mevlana International Journal of Education; Member of the Editorial Advisory Board of International Journal of Education. Dr Letseka is Principal Investigator and National Research Foundation (NRF) grant holder for the 'Archaeology of Ubuntu' study. The study is conducted in Botswana, Lesotho, Namibia, Swaziland, Zambia, Zimbabwe, and provinces in South Africa. Dr Letseka has over 70 publications.

Vimbi P. Mahlangu holds a B.A.Ed. (Vista University); B.Ed.; MEd; & Ph.D. degrees from the University of Pretoria. He is an Associate Professor at the University of South Africa, Department of Educational Leadership & Management. He is responsible for teaching and research. He presented papers at national and international conferences. He is a recipient of Dean's Award for Excellence in Teaching in the Faculty of Education (2011) at the University of Pretoria. He has published extensively in accredited journals and contributed a book and book chapters.

Stephen Marshall is Senior Lecturer in Educational Technology at the Victoria University of Wellington Centre for Academic Development and President of the Australasian Council on Open and Distance Education. Stephen leads the Victoria University Digital Vision and Strategy for Learning and Teaching initiatives and researches in the areas of e-learning benchmarking, plagiarism and academic integrity, intellectual property, and the development of educational policy and strategy supporting and encouraging the effective use of technology. He is co-creator of the internationally recognised and applied e-learning maturity model (eMM, http://e-learning.geek.nz/emm/).

Luka Mathayo Mkonongwa holds a doctoral (PhD) degree from the University College Dublin, Ireland. He also holds a Master of Arts in Applied Social Psychology degree and Bachelor of Arts with Education degree, both from the University of Dar es Salaam, Tanzania. He also holds a Diploma in Teacher Education from Morogoro Teachers' College. Formerly, He worked as a secondary school teacher. Currently, Dr Luka Mathayo Mkonongwa is a Lecturer in the Department of Educational Psychology and Curriculum Studies, Dar es Salaam University College of Education, Tanzania.

Ebba Ossiannilsson is the V President for the Swedish Association for Distance Education (SADE), and the V President for the Swedish Association for E-Competence (REK). She is the founder and owner of Ossiannilsson Quality in Open Online Learning (QOOL) Consultancy. Dr. Ossiannilsson was awarded the EDEN Fellow title in 2014, and she became Open Education Europa Fellow in 2015. Since 2016 she is ambassador for GLOBE, the Community of digital learning. She is nominated in 2017 to become Open Education Europa Ambassador and also for the board for Open Education Consortium. Since the year 2000, she worked at Lund University, Sweden, as an e-learning, open online learning expert, and advisor with special focus on quality. Ossiannilsson is a researcher, advisor and consultant. She has worked as a consultant at several of the prestige national universities. She is frequently invited as keynote speaker for international, and national conferences, within the area of open, online, flexible, and technology enabled teaching and learning (OOFAT) and quality. She is board member in national and international associations, in the area of open online learning and education (EDEN EC, former EFQUEL, earlier in EUCEN). Ossiannilsson is on behalf of SADE in the ICDE Focal Points of Quality. She was the research leader for the ICDE research study on global overview of quality models, and the evaluator of the SEQUENT project on quality. Ossiannilsson collaborated with the EC ET working group on digital and online learning on quality in OER, MOOCs and open education and with Commonwealth of Learning. She was an expert for IPTS on their work on the framework for open education. Ossiannilsson is a quality reviewer for both ICDE as well as for EADTU, ECB Check, and also for former EFQUEL. She was in the board for LANETO, and was among the founders of EPPROBATE. Ossiannilsson is coordinating the ICDE_ON_BOLDIC on behalf of the Swedish Association for Distance Education (SADE). She is in the Board for several scientific Journals and the Editor in the Education Sciences Journal, the topical collection on MOOCs. Ossiannilsson is representing EDEN in ISO, and she works at national level in SIS/ISO (Swedish Standards Institute /ISO. She has a passion to contribute to open education for a Future We Want for All, as is emphasized by UNESCO for 2030. Ossiannilsson has conducted several research studies in open online learning, including flexible learning, OERs and MOOCs, she has conducted several national overview reports, for example, the POERUP, ADOERUP, Global OER Mapping, the IPTS Member States Case Studies on Policies for Opening up Education, and for the Open Education Working Group. She was one of the promoters for introducing MOOCs in Sweden, and she has finalized some 40+ MOOCs herself, since its start in 2008. She was invited as Quality expert for the investigation on MOOCs by the Swedish Higher Education Authority (UKÄ). Ossiannilsson earned her PhD at Oulu University, Finland in 2012 with a dissertation on Benchmarking e-learning in higher education: lessons learned from international projects. Her dissertation has fortunately had a very large outreach and is often cited. Ossiannilsson's publications comprise over 200 publications: Conference papers, Journal articles, Book Chapters, Reports, Editor for books, a forthcoming book (Springer on open education) and her dissertation. Please see links to her LinkedIn and to her ResearchGate.

Nilgun Ozdamar Keskin received her Ph.D. from the Department of Computer Education and Instructional Technologies of the Graduate School of Educational Sciences of Anadolu University in the year 2011. She was a visiting scholar at University of Central Florida from 2009 to 2010. She got the best paper award at m-Learn Conference 2011 in China. Her research interests are Massive Open Online Courses, Global Education, Lifelong Learning, Mobile Literacy, Online Learning, Mobile Learning, Open and Distance Education.

Victor Pitsoe is employed as Full Professor in the Department of Educational Leadership and Management, University of South Africa. Among others, he is a Deputy Editor of Africa Education Review; and a member of The World Institute for Nuclear Security. He has published more than 40 articles and 10 book chapters; and edited two books. He has published extensively in the areas of classroom management, citizenship and human rights education, philosophy of education, open distance learning (ODL), teacher education, teacher professional development, management and leadership in education, and policy studies.

Yusuf Levent Şahin graduated from an undergraduate program in "Computer Education and Instructional Technology" at Anadolu University and the doctorate degree of the same program. He has been working as a assistant professor at the Anadolu University Education Faculty. He works such as gamification, social network analysis.

Hasan Ucar is an English language instructor and coordinator for distance English courses at Bilecik Seyh Edebali University, Turkey. He received his Ph.D. (2016) and Master' (2012) in Distance Education from Anadolu University, Turkey. Hasan's current research agenda is the motivational design of instruction in online learning environments. Additional areas of research include distance learning and teaching, online learning, instructional design/technology, teaching and learning in online technologies, and motivation and engagement of online learners.

Serap Uğur graduated from an undergraduate program in "Computer Education and Instructional Technology" at Anadolu University and the master degree of the same program. Since 2002, she has been working as a lecturer at the Distance Education Department of Open Education Faculty. She works research and development activities and projects in fields such as e-learning content types, animation, gamification, social network analysis, instructional design, individual differences and human-computer interaction.

Index

Ensure Quality Research is Introduced to the Academic Community

Become an IGI Global Reviewer for Authored Book Projects

The overall success of an authored book project is dependent on quality and timely reviews.

In this competitive age of scholarly publishing, constructive and timely feedback significantly expedites the turnaround time of manuscripts from submission to acceptance, allowing the publication and discovery of forward-thinking research at a much more expeditious rate. Several IGI Global authored book projects are currently seeking highly-qualified experts in the field to fill vacancies on their respective editorial review boards:

Applications and Inquiries may be sent to:
development@igi-global.com

Applicants must have a doctorate (or an equivalent degree) as well as publishing and reviewing experience. Reviewers are asked to complete the open-ended evaluation questions with as much detail as possible in a timely, collegial, and constructive manner. All reviewers' tenures run for one-year terms on the editorial review boards and are expected to complete at least three reviews per term. Upon successful completion of this term, reviewers can be considered for an additional term.

If you have a colleague that may be interested in this opportunity,
wc encourage you to share this information with them.

www.ingramcontent.com/pod-product-compliance
Lightning Source LLC
LaVergne TN
LVHW062155300926
849161LV00010B/2666

9781799810056